D1237986

EDWARD MINER GALLAUDET
MEMORIAL LIBRARY
Gallaudet College
Kendall Green
Washington, D.C. 20002

Soviet Russian literature since Stalin

FOR GLENORA

Soviet Russian literature since Stalin

DEMING BROWN

Professor of Russian Literature, University of Michigan

CAMBRIDGE UNIVERSITY PRESS

CAMBRIDGE

LONDON - NEW YORK - MELBOURNE

Edward Miner Gallaudet Memorial Library
Gallaudet College, Washington, D. C.

Published by the Syndics of the Cambridge University Press
The Pitt Building, Trumpington Street, Cambridge CB2 1RP
Bentley House, 200 Euston Road, London NW1 2DB
32 East 57th Street, New York, NY 10022, USA
296 Beaconsfield Parade, Middle Park, Melbourne 3206, Australia

© Cambridge University Press 1978

First published 1978

Printed in the United States of America
Typeset, printed and bound by Vail-Ballou Press, Inc., Binghamton, New York

Library of Congress Cataloging in Publication Data
Brown, Deming Bronson, 1919–
Soviet Russian literature since Stalin.
Bibliography: p.
Includes index.
1. Russian literature – 20th century – History and criticism.
I. Title.
BG3022.B68   891.7'90'0044   77-73275
ISBN 0 521 21694 X

891.709
B7s
1978

CONTENTS

180098

ACKNOWLEDGMENTS

I am indebted to a number of institutions for help in my work on this book. The Horace H. Rackham School of Graduate Studies and the Center for Russian and East European Studies of The University of Michigan have provided generous assistance over the years. A summer research grant from the American Council of Learned Societies gave crucial support at an early stage. A Fulbright – Hays fellowship enabled me to spend the year 1969 in Oxford, England, where I worked as a visiting fellow at St. Antony's College.

A great many individuals have helped in a great many ways. Most numerous are my students – and especially graduate students – with whom I have tried out most of the ideas in this book, and who have shared their ideas with me. My debt to my colleagues in the Department of Slavic Languages and Literatures at The University of Michigan is large. Every one of them, at one time or another, has been helpful. Some of the material in the chapters on poetry is adapted from an article written in collaboration with Professor Mark Suino. Six persons read the manuscript in its penultimate version, and each of them made valuable corrections and suggestions. They are Patricia Carden of Cornell University; Max Hayward of St. Antony's College, Oxford; Geoffrey Hosking of The University of Essex; David Lapeza of The University of Michigan; Lev Lifshitz of The University of Michigan; and Richard Sheldon of Dartmouth College. I cannot thank them enough. I am particularly indebted to Max Hayward for his friendship and encouragement over the years, and for his example of wise and rigorous scholarship. My most constant and valuable helper has been the lovely and brilliant woman to whom this book is dedicated.

1

The literary situation

In recent years the term "Soviet literature" has become an increasingly awkward one. Soviet authorities insist that a monolithic, multinational literature has been created, embracing all the peoples of the Soviet Union, including numerous minority linguistic and ethnic groups. Nearly all of the noteworthy literature in the USSR, however, has been written in the Russian language.

It can be argued, moreover, that the community of good writing has become so disorganized and fragmented that the term Soviet literature is virtually meaningless. If one is to accept official judgments from the Soviet government, for example, Aleksandr Solzhenitsyn can no longer be termed a Soviet writer. Many others have gradually been excluded, and we are now faced with a situation in which a great deal of the most interesting writing in the Soviet Union is not published there. Numerous writers living in the USSR, such as Vladimir Voinovich, have had to resort to *foreign* publication of their best works. But are these works not Soviet literature? Likewise, are we to consider the works of such persons as Nadezhda Mandelstam and Andrei Amalrik, who have *only* been published abroad, as being beyond the scope of Soviet literature? Finally, what do we call the writing of such persons as Solzhenitsyn, Viktor Nekrasov, and Naum Korzhavin, who are now in exile? Did it cease to be Soviet literature the moment they crossed the border?

If all of these questions are answered in the affirmative, what remains is that which is currently published in Soviet books and periodicals, and it immediately becomes evident that this remainder is largely a literature of pretense, if only because it is heavily screened and censored, and governed by complex and crippling inhibitions and prohibitions. In it one often finds the same concerns and themes as in literature that has to be published abroad although, as a rule, these domestic publications cannot be as candid and comprehensive in their exploration of social, moral, and ideological problems. But, regardless of whether works are published inside or outside the USSR, all of them have emerged from the same society. The kinship among them is so close that, for the purposes of the present book, the term Soviet literature will be applied to all of them.

In the period immediately preceding the one with which this book is concerned, Soviet literature reached its nadir. During World War II official controls had relaxed somewhat, but within a year after the war's end they were retightened to an unprecedented degree of harshness and viciousness. In an atmosphere of extreme cultural isolation, the authorities demanded that literature perform the narrow educational and organizational role of instructing the reader in detail about ideological values and standards of social behavior. Writers who failed to conform were denounced and silenced. The Party leaders selected the main themes and topics of literature and carefully supervised its ideological content, of which the chief ingredients were chauvinism (of both a Soviet and a Great Russian variety), hatred of things foreign (especially Western), praise of the superior "new Soviet man" and, last but not least, glorification of Stalin.

The genres that best lent themselves to these demands were the long novel and the narrative poem of epic proportions. For their material, writers and poets had a number of immediately utilitarian topics from which to choose. Among them was the recent war, which not only provided limitless examples of patriotic heroism on the part of Soviet man but also could be used to demonstrate the leading role of the Party, the personal greatness of Stalin, and the beneficence of his regime. Another topic was the corrupt West – most notably America – morally degraded and effete but still a hotbed of anti-Soviet conspiracy and atomic warmongering guided from Wall Street. Postwar reconstruction was a major topic: the fulfillment of the new five-year plans and rehabilitation of collective farms through socialist competition, in the face of obstacles from socially backward elements. Here again, writers emphasized the guiding function of the Party, and work as a measure of devotion to society and the most noble expression of the human personality.

Writers were allowed to concern themselves with problems of personal postwar adjustment, such as the disruption of families, shifts of affection among husbands and wives, and the search of returning soldiers for peacetime vocations. The welfare and felicity of the individual in these respects, however, was clearly a matter of secondary importance. What counted most was the individual's sense of social discipline, his freedom from materialistic longing for consumer goods and "bourgeois" comforts, and his willingness to get back to work without pausing for a rest after the ordeal of the war.

A few good novels and poems – one thinks of Vera Panova's *Fellow Travellers* (*Sputniki*, translated as *The Train*) and Aleksandr Tvardovsky's *The House by the Road* (*Dom u dorogi*) – did emerge during this period. But for the most part a vast, dull, mass literature of make-believe was produced under the guise of socialist realism. Writers either avoided dealing with moral and social evil in its real quality and dimensions, glossed over it, presented it in such a way as to mislead the reader about its causes, or tried to create the impression that it was being eradicated through the relentless march of progress of the Soviet state. Working under tight restrictions, they were frequently forced to revise and rewrite to insure exact conformity. It is surprising that under such circumstances Soviet literature was not killed outright.

It would be inaccurate, however, to portray Soviet writers in the Stalin period merely as a group of slaves, forced against their will to follow a set of formulas. There were then, as now, opportunists who cynically accepted the formulas as the price of wealth and literary prominence. A far larger number, sharing the illusions of a multitude of their compatriots, sincerely and willingly submitted to the prevailing doctrine and its concomitant discipline, wholeheartedly believed that what they were writing was essentially the truth, and were firmly convinced of the aesthetic superiority of current Soviet literary ideology. But there existed all along a cultural substratum: a small, embattled minority of individuals who maintained a creative interest in good literature.

The first public stirrings of this continued interest became evident shortly after Stalin's death in March 1953. The following month, the poet Olga Berggolts published an article deploring the absence of lyricism in contemporary verse and pleading for more attention to personal feeling – love, for example.[1] In October 1953, Ilya Ehrenburg proclaimed in an article that the writer has an obligation to explore the inner world of man and not merely to engage in dutiful descriptions of social and economic life.[2] The most outspoken and challenging expression of dissatisfaction with the contemporary situation, however, appeared in December in Vladimir Pomerantsev's essay "On Sincerity in Literature,"[3] in which the critic attacked the ingrained conformism among Soviet writers, the wooden didacticism of their works, and their habit of prettifying, "varnishing," the reality of the Soviet scene. Pomerantsev's article – both attacked and defended in the following months – became the landmark of a new era of increased freedom in literary discussion and creation.

Within a year after the death of Stalin, works had begun to appear that indicated that Soviet literature was indeed becoming more sincere, humane, and truthful. Examples were Vera Panova's *Seasons* (*Vremena goda*, translated as *Span of the Year*), Viktor Nekrasov's *In One's Home City* (*V rodnom gorode*), and the first part of Ehrenburg's *The Thaw* (*Ottepel'*). The journal *The Banner* (*Znamya*) published poems by Boris Pasternak which, it later turned out, were part of the novel *Doctor Zhivago*. These works, however, constituted merely a modest outpouring of newly oriented literature, and when the Second Congress of Soviet Writers met in December 1954, various speeches made it evident that the Party leadership was prepared to tolerate only a severely limited liberalization in literary publication. Speakers at the Congress also spotlighted the existence of two broad factions in the literary world – liberal and conservative – which were destined for hot contention in the ensuing years. But, for the time being, these two camps maintained a nervous standoff.

The most dramatic change in the literary climate came in 1956. Encouraged by the reformist message of the Twentieth Party Congress and the relative candor of Khrushchev's secret speech to the Congress in which he denounced some of the iniquity of the Stalin regime, writers increasingly insisted on telling the truth about the quality of Soviet life. Numerous stories and novels appeared, protesting against the blatant injustice that prevailed in the country and emphasizing the immense gulf that existed between the Soviet people and their leaders. Vladimir Dudintsev's novel *Not By Bread Alone* (*Ne khlebom edinym*) caused an enormous uproar by emphasizing these themes, and two large almanacs entitled *Literary Moscow* (*Literaturnaya Moskva*) contained a number of similarly disturbing shorter works. Such writings, it should be added, implicitly questioned the viability of socialist realism as a guiding doctrine. At the same time, verse by previously suppressed poets such as Anna Akhmatova, Nikolai Zabolotsky, Leonid Martynov, and Boris Slutsky began to appear, together with poetry by challenging youngsters such as Andrei Voznesensky and Evgeny Evtushenko.

By late 1956 the authorities (who had also been profoundly disturbed by the libertarian rebellion in Hungary) had taken fright at these manifestations of protest and liberalism. The year 1957, then, produced a series of reflexes to counter such manifestations. A number of the writers and publications mentioned above, along with many others of similar inclination, were subjected to official attacks in the press, in public meetings, and in closed meetings within the Writers' Union (although their defenders were also given some voice). Khrushchev personally intervened in literary affairs, addressing groups of writers and supporting the reactionaries among them, admonishing the literary community to adhere to the principles of socialist realism and warning them against the cardinal liberal sin of "revisionism." In addition to such attempts at direct political intimidation, the authorities undertook a series of administrative measures to keep literature in line. They shuffled the editorial staffs of certain offending publications and closed down others; they created new, more tractable literary newspapers and journals; and they manipulated the organization and leadership of the Writers' Union to combat the upsurge of liberal influence.

The events of 1956 and 1957 dramatized as never before the opposition between two loosely grouped but clearly discernible literary camps. A period of open warfare lasting nearly a decade ensued between the liberals (pejoratively called "revisionists") and the conservatives (pejoratively called "dogmatists"). Conservative writers, editors and critics such as Anatoli Sofronov, Vsevolod Kochetov, and Vladimir Ermilov used the press and various Party organizations to attack the ideas and question the loyalty of such writers as Dudintsev, Vasili Aksenov, and Voznesensky. Vehement counterattacks through the same media came from such liberals as Konstantin Paustovsky, Viktor Nekrasov, and Aleksandr Tvardovsky. A prominent center of the struggle was the Writers' Union, not only in its open meetings and congresses but, even more influentially, in the process of appointing editorial boards and allocating administrative and advisory posts.

The liberals, who considered themselves loyal Communists, argued in general for a moderately flexible interpretation of communist ideology. In urging the creation of a more "truthful" Soviet literature, they specified more freedom of experimentation, greater topical latitude and variety, and a less paternalistic concern over what the Soviet reader should and should not be permitted to know. They were therefore inclined to oppose official coercion of writers and state control over literature in general, including censorship. Dogma, they believed, should be replaced by the writer's personal, individualized quest for the truth. In contrast, the conservatives emphasized the obligation of literature to serve the Party and to maintain a strict devotion to the Party line. This meant, of course, the observance of severe official controls over literature. Believing that de-Stalinization had gone too far, the conservatives felt that, just as the Stalinist social system had been basically a good one and should not be fundamentally changed, so there should be no relaxation in the administration of literature. The style and content of Soviet writing, moreover, should remain hortatory, heroic, and dutifully propagandistic.

By 1958 the Party leadership had arrived at a policy of cautious tolerance of the contention between liberals and conservatives. Although the authorities continued to be inflexible on major issues – for example, refusing to allow Pasternak to accept the Nobel Prize – they distributed political favors between opposing factions with a more-or-less even hand. At the Third Writers' Congress in May 1959, Khrushchev urged the writing community to settle its disputes internally and, although he made it clear that writers would not be given freedom to create as they pleased, he affirmed that literary criticism was the province of professionals, not the government, and that erring writers should be guided to the correct path gently, not castigated. In the next few years this policy of moderation encouraged the best writers of the Soviet Union, including many who had only recently been chastised and silenced, to publish works of great interest.

Although the government was guarded and tentative in relaxing controls over literature, and sporadically tightened them on occasion, the change in the literary climate was dramatic. The liberal intelligentsia was experiencing a new sense of identity and purpose, and the literary atmosphere had become lively. The search for new values and positive ideals involved not only open contention between two broadly defined literary factions but also a fresh definition of the civic mission of the writer. Informed and inquiring readers now expected the writer not merely to affirm and document official theses but to think critically, to question, to stir things up. As both writers and readers were permitted to learn more of the truth about the past and present, the literary scene – the main locus of national self-examination and moral reevaluation – became genuinely exciting.

The high point in the period of relative tolerance came in the autumn of 1962, which featured public readings by liberal poets before huge and enthusiastic audiences, the publication of such unprecedentedly frank works as Solzhenitsyn's *One Day in the Life of Ivan Denisovich* and Evtushenko's "The Heirs of Stalin," and increased representation of liberals on editorial boards and in the Writers' Union. By December of 1962, liberal activity and influence had assumed the proportions of a revolt, and once again Khrushchev and his cultural advisers intervened, holding disciplinary meetings with leading writers and editors and encouraging press attacks from conservatives. Repressive measures continued through the spring of 1963, but the liberals remained defiant. By June of 1963, Khrushchev had

largely abandoned his attempts at intimidation. However, the publication
of works of liberal orientation never again reached the intensity of the autumn of 1962.

(A factor that always influenced official policies on literature was the
Soviet position in international affairs at any given time. For example, not
only the Hungarian uprising of 1956 but also the Cuban missile crisis in
the fall of 1962 affected the government's behavior toward writers. The influence worked in various and often strange ways. The publication in
Pravda on October 21, 1962 of Evtushenko's liberal "The Heirs of Stalin,"
a poem warning against a return to Stalinism, was a feature of Khrushchev's attempt to combat his hardline critics following his loss of face in
the confrontation with President Kennedy over Cuba. On the other hand,
this loss of face on the international scene caused the general tightening of
literary controls in December 1962. When foreign affairs place the Soviet
leaders in difficult situations, they seem invariably to crack down on literature. Thus, it might have been expected that the policy of détente in the
1970s would have encouraged a relaxation at home. The opposite oc-
curred: the increase in traffic and communication between East and West
spurred the authorities to increased ideological and political vigilance and
correspondingly severe control over literary publication.)

Although liberals continued to be aggressive and, when possible, vocif-
erous, their influence was gradually eroded after 1963. They continued to
press for a relaxation of the principles of socialist realism, and Soviet literature quietly continued its self-liberation from those principles. On the
other hand, the government did nothing to encourage the expression of
liberal opinion, preferring to cope with it through a policy of containment.
In anticipation of the Fourth Writers' Congress in 1967, for example,
Solzhenitsyn launched a passionate appeal for the abolition of censorship,
and petitions were circulated supporting him, but the Congress itself was
prohibited from discussing this or any other controversial issue of importance. When Soviet troops occupied Czechoslovakia in 1968, the liberal
writing community was forced to remain virtually silent.

Meanwhile the post-Stalin intellectual ferment had produced new literary phenomena. Encouraged by the partial loosening of controls, a
number of writers had ventured beyond permissible ideological, political,
and aesthetic limits. One result was the phenomenon of *samizdat* – the
wide circulation of unpublishable manuscripts and even underground
magazines. Also, writers who despaired of seeing their works in print in
the USSR began sending them abroad for publication. The first of those
to be apprehended were Andrei Sinyavsky and Yuli Daniel, who in 1966

were tried and given harsh sentences in concentration camps. A number of their supporters, and subsequently the supporters of *those* supporters, were similarly sentenced. Protest against these and other manifestations of tightening political screws led in turn to an official policy of selective terror, directed against expressions of dissent. The KGB became increasingly active in literary affairs. The year 1966 was pivotal, marking the end of the period that had come to be known as the Thaw. The trial of Sinyavsky and Daniel set in motion a series of repressive measures that not only forced dissidence underground but also adversely affected the quality of published literature.

A decade after the 1962 flowering of liberal literary activity, the situation had changed markedly. Although the general sympathies of writers had probably not changed as greatly as appeared on the surface, the authorities had succeeded in muffling the arguments between liberals and conservatives, and the seeming absence of disagreement created the impression of a monolith. On the other hand, it was clear that although some erstwhile liberals, such as Evtushenko, had been tamed, others had become radicalized by attempts to intimidate them. Many of these were so disaffected that they either wound up in prison or were forced to emigrate.

The relationship between literature and politics in the Soviet Union has been, and remains, Byzantine. Decisions to publish or not to publish a given work, to promote or not to promote the cause of a certain writer or periodical, are often the result of complex and carefully hidden intrigue that involves not only the Central Committee of the Communist Party but also the leaders at the very top. Some prestigious writers have great personal influence with political insiders and have used it to defend their literary friends and harm their literary enemies. The events of the two decades with which the present study is concerned have shown that literature has not been as easy to manipulate as it was under Stalin. Nevertheless, although the elaborate machinery of control is often creaky and inefficient, it works.

The most visible and prominent instrument of control is the Union of Soviet Writers, which holds a monopoly on all official literary activity. Nominally the Union's policies are set and its administration democratically elected at regional and nationwide writers' congresses. In a strictly formal sense the Union is run by a board elected at the congresses. The board in turn elects a secretariat, which in actual practice administers the Union. Even closer to actuality is, within the secretariat, an uncharted inner circle of five or six who meet daily and make the key decisions.

These decisions are guided primarily not by the opinions of the board, its chairman, or the secretariat, but by the Central Committee of the Communist Party and its Politburo. And many, if not all, of the members of the inner circle are also representatives of the KGB. Moreover, the censorship apparatus, Glavlit – with which the Union must deal constantly as proprietor of all literary magazines and newspapers and as owner of the largest literary publishing house – is also influenced by the KGB.

A great deal of the Union's activity involves the supervision of the editorial policies and operation of its publishing network. The Union runs a literary institute, which gives a five-year training course to young writers, poets, and critics. A considerable amount of Union administrators' time is spent in examining and discussing manuscripts, because they have assumed the all-important ideological responsibility for deciding how individual works should be shaped. Although the preliminaries may be complicated, the essential process is simple: a writer is called on the carpet and told how he must change his book if he wants it published.

The Writers' Union handsomely rewards obedience and conformity. Members in good standing enjoy benefits vastly exceeding those of ordinary citizens – access to foreign films never available to the general public, a special tailor shop, clubs with excellent restaurants, preferential treatment in hotels. More fundamentally – depending on their incomes, which are usually quite respectable and often very large – they enjoy greatly superior living and working conditions. These include hard-to-get new apartments or loans to purchase units in cooperative apartment buildings for writers, summer cottages, seaside resorts, and Houses of Creativity – pleasantly located rural working hideaways with full hotel services. Even in fallow periods a writer of demonstrated talent is assured of liberal monetary allowances, to be repaid from future royalties. If he needs a field trip to gather material and atmosphere, the Union will provide a generous advance.

Not all of this largesse comes, strictly speaking, from the Union itself. Much of it is provided by a subsidiary organization called the Literary Fund (Litfund), whose huge income is derived from members' dues. Its expenditures include not only the above-mentioned advances for field trips, loans, clubs, and apartment buildings but also sanatoriums, special bookstores, resorts and medical clinics for writers, as well as nurseries, kindergartens, and summer camps for their children.

Loosely grouped together as a kind of institutionalized élite, Union members not only are encouraged to develop feelings of social and political solidarity but are also subtly induced to regard their way of life not as a privilege but as a right. Their favored position ties them closely to the establishment, tends to cushion them against the sharper edges of Soviet society, and can also screen them off from the masses whose teachers and spokesmen they purport to be. Only a strong penchant for independent thinking, dedicated curiosity, and persistent effort of will can save them from a smug, pleasantly narcotized conformity.

Many Union members, however, have been alertly independent and in intimate contact with social reality. As we have seen, they have taken advantage of their relative affluence and favorable working conditions to write unorthodox works that cannot be published and either remain "in the drawer" or circulate clandestinely. Moreover, the doctrinal squabbles that have come to the surface have shown that there has sometimes been a formidable amount of bold and stubborn dissidence within the Union. Over the years the authorities have developed various means of dealing with overly independent or recalcitrant writers.

The mildest device is appeasement. Sometimes editors in Moscow or Leningrad are permitted to publish controversial authors just to boost the circulation of their magazines, to compete commercially. Works that cannot be printed in these large central journals sometimes find a haven in provincial journals – in Georgia, Kazakhstan, or Siberia. Also, there are magazines of high quality but low circulation in which a writer can say relatively daring things to a limited audience. Publication under all these circumstances is a carefully controlled safety valve.

Consultation of the writer with Union representatives and committees constitutes another relatively tender means of guidance. The writer is expected to submit to their "comradely" review of his manuscript, including a scrutiny of his themes and topics, his manner of writing, and its political and ideological tenor – and to heed their advice. Suggestions and criticism of this nature may indeed be beneficial to a conformist or politically prudent writer – they are, among other things, one form of self-censorship by the writing community – but clearly many writers would prefer to dispense with this corporate assistance.

When dissident writers unite to form factions within the Union, more abrupt and sweeping measures can be taken. By 1958, for example, the Moscow branch had become a hotbed of liberalism, and the Moscow dissidents were strongly influencing the central policies of the Union. Accordingly, the authorities stepped in and organized a Russian Republic Writers' Union, which partially engulfed the Moscow branch and replaced its malcontents with more tractable, if less gifted, provincials.

Like most other Soviet institutions, the Union has its Party organization, which serves as a collective cheerleader, troubleshooter, and watchdog. One of its functions is to insure that Union members engage heavily in public activities. Writers have enormous prestige just by virtue of being writers, and the Union makes sure that they are kept visible. They are expected to attend numerous meetings, sit on committees, give public lectures, and participate in various ceremonies and celebrations. Their views on the most diverse topics are solicited in newspaper and television interviews and commissioned articles, and they are urged to sign a variety of proclamations and declarations. Many of them perform official political duties: thirty-six writers were delegates to the Twenty-fourth Congress of the Communist Party in 1971, and twenty-seven were members of the Supreme Soviet.

Although the Party plays an important role in the Union, responsibility for crucial policies and disciplinary measures in recent years has fallen increasingly, if covertly, on the KGB. The reason, no doubt, is that the authorities have seen what can happen when the literary community in a communist country is really free to express itself. The Writers' Unions in the countries of Eastern Europe since World War II have been patterned on the Soviet model. Yet in Czechoslovakia in 1967 a determined band of liberal writers, most of them Party members, gained control of their Union, mobilized public opinion through its newspapers and magazines, and spearheaded a movement toward political and cultural freedom that culminated in the Prague Spring of 1968 and, a few months later, in the tragic Soviet invasion of their country. Increasing KGB control of the Union of Soviet Writers undoubtedly represents, in large measure, an apprehensive reaction by Soviet leaders to the Czechoslovak episode.

The Union has developed, on its own, some fairly effective means of dealing with erring or recalcitrant writers whom the ordinary processes of coddling, flattery, censorship, and special persuasion have not kept in line. For the writer who makes a small mistake or is mildly unruly there is, first of all, a private, fatherly word to the wise, with an implied threat of further unpleasantness. When this does not work, the Union can demand, and usually gets, a public recantation and promise to behave. Because these means are not always successful, a number of harsher devices are also in use. Among these are press attacks on individuals and denunciations in meetings like the one in September 1967, in which the secretariat pilloried Solzhenitsyn. Writers are sometimes fired from Union posts for disciplinary reasons. Mavericks are nearly always denied permission to travel outside the Soviet Union, and particularly to the West.

The penultimate weapon for dealing with troublesome writers is expulsion from the Union. (A list of those expelled includes some of the greatest names in Soviet literature – notably Akhmatova, Pasternak, Solzhenitsyn, and Sinyavsky – as well as numerous lesser-known writers with whom the present book is also concerned.) One of the immediate consequences of expulsion is, first of all, a painful loss of income, for the writer finds it extremely difficult, and often impossible, to publish his work, although some do manage to publish under pseudonyms. The writer also loses many rights, privileges and benefits – for example his travel opportunities. And usually he must find some nonliterary job to keep himself alive. If he does not have officially approved employment, he may be arrested for "parasitism."

As we have seen often in the last few years, the ultimate weapons for dealing with uncooperative writers are imprisonment and exile.

Open defiance in the presence of pressures such as these is obviously an extremely painful, if not downright ruinous, mode of behavior for the individual. Increasingly in recent years, therefore, Soviet writers have resorted to the time-honored Russian practice of writing between the lines, of using so-called Aesopian language as a means of evading the censorship. Sophisticated Soviet readers trained in this convention, with its use of hints, code words, and special intonation, have learned to examine the censored, printed page for hidden meanings, and writers have often found that dissident messages increase in aesthetic power when masked in this fashion. In this connection, one of the reasons for the extreme popularity of poetry during this period, no doubt, is that verse has more license to be ambiguous and flexible in its connotations than does prose in the Soviet Union. Its ideology is harder to pin down, less readily censorable.

It is ironic that camouflage techniques of writers, on the one hand, and repressive disciplinary measures by the state on the other, should have increased during a period when the literary climate on the whole remained much better than it had been during Stalin's lifetime. By the early 1970s, it is true, the situation of writers had become neo-Stalinist in several important ways. But by no means had conditions fully reverted to those of Stalin's lifetime, when the price of nonconformity was terror, imprisonment, and often death. Halting and incomplete as they were, the post-Stalin reforms had brought about a net improvement in the literary atmosphere, a gain that could be eradicated only by the most extreme measures.

A prominent indication of this gain was the decrease in the isolation of the literary community from the Russian cultural heritage and from the twentieth-century literature of the West. The authorities have permitted the gradual and fitful rehabilitation of many of the best writers, such as Isaac Babel, Mikhail Bulgakov, Andrei Platonov, and Osip Mandelstam, who had been previously suppressed or consigned to oblivion and whose reappearance in print, although selective and incomplete, has enriched the literary atmosphere. Likewise, some writers who emigrated after the October Revolution, such as Ivan Bunin and Konstantin Balmont, are now published in the Soviet Union. The poems of Marina Tsvetaeva, who lived for years in emigration and returned to Russia but was cruelly neglected and died a suicide, are now available in part. Perhaps the most significant phenomenon in this respect is the fact that Soviet Russians, after years of officially induced inhibition, are now able to read and discuss, unabashed, the works of Fyodor Dostoevsky.

Also selective, but nevertheless extensive, has been the increased translation and publication of Western literature. This includes many important, even seminal, writers who had previously been anathematized for ideological reasons, such as Franz Kafka and William Faulkner, writers such as Ernest Hemingway who had once been popular and then had been interdicted in the depths of the Stalin period, and gifted and provocative new writers such as Eugene Ionesco and J. D. Salinger. Russian readers and writers also received a small taste of avant-garde writing through the very limited translation of such Western Slavic modernists as Slawomir Mrożek and Ivan Klima. (Modern Polish and Czechoslovak writing, however, is translated much more extensively into the minority languages of the Soviet Union – especially Ukrainian and the Baltic languages – than into Russian.) The literary situation has improved in this respect, but it is clear that some Soviet writers are still not well acquainted with the work of their Western contemporaries.

An enormous amount of commentary on literature is published in the Soviet Union. In sheer volume – in books, newspapers, and numerous fat monthly journals – it may well exceed that of any other country. In the first decade with which the present study is concerned, however, the average number of new ideas and fresh observations per page may well have been the world's smallest, for Soviet literary criticism was still just emerging from the Stalinist doldrums, and most of it was depressingly uninspired and repetitive.

Ten years after the death of Stalin, critics still dealt in the formulae that had become frozen in his time. No longer, of course, did critics attempt to reinforce their judgments and arguments with quotes from Stalin or with other appeals to his authority. It was possible, in fact, for a critic to write without genuflecting to *anyone*, as if he were relying on his own autonomous opinion, and some of them did affect this manner. Nevertheless, the need to invoke some central authority remained a strong one, and that role was now played by Lenin and the Communist Party. Every remark that Lenin ever made about literature – including some that were suppressed in Stalin's time – had been gleaned, collated, and classified. Even his most casual, cryptic office memoranda were cited if they contained the tiniest scrap of comment that was remotely related to literature. All of this was done in the name of *partiinost'*, an untranslatable Soviet coinage meaning, roughly, "Party-spiritedness." Under this concept, the authorities attempted to tolerate mildly liberal reforms in literature while maintaining the militantly utilitarian attitude that was bequeathed to them by Lenin and reinforced in Stalinist practice.

One reason for the uniformity of Soviet criticism in those years was that the conservatives dominated all but a handful of the editorial boards of Soviet literary periodicals and controlled most of the publishing houses. Consequently, the liberals published relatively little criticism. Their arguments, moreover, were often presented only inferentially, for it was foolhardy to attempt a frontal attack on a fundamental tenet of Soviet orthodoxy. In contrast, the conservatives' opinions were published abundantly, frankly, and in detail. It was this very abundance and blatancy that rendered Soviet criticism so tiresome and stale even in such a period of comparative flux.

One of the main obligations of literature, as we have seen, was to educate and persuade the reader to work for the Party's program. A mission of Soviet criticism was to determine how well literature performed these combined reportorial and didactic tasks and to suggest ways in which the performance could be improved. At their worst, the critics could be extremely assiduous about this mission. Olga Berggolts complained, for example, of having seen a review of a novel on a collective farm theme in which the critic "praised the novel, but added that the love of Afrikan and Agafya was depicted broadly at the expense of a portrayal of melon-gardening culture."[4] Berggolts was not joking. She was reflecting on the fact that literary criticism had great weight and influence in Soviet society, that critics could ensure a book's success or kill it, and that the general reception of a book was based first of all on political and ideological considerations.

Another function of Soviet criticism was to participate in and comment upon the struggle that was then taking place between the forces of Stalinist tradition and the forces of innovation, under close Party scrutiny and with frequent Party intervention. In view of the increased contact both with foreign literature and with previously suppressed Russian literature, criticism had the related task of distinguishing between those influences that would be legitimate and acceptable and those that would be harmful. Soviet critics had always been inspectors of ideology, and there was nothing fundamentally new about their current tasks. What was new, however, was the relative strength and influence of the forces of innovation. Despite the fact that they lacked sufficient political power to command their fair share of the forum, the liberal critics spoke on Soviet aesthetics for an increasingly dynamic element of the literary community.

Under these circumstances, "revisionism" in literary criticism meant an ideological softening-up that paved the way for various tendencies that came under the heading of "modernism." Often used synonymously with "decadence," this term designated nearly all strains of twentieth-century literature that conflicted with socialist realism. The critics recognized that modernism is not a unified, harmonious movement, with an "accurately and broadly formulated program," as it is "confused and changeable," and its "separate schools are contradictory."[5] Modernism, for example, refers to Freudian thought, to Gide, to Joyce, and to Imagist poetry. It means the Russian Symbolist movement that flowered and died before the Revolution, as well as Russian Futurism and numerous schools that sprang up in the twenties and were shortly outlawed.

Whereas socialist realism advocates an art down-to-earth and perfectly communicable, modernism means, first of all, abstract art. Thus it represents a "complete divorcement of art" from "any living content," because the artist "hides from reality" in a "ghostly ivory tower," or flees into the "unreal world of the imagination."[6] While socialist realism advocates absolute clarity, based on simple and evident logic, modernism assumes that "between the appearance of phenomena and their real essence is an uncrossable gulf."[7] Therefore modernist art emphasizes the elusiveness of reality and is obscure, blurred, and formless. Samuel Beckett, for example, creates a "delirious mirage, a phantasmagoric distortion of reality."[8] Socialist realism has absolute confidence in its own ideological correctness; modernism shows a "lack of understanding of the historical process, perplexity, the loss of historical perspective."[9] Socialist realism is rational and devoted to objective truth. Modernism assumes the "helplessness of human feelings in the cognition of certain spheres of the world surrounding us";[10] it is subjective and antirational. In the works of such writers as Kafka and Ionesco, "the irrational is also the chief reality,"[11] and "the fundamental source of evil in the world is irrational and will not submit to any kind of logical or artistically satirical analysis."[12] Finally, modernism is ugly. While socialist realism aspires to order, harmony, health, and beauty, modernism involves "the savoring of all sorts of deformity, coarseness, the perversion of the external and spiritual visage of man."[13] It is both amoral and antiaesthetic, because it obliterates the distinction between the disgusting and the beautiful and requires the artist to "free himself from social and moral ideals, emotions, elevated aims, humanism."[14]

Conservative critics copiously and reverently quoted such nineteenth-century prophets of socially dedicated art as Dobrolyubov, Chernyshevsky, and Belinsky to justify the catchwords *partiinost'*, *narodnost'* (closeness to the people), *pravdivost'* (truthfulness), and *svyaz' s zhizn'yu* (connection with life) – slogans that formed an oft-repeated litany. With equal frequency they called monotonous rolls of Soviet writers whom they had endowed with reputations as foremost socialist realists – Gorky, Furmanov, Fadeev, Nikolai Ostrovsky – as if the mere repetition of such names would convince. They produced floods of reviews, articles, and symposia designed to discourage daring literary experimentation, and their tireless examination of current works to determine the exact degree to which they conformed to current Party requirements could only be inhibiting to writers with a taste for exploration. At its most reactionary extreme, this wing of Soviet criticism was no less bigoted than superpatriots anywhere. A hate word employed among the conservatives, for example, was "isms," which meant what it does everywhere: dangerous foreign ideas. (There was a special sanction for the term: Lenin once employed it in a mood of ideological irritation.) The job of the conservative critics was to stamp out ideological fires started by the various "isms."

By 1964, however, the conservatives, although still in power, were clearly on the defensive. Their hold on public opinion was not nearly as strong as it seemed to be, for the millions of words they printed were not read nearly as extensively as they were intended to be. Like official propaganda in most spheres of Soviet life, the mass of verbiage poured out by the conservatives was wearily, passively, but nevertheless effectively ignored. The conservatives, then, were insecure – knowing that they did not have the support of cultivated, intelligent, and sophisticated Soviet readers. One consequence of this situation was that they began to adopt a more polite, circumspect, less abusive tone in their polemics against liberal tendencies. They still hewed to the same stale line, but they were trying painfully to be more civilized about it.

Diverse and disunited, liberal critics represented no single literary philosophy. What they did have in common was an ambition to increase the variety and profundity of Soviet literary expression through free experimentation, through open access to all possible creative influences, and especially through increased communication with the literature of the West. By their preference for iconoclastic young writers, by their very avoidance of orthodox clichés and ponderous dialectical formulations, and by their penchant for writing about literature as literature and not as social documentation, these critics implicitly protested against everything that was hidebound in Soviet culture.

In stating their disagreement with the conservatives, the liberals attempted to preserve the appearance of agreement on fundamentals, as if the actual disagreement only concerned peripheral matters. The age-old Russian technique of expressing oneself obliquely, of surrounding one's argument with so many qualifying phrases taken from official cant that one could be understood correctly only by the initiated, was developed into a formidable weapon. Working within the semantic and linguistic heritage of Leninism, using catchwords and clichés that had long been established, the liberals in fact used the language of the conservative to combat the conservatives. The endless discussions of the history of realism, for example, sometimes included subtle and indirect arguments aimed at a radical widening of the concept of socialist realism. As the term itself was still sacrosanct and had to be lived with, the only thing the liberals could do was quietly undermine its more objectionable precepts in the hope that eventually it could be divorced from its most odious connotations. The more favorable climate for liberal criticism was to some extent a tribute to the painstaking tactfulness of its adherents. As a result of their efforts, criticism in general had become, by the late 1960s, much more varied and concerned with purely literary values than it had been in Stalin's time.

Nevertheless, the ostensible ideological monopoly of socialist realism as the guiding theory of Soviet literature remained a major obstacle to the development of criticism. Reduced to its essentials, this theory holds that the function of literature is to serve as an instrument of the Party in shaping social attitudes and motivations. Literature should portray reality on the basis of an underlying faith in the ultimate victory of communism, that is, the elimination of all man-made impediments to human happiness. Its basic orientation, therefore, should be optimistic: life should be pictured partly as it is, but mainly as it *should* be. A keystone of socialist realism is the concept of the "positive hero" – a vigorous, fearless, self-sacrificing, optimistic and, above all, socially dedicated activist who serves the reader as an inspiration and model of communist behavior. As a consequence of the stress on the need for positive heroes, characters in Soviet novels, stories, and plays were discussed by the critics, more often than not, as if they were real people described by a biographer, and not simply characters of a fiction. On going through half a dozen reviews of a single novel, one gets the impression not of reading a series of literary commentaries but rather of attending a meeting to appraise a candidate for some Party honor roll.

Theoreticians of socialist realism argue that, despite its obligatory optimistic bent, it also allows room for tragedy. Humans suffer, are defeated and destroyed – but, if they are striving for the cause of a better future, their personal tragedies are transcended. Likewise, the theoreticians argue, there is room for satire within socialist realism. Its function is to ridicule those elements that impede social progress. The critics became particularly solemn when discussing humor and satire, whose purpose, in the words of one of them, is to "help us to struggle with social evil and to affirm the moral principles of communism."[15]

Although official pronouncements on literature, echoed by many dutiful critics, still pay lip service to socialist realism, in the past two decades there have been so many inroads into this doctrine in actual practice as to render it virtually inoperative. At times critics have been so bold as to point out that many of the best Soviet writers are *not* socialist-realists and have politely questioned the official pretense that they are. Occasionally the authorities attempt in gingerly fashion to cope with this situation, but they obviously avoid a frank and open discussion of the problem. As they continue to evade a genuine ideological confrontation, the erosion proceeds. The positive hero is disappearing from all but the most puerile writing, and pessimistic attitudes are increasingly evident — even among political conservatives, who previously could be counted on to keep a steady eye on the sunny future. The only essentials of socialist realism that have been retained since Stalin's time are a strong inclination toward moral didacticism and an avoidance, on the whole, of formally modernist modes of writing.

This is not to say that all of Soviet literature has shed the essential traces of socialist realism. Among Soviet writers the number of diehards who cling to the Stalinist heritage is large, and many of them enjoy powerful support from the editors of periodicals and from publishing houses, which print their books in huge editions. They also apparently enjoy a large audience among unreconstructed readers. As a rule, their fiction and poetry is journalism dressed up as literature, written to popularize reactionary points of view in unambiguous terms. One can find a certain perverse fascination in the writing of Vsevolod Kochetov, Vadim Kozhevnikov, and Aleksandr Chakovsky, who contrive intricate plots and puppet characters in elaborate novels to polemicize against revisionist notions. Kochetov, for example, appears to have built his novels on the basis of long catalogues of timely, ideologically significant phenomena in Soviet life, which he wished to attack or defend, and to have managed to drag in all of them. Writers of this type are not discussed in the present study. The literary level of their works is low, and when they are not boring they are simply ludicrous.

In the post-Stalin years, writers have been permitted, largely as the result of their own persistent initative, not only to deal with a larger number of social evils but also to deal with these evils in greater profundity and with increased candor. The range and depth of permissible inquiry have been increased to allow a more comprehensive and elastic understanding and a more subtle and resonant expression of "truth." It is possible, for example, to question the wisdom and morality of certain official Soviet policies in the past. As a result, socialist realism, which has always operated on shaky theoretical foundations with its obligation to affirm, indoctrinate, educate, and reassure, has largely been replaced by critical realism, with its inclination to question, evaluate, and negate. Conservative critics, fortified by the knowledge that socialist realism is still the only officially recognized literary credo, vehemently deny this fact. Liberal spokesmen such as Ehrenburg and Aleksandr Tvardovsky, on the other hand, have subtly insisted that in actual practice socialist realism, in its traditional sense, has been eroded beyond recognition. For Party ideologists, who still cannot frankly admit that this transition has taken place, the obvious gulf between theory and practice has created an increasingly serious ideological dilemma.

Many leading Party intellectuals no doubt realize that socialist realism has run its course and are trying to contain and guide an ideological evolution that they know to be inevitable, so as to prevent the collapse of discipline that would ensue from a frankly acknowledged ideological chaos. They must cope, for example, with critics who attempt to study contemporary world literature as if it were a single entity, not divided into ideological camps. This urge to get away from Soviet exceptionalism and to study literary ideas as such, because they have validity and interest regardless of their place of origin, to conceive of some "contemporary style" that leaps across East–West political boundaries, has been labeled revisionist. Even within the framework of realism there can be no "pan-human style," for, as Khrushchev was fond of reminding Soviet intellectuals, "peaceful coexistence does not mean ideological coexistence," and the notion of "realism without prefixes" is incipient heresy. Furthermore, critics and theoreticians who have suggested that there is now room for two realisms – "critical" and "socialist" – have been firmly reminded that this would require a major ideological revision by the central cultural authorities and that such a decision is not about to be made.

Critics are supremely aware, nevertheless, that Soviet literature faces two broad alternatives. Either it will return to the narrow and stifling confines of socialist realism, or its latitude will expand to include new interests, topics, and ways of looking at things, will permit approaches to writing that are characteristic, in their variety, of the contemporary West and that *were* characteristic of Russian literature in the first three decades of this century. The conservatives stubbornly maintain that the concept of socialist realism is a substantial and fertile philosophy of art, sufficiently elastic to permit the total range of literary expression that is needed in twentieth-century society. They still spend a great amount of time defining realism, studying the history of its development, and describing its relationship to other strains in the literature of the past and present. These critics have a particularly strong stake in refuting the accusation that socialist realism does not permit an adequate opportunity for literary innovation.

The conservatives, who speak directly or indirectly for the political authorities, want above all to preserve the immediate and practical function of literature as a device for molding public opinion and maintaining social discipline. They realize, however, that they can no longer rely on coercion to achieve this end and at the same time produce a literature worthy of the name. Recently, therefore, they have been suggesting a series of accommodations. Some have argued that socialist realism, although recognized as the *leading* theory of Soviet literature, should not enjoy a monopoly of critical attention by being considered the *only* legitimate theory. Open competition between socialist realism and other theories, it is argued, would be healthy and would only serve to strengthen socialist realism itself and prove its supreme validity. Others have recently argued, however, that socialist realism has never been as narrow and limiting as it has been made out to be, and that it can encompass a variety of literary styles, approaches, and ideas. This argument for an expanded interpretation of a single doctrine would also seem to point in a more liberal direction. But it is manifestly a move of ideological desperation: theory must somehow be made to correspond, more or less, to the facts.

Meanwhile, Russians have come to know much more about their literature, past and present, than they did twenty years ago. This rise in the general level of literary culture is largely the result of a marked improvement in the quality of scholarship and criticism, coming from a generally increased freedom to investigate and interpret. An example of the improvement is the *Short Literary Encyclopedia (Kratkaya literaturnaya entsiklopediya)* (the term "short" is relative – it consists of eight large volumes), of which the first volume was published in 1962, and which presents on the whole, despite some distressing omissions, an informed and balanced picture of Russian and world literature. Full, meticulously prepared and sometimes even handsome editions of Russian classics – Dostoevsky, for example – have appeared. Scholarship on classical writers has greatly improved, as in several studies of Dostoevsky, Mikhail Bakhtin's book on Rabelais, and the continuing publication of important documents in the series *Literary Heritage (Literaturnoe nasledstvo)*. Several good critical works on rehabilitated or semirehabilitated writers – such as Yuri Olesha, Andrei Platonov, and Mikhail Bulgakov – have been published. Memoirs about these and other partially restored authors, such as Marina Tsvetaeva and Osip Mandelstam, have appeared. It is even possible to mention without abuse – although usually only in passing – such officially disparaged writers as Alexei Remizov, Evgeny Zamyatin, and Boris Pilnyak. There are perceptive and informative critical introductions to new (although not complete) editions of important but often suppressed and neglected poets such as Pasternak, Tsvetaeva, Nikolai Zabolotsky, and Andrei Bely. Important works of criticism, out of print for decades, by Yuri Tynyanov and Aleksandr Voronsky, have appeared.

Many recent critics are more eclectic than their predecessors in their approaches to literature. Benedikt Sarnov, Andrei Sinyavsky (until his imprisonment), and Lev Anninsky, for example, bring a new richness of cultural background to bear on their comments about contemporary writers. Criticism of foreign literature untainted by extraliterary considerations has increased, as in the commentary on American and English writers by Inna Levidova. Nevertheless, the best critics, like the best poets and prose writers, must often turn to provincial journals of comparatively small circulation for publication of their most interesting and provocative pieces. Similarly, critics often feel it necessary to resort to Aesopic language to express their boldest ideas. It is doubtful, however, whether such "covert" literary criticism can really be communicated beyond a severely limited audience of initiates.

Scholars and critics have recently paid increased attention to the relationship between poetics and linguistics. Studies in this area, centering at the University of Tartu in Estonia under the leadership of Professor Yury Lotman, attempt to analyze works of literature on the basis of the patterns of language therein. The theory and methods associated with this approach to literature are identified by the term "structuralism." A relationship exists between structuralism and Russian formalism – a promising and imaginative school of criticism that was driven underground in the Soviet Union in the early thirties and has been under official interdict ever since. Conservative critics complain that just as formalism was "at the very least the dead classification of purely external phenomena, which tightly closes off the road to genuinely substantial ideological-aesthetic analysis,"[16] so structuralism displays an "aloofness from the content and ideological tendency of a work."[17] Although structuralism is indeed largely involved with pure literary theory at present, the conservatives' condemnation is much too narrow and categorical. Structuralism, which displays a sophisticated awareness of contemporary international scientific and intellectual discoveries, has already produced interesting and valuable analyses of individual works and, if given a chance, might greatly expand the horizons of Soviet literary scholarship.

2

The oldest poets

In 1956 Nikolai Aseev complained that Soviet poetry in recent years had consisted chiefly of "rhymed information about events which do not arrest the attention of the reader and do not become events in his life," because it simply "explains, narrates, reports that which has already been heard, understood, known from other sources." Lyrics, the veteran poet continued, had become merely illustrative, trivial commentary. Critics who tried to talk about the *quality* of poetry were deemed guilty of "formalism" and "aestheticism," which, Aseev said, "dooms the accused to a cataleptic silence." Poets had become fearful and cautious, writing only for the approval of editors, who in turn were governed by a "single taste," a single standard – that of the late Iosif Stalin.[1]

Aseev was merely saying, rather boldly, what every cultured Russian had long since realized. Poetry had been vulgarized and oversimplified, its field of vision narrowed, and its quality reduced to the schoolboy level. Words had been cheapened and, under the influence of the Party's notions about the educational mission of art, had degenerated into pure rhetoric. Dull and repetitious, lacking in the stimulating complexity of multilayered metaphors and symbols, poetry had been reduced to a state where even elementariness in stanza design was considered a virtue.

In these circumstances lyric poetry had been the major victim. The demand that poetry promote official views and popularize Party dogma implied a verse that did not require meditation or study, much less an expression of the poet's personal emotion. Detailed expressions of individual sorrow, love, melancholy – even the appreciation of a landscape for its own sake – had come to be considered suspect, if not downright inimical, and it had become extremely dangerous for a poet to express a unique reaction to his social surroundings. One of the fundamental developments in the latter half of the fifties was the partial restoration of the lyric, of the poet's right to meditate independently and express his feelings on love and nature, life and death.

The birthdates of the poets in the present chapter range from 1887 to 1906. Not only were they individuals with widely varying social and cultural backgrounds and sharply divergent personalities but also, many of them, with vastly dissimilar personal and literary careers. At the time when they began writing – the 1910s in some cases, the 1920s in others – the world of Russian poetry was rich and motley. During the formative years of some of these writers, Russian Symbolism was the dominant school of poetry; for others, Symbolism was in its twilight. But all of them were exposed to it, if only to reject it. One of them, Anna Akhmatova, was a founder of the Acmeist school, a highly refined, classically inclined reaction against Symbolism and successor to it. Others, such as Aseev and Semyon Kirsanov, became attached to the other major group rebelling against Symbolism – the Futurists – and, at an early stage in their careers, became affiliated with LEF (The Left Front of Art), an offshoot of Futurism ostensibly dedicated to a socially useful, practical art based on "facts." Another, Vladimir Lugovskoy, identified himself at first with Constructivism, a school dedicated to a poetry of socialist technology. On the other hand, Boris Pasternak, the most gifted of them all, constituted by himself, at a relatively early stage, a school all his own. The point is that these poets grew up in an exciting, variegated, and turbulent literary milieu.

What is most important, however, is that all of these poets lived through the entire Soviet era and into the post-Stalin years. They witnessed the Revolution; the halting, contradictory, but often exhilarating twenties; the thirties, in which industrialization was achieved through enormous hardship and at the cost of increasing regimentation, police terror, and repression; the grim forties and early fifties, marked by the most devastating war in Russia's history and a reconstruction period demanding not only further sacrifice but also further submission to the machine of a callous, willful, and increasingly paranoiac dictator; and, finally, a period of limited relaxation complicated by the anxieties of the atomic age. All of these poets survived to bear witness to public events and personal experiences that were virtually unprecedented in the intensity, complexity, and awesomeness of their development.

Despite the large historical experience they had in common, these poets viewed the world with vastly different eyes. Some of them, such as Akhmatova and Pasternak, were deeply rooted in the Russian culture that flourished on the eve of the Revolution and interpreted events largely from that perspective. The aesthetic attitudes they acquired in their youth, their ideologies, and their sensibilities, were such that the new literary standards that the Soviet regime imposed left their poetry fundamentally untouched. Others, with somewhat different cultural backgrounds and temperaments, found the new Soviet standards and practices more congenial and suitable, or at least proved to be more adaptive and malleable. Likewise, while certain poets tended to focus on the timelessness and continuity of Russian culture, others stressed the Revolution's break with the past, and the changes signified by Soviet developments.

The personal fates of these poets varied greatly, and this is reflected in their writing. Some conformed, with varying degrees of willingness and enthusiasm, to the demands of a state-controlled civic literature and were permitted to flourish under its terms – although even these poets clearly experienced moments of frustration and silence. Others refused to knuckle under and were hounded, interdicted, and even imprisoned. All of them lived under the constant threat of a police state apparatus that often seemed capricious in the choice of its victims. Some were seized, others were spared – in certain cases inexplicably, as if by accident.

The poets in the present chapter are those of their generation who survived – through luck or calculated self-preservation and, of course, through sheer longevity – to write after the passing of the Stalin era. All of them are poets who are generally recognized in the Soviet Union as being prominent and significant. Here it should be mentioned that I have omitted several poets – the most prominent are Ilya Selvinsky, Vera Inber, Aleksei Surkov, and Aleksandr Prokofiev – who also survived but who, in my opinion, wrote little or nothing of significance in this period. My criterion has been, in most cases, the degree to which the individual poet continued to grow and write originally, and particularly the degree to which, in the light of his increased freedom of expression, he took the opportunity to evaluate the moral, psychological, social, and cultural experience of his generation.

In the last few years of her life, Anna Akhmatova (1889–1966) was the sole surviving major representative of prerevolutionary Russian literature. Her pen served as a constant reminder of a precious poetic heritage, which official Soviet cultural practice had frequently threatened with extinction. Enormously erudite, deeply cultured, familiar with many classical and modern languages and literatures, and a scholar of Russian literature in her own right, she became not only the symbol of a rich and vanished era but also an aesthetic touchstone and unique inspiration for her younger contemporaries. When she died in 1966, the last direct connection to a great and tragic tradition was severed.

Most of the poetry Akhmatova wrote in her last ten years had a retrospective cast. Her seeming preoccupation with the past was an aspect of her own steady, quietly stubborn assertion of her integrity as an artist. Lyrical recall, the spiritual evaluation of echoing personal experience, had always been her bent. Now she reminisced about her youth – musing over an oil portrait of herself at age twenty-five, recalling her girlhood at Tsarskoe Selo and walks in the Summer Garden in St. Petersburg. She wrote in memory of dead friends and colleagues, and of her sense of loss in parting with them. And in continuing to write on her favorite theme of love (especially its disappointments and sorrows), about music, her religion, and nature, she implicitly insisted on her *right* to cultivate these themes and on the worth of her own personal culture.

In these last years Akhmatova wrote as the conscious representative of an epoch, and her personal recollections were designed to embody the historical memory of a whole generation. The subjective impressions in her poetry were now endowed with a generalized cultural and civic intonation. Despite the attempts of hostile orthodox critics to make her seem *passé*, she was never so, for her intimate themes were timeless, and her sense of history made them immediate and significant. The essence of her poetry was *continuity*. When most Soviet poets were developing "modern," "contemporary" thematics, Akhmatova, in the words of Evtushenko, "returned from Leningrad to Petersburg." But her own maturing, and history itself, had prevented her from sealing herself in a time capsule, so that her poetry was never archaic and always had contemporary relevance.

Akhmatova had first appeared in the 1910s as a writer primarily of delicate, intimate love lyrics, exquisite in form but confined to a personal emotional sphere. By the 1920s the experience of war, revolution, and cultural upheaval had made her poetry less egocentric, and her emotions had become much more closely identified with the fates of the Russian people and nation. For the rest of her career, politically suspect and unfairly stigmatized as a "pure aesthete," she was subjected to long periods of forced silence. But her literary activity never ceased. In the latter half of the 1930s she wrote the majestic, bitter, and sorrowing *Requiem (Rekviem,* 1935–40) – a cycle (never published in the Soviet Union) inspired by her son's arrest and imprisonment in a concentration camp.

During World War II she published a considerable amount of poetry, much of it intensely patriotic. In 1946 the postwar Stalinist repression drove Akhmatova out of the literary world, to which she was able to return only in 1950. Her powers undiminished, she reached her zenith in the post-Stalin period. Although she was never fully rehabilitated by the authorities, Akhmatova was readmitted to the Writers' Union and allowed to be published, and was permitted brief visits to Italy and England, where she received high honors. The brief official notice of her death was accompanied by wide, but unofficial, mourning.

Akhmatova's poetry is disciplined, precise, clear and concrete, in the classical Russian tradition of Pushkin. Her voice is quiet, and her simple, colloquial language conceals a rich emotional and intellectual complexity. Although Akhmatova is a musical poet whose lines are intricately orchestrated, her reticence and austerity seem to have prevented her from influencing the relatively flamboyant young poets of the fifties and sixties. (An exception is Bella Akhmadulina, whose intensive use of classical iambic meters, intimate tone, feminine viewpoint, and exploration of emotional problems echo the early Akhmatova.) On the other hand, Akhmatova was clearly revered by her contemporaries, old and young alike – many of them dedicated verses to her during her lifetime, and many wrote elegies upon her death.

The strong sense of history that governs most of her later poetry is particularly prominent in the long and complex *Poem Without a Hero* (*Poema bez geroya*) on which she worked from 1940 to 1962. (The poem was published only in sporadic fragments during her lifetime and has never been published in full in the USSR.) Fluctuating among three time planes – 1913 (a twilight year, when the old regime was on the eve of its final catastrophe), 1941 (the year of Russia's entry into World War II), and the years 1946–56 (the Stalin "epoch of the great Silence") – the poem is an intricate chronicle of the age in which she lived, with numerous intersecting, interwoven, often hidden currents. The setting is St. Petersburg-Leningrad, perceived in mixed fear and admiration, in the spirit of Pushkin's *The Bronze Horseman*. The work is "without a hero" in the sense that there is no individual central figure; rather, there is a *generalized* hero, which might be called Time, or the Age in which Akhmatova lived, as it represents the developing fate of the nation through the clash and contrast of epochs:

> As the future ripens in the past,
> So the past decays in the future.[2]

Poem Without a Hero is musical in conception, polyphonic in structure. Intensely allegorical and laden with echoing leitmotifs (windows, an old maple, a magic mirror which, like the poet, is a participant in the life it reflects), it features the themes of time, death, and repentance. The basic mood is a mixture of regret and nostalgia. The epoch of 1913 is shown as one of heedless decadence – sinful and prodigal, but also captivatingly bright and colorful. The portrayal of succeeding epochs is marked by images of devastated suffering and retribution involving both the innocent and the guilty. For the purposes of this poem, Akhmatova employed a complex and varied stanza structure and a unique poetic line of irregular anapestic trimeter, with much interior rhyming and subtle alliteration, for example:

> I ot*klik*netsya izdaleka
> . . . .
> *Klok*otan'e, ston i *klyo*kot³

The rhythm of the poem, in keeping with its subject matter, is agitated and intense.

An important theme of *Poem Without a Hero* is – poetry. This is in keeping with Akhmatova's lifelong preoccupation with the world of poetry as a self-contained and self-justified entity. It was in these later years that she completed the cycle *Secrets of the Trade* (*Tainy remesla*, 1936–60) on the nature, origin, and inspirational sources of poetry, and on how different kinds of verses come to the poet. Likewise, she continued to commune in verse with her nineteenth-century predecessors – Lermontov and especially Pushkin, who remained her idol to the end. She evoked the memories of the contemporaries of her youth – Blok, Mandelstam, Pasternak – heard echoes of the voices of her departed poet friends, and conducted conversations with them. In a poem of 1961 she feels the presence of Marina Tsvetaeva and communicates with her shade.⁴

Although it retained its personal intimacy, Akhmatova's poetry of this period was informed by a tragic sense that seemed to ignore the Soviet framework and to stress the continuity of Russian history and culture. Even in her last years she was not a political poet, but the political events of five decades had made her a *civic* poet, almost against her will. In a famous poem of 1922, addressed scornfully to Russian émigrés who had fled the Revolution, she had asserted her determination to remain at home and share the fate of her nation. In 1961, this poem provided an epigraph for a sonnet entitled "Native Land." Of the Russian soil, she wrote:

Yes, for us this is mud on galoshes,
Yes, for us this is grit in our teeth.
And we powder, and knead, and crumble it
This dust, unmixed with anything.
But we lie down in it and become one with it.
That's why we call it so freely our own.[5]

Akhmatova wrote of her own old age in sorrow but with characteristic dignity. In a poem of 1964 she observed, perhaps erroneously, that three-fourths of her readers were already dead. As for the rest, however:

But you, friends! A few of you remain, –
Therefore you are dearer to me each day . . .
The road has become so short,
Which seemed longest of all.[6]

She increasingly felt the presence of death and pondered its imminence. Writing in memory of a lifelong friend, she observed:

But your ringing voice calls me from beyond the grave
And asks me not to grieve, and to await death as a miracle.
Well, why not! I'll try.[7]

Worn out by a lifetime of suffering, she retained, to the end, her love of beauty. In "The Last Rose" (with an epigraph from a poem written to her by the young Joseph Brodsky), she wrote:

Lord! You see, I am tired
Of rising from the dead, and of dying, and of living.
Take everything, but let me once again
Feel the freshness of this red rose.[8]

Although Vladimir Lugovskoy (1901–57) was only twelve years younger than Akhmatova, he seemed light-years removed from her. He wrote as a fully committed Leninist, a totally engaged son of the Revolution, stirred by its heady romanticism and fully believing in its utopian promises. Lugovskoy was captivated by the heroic atmosphere of social change and industrialization, and by the dreams of progress, equality, and justice that the Revolution inspired. He was especially fond of exotic Central Asia and the Caucasus – their peoples, history, and legends – and fascinated by their revolutionary transformation.

For the most part, the poetry of Lugovskoy is popularly oriented, intellectually uncomplicated, and often pedestrian. In his early verses about the Civil War there is a romantic, balladlike lilt. This was largely replaced in the late twenties by a dry, matter-of-fact tone in keeping with the Constructivist school to which he belonged for a time, and in the early thirties by a rhetorical, declamatory, socialist-realist style. He wrote many poems about Europe, stressing its decadence and affirming the political and moral superiority of the Soviet Union over the capitalist West. At the same time, however, he wrote nature poetry and, occasionally, meditations on love and on his own subjective orientation to life. His later poetry shows, moreover, that during his long period as a strident, affirmative, utilitarian versifier observing Stalinist formulas, Lugovskoy was troubled by moral and intellectual doubts.

The passing of Stalin and the spiritual release that accompanied the Twentieth Party Congress brought about a flood of poetry from Lugovskoy – three volumes in the last three years of his life. It was remarkably different from most of what preceded it – deeper, more personal and reflective. The poet emerged as a painfully honest thinker, burdened by misgivings, and sensitive not only to the natural environment but also to the injustices and contradictions of the times he had lived through. Two of the three volumes – *Summer Equinox* (*Solntsevorot*, 1956) and *Blue Spring* (*Sinyaya vesna*, 1958) – consist of lyrical meditations based chiefly on nature symbolism. The third, *Middle of the Century* (*Seredina veka*, 1958), is a collection of twenty-five long poems in blank verse, which Lugovskoy called an "autobiography of the age."

The book is designed as an epic: the poet writes as a man from the ranks, evaluating a combination of public events and personal experience from 1908 to 1956. Although it is not entirely successful in its attempts to synthesize publicistic and lyrical elements, *Middle of the Century* nevertheless contains a variety of interesting material – sketches, stories, landscapes, odes, folklore, and philosophical essays. Its central theme is the fate of the individual, as a representative of his people, in a time of turbulently developing history. A major virtue of the work is its sincere attempt to grasp the complexity of good and evil in the Revolution and its Stalinist aftermath. (Lugovskoy began *Middle of the Century* in 1942, but revised it thoroughly in the relatively liberal climate of 1956; it was first published in 1958.) Its message is affirmative and, for its time, not at all unorthodox – the Soviet people have suffered tragically, but they have never ceased to *believe*, and now history has justified their faith and endurance. The poet asks:

Tell me, how will it end, the eternal quarrel
Between the individual, unique in the world,
And the state.
                    Between personal happiness
And the state.
                    Between personal freedom
And the state.
                    Between personal truth
And the state?[9]

The answer is in a reaffirmation of the original, unperverted ideals and principles of the October Revolution:

We have walked behind him.
                              Always, always behind him.
Behind Lenin. Behind our man,
Not bronze, not marble, not bound in books –
Alive, as long as there is a breath in our breasts . . .[10]

This is, of course, a rather rhetorical answer to a set of complicated, although precisely stated questions. For Lugovskoy's liberal audience, however, its anti-Stalinist emotion was infectious and welcome.

A more gifted, original and technically versatile poet than Lugovskoy, Nikolai Tikhonov (1896–   ) has devoted the major part of the past four decades to propagandistic writings and to his career as a literary bureaucrat. As an official poet, he has traveled extensively both inside and outside the Soviet Union and has produced large amounts of journalistic verse and prose. Unlike Lugovskoy, he seemed basically unchanged by the liberalization of the fifties, although some poems of 1967–9 express fashionably mild and timid regrets over past iniquities. His direct contribution to post-Stalinist literature has been small. Although he is now prominently featured in official histories of Soviet literature, he will probably appear in subsequent histories as a poet-who-might-have-been.

Tikhonov's poetic beginnings in the early twenties were auspicious. In the spirit of the times he wrote rebellious ballads full of revolutionary zeal, stressing the strength, daring, and self-sacrifice of iron-willed warriors struggling to build a new, just society. Soon, however, he was engaging in refined technical explorations, under the influence of Pasternak and Khlebnikov. His poetry became complex, with intricate sound play, startling metaphors, deliberately jarring mixtures of language levels, arresting and puzzling semantic shifts, and difficult juxtapositions of realistic detail and abstruse symbols. To this day his best poetry retains the technical virtuosity he acquired in the twenties, but without the superfluous verbal fireworks.

In the thirties Tikhonov curbed a certain strain of lonely lyricism, as well as his experimental "formalistic" tendencies, to become a militant, orthodox Party poet. He wrote simple, concrete, enthusiastic poetry from "socialist construction sites" and sounded the alarm over the rise of fascism. Especially fond of exotic lands and customs (about which he wrote prolifically even in the twenties, without having observed them), he now traveled in Europe, Asia, and Soviet Central Asia, recording his impressions in verse. During the war he wrote quantities of hortatory, patriotic poetry; after it he traveled widely as a delegate to various peace congresses, and again wrote copiously, tendentiously, and often obtusely of what he saw – notably in India, Burma, Pakistan, and Afghanistan.

In recent years Tikhonov has been attempting a lyrical and philosophical summing-up of his life experiences. With a few exceptions – for example, one taut and moving poem in tribute to a woman with whom he shared the horrors of the siege of Leningrad – these efforts are heavily sentimental and have the ring of political journalism. As a literary official close to the center of things for decades, Tikhonov has been intimately acquainted with, and sometimes an active participant in, the persecution of fellow writers. There is an unmistakable hollowness, therefore, about such lofty and abstract philosophizing as the following, written in 1969:

> Our age will pass. The archives will be opened,
> And everything that has been hidden until now,
> All the mysterious windings of history
> Will disclose to the world glory and shame.
>
> The images of some gods will then fade,
> And every misfortune will be bared,
> But that which was truly great
> Will remain great forever.[11]

Not a shadow of personal remorse, or even of regret, is to be found in these lines. They could have been written in any age and about any set of historical circumstances. They are so unspecific and so disingenuously detached as to mean virtually nothing.

Nikolai Aseev (1889–1963) was early associated with the Futurist school of Russian poetry, and throughout his career he remained versatile and technically ingenious in the manner of Mayakovsky and Khlebnikov. He served as a living link between prerevolutionary experimental poetry and that of the post-Stalin generation. The concentrated interest in phonetics of Voznesensky and Tsybin has much in common with that of Aseev; both the antiquarian subject matter of Viktor Sosnora and his extravagant sound play stem largely from Aseev, who wrote a warm introduction to a volume of Sosnora's poems in 1962.

The emotional idealist and dreamer, with concomitant excesses, are nearly always evident in Aseev. His poetry of the twenties shows a "maximalist" enthusiasm for the Revolution and a sometimes petulant hatred of lingering bourgeois attitudes. There were also formal excesses, notably a weakness for extremes of alliteration. As an activist in the LEF organization, he early developed a penchant for agitational poetic feuilletons. These – often rhetorical and rather vapid – he continued to write all his life.

At the same time Aseev was a learned philologist with a pronounced interest in Russian literature, history, and folklore. His best poetry is deeply embedded with learning and shows a wide cultural reference; he also wrote interesting theoretical works on poetry. As a man of culture, Aseev was evidently depressed and virtually silent during the last years of Stalin. However, his last two volumes, *Reflections* (*Razdum'ya*, 1955) and *Harmony* (*Lad*, 1961), although they contain a prominent ingredient of traditional "official" poetry, also include much that is fresh, original, and individual.

This is particularly true of *Harmony*, which is a kind of summary of the poet's career. It is an evident attempt to draw together all the varied strands of his thought and experience – a mixture of wistful autumnal musings, orthodox political statements, philosophical speculations on man and history, and delightfully ingenious, melodic lyrics. The title *Harmony* refers not only to harmony in personal relationships and peace on earth but also to the book's musical element and its aesthetic and intellectual structure. It is a broad evaluation of existence and an optimistic statement of faith in the future of mankind, including aphoristic treatments of the past, present, and future, and speculations on the possibility of personal immortality.

The section "Today" includes verses on poets and poetry, nature, and the present human condition. There are a number of particularly charming love poems – warm, witty, and marvelously adroit. Perhaps the most revealing poem, although technically not the most interesting, is "People Still Covet Money," which begins with an account of the lingering human thirst for wealth, power, and glory, and concludes:

> Since
> > the earth began to spin,
> continuously rushing
> > > through eternity,
> the great
> > fraternity of humans
> for the first time
> > > has begun to show itself.
> Let all – whites,
> > and blacks,
> and yellows
> > of the earth brotherhood –
> enter the wide,
> > > spacious
> region
> > of universal riches.[12]

The section "Yesterday" features folklore motifs and styles in poems about mythological Russian folk heroes, combining images of the ancient past with those of the atomic age in an attempt at a broad historical synthesis. The section "Tomorrow" is the weakest, because of its abstract rhetoric, essentially mundane ideas, and lofty topical pronouncements tied too evidently to the current Party line. There is one excellent poem in this section, the bitterly ironic "Song About Garcia Lorca," which gives an account of the tragic execution of the Spanish poet, and concludes:

> And the gendarmes sat
> > > pouring out lemonade,
> humming the words of his songs
> > > > to themselves.[13]

The volume is a fitting valedictory by a poet who, perhaps, wasted talent in the service of his state but who retained enough of that talent to write genuine poetry of a high order.

Semyon Kirsanov (1906–72) was one of the most interesting poets of his generation – a brilliant, erratic experimenter in verse who also dutifully wrote vast amounts of propaganda directly useful to the Soviet government. In 1956, and occasionally thereafter, he wrote allegorical poems of strong liberal protest without, however, fundamentally jeopardizing his status as an officially accepted member of the literary community.

Like Aseev, Kirsanov had been a friend and disciple of Mayakovsky in the twenties and a member of LEF. His verse is in the Mayakovskian mode, both in its formal aspects and its topical content, inspired by daily newspaper headlines. The socialist enthusiasm of his works in the twenties and thirties is suggested in titles such as *Taking Aim*, *The Shockworker Block*, *Lines of Construction*, and *The Party Aktiv*. At the same time, Kirsanov showed strong inclinations toward lyric poetry and formal inventiveness (both of which brought on attacks for "petty-bourgeois tendencies").

In one poem he calls himself a "Michurinist of words" – a reference to the Russian plant breeder who, like Luther Burbank, created new varieties of fruit trees. He goes to great lengths to shape his lines phonetically in correspondence to the thing described, as in stanzas on tuberculosis whose words are full of coughing sounds! At times his experiments were purely technical, at the expense of meaning, and his themes provided a merely passive support for verbal acrobatics. There is a tongue-in-cheek poem devoted to the letter R,[14] and another in which every word in thirty-six of thirty-nine lines begins with the letter M.[15] (In the other three lines he comments on what he is doing.) His verse is loaded with puns, neologisms, clever inventions in rhyme and meter, and extraordinary metaphors.

As an innovator, Kirsanov exerted a powerful attraction on the young poets of the postwar generation, many of whom were accused of having imitated him slavishly; conservative critics called him a "decadent" influence. Evtushenko reports in his *Precocious Autobiography* that, as a beginning poet, he thought he was learning from Mayakovsky but then discovered he was actually borrowing from Kirsanov. And many of the excesses of the young Voznesensky probably come from phonetical and rhythmic exercises of Kirsanov.

Kirsanov's poetry contains a prominent element of fantasy. In 1936 he successfully combined fantasy, lively verbal experimentation, and political message in the long poem "Cinderella" – a socialist version of the ancient fairy tale. His lyric talent achieved its full development in 1938 in "Thy Poem," a deeply mournful outpouring of feeling for a young woman he loved who had died. During the war and postwar years Kirsanov continued to oblige as a timely civic poet, and in 1951 he received a Stalin Prize.

A prominent literary event of the year 1956 was the appearance of Kirsanov's fiercely satirical fantasy, "Seven Days of the Week."[16] An allegory with multiple meanings, the poem tells of its hero's invention of a perfect human heart which can be mass produced to replace worn and ossified Soviet hearts that have lost their integrity and their capacity for feeling and communicating with one another. While bureaucrats are giving him the runaround in his attempts to have his invention accepted, he discovers that one of them has stolen and cheapened his idea. His notion of "honest" hearts has been supplanted by one of "useful" hearts. Packed with richly ironic detail, the poem is an amazingly frank and sweeping indictment of Stalinism and, by implication, neo-Stalinism.

In 1967 Kirsanov published another, more elaborate fantasy, "Mirrors," based on the idea that mirrors retain and preserve in themselves everything that has ever been reflected in them. Mirrors thus become a metaphor for history. But the poem further argues that all manmade objects – doors, ceilings, coins, the pages of books – are also "mirrors" that witness and record for posterity all gestures, words, and deeds. Thus,

> He who wants to hide
> the essence of events from reflection,
> beware of mirrors,
>> don't look:
> they can disclose everything.

Although the past may seem to vanish without a trace, and although the guilty may attempt to hide their crimes by destroying mirrors, there will always be those who can decipher the true course of past events, even if they are forced to interpret fragments:

> You cannot avoid
>> the evidence.
> Mirrors
>> remember it all.
> They may fall
>> from the walls,
> But from the splinters –
>> No one ever escapes
>>> No one –
> No matter who he may be.[17]

The poem is a polemic against official Soviet falsification of history, and more precisely against the trend toward rehabilitating Stalin through continued concealment of the crimes and tragedies of his era.

A parable, "The Cage," published in 1969, would seem to indicate that Kirsanov felt remorseful, or at least ironically frustrated, after a lifetime of service as a state poet. The poet feels sorry for two goldfinches he keeps in a cage:

> The goldfinch and his friend
> Grieve over prison life.
> I too
>   am no lover
> of bolts and latches.
>
> . . .
>
> Captivity
>   is not a life.
> A bar is a bar
> even if you gild it.

Summer is approaching, and he decides to free the birds. He opens their cage and puts it by the window, but the birds refuse to leave. The poem concludes:

> Well, stuff your craws
>   with grain
> At the feeding trough.
> Habit
>   is habit:
> Home is where you're fed.[18]

One cannot say for certain that Kirsanov's goldfinches are intended as a metaphor for their master but the Russian word for "feeding trough" is *kormushka*, which also means "sinecure."

The fame of Samuil Marshak (1887–1964) is based chiefly on his poetry for children and his translations from English literature – Blake, Shakespeare, Shelley, Byron, Burns, Kipling, and Scottish ballads. Like Aseev and Kirsanov, he performed state duties – by writing political satire on desired international themes and, during World War II, texts for propaganda placards. For the most part, however, he stood apart from public matters and literary politics and cultivated his small garden – public events after 1953 seem to have had no perceptible effect on his poetry.

Marshak's poetic style is conservative and classical in the manner of Pushkin, and his diction is conversational and clear. His lyrics – mainly on nature, life and death, art, and time – are pensive, pleasant, and mildly thought-provoking. In the last decade of his life, Marshak devoted himself increasingly to sunset poetry – meditations on the value of existence and the finality of death:

> Love life, while you live.
> Between it and death there is only an instant.
> And there will be neither nettles there,
> Nor roses, nor ashtrays, nor books.
>
> And the sun will not even notice,
> That in the depths of one pair of eyes
> On this little planet
> The light has died forever.[19]

He expressed no terror of death and no remorse – merely an intensified sense of tragedy in the passage of time and a feeling of sadness in the realization of his own aging:

> How many times I have tried to speed up
> Time, which has carried me forward.
> Whip it up, startle it, spur it on,
> To hear how it passes.
>
> And now I go unhurriedly,
> But hear each step,
> I hear oaks in conversation,
> A forest stream rushing into a ravine.
>
> Life goes not slower, but quieter,
> Because the evening forest is quiet,
> And the farewell rustle of branches I hear
> Without you – I alone for the two of us.[20]

These dignified, sensitive, and graceful lines, coming naturally from an aging poet, are entirely admirable. One marvels, however, that this is *all* he has to say, and that he has apparently been able to seal himself off from the communal accomplishments, troubles, and anxieties of his era.

Mikhail Svetlov (1903–64) became identified in the twenties as a "kom-somol poet." His ballad "Granada," an expression of youthful, romantic enthusiasm for the Revolution, is one of the most popular and widely remembered poems of that decade. Until the end of his days, Svetlov re-tained, to a great extent, the idealistic spirit and temperament of a *kom-somolets* of the twenties. His poetry is unpretentious, conversational in in-tonation, gentle, and warm.

While many Soviet poets in the late twenties and early thirties "learned to accept the prose of life," became factual, descriptive, and utilitarian, and replaced lyricism with a kind of hortatory reportage, Svetlov retained a tender concern for the individual human being. A poem of 1927 ex-presses his reservations about the "social command": an old woman is making her way through the streets of Leningrad, walking to save carfare. The poet gives her seven kopeks for her trip and then exclaims:

> Comrade! Singer of attacks and cannons,
> Sculptor of red human statues,
> Forgive me! – I pity old ladies,
> But this is my only shortcoming.[21]

The self-mocking humor of this passage is typical of much of Svetlov's subsequent poetry. In the literary world of socialist realism he became a romantic ironist. Unable either to accept or repudiate the prosaic reality of the Russia of the five-year plans, mistrusting the hollow grandiloquence of officially cultivated poetry but still harboring lofty dreams of a beautiful future, he resorted to a paradoxical combination of the exalted and the vulgar, the tragic and the satirical, the fantastic and the ordinary. Through this puzzling play of contrasts, presented with a sly smile and often in a bantering tone, Svetlov was able to preserve his youthful dreams without exposing them fully to possibly scornful or uncomprehending public scrutiny.

In the middle thirties Svetlov became a dramatist, and he combined po-etry with playwriting for the rest of his career. In World War II he be-came a front-line correspondent and was twice decorated for bravery. Subsequently, for undisclosed reasons, he seems to have suffered hard times and was periodically inactive until the middle fifties. At that time he experienced a kind of creative rebirth and began reasserting the frank ide-alism of his youth – now as a somewhat avuncular poet of the komsomol.

> We – my comrades and I –
> Are discovering new regions.

With bitterness I feel now,
How many losses there were along the way!
And let obelisks be raised
Above the people who perished on the way, –
Everything distant you will now make near,
To march forward again into the distance.[22]

The past had been difficult; there had been tragedies; but now was a time for moral renewal, for a romanticism refreshed:

And, greeting the new day kindly,
Cast off inertia, leave terror behind,
Meet poetry, alongside the epoch
At full speed,
At a gallop,
Full steam ahead.

And remembering my former youth,
I desert the post of old man,
And the rosy cheek of youth
Presents herself again for me to kiss.[23]

Svetlov experienced the sadness of old age, of course, but he faced it with his usual mild self-disparagement and mischievous irony. The poem "In the Hospital" begins:

What more is there to count on?
Every day they meet me, see me off . . .
It seems I've now been wreathed with respect,
Like a herring, garnished with onions.[24]

More than a decade after his death, Boris Pasternak (1890–1960) has yet to receive the critical acclaim he deserves in the Soviet Union. In the Soviet literary world he is recognized, unofficially, as a great Russian poet. But lingering political and ideological inhibitions, largely resulting from the controversies surrounding the novel *Doctor Zhivago* and the abortive award of the Nobel Prize, have caused conservative or cautious critics to slight him. There is no complete Soviet edition of his poetry, let alone his novel.

His influence on contemporary Russian versification has been great. A pioneer in the use of Russian "deep" rhyme and of relaxed, conversational diction and lexical style in the treatment of serious topics, he has been studied assiduously by the best poets of the younger generation. Andrei Voznesensky, for one, learned many of his stylistic principles from personal instruction by Pasternak. The originality and boldness of Pasternak's poetic strategy, and the stubborn independence and integrity of his creative spirit, have won him countless disciples.

Pasternak's poetry is tight and disciplined, employing classical meters, rhyme schemes, and stanza forms. Within these conservative structures, however, tremendous energies are at work, which give the poems a unique, complex inner resonance. One source of this resonance are subtle patterns of sound repetition, of interior rhymes and assonances, which not only produce musical effects but also create and reinforce all-important semantic associations. Daring and arresting metaphors, which disclose connections between phenomena that are not ordinarily thought to be associated with each other, are another source of resonance. An easy, graceful mixture of language levels enables Pasternak to endow "prosaic" images with startling and profound poetic significance. In Pasternak the reader discovers a variety of unusual and uniquely revealing angles of vision.

In Pasternak's early, most radically innovative years – the 1910s and 1920s – these qualities were a source of great complexity, and his poetry had the reputation of being brilliant but difficult, abstruse, and esoteric. Moreover, despite his attempts to deal with revolutionary themes in the epic poems *1905* (1926) and *Lieutenant Schmidt* (*Lietenant Shmidt*, 1927), Pasternak was constantly accused of being excessively individualistic, aloof, and detached from social reality. Beginning in the thirties, because of his own changing aesthetic convictions, and not in response to pressure from critics or authorities, he strove to simplify his poetry, chiefly by making it less intensely metaphorical. However, his verse remained essentially lyrical; he was attacked repeatedly for not responding to the collective, civic spirit of the times, and from 1936 to 1943 he was almost totally prohibited from publishing original poetry. As a consequence, for a number of years he made his living by translating, and produced distinguished renditions of Shakespeare's plays, as well as of English, German, French, and Georgian poetry. In the late thirties he also began working on the preliminary versions of *Doctor Zhivago*. Some of Pasternak's wartime poetry was acceptably patriotic, but after the war he was again attacked for having remained too far above the battle. Meanwhile, he began working intensively on *Doctor Zhivago*, which he completed in 1955. The poems in this novel, and the numerous lyrics he wrote in the last five years of his life, are perhaps his finest accomplishment.

Pasternak did indeed respond to the amelioration of the social and intellectual atmosphere of the fifties, although his poetry remained characteristically free of journalistic or publicistic notes. In the sense that his verse still consisted mainly of intimate and "individualistic" meditations on such eternal themes as nature, life, and creativity and was not explicitly civic or timely, it was unchanged. But it became plainer and clearer, and expressed a sensation of liberation and renewal. A major trait of Pasternak was always to pack a variety of traditionally disparate materials into an individual poem and to surprise and delight his audience by reconciling these items and justifying their presence. Without fundamentally abandoning this practice, he now modified it to make his poems more discrete and monothematic.

Nature had always been the core of Pasternak's poetry, and it remained so. It is portrayed dynamically, in the process of changing and developing. Even relatively static and quiescent landscapes are endowed with an incipient explosiveness, are captured in such a way that one feels both the preceding and future life and movement inherent in them. In "Spring in the Forest" he writes:

> The awful cold spells
> Hold back the thaw.
> Spring is later than usual,
> Thus more surprising.
> . . . .
> Steaming and baking
> Have gone on for weeks,
> But ice fetters the road
> In a blackened crust.
>
> In the forest litter, debris of fir,
> And all is buried in snow.
> Thawed patches are flooded
> Half in water, half in sun.[25]

The poet puts himself so deeply into the natural world and identifies himself with it so closely that often nature itself seems to be the narrator, endowed with a personality of its own and a full range of emotions. Nature not only is the center and source of activity but also seems to displace the traditional lyrical hero, with its own point of view, sensations, and set of moral norms and judgments. It is depicted in imagery, sometimes bor-

dering on the surrealistic, that lends it human attributes and thus personifies it:

> The frost is covered with goose-flesh,
> And the air is deceitful, like a layer of rouge.[26]

It can be seen, then, that nature is not a separate entity or group of enti-
ties external to the poet's psyche, and that its phenomena are so intimately
familiar that they seem inextricably blended with his spirit. The poet's joy
in nature seems to become nature's own expression of delight in itself. It
should be emphaized that, in Pasternak, "nature" means the total environment, consisting of all things living and dead, human and nonhuman, conceived as a wondrous unity, in which diverse phenomena reflect, echo and
communicate with each other. Thus, in the poem "Hayricks," a series of
metaphors creates a close identity between human activity, inanimate objects, and the rhythm of day and night:

> Each rick in evening dusk assumes
> The likeness of a lodging hut,
> Where night lies down to rest upon
> A bunk of clover freshly cut.

> At break of day the hayricks loom
> Like lofts in ashen morning light,
> Where the harvest moon has dug itself in
> While stopping over for the night.

> At early dawn cart after cart
> Rolls creaking on in murky air
> In twilight fields, and day crawls out
> Of bed with hayseed in its hair.[27]

Much of the nature poetry of Pasternak's last years is purely an exquisite, worshipful celebration of the beauty and miracle of life. He writes extensively of the changes of seasons, of various kinds of snows and snow-
storms, of transformations in the skies and in the fields. Nature is
creativity, the source of the poet's aesthetic principles and his faith in life.
But nature's implications are not merely aesthetic or emotional. Its portrayal is frequently laden with allegorical overtones relating more or less
specifically to individual areas of human belief and endeavor. One of these
is religion, which is the burden of many poems in *Doctor Zhivago* and also
of later ones, such as "When it Clears Up":

> The whole wide world is a cathedral;
> I stand inside, the air is calm,
> And from afar at times there reaches
> My ear the echo of a psalm.[28]

Pasternak's poetry is in fact so intensely metaphorical in spirit that one finds multiple meanings in nearly every line. At times he is quite simple and candid, as in "After the Storm" (1958), where nature imagery is directly translated into a commentary on history in the light of Stalin's demise:

> The air is full of after-thunder freshness,
> And everything rejoices and revives.
> With the whole outburst of its purple clusters
> The lilac drinks the air of paradise.
>
> The gutters overflow; the change of weather
> Makes all you see appear alive and new.
> Meanwhile the shades of sky are growing lighter,
> Beyond the blackest cloud the height is blue.
>
> An artist's hand, with mastery still greater
> Wipes dirt and dust off objects in his path.
> Reality and life, the past and present,
> Emerge transformed out of his color-bath.
>
> The memory of over half a lifetime
> Like swiftly passing thunder dies away.
> The century is no more under wardship:
> High time to let the future have its say.
>
> It is not revolution and upheavals
> That clear the road to new and better days,
> But revelations, lavishness and torments
> Of someone's soul, inspired and ablaze.[29]

But, knowing Pasternak's ideological inclinations, one is also tempted to find historical or political relevance even in innocent lines about changes in the weather.

In nature Pasternak also finds the ultimate moral guidance. From nature the poet learns humility, the value of quiet contemplation and intelligent discovery that constitute real service to humanity, as contrasted to arrogant and pompous law giving. One of his most outspokenly ethical poems of this period begins, "It's unbecoming to be famous," and counsels poets:

> Then pass into your deep seclusion,
> A man alone and unespied,
> As vanishes the evening mist
> And sudden dark the countryside.[30]

The seriousness and quality of his dedication are suggested in a poem that begins:

> I want to go into everything,
> To its very essence:
> In work, in seeking a path,
> In the heart's turmoil.[31]

and in the poem "Night," in which he admonishes the artist:

> Don't sleep, don't sleep, work,
> Don't interrupt your labor . . .[32]

His object was no less than to find the meaning of life and man's place in the universe. In his last poems there are bitter, gloomy, and tragic notes, especially in the unrelievedly melancholy "My Soul." But in others he wrote in joyous appreciation of the things that had gladdened his heart over the years – landscapes, music, the beauty of woman and, above all, the marvel of existence.

In 1943 Pavel Antokolsky (1896–) wrote a long poem in memory of his only son, who had been killed in action the year before. Entitled "Son," the poem describes the boy, who will remain "forever an eighteen-year-old," tells how and why he died, commemorates the generation that perished in the war, and presents the personal tragedy of a father as a symbol of the tragedy of the entire nation. For this work, Antokolsky was awarded a Stalin Prize in 1946.

Ten years later Antokolsky wrote an anguished poem of remorse over the behavior and fate of writers under Stalin:

> We are all laureates of prizes,
> Accorded in his honor,
> Having peacefully passed through a time
> That is now dead.
>
> > We are all his brother-soldiers,
> > Were silent, when
> > Out of our silence there grew
> > A huge calamity.

Hiding from one another,
Not sleeping at night,
While from our own circle
He created hangmen.

> We, sowers of eternal, good,
> Wise axioms,
> Bear responsibility for
> The blood of Lubyanka, the hell of
> interrogations.

Antokolsky concludes:

> And it is not the dead one who is hateful
> to us,
> As much as our own silence.[33]

It is not surprising that this testament has never been published in the Soviet Union.

Although Antokolsky is by no means lacking in emotional strength, he is a cerebral, cultured poet whose verse relies heavily on references to allied arts and on literary and historical allusions. For many years he was an actor and director in Moscow's Vakhtangov Theater. He is a learned man, of Western orientation, and many of his best works (notably "Francois Villon," published in 1934) are on themes from French culture and history. He has translated poetry extensively from French and from several of the languages of the Soviet Union. His own verse is conservative in form, deft, and disciplined.

Like many liberal poets of his generation, Antokolsky experienced a renewal of creative activity in the mid-1950s. In the last fifteen years he has produced several volumes of poetry. His chief preoccupation has been a generalized, analytical treatment of the problem of time, as it relates to history, the age he lives in, the lives of persons he knows, and his own personal life. *The Fourth Dimension (Chetvyortoe izmerenie)*, a volume published in 1964, is written in the form of monologues and dialogues by abstract characters, such as History, Time, and Earth. It is a complicated attempt to solve the puzzle of all-powerful time, including meditations on the future of humanity and dreams of mankind's victory over death.

A more impressive achievement is his *Tale of Bygone Years (Povest' vremennykh let*, 1964). (Its title is identical with that of Russia's medieval *Primary Chronicle.*) Combining lyrical evocations of his personal experience with reflections on public events that took place in his lifetime, it chronicles the history of the past seventy years as it affected a sensitive, alert, meditative man of wide interests. The poem weaves together facts, names, episodes and conflicts in the development of Russian society and culture of his era, and at times seems to embrace past, present, and future all at once. The work is true poetry, cleaner, sharper, and more sparkling than Lugovskoy's *Middle of the Century*, which seems heavy, ponderous, and verbose in comparison.

Antokolsky's most recent verse is equally arresting. In 1968 his wife, Zoya, died, and he began a long cycle of poems in her memory. The poet faces and accepts the fact that she is gone forever:

> There is no end. No beginning.
> My world has left without a word.

But he asks, "Why have you become silent?", and there is a reply: "THE SILENT ONE IS NOT I, BUT DEATH." With this understanding, he conducts tender, proud, one-way conversations with her:

> Forgive me that I am so old,
> So poor and savage and bent
> And yet did bear the blow
> And was not choked by stifling sorrow;
> . . . .
> Forgive me for the futile "forgive me,"
> That remains unanswered
> At that frontier, on that path,
> Where there is neither air nor light.[34]

Without describing Zoya directly, the poet gives a feeling of what she was like by going over her life, and their lives together, and showing what her existence meant to others and to him.

A sonnet written in 1969, with its melancholy awareness of time and history, its political disillusionment, and the sadness of advancing age, serves Antokolsky as a bitter valedictory:

> History is in me, in its entirety,
> All in a tangle of false analogies,
> It arises, like an ancestor from a forest lair,
> Like a martyr of the Roman catacombs.
>
> In whose memory, in what tongue,
> What verb in passive voice
> Sounds as a refrain in our dialogue
> And comes, like a lump, to the throat?

The years creep on. Century flies after century.
But, in the dust of libraries, I dream of
Bonfires of books, concentration camps, roundups.

I, the same age as my century, will endure much –
Not sleep at night, write, squeak the pen,
Sweat, scrape, accumulate dry chapters.[35]

Persecuted, imprisoned, and silenced for over a decade, at a time when his powers were at their height, and virtually ignored by Soviet literary criticism for an even longer period, Nikolai Zabolotsky (1903–58) has now become one of the most thoroughly respected, studied, and influential of Soviet poets. The work of younger poets as diverse as Vinokurov, Soloukhin, Akhmadulina, and Kushner, in one way or another, all bears his stamp. Although gravely interrupted, Zabolotsky's career as a poet was extraordinarily varied and fruitful.

He began in the twenties as a writer of grotesquely fantastic portraits of urban life, satirizing the petty acquisitiveness and cheap materialism of the ordinary Soviet citizens under the New Economic Policy. The imagery of these poems is vivid and concrete, but the relationship between images is vague and irrational, as in a nightmare. An ironical primitiveness and ambiguous humor, combining the comic with the tragicomic, convey a sense of dislocation and unreality in which playfulness is mixed with distaste, and pity with horror. Zabolotsky's fondness for strangeness and illogicality in this period comes largely from the influence of Khlebnikov and relates him closely to the strain of modernist experimentation in many poets of the twenties. At the same time, these bizarre visions are presented in classically precise, carefully perfected verse.

The phantasmagoric stream in Zabolotsky's poetry of these years, however, was paralleled by, and in the thirties gave way to, a stream of philosophical lyrics involving nature. He abandoned surrealistic imagery, for the most part, and strove for intellectual clarity, employing rational, analytical concepts and scientific terminology for the cognition and interpretation of natural phenomena. In this poetry the processes of nature are both a romantic source of beauty and the object of metaphysical investigation. Zabolotsky is captivated by an instinctive belief in the relatedness of all living things, akin to pantheism. Man, he suggests, is only a development of that which is already embedded elsewhere in nature: in the animal world there already glimmers something intelligent and spiritual. The knowledge that the original elements of which any living organism consists have always existed and will exist eternally, leads to the comment:

> How everything changes! What was formerly a bird,
> Now lies a written page;
> A thought was once a simple flower;
> A poem slowly plodded as a bull;
> And that which was I, perhaps,
> Will again grow and multiply the world of plants.[36]

Like Pasternak, Zabolotsky finds that nature and human feelings often echo each other so closely as to be inseparable. To express his wonder at nature's complex harmonies he uses the images "organ" and "orchestra." More than Pasternak, however, he is interested in the dialectics of nature, its constant change and alternation, the eternal struggle of opposed phenomena:

> Lodejnikov listened closely. Above the garden
> Went the vague rustle of a thousand deaths.
> Nature, transformed into a hell,
> Did its business simply.
> A beetle ate grass, a bird pecked the beetle,
> A polecat drank the brain from the bird's head,
> And the features of night creatures,
> Twisted in terror, gazed out of the grass.
> The eternal winepress of nature
> United death and existence
> In one lump, but thought was powerless
> To unite her two sacraments.[37]

In the thirties Zabolotsky's poetry was generally remote from the practical world of people and events. His few attempts to write on contemporary affairs and currently fashionable themes were too elevated and abstract to find official favor, and when he did become specific he got into trouble. A dutiful poem in honor of Stalin was severely criticized for inadequacies in its portrayal of the Leader's childhood. His long poem on collectivization, *The Triumph of Agriculture* (*Torzhestvo zemledelie*, 1933), was ideologically so ambiguous that it was first denied publication and then, when it came out, attacked repeatedly. Finally, in 1938, Zabolotsky was arrested and sentenced to forced labor. He spent six years in concentration camps in Asia and the Far East and another two as a laborer in exile – experiences that broke his health. He was not officially rehabilitated until 1951.

Zabolotsky's first publications after returning from camp and exile reflect his bitter experiences only indirectly (the censorship at that time could not have had it otherwise) and without self-pity. Into poems such as "City in the Steppe" and "Creators of Roads," which ostensibly celebrate socialist construction in Central Asia, he inserted notes of compassion and respect for those who are forced to labor there. The poem "In the Taiga" employs a cedar tree as a symbol of man's proud suffering and endurance. It was not until 1956, however, that his most candid treatment of the concentration camp theme appeared, in the poem "Somewhere in a Field Near Magadan." Two old prisoners, sent to town in dead of winter to procure flour for their camp, are thus described:

> All the soul had burned out in them
> Far from friends and dear ones,
> And the fatigue that hunched their bodies
> Consumed their souls that night.
> Life, with its sequence, moved
> Above them in images of nature.
> Only the stars, symbols of freedom
> No longer gazed on people.[38]

A blizzard comes up and, rather than save themselves for more camp existence, they simply sit down on frozen stumps to die.

Like so many others, Zabolotsky markedly increased his poetic activity in 1956. The last two years of his life, in fact, were his most productive. However, his productivity had been growing steadily since shortly after his return from exile. He had translated extensively, from Serbian, Ukrainian, German, Italian, Hungarian, and especially from Georgian poetry. Moreover, the scope and thematic variety of his original works had increased. Although he continued to write prominently about nature, he now wrote frequently about people and displayed a warmer concern for the human race. Quite uncharacteristic of the earlier Zabolotsky, for example, is "The Ugly Little Girl," a poem of 1955 in which he describes an urchin who is so misshapen, unattractive, and awkward that she reminds him of a frog. Ignored by other children at play, she still delights in their joy, without a shade of spite or envy. The poet wonders about her future:

I'd like to believe that this pure flame
Which shines within her depths
Will overcome her pain
And melt the heaviest stone!

And though her features are plain
And there's nothing to charm the imagination, –
An innocent grace of soul
Shines through in her every movement.
And if this is ugliness, then what is beauty,
And why do people idolize it?
Is it a vessel of emptiness,
Or a fire, glimmering in a vessel? [39]

Although Zabolotsky continued to avoid direct reference to current events, the implications of his verse were politically liberal. A poem of 1954 is on the theme, later to become extremely fashionable, of Lenin's democratic spirit and closeness to the people (in implied contrast to Stalin). Three old men journey from a remote village to see Lenin at his Smolny headquarters. Tired from overwork, Lenin nevertheless takes time to explain the Revolution to them, and its promised benefits for the peasantry. The old men then open their knapsacks and Lenin shares their simple peasant bread. The use of folklore rhythms and popular language lends the poem an intrinsic interest that makes it something more than a purely political tract. All the same the poem is sentimental, obvious, and by no means as strikingly original as Zabolotsky's earlier poetry.

Throughout his entire career Zabolotsky was a masterful, technically versatile poet. Among other things, he was strongly influenced by painting, and particularly by the fantastic compositions of Chagall and Henri Rousseau. His imagery was sharp and concrete, and the interplay and association of images – in both his early surrealistic period and his later, more rational poetry – was lively and complex. There is great euphony in his verse: the alliteration is delicate and deft, and the use of internal rhyme, anaphora, and various syntactic parallelisms often endows his verse with a lofty sonority. In form Zabolotsky's poetry is conservative, eschewing the free verse and tonic verse of many of his contemporaries in favor of classical binary and ternary meters; his rhymes are similarly exact and orthodox. In his later verse there is often a calculated choice of archaic words and locutions, a use of mythological and antique images, and a clarity and stately harmony that make it seem deliberately old-fashioned. But there is great technical variety even in the fifty-odd lyric poems Zabolotsky wrote in his last two and one-half years.

The thematic variety in the poetry of Zabolotsky's last years suggests that he may have been groping for new paths. His first love lyrics belong to this period, and he wrote of death without fear – death is sad because it is the end of human communication, but it is merely a transformation of eternal matter. Although his verse gained in human interest and social significance in comparison to his works of the twenties and thirties, there was some loss of intellectual complexity and aesthetic verve. Cosmic imagery, which formerly was material for metaphysical speculation, was now used at times for simple allegory. Thus, in the poem "The Opposition of Mars," the planet Mars not only symbolizes war but is also made to stand for Stalinist authoritarianism, in dialectical opposition to the planet Earth, which stands for spiritual humanity. Mars is:

> The spirit that built the canals
> For ships unknown to us
> And glassy railroad stations
> Amidst Martian cities.
> A spirit full of mind and will,
> Devoid of heart and soul,
> Which cares not for others' sufferings,
> To which all means are good.

As for earth:

> But I know that in the universe
> There is one small planet
> Where from century to century
> Other tribes exist.
> And torment and sadness are there,
> And food for passions is there,
> But people there have not lost
> The soul which nature gave them.[40]

The abundant nature poetry of these last years is less detached and philosophical, more purely descriptive and lyrically enthusiastic over nature's beauty. But Zabolotsky still retained a pantheistic aspiration for identity with all things:

I lay in the oak-adorned meadow,
And dissolved in its blazing flame,
Like countless pipes and harps,
The shrubs parted and concealed me.

I was made the nervous system of the plants,
I became the meditations of stone cliffs
And wished to give to humanity
The experience of my autumn study.[41]

Among senior poets, the most popular and widely published in this period was Leonid Martynov (1905–   ). The main reason may be that more than any other major poet of his generation he refused to write retrospectively, and focused not on an autumnal consolidation of his lifetime experience but rather on change, the future, and new discovery. His versification is stimulatingly "modern," and his political views – especially his venomous, ironical, relentless anti-Stalinism – correspond closely to those of his younger liberal contemporaries. His techniques of using the phenomena of nature as complex political and social metaphor, his fondness for hyperbole, and his aphoristic style, seemed especially timely in the climate of the fifties and sixties, and it influenced many of his juniors – notably Evtushenko, Voznesensky, Boris Slutsky, David Samoilov, and Evgeny Vinokurov. At times he seemed to be somewhat aggressively trying to be youthful, but in the main he wrote with dignity, balance, and maturity and was free of the extravagances of the young.

Much of Martynov's prewar poetry is about his native Siberia – its history, folklore, peoples, and landscapes. He was chiefly known in the thirties and forties, however, for his cycle of poems about the romantic land of "Lukomore," a fantastic, fairy-tale place that combined the beauties of Russian nature with the finest qualities of the Russian folk. Shortly after the war, largely on the basis of "Lukomore" (1945), Soviet criticism indicted Martynov's poetry for being "apolitical" and "timeless," and he was prevented from publishing for over a decade. Soviet printed sources also suggest that there were attempts to make him a pariah, although there is no mention of imprisonment. By the time his first new volume came out in 1955, he was clearly not an apolitical creator of fantasies but an angry, engaged, genuinely contemporary civic poet.

But the term "civic poet" does not at all describe or do justice to Martynov, for his field of topics and intellectual concerns is extensive, and the very texture of his verse has great intrinsic interest. He is often playful and fanciful, with a wry humor and propensity for far-fetched, startling puns and, occasionally, a kind of rhymed free verse that remind one of Ogden Nash. An informal, conversational style enables him to write unpretentiously and intelligibly about complex matters without over simplifying them. The confidential intonation of his poetry protects it from creating the impression of purely analytical, abstract wisdom. He often begins a poem with an exclamation, a flat statement of opinion ("I like . . ." or "I don't like . . ."), or an announcement that he has solved a problem ("I have figured out what it means to be free . . ."). The schemes of his poems are highly original: he frequently begins with a stimulating, sharply formulated question or surprising proposition, then temporarily perplexes the reader with clashing images or sudden transitions from one spiritual condition to another, or from concrete events to abstract judgments, and then adds new developments that resolve the poem.

Martynov's vocabulary is an interweaving of elevated poetic and popular prosaic speech, a mixture of opposites that creates a restless tension and suggests the nervous pulse of contemporary life. He can combine scientific terminology, local idiom, archaic words, and everyday diction, and make them seem natural and harmonious in a single poem. His imagery brings into conjunction things that are normally considered strange and remote from one another, and makes them exciting through unusual but convincing associations. His ability to bring together and organize the most various impressions, to combine ordinary detail with refined intellectual concepts, and objective data with subjective interpretations, is one of his greatest sources of strength and liveliness. Martynov's juxtaposition of images is occasionally so idiosyncratic and apparently accidental that his poetry seems misty and whimsical. As a rule, however, his verse is logical, clear, lean and spare, with a minimum of decoration and melody.

Metaphors in Martynov are condensed and laconic, but are drawn from a wide range of elements – often from nature imagery but most recently, in keeping with his interest in modern science and technology, from such realms as cybernetics, medicine, nuclear research, and space exploration. At times, however, his search for original imagery makes his metaphors appear contrived or bookish, or as an artificial product of his love of puns and peculiar word combinations. And, although his poetry is primarily cerebral, he is also fond of sound play, as in a poem about an olive tree, which is full of assonant echoes of the word "*oliva*" and of sibilants suggesting the rustle of leaves in the wind. Rhyme is extremely important in Martynov. It is an active force in promoting the ideas of a poem, augmenting its semantic structure by helping to disclose the connections between diverse images and thus emphasizing its thematics. Although he writes tonic verse and free verse, his poems are usually metrical in traditional fashion. To reduce the danger of rhythmic inertia, however, he uses a number of graphic devices to break up the line, and his stanzas often appear as long, thin but irregular columns, with key words arranged on the page for maximal effect.

Martynov seldom writes directly about private experience or the ebb and flow of his own moods. He exposes his individual psyche with reticence and, often, a kind of tight-lipped, sly irony. In the poem "Success," for example, he begins with the statement:

> My life is getting shorter and shorter,
> My death is nearer and nearer.

After a few bittersweet lines in which he indicates that aging had made him richer in understanding, he concludes:

> They say I have achieved success.[42]

He can also express feelings of ambivalence and inadequacy in the role of civic poet, as in lines written in 1963 in which he confesses an occasional sense of apprehension and guilt because he "sings rather sweetly" and does not sufficiently "agitate people," and because "I am not very fit to be a prophet, perishing at the stake."[43] On the other hand, he has convictions about the indispensability of the poet's freedom, independence, and integrity. In a poem, "Voices" (1954), he draws conclusions from his own period of interdiction:

> This
> My voice,
> Great or small,
> Not fearing reverses,
> I have stubbornly raised,
> I have lifted it, –
> O, no, I did not keep silent, –
> And though it was not decisive,
> Still it sounded,
> Encouraged, stifled,
> Now in secret, now overt,
> No matter what,
> It's mine,
> It's mine,
> It's mine!

> And I'll not let it
> Stifle you,
> And I'll not allow anything
> Decide for me.[44]

Martynov is equally firm in his belief in the spiritual mission of poetry. In 1954, anticipating the prominent part poetry would play in the moral renewal of the next few years, he wrote:

> There is something
> New in the world.
> Humanity wants songs.

Song he associated with rebirth:

> The naked slave stands erect,
> The leper is healed,
> The executed innocent is resurrected,
> He can't understand what has happened:
> – It's me! – he says – It's really me!

The poet concludes:

> The whole affair smells of art.
> Humanity wants songs.[45]

Despite an inclination toward detachment and ironic noninvolvement, he expresses a genuine sense of civic obligation. The poet must be clear-sighted, and he must try to show others how to live by redefining familiar words and concepts that have been debased:

> And do you know what it means to be free?
> It means to be responsible for everything!
> I answer for everything in this world –
> For sighs, tears, sorrow and loss,
> For faith, superstition and unbelief.
> I must do this at least,
> Since I myself am no longer bound to anything
> And have become, as they say, free as a bird.
> I am obligated to help everything and everyone
> To free themselves![46]

Images from nature in Martynov are often employed for metaphorical commentary on moral, social, and political issues. Particularly prominent are images of dawn, spring, and thawing, which indicate fresh hopes of lib-

eration, new awakenings, and renewed expectations. In the poem "Cold"
(1961) he describes vividly an "experiment" to freeze the whole world
solid. Then, the consequences:

> But this experiment –
> Quite understandably – called forth grumbling . . .
> And a breakup of the ice.
> And a hunger for heat and light
> Enveloped the whole world:
> The seas, and the dry land,
> And the human
> Soul.[47]

Martynov also makes figurative or allegorical use of a wide variety of other
materials. As early as 1946 he wrote satirically, but unspecifically, of
swarms of nameless, cowardly "gnomes" threatening decent society –
very likely a reference to the secret police and informers, then ubiquitous.
In "The Diary of Shevchenko," which lauds the endurance of a nineteenth-century poet under persecution, he uses the device of tacitly com-
menting on the present while apparently describing the past. His preference for allegory in dealing with the enemy is understandable in the
conditions under which he writes, but it is also a source of weakness
because it avoids candor. On the other hand, in entering into polemics
with unnamed adversaries, he often attains an extra dimension of vivid
abusiveness, as in this poem, quoted in full:

> And casually a snake remarked to me:
> – Everyone has his own destiny! –
> But I knew that one cannot live that way –
> Wiggling and sliding along.[48]

Scientific imagery is another favorite source of metaphor for Martynov.
In "Microbes" (1962) he attacks cowardly rumormongers who half-
fearfully, half-wistfully whisper of a return to Stalinism, and character-
izes them as "germs who dream of growing into giants." Of their sneaky
manipulations he writes:

> I know
> Who likes these fables,
> I can smell where these songs come from,
> In what sense, in what spirit
> These fears are inspired:
> – But if, but if

The dead are not dead, and we have not been resurrected! –
I know in what armchair this is being dreamed.[49]

Most of Martynov's scientific imagery, however, is nonpolitical; he is chiefly concerned with the implications of science and technology for the future of the planet – human welfare, war and peace, and man's moral state in general. The titles of some of his poems of the sixties show this emphasis: "Radioactive Island," "Higher Mathematics," or "Plasma," in which the image of plasma is used as a metaphor for the latent "turbulent condition" of history and the human personality. He is greatly interested in the phenomenon of *time*, and calls his own feeling for the future a "seventh sense." The fourth dimension, he insists, is just as real for him as the other three: time is something almost visible, which endows everything with a new significance, as if solidly tangible, and he therefore tries to apprehend concrete facts as conditioned by the moving stream of time, in mutual interaction with it. Unlike many of his contemporaries, he looks on antiquity without any special respect, and he places no special value on ancient churches and monuments of the Russian past.

Oriented to the future, he tries constantly to get a perspective on it. In the poem "Boundary" he writes:

Don't
Think of yourself
As standing
Just here in the real,
In the present,
But imagine yourself moving
Along the border of the past and the future.[50]

But although he is fascinated by superspeeds, space exploration, and the wonders of the age of accelerated scientific discovery, and expresses joyous surprise at the constant newness of physics and biology, he has no automatic, teleological faith in progress. One of his chief themes is his fear of atomic disaster:

The main thing is
The atomic reactor!
This is what we must carefully, with tact,
Convey, without breaking contact,
Across the border between the past and the future.[51]

Whether he is writing about the ruins of Pompeii or the splitting of the atom, Martynov is constantly in search of truths that are relevant to the times. It is this search, conducted with sparkling talent, that has made him, of all his contemporaries, the single most influential bridge between the oldest living generation of Soviet poets and the youngest.

For the writers of this oldest generation the period of the middle fifties has been called a "second Spring," in which they regained their lyrical voices, reasserted their individualism, and even took on new qualities. Surely this was true, particularly after the Twentieth Party Congress in 1956, of such poets as Lugovskoy, Zabolotsky, Svetlov, Pasternak, and Antokolsky, all of whom were affected positively but in various ways. In general, the changes that took place in their poetry were of a moral, psychological, or ideological nature, and involved matters of form and style little, if at all.

Yet the very fact that these poets could now write more or less as they wanted to, and could show their wares without the previous degree of inhibition, helped to bring about a general improvement in the cultural level of contemporary poetry. The knowledge that Akhmatova could write once again like Akhmatova, Pasternak like Pasternak, and Zabolotsky like Zabolotsky, encouraged younger poets to be themselves. Also now that these venerable masters once again "belonged" in Soviet literature, were published and respected, younger poets could delve with greater confidence into the *early* Akhmatova, Pasternak, and Zabolotsky and learn from the ideas and formal experiments of their most innovative works. These are the chief ways in which the oldest poets helped to restore the legitimate heritage of twentieth-century Russian literature.

Largely as a result of their presence, a general aspiration to regain the pre-Stalin level of excellence in poetry, to reattain the heights of Russian verse of the 1910s and 1920s, became evident. Such poets as Aseev and Kirsanov now increased in importance as living links with a brilliant past. The republication – although usually selective and far from complete – of neglected or suppressed works by Akhmatova, Pasternak, and Zabolotsky, as well as those by long-deceased members of their generation such as Khlebnikov, Tsvetaeva, and Osip Mandelstam, provided a strong incentive for younger poets to emulate the best achievements of the early twentieth century.

The opportunity to be themselves, to write more or less candidly for the first time in decades, produced varying responses from these senior poets. The majority of them, of course, had continued to write and be published even in the darkest Stalinist years, turning out serviceable, propagandistic verse on demand. Certainly some of them had written out of genuine, enthusiastic belief, but others had done so out of cynicism, or in response to unbearable pressure. Many, such as Aseev, Tikhonov, and Marshak, continued in the late fifties and sixties to write orthodox publicistic verse on officially desired topics. Through the habits and discipline of decades, such activity had become second nature to them. Any misgivings they may have had in the past, moreover, could now be overcome relatively easily because the state policies that their works were currently promoting were comparatively sensible and therefore congenial. In any event, there were safe areas, such as antiwar propaganda, on which everyone could agree. As a result of these factors, the fifties and sixties brought about no fundamental change in the publicistic writing of several senior poets.

Differing patterns of thought and sentiment, however, are apparent in the poetry that takes stock of the past from the perspective of these poets' advanced years. Sincere feelings of a generation's guilt and remorse are evident in the writings of Antokolsky and Kirsanov. Even Tikhonov, who gives no evidence of dissatisfaction with his own behavior, loftily admits that there are interesting moral lacunae in the era through which he has lived. Akhmatova and Pasternak express profound sorrow over the past, and others, such as Antokolsky, Lugovskoy, and Zabolotsky, also strike bitter and tragic notes. On the other hand, there is a prominent strain of romantic nostalgia, particularly for the Revolution and the twenties. In large measure this is simply the poet's sentimental evocation of his own and his generation's youthful élan. But it is also a device for suggesting that the Bolshevik dream was betrayed, and for reasserting faith in a democratic and humane Leninism, whose presumed purity was sullied by Stalin.

One of the most interesting features of the poetry of this generation is its preoccupation with time. For most of them, of course, the passage of time is associated with the loss of friends and loved ones and with the approach of old age and death. But for some of them the phenomenon of time has a special intrinsic fascination. Aseev, Kirsanov, Lugovskoy, and Antokolsky are subjectively preoccupied with the problem of what time *means*, and they attempt to grapple with the puzzle by examining the period in which they have lived in the light of their own personal experience. Akhmatova does much the same thing, although she mixes temporal planes much more intricately than the others. Many of them are clearly concerned with the moral implications of time and, most significantly, seriously question the notion that the passage of time inevitably ensures historical progress. Even the final affirmative notes of a Lugovskoy fail to answer completely the doubts he raises. And Martynov, the most concerned with the future, remains basically skeptical.

With the exception of Tikhonov and Marshak, this group of elder poets seized the chance given them by the break with Stalinism to say new and important things. Even under improved Soviet conditions their collective testament could not be thorough and frank. Through their years of frustration and suffering, however, most of them had gained a tragic wisdom and had managed to preserve both talent and sensitivity. The efforts of their last years demonstrated that although Russian poetry had been severely damaged during the years of cultural blight, it had survived.

3

The first Soviet generation of poets

The poets in this chapter developed their talents during years when the Soviet state was engaged in a vigorous and ruthless effort to efface prerevolutionary culture. They were born between 1907 and 1915, and by early adulthood in the 1930s most of them were writing as convinced and enthusiastic supporters of the new regime. Whatever their views of the Russian cultural heritage, whatever their ties to the past, they seemed to have made an easy and positive accommodation with prevailing official values. In the period of liberalization that followed the death of Stalin, however, it turned out that members of this age group had survived that accommodation. Through the years of Stalinist terror, war, and postwar repression each had suffered doubts and losses, and each had evidently preserved an individualized set of moral and aesthetic values. In maturity, moreover, they demonstrated strong links to prerevolutionary poetic tradition.

Olga Berggolts (1910–1976) was born in St. Petersburg and spent most of her life in her native city. Leningrad is the setting, and often the subject, of much of her poetry. She lived there during the whole of World War II, broadcasting her poems, sketches, and articles on the radio and reading them at factories and military installations. Although her first book of verse was published in 1934, her real literary prominence began with the moving war poems she wrote during and after the siege of Leningrad. Her "February Diary" (1942), for example, is a portrait of the city under blockade – miserable, freezing, and starving but proud and defiant. A harshly vivid account of her compatriots' suffering, the poem combines sorrowful compassion with a strange, fierce joy:

> In mire, in gloom, in hunger, in sorrow,
> Where death, like a shade, dragged along at our heels,

We were so happy,
Breathed with such wild freedom,
That our grandchildren would have envied us.[1]

Much of the warm sympathy that Berggolts expresses for the sufferings
of others comes, no doubt, from her own abundant experience of misfortune and misery. Her two daughters died in childhood; her first husband,
from whom she had been divorced, was arrested in 1937 and died in
prison. Her second husband died of starvation in Leningrad in 1942.
Berggolts herself was arrested in 1937 on a charge of "association with
enemies of the people" and imprisoned for a year and a half. Despite her
evident patriotism (she had been allowed to join the Communist Party in
1940), she remained under suspicion in the early postwar years because of
the lingering gloom and sorrow in her verses at a time when the authorities
were urging uplift and joy. Her concern for the human heart further an-
tagonized hard-liners in April 1953, when she published the article "A
Conversation About Lyric Poetry" – the first strong plea, following the
death of Stalin, that poets be allowed to express individual emotion and
explore their own inner experiences: to write, for example, about love.
Nevertheless, she had strong support in the writing community. Her long
poem *Pervorossiisk* was awarded a Stalin Prize in 1950, and her verse tragedy *Loyalty* (*Vernost'*, 1954), about the defense of Sevastopol in 1941–2,
was widely heralded. Active in the Writers' Union from the mid-fifties,
she was an outspoken advocate of literary freedom.

In her poetry Berggolts conveys strong and deep emotion without the
aid of striking devices. Her verse is classical, spare, and restrained in the
spirit of Akhmatova, and at the same time has some of the compactness
and allusiveness of Pasternak. In her lyrics she is direct and frank, disclosing her intimate feelings and attitudes without half-tones or ambiguity.
Berggolts is a passionate poet, fully committed emotionally and strongly
inclined to identify her personal concerns with those of the Russian people
at large, of the motherland. Ultimately she is concerned with the moral
and spiritual significance of experience; in her poetry small episodes, concrete objects and everyday detail tend to be raised to a symbolic level. She
has a prominent sense of history, and her writing, tragic in its essence,
often imbues autobiographical material with historical meaning.

In 1965 Berggolts published the volume *The Knot* (*Uzel*), containing
poems dating from 1937 to 1964. The collection, both retrospective and
contemporary, draws together the best lyrics of her career and constitutes
the powerful testament of a life of oppression, loss, torment, and coura-

geous thought. Although *The Knot* is a tragic book, an intimate confession embracing the most painful years of her life, it has a tone of proud strength and dignity and displays a keen historical awareness of the poet's inseparability from the public events of her time and from the destiny of her motherland. The poems are arranged not chronologically but thematically in accordance with the subjective association of the poet's memory – in much the same fashion as her remarkable work of prose memoirs, *Daytime Stars* (see pp. 256–7).

Many of the verses in *The Knot* are about love – usually a difficult and painful love, considered not at the moment of its onset or its flowering, but at the point of termination or as a memory. Thus, the poem "Before Parting" (1956–60) is a sad but affirmative elegy:

> We shall never know again – neither you nor I –
> Such happiness as that which possessed us.
> But I believe that my best song
> Will preserve its worn out banner . . .
> . . . .
> Farewell, my generous one! I loved you strongly.
> You shall be richer – I shared too.[2]

"Indian Summer" (1956–60) describes the season, strikes a note of bereft melancholy, and concludes:

> You see . . . the time of falling stars is passing,
> and, it seems, it is time to part forever . . .
> But only now do I understand how one must
> love, and pity, and forgive,
>   and take leave . . .[3]

The poem "That Year" (1955) refers to prisoners, arrested in the terror of 1937, who were released after the death of Stalin – to "that year when from the bottom of the sea, from the canals, friends began to return":

> Why hide it – few of them returned.
> Seventeen years is always seventeen years.
> But those who returned came first of all
> to get back their Party cards.[4]

In the above verses Berggolts gives expression, as she often does, to feelings of inseparable and proud identity with her countrymen, their anguish and their destiny. Her consciousness of history is illustrated in the poem

"International Prospekt" (1956–63), which traces the changes in a familiar Leningrad boulevard from the moment it was renamed after the October Revolution to the present when, out of the war ruins, a Park of Victory has been built along it.[5]

A poet frequently mentioned in association with Berggolts, chiefly because of her wartime verse, is Margarita Aliger (born 1915). Her poem "Music" (1942) is a requiem for her husband, a young composer killed at the front in the first months of the war. The work is distinguished by a restraint and simplicity that dignify its deep and powerful underlying emotion. Aliger's most famous wartime work is "Zoya" (1942), a long narrative poem about the Moscow schoolgirl Zoya Kosmodemyanskaya, who became a partisan and was captured, tortured, and hanged by the Germans. Since the war and continuing to the present Aliger has been a prolific poet, with a range of topics considerably wider than that of Berggolts. She has also been active as a translator of poems from various Slavic and non-Slavic languages.

Emphatically emotional and romantic, Aliger scorns a rational or cautious approach to life. In "Conversation on the Road" (1965), she disagrees with a chance train companion, an intellectual who has argued that one must carefully *study* life. Aliger asserts:

> . . . never have I studied life,
> I have simply breathed and lived . . .
> . . . .
> No matter how I try, I cannot
> study people, like algebra.[6]

At times her romantic enthusiasms take on a shade of scolding, schoolmarmish didacticism, as in "First Steamship," where she writes:

> Live courageously, don't fear the answer.
> Believe in happiness, don't fear adversity.[7]

Love is one of her favorite themes. She writes that there is "no such thing as unhappy love!" and urges her readers: "Only dare to love!" She speculates about the role of love in the lives of others: a well-to-do but loveless couple; a woman who loves an unworthy husband but benefits from it nevertheless; a pair of lovers arguing:

Once again they've quarreled in the streetcar,
not holding back, in public, unashamed . . .
Involuntarily I envy them
And gaze at them in wonder and concern.

They're not aware of their own happiness.
Thank God for this! They have no cause to know.
Just think! they are together and alive,
and they can surely patch it up in time . . .[8]

Like Berggolts, Aliger writes a spare line largely free of metaphor, unambiguous and without notable density. Her language is conversational and concrete. Although she employs a variety of verse forms and often writes free verse, she is fundamentally conservative in stylistic matters. One of her favorite topics is poetry itself, as in "To The Builders" (1959), which compares various kinds of poems to various forms of architecture. Architecture – especially as a symbol of building for a better future – is another of her interests. On the whole, Aliger is quite eclectic in what she writes about – sputniks, Shakespeare, nature and its lessons, her friend Pablo Neruda, themes from Pasternak, and people in numerous occupations and walks of life.

In much the same spirit as Berggolts, although with a greater amount of immediately evident emotion, Aliger combines her own personal concerns – her autobiography and spiritual development – with an awareness of history in the making and an interest in public matters. A member of the Party since 1942, she has often been identified with its more liberal members. In "Rightness" (1954–6) she describes an encounter with an old friend, unjustly arrested, who has just returned from seventeen years' imprisonment. At the time he was seized, she and his other Komsomol comrades had stood by helplessly, and she wonders

> who will understand how ashamed I was
> That I was unable to defend him.[9]

Aliger has been periodically, although relatively mildly, disciplined for her occasional outspokenness. She nevertheless has insisted that such pressures not be allowed to inhibit or discourage the poet:

You want to write in epic form
the history of your soul,
in which time will be reflected
as in a pure drop . . . Well, write!
. . . .
Write immediately, write, don't dawdle,

Don't let anyone
say with an unkind smile:
"They won't print it . . . Why do it?"[10]

In her "Poem About the Young" (1962)[11] she expresses alarm over still vigorous manifestations of Stalinism.

Aliger has written many poems about her travels within the Soviet Union. In recent years, however, she has become an extensive globetrotter and has written cycles about her visits to Italy, France, England, Japan, and Latin America. Her eye-witness poems about East and West Germany, with their nagging speculations on the fascist past, are particularly arresting.

Although he printed his first poem in 1934 and has been very prolific, Viktor Bokov did not develop a prominent reputation until 1958, when the first two volumes of his poems came out. Since then he has been widely published, and many of his verses have become popular songs. Bokov was born in a peasant family in the Moscow region in 1914, and writes that his illiterate mother, a fine singer of folk songs, was his most important literary instructor. He also pays tribute to Mikhail Prishvin, who first recognized Bokov's poetic talent and took him into his home at age fifteen, and to Andrei Platonov and Boris Pasternak, who gave him early encouragement.

A sunny poet, Bokov is genial and fun loving. His dominant mood is one of energetic, joyful optimism, of impetuous, somewhat naive desire to share his discoveries about life, people, and the world about him. He writes about many things – love, interesting characters, his war experience, nature, the Russian people. Many of his poems are pronouncedly patriotic. In "Distant Archepelagos" he says that he would like to visit distant places – Thailand, Australia, Sumatra – and there to sing his native songs from Zagorsk and Vyatka, just to show how warm the Russian heart is (and, incidentally, to make Leninists of those foreigners!). He loves to write about even the most prosaic objects and phenomena, to the extent that his poetry at times descends to playful triviality.

Bokov's favorite topic, however, is nature, with which he is quite evidently on intimate terms. He addresses the seasons, the separate months, warmly and lovingly apostrophizes the Volga, reports on a conversation between the sun and the earth. His landscapes are animated, their elements frequently personified and given human attributes. A cloud that passes without dropping moisture on thirsty vegetation is characterized as a "miser." Birds and animals induce bemused speculations. In one poem he describes the predatory bird known as the kite, notes that although its fledglings are innocent like all babes, they too will grow up to plunder, and asks: "Is evil in the world really deathless?" About eagles he asks:

> Why don't eagles sing
> And why aren't they merry?
> Or do they see very well from the mountain
> And know more than we? [12]

He speculates at some length on the "lilac-tinge and avidity" of the white of a horse's eye, remarks on its mysterious profundity, and then swerves to a surprising conclusion:

> In the equine hugeness of that eye
> Is only a path, an endless path.
> And a single constant phrase:
> "Hurry up with the oats!" [13]

Bokov loves to write about people. Visiting a market place, he admires its colorful sights and then notices a beautiful Russian peasant woman with her Tatar husband, and concludes that the strength of his nation will be in the blend of its races. He is especially fond of folk speech, and proclaims that

> I live not in the city
> But in the sound of voices.

Bokov has traveled widely in Russia, collecting folk songs and locutions, tales, and especially *chastushki* —short, rhymed folk ditties, of which he has assembled more than ten thousand. His interest in folk forms has strongly influenced the style of his verse.

The influence of folk poetry is evident in Bokov's melodiousness, his usage of archaic, colloquial, and regional verbal forms, and his fondness for the rhythms and word play that are characteristic of *chastushki*. His imagery is vivid, and he is given to ingenious verbal ornamentation, phonetic tricks, and experiments in rhyme. Often, however, his love of startling the reader, and his penchant for pyrotechnics and verbal trickery, lead to a neglect of semantic values and the loss of a sense of measure and taste. Despite these excesses, Bokov stands as a highly original poet whose best verses are a charming mixture of folk elements and invention along contemporary lines.

Another poet who took much of his inspiration from the rustic folk idiom was Aleksandr Yashin (1913–68). Born and raised in the dense forest region of Vologda in Northern Russia, he frequently returned to his native haunts and spent his last few years there. (For a consideration of Yashin as a prose writer on rural themes, see pp. 231–3.) The verse of his early and middle years, including the long narrative poem *Alyona Fomina* (1949) which won him a Stalin Prize in 1950, is largely descriptive of rural life and nature and, stylistically, is based on the cadences of folk poetry. In the last ten or fifteen years of his life, Yashin developed an introspective, lyrical style, often employing free verse, to express feelings and judgments that were – socially and morally – considerably more profound than those in his previous poetry.

Yashin's nature poetry is colorful and lyrical. Often it expresses merely a simple, heartfelt appreciation of the beauty of living things. He worships the sun. In the title poem of the volume *Barefoot Over the Earth* (1965), he describes a walk along a stream:

> Birds fly up under foot,
> Rabbits scatter as fast as they can.
> But I touch none of them:
> I go my own way, like a kind god,
> Through the meadows, the forests.
>
> And I eat berries,
> And nibble grass,
> I kneel before the brook.
> I love water,
> I love earth,
> As after a convalescence.[14]

In the poem "Day of Creation" (1966) he tells of how he helped a chick, abandoned by the hen who was hatching it, to break out of its shell.[15]

Nature imagery in Yashin often has social and political implications. In his later prose writings life in northern villages is portrayed as harsh and depressing. Similarly he describes a Russian birch tree in winter when it is drooping and drowned in snow:

> I know all its scars and wounds,
> All the flaws on its bark.[16]

Yashin responded strongly to the spirit of the Thaw. His poetry of the late fifties and sixties includes many fervent appeals (at times, unfortunately, sweepingly banal) for increased brotherhood and honesty among the people, for kindly deeds. In the poem "In One's Own Orbit" he asserts that he has been born anew and can "never again deceive either myself or others."[17] Another poem, written in the same year, proclaims:

> We washed the windows
> With fresh, ice-cold water, –
> The whole world seemed wan,
> Now it is young.
>
> As if we had washed
> Our own eyes
> . . . .
> And what is dearest of all –
> In the homes of my friends
> It has also become brighter,
> The windows are all clean.[18]

In 1965 Yashin stated flatly that

> I'm fed up with being afraid,
> My soul is bare.[19]

Concomitantly, the theme of conscience became prominent in his poetry, even to the point of self-laceration. In 1958 he wrote:

> Oh, how many of our people
> Still sleep badly at night![20]

"Insomnia," from which these lines are quoted, became the title poem of a volume published in 1968. It had been preceded by the volume *Conscience* (*Sovest'*, 1961), whose poems similarly emphasized the need for moral renewal and clean hands.

The last poems of Yashin, as published posthumously in *Insomnia* and *Day of Creation* (1970), are largely personal and melancholy – about loneliness, growing older, and bereavement – and express a grief both specific and generalized. The poet worries over the future of his son and daughter, who are his "dear sorrow," he writes about divorce, and ends a poem entitled "My Wife No Longer Loves Me":

> I am defenseless,
> like an open city.
> Even self-esteem does not raise my head.
> It is silent and empty all around,
> As before the creation of the world.[21]

Among the poets featured in this chapter, the most profoundly meditative and intellectually complex is Arseni Tarkovsky (born 1907). His style is severely compact, the imagery rich, dense, and resonant. Most evident are his ties with the tradition of Russian philosophical poetry of the nineteenth century, notably that of Tyutchev, and with such poets of the early twentieth century as Pasternak, Mandelstam, Tsvetaeva, and Zabolotsky. Tarkovsky distinctly reveres the classical tradition of Russian poetry, as shown, for example, in his verses in memory of Akhmatova. He has also been influenced by the phonetic experimentation of Russian Symbolism.

From 1932 to 1962 Tarkovsky was known by the Russian reading public as a translator of verse from Turkmen, Armenian, Uzbek, Georgian, Arabic, and Hebrew, as a writer of stories for children based on Central Asian folk tales, and as a literary critic. Although he had been writing poetry since his teens, the first volume of his verse did not appear until he was in his mid-fifties. This book, *Before the Snow* (*Pered snegom*, 1962), and two subsequent volumes, *To the Earth the Earthly* (*Zemle-zemnoe*, 1966) and *Messenger* (*Vestnik*, 1969), quickly established his reputation as a major contemporary poet.

Tarkovsky's style is conservative, even somewhat old-fashioned. His rhymes and meters are strictly classical. Although he uses a variety of standard meters with ease, he prefers iambics and often writes in blank verse. He is fond of the sonnet form. Tarkovsky is laconic and economical, but at the same time his verse can be subtly musical, with carefully disciplined alliteration and variations in rhyme. He is never purely descriptive: underlying his sensory detail is a rich play of associations. His vocabulary includes the language of science and philosophical abstraction, as well as classical and mythological allusions, but its basic ingredient is words that are concrete and ordinary.

The dominant tone in Tarkovsky's poetry is one of deep and serious contemplation, tinged at times with bitterness and suffering. His meditations on man's fate combine tender solicitude with a lofty, sad irony. In his poems about love, joy is equated with anguish, and wonder at love's miracle is shadowed by anxiety over the threat of death, separation, and estrangement. The poem "First Rendezvous" (1962) concludes:

> When fate followed in our tracks
> Like a madman with razor in hand.[22]

On the other hand, he refuses to view mortality with apprehension. He feels that man, and especially the poet, continues to exist after death in the acts and works of his life:

I do not believe in forebodings, and omens
I don't fear. Neither slander nor poison
Do I flee. On earth there is no death.
Everyone is immortal. Everything is immortal. One mustn't
Fear death either at seventeen
Or at seventy. There are only reality and light,
There is neither darkness nor death in this world.
We are already on the shore of the sea,
And I am one of those who hauls in the nets,
When immortality runs in schools.[23]

Tarkovsky also finds much consolation in close communion with nature, in contemplation of its beauty and grandeur, and nature imagery is prominent in his verse. Despite the philosophical bent that causes him frequently to contemplate the universe, he feels firmly and comfortably tied to the earth:

If I had been preordained
To lie in the cradle of the gods,
A celestial wet-nurse would have fed me
On the holy milk of clouds,

And I would have become the god of streams and gardens,
Would have watched over bread and grave,
But I am a man, I don't need immortality,
Terrifying – an unearthly fate.[24]

A veteran of World War II, Tarkovsky writes extensively of his wartime impressions, with pride in his fellow soldiers and compassion for his compatriots, but without heroics. He avoids writing about combat itself, preferring to deal with the more mundane aspects of war and eschewing broad and direct conclusions. In "Field Hospital," for example, he writes of the treatment of his wounds and of his recovery, content merely to evoke the experience. Similarly, Tarkovsky often writes about "prosaic" subjects, such as an empty house, but such subjects are likely to have profound significance. The first two stanzas of "Washing Clothes" go as follows:

Marina is washing clothes.
Arrogant, her worker's hands
Fling sparkling foam
Against the bare wall.

> She wrings out the clothes. The window
> Is opened wide to the street, and she hangs out
> A dress. It doesn't matter.
> Let them see this crucifix, too.[25]

The topic ceases to seem ordinary when, later in the poem, fairly clear internal evidence suggests that the person washing the clothes is Marina Tsvetaeva and the location is Elabuga, the town where the poet hanged herself.

Tarkovsky writes much about poetry itself, its nature and mission, and the role of the poet throughout history. He comments quizzically on the ineradicable but inexplicable compulsion to rhyme. In the poem "Lexicon" he writes lovingly of words, especially those of the Russian tongue, speculates on their origin, and adores the beauty of their sounds and the magic of their connotations. In other poems he stresses that words – even the simplest and most basic – are the embodiment of history, and that the poetic word is a key to immortality. It is the poet's function to weigh and examine the word and to disclose its multiple values and meanings, its cultural depths. Poetry, Tarkovsky argues, is a connecting link between the past and the future, and the poet himself is a kind of bridge:

> I am a man, I am in the middle of the world.
> Behind me a myriad of infusoria,
> Before me a myriad of stars.
> Between them I lie full length –
> A sea connecting two shores,
> A bridge uniting two cosmoses.
>
> I am Nestor, chronicler of the mesozoa,
> Of future times I am the Jeremiah.
> Holding clock and calendar in my hands,
> I am moved into the future, like Russia,
> And I curse the past like a destitute tsar.
>
> I know more than the dead about death.
> I am the most alive of the living,
> And – my God! – some sort of butterfly,
> Like a girl, laughs at me,
> Like a shred of gold silk![26]

At his most philosophical level, Tarkovsky strives to synthesize human experience and knowledge, and to observe and understand history and life as parts of a majestic, endless, cosmic process. He approaches this awesome task humbly but with impressive poetic talents, intellect, and humanity.

The career of Aleksandr Tvardovsky (1910–71) has been important for Soviet literature in two respects: as a poet he gave the Soviet Union its favorite literary hero of World War II – the soldier Vasili Tyorkin – and as editor of the magazine *New World* (*Novy mir*) in the years 1950–4 and 1958–70 he brought to light, fostered, and defended against ferocious reactionary opposition, the best literature that was published during these periods. For the latter accomplishment alone he has earned a place of high honor in the history of Russian literature.

Tvardovsky, the son of a village blacksmith-turned-farmer in Smolensk province, began writing verse on peasant themes in his teens, and by the early 1930s had become an enthusiastic poet-propagandist in support of the collectivization of agriculture. The work that brought him prominence was *The Land of Muravia* (*Strana Muraviya*, 1936), a long poem in the style of a folk tale, narrating the adventures of Nikita Morgunok, a peasant who refuses to join a collective farm and sets out in search of a peasants' paradise where he can own his own farm. Nikita, who finally returns home and joins the collective, epitomizes the land-loving, hard-working middle peasant with his dream of a better future, and is presented with warmth and sympathy.

A military correspondent during the Soviet–Finnish war and World War II, Tvardovsky published his masterpiece, *Vasili Tyorkin*, in installments from 1942 to 1945. The work is a long epic poem, written in popular trochaic tetrameter, presenting the war from the point of view of an ordinary combat soldier. Vasya Tyorkin is a genuine folk hero, no larger than life but endowed with the most engaging and admirable qualities of his people – ingenuity and staunchness in the presence of danger, good humor, a robust wit and love of fun, generosity, and a sense of patriotic duty. An unassuming and unrewarded hero, Vasya is brave in battle but shy about expressing his loftier feelings. Tvardovsky presents him with sympathy and affectionate humor and, without sentimental proclamations about Vasya's heroism, manages to suggest that the war was won not by the country's political organization and leadership but by the people. There is not a single mention of Stalin in the entire poem.

Tvardovsky remained, however, a devoted Communist. He had joined the Party in 1938, had written poems in praise of Stalin and, apparently, accepted the Stalinist system without question until the general awakening signaled by the Twentieth Party Congress in 1956. He accepted three Stalin Prizes in poetry – for *The Land of Muravia, Vasili Tyorkin,* and *The House by The Road* (*Dom u dorogi,* 1946), a sorrowful and compassionate long poem about a Russian mother under the Nazi occupation and forced labor in Germany. Tvardovsky's first serious brush with the authorities came in 1954, when he was fired as editor of *Novy mir* for having published Vladimir Pomerantsev's essay "On Sincerity in Literature" – the first appeal for truth in literature in the post-Stalin period. It was not until his second, twelve-year term as editor that he became identified as the most prominent literary figure in the liberal cause and defender of creative freedom.

During the Khrushchev period and to the end of his life Tvardovsky maintained his Party career, which reached its peak when he became a candidate member of the Central Committee in 1961. He never abandoned his faith in the possibility of a truly democratic communism. Even under Khrushchev, however, he had experienced serious vicissitudes as editor, repeatedly forced to defend himself and his journal for encouraging and publishing liberal writers. Following the ouster of Khrushchev, the last six years of Tvardovsky's editorship were increasingly embattled. His authority was gradually undermined (some of his own poetry was repeatedly rejected by the censorship), and the harassment continued until he was forced to resign in 1970. At his funeral in 1971 the official eulogies so distorted his career by failing to mention his most controversial poems and achievements as editor that Solzhenitsyn wrote his own eulogy (unpublished), in which he referred to "sixteen years of insults meekly endured by this hero."

The style of Tvardovsky's long narrative poems is simple, natural, and unpretentious, in keeping with the author's evident aspiration to communicate as directly and widely as possible. Their language is colloquial and relaxed, largely free of ornamentation or musicality. The meters of Tvardovsky are regular; the rhymes do not draw attention to themselves. His metaphors and similes are few and modest, designed to designate rather than to startle. Exactitude in expression and factual precision of imagery seem more important to him than displays of formal virtuosity. As a consequence, his lines seem old-fashioned and unoriginal, in many respects a throwback to the nineteenth century and specifically to the populist poet Nikolai Nekrasov. This is not to say that Tvardovsky's poetry is lacking in color; it is earthy and, like Nekrasov's, subtly flavored with elements borrowed from folklore. The imagery, although not stunning, is heavily laden with meaning, and it serves as a powerful focus of ideas.

One of Tvardovsky's favorite images is that of "the road," conceived of as a highway along which time and history move. It became the central image of the epic poem *Distance Beyond Distance* (*Za dal'yu dal'*), written between 1950 and 1960. The poem consists of fifteen chapters, written in the form of a kind of lyrical diary in which the narrator comments on his life and times and gives a sweeping portrait of his country and its people in a period of increasingly positive but still uncertain transition. The "road" is the narrator's journey by train from Moscow to the Soviet Far East, in the course of which he observes various regions of his motherland and describes characters he meets along the way. Another uniting principle of the poem is the narrator's meditation over the past and present, his reactions – emotional, moral and intellectual – to events of historical significance in which he has participated or which he has witnessed. His dominating concern is the destiny of his vast and sprawling nation, with which he intimately identifies himself. *Distance Beyond Distance* is thus a combination of travelogue, personal confession, and civic musings.

Although the style of the poem is typically relaxed and easy, its language tends to be intellectual and lacks the previous Tvardovskian peasant coloration. The verse itself is iambic tetrameter, similar to that in *Eugene Onegin*, and the texture of the poem – at times descriptive and discursive, at others lyrical and ruminative – also seems influenced by Pushkin. This structural flexibility enables the poet to interweave personal recollections, contemporary observations and reports, and portraits of typical individuals, designed to give a cumulative impression of an era.

Tvardovsky's mixture of the personal and the civic is illustrated in the chapter "Two Smithies," in which he begins by describing, from childhood recollection, his father's smithy and the local folk who gathered there to talk, and concludes by celebrating a different smithy – the Soviet armaments industry in the Urals that helped supply the tools of victory in World War II. In the chapter "Literary Conversation" he converses with his own "internal censor" – a second personality, shaped by a repressive literary environment, that has heretofore inhibited him from writing the truth to his own satisfaction. (There are implicit and explicit pleas for greater literary freedom throughout the poem.) The chapter "Childhood Friend" tells of the narrator's meeting with a friend of his youth who is returning to Russia from long Siberian exile:

> And I look him in the face:
> Everything about him is the same as it was,

> But the grey hair, the weariness of the eyes,
> The dismal gleam of prison dentures –
> . . . .
> And what about me –
> Although I did not cross that threshold,
> Of course I am no younger,
> It's just that I kept my teeth.[27]

The moral center of *Distance Beyond Distance* is its fourteenth chapter, entitled "This is How it Was." Here Tvardovsky attempts to assess the Stalin period and, in rather gingerly fashion, to find the causes behind that melancholy epoch. He insists that the painful past must not be allowed to fade from memory, that its lessons not be neglected. Moreover, he argues against easy scapegoating. All, including himself, he feels, must share the blame for the "cult of the personality":

> Thus on earth he lived and ruled,
> Holding the reins with a stern hand.
> And who did not praise him in his presence,
> Did not glorify him – find such a person!
> . . . .
> And who of us is fit to judge –
> To decide who is right and who is guilty?
> We're speaking of people, and don't
> People themselves create gods?[28]

Thus, the poet seems impartial, but at the same time excessively vague and indiscriminate in allocating political and moral responsibility. His prescription for a better future is equally unspecific: he advises the people to "be like Lenin."

In 1963 appeared *Tyorkin in the Other World* (*Tyorkin na tom svete*), a satirical sequel to *Vasili Tyorkin* in which the hero is conducted through hell by a fellow soldier and finds the place grotesquely similar to the world above. For one thing, the place has separate capitalist and communist sections, but of course the latter is superior:

> In this place beyond the grave, our world
> Is the better and more advanced.
>
> "Their foundation's shaky,
> Ours is solid.
> We have shortcomings, of course –
> But on the other hand we've system."

"In the first place, the discipline there
Is weak compared to ours,
The picture is:
Over here – a marching column,
      over there – a crowd."[29]

Versions of the poem had been known to a very limited circle of readers since 1954, but its printing in 1963 marked a high point in the publication of Soviet satire. Hell, it turns out, is a bureaucratic paradise, bathed in eyewash and governed by absurd administrative formality hilariously familiar to the Soviet reader.

Throughout his career Tvardovsky had written nature poetry, but during the last decade of his life it became less descriptive, more lyrical and ruminative, freighted with introspection and notes of disillusionment and sadness. Delight in the beauty of nature became mixed with anxiety and foreboding. Natural phenomena became metaphors not only for his own emotional states but also for the Soviet political situation. In a poem published shortly after the Soviet invasion of Czechoslovakia in 1968 he wrote:

Windless, warm – almost hot,
Ever shorter, gift-days
Resound barely audible like the gold of the foliage
In Moscow itself, in Moscow's environs
And somewhere else, no doubt, in a Prague park.

Before such an unknown winter
Of such anxieties and shocks ahead
Can this autumn world be so fresh and clear,
My every breathing in and out so sweet?[30]

Tvardovsky's bitterest poem, "By Right of Memory," has not been published in the Soviet Union. He submitted it unsuccessfully to the magazine *Youth* (*Yunost'*) in 1967, and in 1969 decided to publish it in *Novy mir*, only to have it rejected by the censorship in three successive months. The most poignant and unconsciously ironical section of the poem is one in which Tvardovsky – the author of numerous poems in the 1930s supporting the collectivization of agriculture – describes how his own father, a poor and industrious peasant, was unjustly branded a kulak, dispossessed, and deported to Siberia. He speculates on the naive hopes his father must have had in prison:

> And he believed: everything will fall in place
> And soon everything will be reexamined,
> As soon as Comrade Stalin himself
> Reads his letter in the Kremlin . . .[31]

The impact of the experience on Tvardovsky himself is suggested in the following lines:

> O, years of unloved youth,
> Its fierce troubles.
> This was my father, then suddenly – the enemy.[32]

The poem is not only a sad and anxious recapitulation of the injustice, lawlessness, and terror that marked the Stalin period but also a pessimistic warning that if the police regime (including the prohibition of open discussion of Stalin's crimes) continues, this dark era in Soviet history could repeat itself.

4

Poets formed during the war

When the German armies invaded Russia in 1941, all of the poets with whom this chapter is concerned were barely on the verge of adulthood – most of them were still in school. The war thrust them abruptly from youth into maturity and influenced their characters decisively, both as individuals and as poets. During the war itself, most of them were too young, and too preoccupied with the shock of growing up in the midst of holocaust, to write and publish significant verse. A certain distance, therefore, separates their war poetry from the events that inspired it. But the psychological and moral traces of this formative experience are indelible not only in their war poetry but also in verse written two decades later, on themes that seem totally unrelated to the war.

Front-line lyrics written during the war emphasized proud suffering, the heroism of the fatherland's defenders, and the political and national cause for which the war was being fought. A decade later poetry had become more elegiac, had begun to concentrate more heavily on the moral and psychological aspects of combat and the tragic cost of war, and frequently had strongly pacifistic implications. The realization that Russia's appalling losses were partly attributable to Stalin's blundering and callous waste of lives, and the feeling of betrayal caused by the senseless cruelty and injustice of his postwar domestic policies, placed the war itself, for many poets, in altered perspective. The just purpose of the war – the defense of the fatherland – was never in question. But as it became possible to write more candidly and intimately about the war, new notes of reappraisal and skepticism appeared. As they concentrated more heavily on what the war had meant to the individual participant, the poets portrayed its prosaic aspects in greater clarity and detail.

For many poets of this particular generation, the war was also a time of complex spiritual reevaluation. As children of the twenties and thirties, they had been taught to consider themselves the direct heirs of the Revolution and to believe confidently in its promise of social equality and justice. They had been cast in the role of young heroes of a triumphant future. Then, at a stage in life when the psyche is particularly vulnerable, they experienced the disillusionment of a massive retreat in the face of the fascist invaders, the unresisted bombing of their cities, the devastation of their land. Ultimately victory came, at a terrible price. But simultaneously came another disillusionment – the renewed Stalinist repression, with its stifling atmosphere of harsh coercion and suspicion. Under these circumstances, many of these young veteran-poets, oppressed by a sense of betrayal and therefore skeptical of the moral code under which they had been reared, underwent creative crises. It would have been politically unacceptable, of course, for them to call themselves a "lost generation," but spiritually they did have much in common with the Western vintage that had preceded them by three decades.

A poet who stressed the prosaic aspects of the war was Evgeny Vinokurov. Born in 1925, Vinokurov entered officers' training in 1943 and was in command of an artillery battery before he was eighteen. His first volume, *Verses about Duty* (*Stikhi o dolge*, 1951), presented a factual, earthy view of war confined largely to his own personal experience. Avoiding lofty rhetoric (there is little mention of heroism or patriotism), he wrote with a light touch and often with wry humor. One poem recalls a bawling-out he received as a trainee, for his "tactlessness" in being late for a formation. At the same time he conveyed with restraint, and yet directly and intimately, the most profound emotions. Of a schoolboy friend who served in the poet's own regiment, he wrote:

> He was killed near Warsaw in a bayonet charge.
> We parted. Forever.
> He lived on the Arbat, in the big grey house on the corner,
> Opposite the pharmacy.[1]

As he matured, Vinokurov gradually moved on to a large variety of nonmilitary topics. Nevertheless, impressions and attitudes formed at the front have continued to govern his vision of the world and to provide much of the imagery for his reflections on subjects unrelated to the war. In a poem of 1960, for example, he recalled that barracks life had been like "a cold knife, bared for a fight," that its values had been reduced to "food and woman," and that his only true spiritual sustenance had been in "the momentary complexity of a flower and a blue midnight star." He concluded that "there is nothing more horrible on earth than simplicity."[2] Although the poem speaks directly of the brutish, primitive simplicity of military existence, it suggests metaphorically that there is inherent evil in simplistic views of life in general. Vinokurov's major effort as a poet has been to reveal unexpected aspects of that which *seems* mundane and simple, and thereby to disclose the complexity of things that, at first glance, appear to be elementary and obvious. In doing this, his poetry is also a challenge to the dogmatic generalizations and frozen habits of mind that were fostered in the Stalinistic intellectual atmosphere.

Vinokurov's poems are most frequently based on everyday personal experience or direct observation, centering on a concrete object, person, phenomenon, or incident, which becomes the point of departure for a brief, stimulating speculation. He is alert, curious, and deeply involved in the swim of contemporary life. He celebrates the domestic routine – giving the children their baths, his wife washing the clothes. He describes the neighbor who lives across the hall, grumbles about unpleasant features of the circus or the movies, tells how drinking is done in beer halls, explains why he likes statues in parks. But he is seldom purely descriptive. A poem is his way of standing slightly aside, to evaluate and to find the special significance of something ordinary that might otherwise be ignored, insufficiently pondered, taken for granted. His statements of likes and dislikes are clear, strong, original, and often amusing. At the same time, his absorption and delight in the details of existence is an implicit criticism of the official Soviet passion for civic values, and his interest in the stable routine of private life appears as gentle defiance of official insistence that Soviet citizens live for the future.

Two of Vinokurov's collections are entitled *The Human Face* (*Litso chelovecheskoe*, 1960) and *Characters* (*Kharaktery*, 1965) – people interest him immensely. There is an array of personalities in his poems, many of them admirable, others unattractive. In one poem he presents a small gallery of sycophants, timeservers, and sneaks.[3] Another, describing a physically repulsive bore, begins, "This man is obnoxious" and ends:

> At last! He's gone. I hang over
> The railing: – You forgot your briefcase!
> No, why? I'll just throw it down.[4]

What Vinokurov values above all is the sanctity of the individual. By way of stressing the need for solicitude for every human being, he suggests that, just as Soviet railroad stations have complaint books for the public, so should eternity have one for silent, anonymous sufferers such as "that woman I saw crying in the park last night."[5] In another poem he writes:

> There are eccentrics in the world. They live among us.
> Ecstatics. Hair down to their shoulders.
> Their talk is complicated and wise.
> Their actions are surprising at times.
> Wretched eyeglasses. The rims tied up
> with string. Drop into their garrets:
> You'll just throw up your hands: really!
> What a scarecrow! Brother, what a queer fish!
> They dream all the time. At night they pull the covers
> Up to their ears, listening to noises in the chimney.
> And I'm often sorry that I've allowed myself
> So few crazy quirks in this world.[6]

This poem can be interpreted not merely as a statement of wistful respect for eccentricity but as a portrait of persons whose spiritual independence has forced them into the social underground. Vinokurov shows a special interest in the emancipation of the human personality from narrow channels of thought and behavior. His poems seek to define the *individual* and to find the place of the personality in a complicated and perplexing world – many Soviet citizens have not been accustomed to this kind of thinking. The poet is not merely fascinated by human variety; he insists on its importance:

> How good it is to have one's own face . . .
> This fellow looks at you shyly, that one proudly.
> One likes to sit in a boat with a fishing pole,
> Another is crazy about crossword puzzles.
> Everybody has his own way of walking,
> And everyone wears the kind of scarf he wants.
> This one's lips barely tremble at a joke,
> But that one guffaws like a madman.
> How good that everyone is different
> From his neighbor. And marvelous
> That he and I are not the same:
> We stand in different ways. Light our fags differently.
> Oh, how joyous is this haphazard diversity

> Of clothes, hair, habits, color of skin!
> There must be a good reason why we're evidently afraid
> To be as like one another as fish eggs.[7]

In his affirmation of the individual and praise of human variety, Vinokurov is like other poets of his particular generation of veterans. Their delight in the value of a personality that aspires to think boldly and freely seems like a somewhat naive discovery of the obvious – but only if one forgets the painful process that led up to this discovery. Vinokurov is acutely, historically conscious of belonging to this generation, and his works contain constant reminders of its accumulated experience and wisdom. He is particularly sensitive to the passage of time, so that his treatment of the events and experiences of his own life provides a kind of spiritual biography of his generation. Their childhood and adolescence was spent in the years of industrialization, collectivization, and Stalinist indoctrination. In "Poems About Childhood" he writes with amused irony of the "Certificate of Political Maturity" that was awarded him in kindergarten, of how as a schoolboy he drew crude caricatures of *kulaks* and suspected every fat man of being "bourgeois." This early training also imbued him with communist idealism, a feeling of romantic pride in the Revolution (which he has never lost), and overwhelming trust in the nation's leadership. But, in addition, it instilled in him a callow impatience, intolerance, and ideological smugness – a willingness to accept large generalizations and eagerness to sweep aside contradictions. Only much later, as he testified in a poem in 1961, did he realize how rigidly he had been formed:

> I didn't keep a diary. I didn't collect facts.
> I despised the particular.
>   Hated details.
> A huge light had blinded me.[8]

Like the rest of his generation, he had been the intellectual and spiritual prisoner of Stalinism. His reaction to this realization, however, has not been noticeably militant or bitter. When he touches upon civic themes, it is usually by indirection, and his lines do not have the tone of rage that is present in some of his contemporaries. He seems, rather, to be grateful that the worst is over and determined to repair the damage earnestly but quietly.

There is an air of modesty, candor, and artlessness in Vinokurov's poetry that has obviously been carefully cultivated. He repeatedly stresses the importance of simple-heartedness, not only as a virtue in itself but also as a matter of cognitive strategy, for, as he argues in the poem "Ingenuousness," more things can be understood through purity of heart than through rational schemes and dogmas. This attitude is underlined in the very style of his poetry. Technically there is nothing obtrusive or outstanding about it. His metaphors are uncomplicated, his images exact and graphic. Although he is melodious, he avoids obtrusive sound play, and his rhymes are simple and accurate. His syntax is straightforward and natural, usually involving declaratory statements of not more than two lines. For the most part he favors classical metrics, and the greater number of his verses are in iambic tetrameter or iambic pentameter. In recent years, however, he has been increasingly writing free verse. Although his style is frequently elevated and solemn, he is seldom stuffy. His vocabulary is colloquial, and he is not afraid to use crude words on occasion. Moreover, he is capable of subtlety: his poems require study, for often he smuggles his most important ideas in ostensibly accessory or secondary places.

Vinokurov's poems have become increasingly contemplative. Often he writes about abstractions, in poems bearing such titles as "Inspiration," "Appearances," and "Profundity." He alludes frequently to music, and discusses purely aesthetic problems: beauty, harmony, and precision. Much of his verse is devoted to poetry itself – its innermost purpose and the tormentingly difficult lot of the poet. One of his most arresting poems, telling of the agony of speaking gracefully, clearly, and honestly about that which the poet knows to be hopelessly complex, is entitled "Tongue-Tied."

Despite his analytical bent, Vinokurov remains primarily a lyric poet. One suspects that this is why, without making concessions to vulgarity, he has become one of the most *popular* of contemporary Soviet poets. It is true that a quality of emotional and intellectual detachment seems to make him strive to maintain an evaluative distance between himself and the subjects he is contemplating. His is a *tempered* lyricism, governed by a seemingly inborn sense of limitation that prevents him from going to daring extremes. It is clear, however, that this comes not from coldness but from honesty and wise humility. His warmth and modesty are illustrated in two poems written in 1961. In "I Visited That City" he tells of learning of the death of a woman whom he had once loved deeply but who had been "both tender and malicious, both false and dear" to him:

> I cannot resolve the intricate problem,
> The deep enigmas of existence.

> I know nothing. I simply weep.
> How am I supposed to understanding everything?
> > I simply weep.[9]

In the second poem he discusses the art of Picasso, which has "dissected the world into parts." Then, seeing someone crying in a cafe, the poet issues this challenge:

> A tear is trickling down . . .
> > Dissect it! Just try![10]

Boris Slutsky is a less dispassionate poet than Vinokurov, with a more pronounced sense of social mission. In verses recalling his duties as a political instructor at the front, he states that this experience qualifies him "to speak in the name of Russia in a new post – that of poet." The implication is twofold: the poet's function is civic and didactic – the poet is a mentor; and the war veteran has a special right and qualification to perform this function.

The feelings that support this attitude are abundantly evident in Slutsky's poetry about the war itself. It is grim, earthy, anguished poetry, full of pain and trauma. The poet tells of being wounded and of dragging himself back to his lines. In "How Did They Kill My Grandma?" he tells of how the Germans, aided by local collaborators, rounded up a Ukrainian town's Jewish population "light from a year's starvation, pale in the agony of anticipated death."[11] Among them was the grandmother, who screamed defiance and was shot before the pitiful group was herded to its place of execution. In another poem he records his dumb sorrow on learning that a whole family of his aunts, uncles, and cousins was cremated. There are poems to dead comrades and their widows, grim descriptions of the wounded in hospitals, portraits of peasant women receiving parcels with the personal effects of their soldier husbands. The intense horror of the war reinforces the poet's awareness of its issues: the poems resound with hatred for the Nazi aggressors and solemn pride in the self-sacrifice, endurance, and stubborn heroism of Soviet soldiers and civilians. Fighting alongside "the Ivans" (as he calls them in one poem), the poet has become so intimately identified with them that he feels an obligation to become their spokesman.

Slutsky is particularly eloquent about the emotional and spiritual consequences of the war – its residue of heartbreak and fatigue. Although he writes as a loyal Soviet citizen, proud of his nation's accomplishments and confident of the future, in his civic enthusiasm there are discordant notes of weary skepticism. In the poem "1945" he describes the beginnings of reconstruction:

> And gradually the cracks were painted over,
> The strong wrinkles smoothed out,
> And gradually the women grew prettier
> And sullen men grew merry.[12]

The apparent optimism of this poem, however, is laden with irony, all the more bitter because it is cryptic. A passage buried in the middle of the poem reads:

> The tired labored tirelessly.
> The hungry worked as if satiated.
> We sat down to wheat soup without grumbling,
> And no one checked with his spoon: is it thick?
> From all the rocks crunching underfoot
> First palaces, then homes were built . . .[13]

In a seemingly insignificant detail, as if in passing, the poet mentions the priorities Stalin's government observed in rebuilding the country – and their incalculable cost in additional human suffering and disillusionment. In this and other poems there is a suggestion, never explicit but clear enough, that "the Ivans" deserved more for their valiant efforts and that the goals of the war were betrayed. This is undoubtedly one of the reasons why Slutsky was unable to publish a single poem after the war until 1953.

Born in 1919 in the Ukraine, Slutsky grew up in industrial Kharkov. He recalls the psychological atmosphere of the 1930s, with its emphasis on working for the future:

> And, as in a crowded streetcar,
> We dream to make the time pass.
> And tearing a leaf from the calendar,
> We look at the date with hope.
> And why should we, standing in the streetcar,
> Guarding our sides with our elbows,
> Why should we value the present?

As for himself:

> As if I were doing some good deed
> By living in Kharkov,

I dashed to high school,
And later to night school,
Subsisted on cold soy beans,
Read the newspapers about the trials,
Tried to understand everything,
Did not consider myself a prophet.[14]

When the war broke out Slutsky, now a budding poet, was in law school in Moscow. He fought all through the war, and was several times wounded. Evtushenko describes him in the early 1950s, living serenely in a tiny Moscow room on cheap canned food and coffee, supporting himself by writing small items for the radio, his desk drawers stuffed with "sad, bitter, grim poems" which "it would have been absurd to offer . . . to a publisher."[15] As with many Soviet poets who have undergone periods of interdiction, the individual poems in Slutsky's collections are seldom dated. It is fair to surmise, however, that the poem "God" lay long in the drawer. In it he recalls seeing Stalin's motor cavalcade speeding along the Arbat in the grey early dawn; even his guards in their mouse-colored coats were trembling. As for the Leader himself:

He lived not in celestial remoteness,
Sometimes he was seen
In person. On the mausoleum.
He was wiser and more vicious
Than that other, different one,
Who is called Jehovah.[16]

The poems of Slutsky that have been printed in the Soviet Union since he began publishing in 1953 have not, as a rule, been notably dissident. In many respects he seems a model of what the Soviet poet is expected to be – patriotic, affirmative, down to earth, fully committed to the ideals of the Revolution, and one who stresses the moral value of hard work, self-sacrifice, and social dedication. At the same time he manages to preserve an air of wary independence, of striving to expand the limits of orthodoxy, which places him unmistakably in the liberal camp. Attacking ideological conservatives who deny the validity of religiously based art, he writes, of the fifteenth-century icon painter Andrei Rublyov:

No, not everything fits into a scheme,
However much you try . . .
. . . And what's the point
Of trying to turn

His archangels into peasants?
He was saved not by a swineherd
(Symbolizing labor)
But quite simply
                    by the Saviour.

After exposing an absurd fallacy, however, Slutsky is quick to restore the
ideological balance:

As for the Lord, we'll
Finish him off
                    without Rublyov.[17]

Although Slutsky's poems do not lack lyric emotion, he seems to prefer
the role of a hardheaded, commonsense poet given to brief, disciplined utterances. (His most emotional poetry by far is that about the war.) Even
when he writes on intimate, personal themes – as in a rather desolate
poem about his fortieth birthday – he is restrained. He very seldom
writes on love or nature. He favors brief reflections on limited topics,
frequently concerning urban life (city crowds, what it is like to live on the
twentieth floor), or popular intellectual issues (his poem "Physicists and
Lyricists," in which he observes wistfully that contemporary science has
thrust art into the background, caused a flurry in literary circles).[18] As a
rule, the poems contain one discrete idea, raising a question, stating an
opinion, or giving advice, in keeping with his belief (stated repeatedly in
his numerous poems *about* poetry) that the poet is a kind of custodian of
culture whose mission is to express thoughts and feelings that his fellow
citizens share but are less able to articulate.

Slutsky has said that "a poet is not a telephone but a telegraph wire."
Correspondingly, his verse is laconic and sinewy, and his statements are
clear, direct, and event blunt. The language is prosaic and often harsh, the
imagery chiseled like rough sculpture. Formally his poetry is versatile but
conventional, and it has only a modest intrinsic beauty. To make his verse
angular and emphatic (occasionally at the expense of his usual telegraphic
compactness) he often uses repetition, and combines deep rhymes with
the most elementary grammatical, or even homonym, rhymes. At times
his rhymes can be so bad as to seem intentionally grotesque (e.g. *royal'* –
yanvar'). These characteristics are not attributable to prosodic ineptitude
but are in keeping, rather, with Slutsky's concept of beauty. Perhaps the
best illustration is his poem "The Bathhouse," in which he describes the
bodies of bathers, with their wound scars, calluses, tattoos, and burns,

each telling something of its owner. In this poem the human body is something ugly, but its blemishes indicate a spiritual beauty that transcends the
physical.[19]

Despite his straight-from-the-shoulder pundit's manner, Slutsky is
clearly a troubled and contradictory poet. He fluctuates between eloquent
outpourings and guarded mutterings. At times he is genial, witty, and
playful, at others wry and caustic. One must be constantly on the lookout
for the single subtly sarcastic, almost hidden line, that is the real burden of
the "telegram." Behind his tart, sometimes skeptical aphorisms there is
discernible the discontent of a strongly frustrated moral sense. For all his
earthiness, he seems to be ultimately worried about the destructive effects
of rigid institutions on the human soul:

> Using the metric system
> It's easy to measure a neck or a belly.
> But you can't trust spiritual measurements:
> That's a tailor's idea.[20]

One of the most widely published poets during this period was Konstantin Vanshenkin, who was born in Moscow in 1925, fought in the war, and
is closely identified with the poetic circles of his veteran contemporaries.
Perhaps the least gifted of the poets mentioned here, he nevertheless deserves attention because he is a popular favorite and because he represents
a nostalgic (although by no means militaristic) strain in Soviet war poetry.
Vanshenkin's poems, for the most part, neither require nor inspire much
intellectual effort, but they have an infectious lyric sincerity and modest
beauty. A number of them have been set to music.

Vanshenkin writes pleasantly about nature and human beings; his speculations on life are rather mundane. One of the reasons for his wide appeal, no doubt, is that he is assiduously democratic: he writes of ordinary
humans, often of blue-collar workers, and in his war verse he writes particularly warmly of the common soldier, engaged in humble occupations.
Although his war poetry is on standard themes (the loss of friends, the
ghastly waste of life, the unpleasantness of the trenches), two features
stand out particularly: he does not emphasize or linger over suffering and,
rather more than other poets, he seems to treasure his youthful military
experience to the point of romanticizing it. For all its horror and sorrow,
the war brought comradeship, understanding, and a basic set of human
values. Above all, it was the time of his youth. He has continued to write

war poetry well into middle age, and it is clear that he recalls some features of military life with genuine affection – even, in one poem, peeling potatoes.

Vanshenkin's greatest strength is his ability to describe things deftly and naturally. The poem "The Worker," written in compact, rhymed iambic pentameter, pictures a metalworker just home from his shift, as he cleans up and eats his dinner (the lines lose much of their vividness and precision in literal translation):

> He washes, scraping the grime off his palms,
> At first the suds are black,
> But in the second washing they are grey,
> And the third suds are iridescent.[21]

The poem, in the traditional "proletarian" mould, suffers esthetically from two closing stanzas containing gratuitous generalizations about Soviet working men. Although the poem is dignified, devoid of false notes, and packed with trenchant detail, it is ultimately rather shallow because Vanshenkin seems unable to endow his images with figurative significance. The same is true of other poems about carpenters, oil drillers and arc welders.

It is notable, however, that Vanshenkin can be less sanguine about the "poetry of labor." In "Weekdays" he writes about the daily grind, comparing the laborer to the propeller of a ship sailing on a sea of monotonous weeks "between islands of Sundays."[22] Although the poet insists that "there is something in such a tenor of life that gives strength," there is an unmistakable feeling of hatred for the worker's discipline, a wistfulness and discontent and feeling of unfulfillment. Vanshenkin's wide appeal for Soviet readers undoubtedly comes from his honesty and his striving to avoid the ideological cliché.

A poet of much greater culture than Vanshenkin, but one who shares the same lingering awareness of having been formed by the war both as a person and as an artist, is David Samoilov (born 1920). For Samoilov the themes of youth and war are inextricable. He writes with great sorrow and tenderness of "Pavel, Misha, Ilya, Boris, Nikolai," who did not return. Still, he insists that the war did not cure him of romanticism: "We were not a lost generation. It is simply that many of us died."[23] He is grateful, he writes in one poem, for the fact that he was not killed, but also for having experienced hardship, anxiety, and misfortune. These tough-

ened him "for different circumstances, perhaps psychologically more difficult than war."[24] Although he does not say so specifically, it seems clear
that he is referring to the postwar Stalinist terror.

In 1941 Samoilov was a philology student. He entered the war "laden
with literary associations" and brought to the experience a special awareness of his literary heritage and the sanctity of words. One of his poems
concerns a front-line censor who, under the pressure of obliterating all the
truth from soldiers' letters home, undergoes a mental breakdown and
begins obliterating the lies.[25] Samoilov safely stipulates that this is a
German censor, but the implication is much broader. There is something about words, the poet argues, that ultimately compels the truth.

Concern for the purity, honesty and integrity of the *word* is something that Samoilov shares with a great many of his liberal contemporaries, who see it as one of their major functions to restore the semantically
corrupt Russian language as a means of thought and expression. It is both
an aesthetic and a social matter:

> I love ordinary words,
> Like unexplored countries.
> They are comprehensible only at first,
> Then their meaning is cloudy.
> But they can be wiped like glass.
> And that is our trade.[26]

But this is not easy. His awareness of the historically difficult role of the
poet, and the painful price of the poet's integrity, is shown in his elegy to
Anna Akhmatova, published in 1967:

> But for being the embodiment
> Of the finches of Tsarskoe Selo
> She paid full ten times over.
> For this she had to traverse
> All the stages of a silent Hell,
> To turn herself into a songster.[27]

As befits a poet who so reveres the clear and precise Akhmatova, Samoilov strives to write simply, exactly, and naturally. Except for a tendency
to use modern inexact rhymes, his verse is conservative in form. His
themes are varied: some poems are purely descriptive – melting snow-
flakes on one's hand, impressions of Leningrad, a portrait of an old man.
There are poems of love and parting, and one particularly fine expression
of autumnal, quiet joy, comparing himself to a beech tree shedding its

leaves as he approaches middle age. Samoilov is particularly sensitive to the color and feel of nature. In "The Black Poplar" he delicately captures the atmosphere of the Russian April, when everything is grey, ugly, and gloomy but when a sixth sense can detect approaching spring. Samoilov's spare, clean, nature poetry is refreshing in its unabashed lyric intensity, strongly identifying the poet's emotion with the things he sees in the sky, woods, and fields.

History, however, is the dominant theme in Samoilov's poetry. In his war poetry there is an omnipresent sense of the interaction of past and present, of the soldier as a figure in an age-old process. His verse drama "Ivan and the Serf" implies not only that the moral problems of history are eternal but that Russian despotism, tragically, has always solved them in the same way. The poem features a dialogue between Ivan the Terrible and a peasant whom he is about to execute. Although the Tsar fully recognizes the cruelty and injustice of the execution, he argues that it is necessary and justified in the name of historical progress. The peasant simply answers, "God will decide." [28]

Samoilov also concerns himself with cultural and literary history, and specifically with the poets. A particularly fine poem is "Alexander Blok in 1917," speculating on the complex historical forces and moral and spiritual concerns that drove the poet to write "The Twelve." [29] History is put to satirical, ironic use in the poem "House-Museum" – the boring, indifferent monologue of a museum guide conducting a tour through the house in which a great poet lived and died. In his lifeless, unseeing, monotonous recitation of facts, the guide obscures all the significance of the poet's career. With its illustration of gross insensitivity the poem emphasizes, by implication, the very importance of historical awareness. It further suggests the presence of a soulless, formal, bureaucratic element in some Soviet attitudes toward culture. The poem ends:

> The last section shows the death of the poet,
> Don't crowd in front of the coatroom. [30]

Naum Korzhavin is another who makes use of historical material for the light it casts on the present. Many of his poems first published in the post-Stalin period were actually written earlier, several of them in Siberian exile. Born in Kiev in 1925, Korzhavin was, according to the testimony of Evtushenko, the only poet who openly wrote and recited verses against Stalin while Stalin was alive. That is what probably saved his life, for the authorities evidently felt he must be insane. (Many years later, in 1974, Korzhavin emigrated, and he now lives in the United States.)

Three poems written in the early fifties illustrate Korzhavin's use of historical materials. "Borodino" speaks of Napoleon's attempt to aggrandize himself by enslaving the Russians, using their nation as a pedestal to support his own glory. The poet assures his countrymen that "the lie about freedom and brotherhood will not bedazzle you."[31] "The Decembrist's Fiancée" pictures a girl whose impending marriage is cut off by the political exile of her groom. She will marry another but will dream of the "snowy cold, the spacious air . . . the silvered pines" of Siberia.[32] In "The General" a distinguished Tsarist officer refuses the reward of a plush appointment in the gendarmes, preferring an "Asiatic Sahara" to a sinecure in the political police:

> He would have passed for a nihilist,
> But he was already too old.[33]

All three poems are set deep in the nineteenth century, but to a perceptive Soviet reader the parallels with modern times are obvious.

In dealing directly with the history of the Soviet period, Korzhavin is less detached, more ironical, and more anguished. He wonders where the "commissars of nineteen twenty" have gone, ponders the contradictions of an era that is "moving toward freedom" but "strengthens its laws," that in the name of democracy maintains a system of ranks. Historical time pitilessly ignores human suffering, but he asks, gravely:

> . . . is it easy
> To experience constantly
> The pain of unceasing growth?

In a poem of 1956, he evokes the spiritual and intellectual atmosphere of Stalin's times:

> Day seemed night, frost seemed heat,
> All outlines melted at times.
> Object was indistinguishable from shadow,
> And suddenly the pygmy was made huge.
>
> And every day your reason had to redefine
> What light and darkness meant.
> What night and day, what swamp and road,
> Define again the simple things.[34]

For the poet, Korzhavin insists, the effort to understand human history must involve the deepest agony. The search for truth, he writes in "The Nightingale," is inevitably painful and lonely, and it is seldom acclaimed.[35] In his poem "Inertia of Style" (which closely resembles, in a formal sense, poems by Akhmatova and Pasternak on the same theme), he equates poetic style with courage itself.[36] His intensity of feeling in this respect comes from the fact that he is by nature a poet who broods on the darkest paradoxes of man's collective behavior. "The Children of Auschwitz" describes, for example, the feature of the war that seems to have impressed him most deeply:

> Men tormented children.
> Cleverly. Intentionally. Skillfully.
> They made it an everyday affair.
> They worked at it – tormenting children.
>
> And every day over again:
> Cursing, swearing senselessly . . .
> And the children couldn't understand
> What the men wanted of them.
>
> Why the insulting words,
> Beatings, hunger, snarling dogs?
> And the children thought at first
> That it was for disobedience.
>
> They couldn't conceive of that
> Which was obvious to everyone:
> By the ancient logic of earth,
> Children expect protection from grownups.
>
> But the days went on, terrible as death.
> And they became model children.
> But they still beat them.
> > > The same.
> > > > Again.
> And didn't relieve their guilt.
>
> They clung to people.
> They implored. And they loved.
> But the men had "ideas,"
> The men tormented children.

I'm alive. I breathe. I love people.
But life is repellent to me,
Whenever I remember: this – happened!
Men tormented children.[37]

As we have seen from the example of Olga Berggolts and Margarita
Aliger, the war poetry of Soviet women was imbued primarily with a
tragic sense of loss but also with resolute determination to endure. These,
however, were women who had already reached emotional maturity before the war began. Yulia Drunina, on the other hand, was born in 1925,
volunteered for the army at the age of seventeen and, in her own words,
"went directly from childhood into a filthy army hut, into an infantry ech-
elon, a medical platoon." In a poem written at the close of the war she
notes that she was a city girl who had grown up ignorant of the countryside and adds, not without irony, that "at seventeen, roaming about the
trenches, I saw my motherland."[38] It would appear that she saw everything: she writes of the forgotten grave mounds of comrades killed in bayonet fights and of her battalion commander who, having shot two of his
men who turned back in an attack, writes letters to their mothers praising
them as heroes. Drunina herself was gravely wounded and decorated for
bravery.

Largely an autobiographical poet, Drunina has gone on to record in
graceful, sometimes slightly experimental but generally unspectacular
verse, her life as a wife, mother, and busy, apparently well-adjusted, and
contented Soviet citizen. Some of her poetry is topical. She writes with
enthusiasm of Fidel Castro, and with disapproval of a Paris where movie
queens travel in Rolls-Royces and their less fortunate sisters must prosti-
tute themselves to pay the rent. On the other hand, although clearly not a
rebel, she does have liberal views. In a poem of tender advice to her
daughter, she tells her that any mistakes she makes must not, above all,
come from pettiness of soul. In another she pleads for public tolerance of
girls whose efforts to dress stylishly lead them to extremes.

A totally feminine poet, Drunina has devoted much of her verse to her
husband, expressing mature, dignified feelings of deep conjugal love. At
times there are notes of gentle sarcasm. She theorizes, in one poem, that to
wait for a tardy husband is a wife's "profession." She predicts, in another,
that some day Martians will land on earth and that a blue-skinned Martian
girl will fall in love with one of Drunina's own descendants:

> His sinful earthly love
> And the blue heart of the Martian girl –
> How difficult it will be for people of two worlds! . . .
> Almost as difficult, my dear, as it is for me and you . . .[39]

This, however, can be dismissed as mild feminine waspishness. A more accurate indication of her feelings would seem to be a sonnet in which she recalls that, at the front, her only peace came in the trenches in the moments before a battle. Now, years later, the calm constancy of her happy devotion to the husband she has loved for so long brings her a similar peace.

What is particularly significant about this poem is that it is dated 1960 and that the poet still thinks in images from the war fifteen years after its end. Like so very many Russian poets of her particular generation, Drunina finds that, despite the many subsequent developments in her life, the war remains the matrix of most of her impressions, and that her whole autobiography must be framed in its terms. In 1948 she was writing of how she had been three years before:

> Returning from the front in forty-five,
> I was ashamed of my worn-out boots
> And my rumpled coat,
> Filthy with the dust of all those roads.
>
> Now I cannot even understand,
> Why I was so tormented by
> The powder burns on my hands
> And the traces of iron and fire . . .[40]

A poem about her childhood, dated 1958, is again written in terms of the war. She recalls that, as a little girl, she was protected by not being allowed to climb on the roof like the boys. But she went to war: "Thank you, Motherland, for this happiness – to be equal to your sons in battle!" In a poem of 1959, she thinks of students leaving on their summer expeditions and asks:

> What was my youth like?
> The deaths of friends, bombardment,
> Cities and villages drowned in smoke . . .
> Perhaps because youth was not lived as it should have been,
> The hearts of soldiers remain eternally young . . .[41]

The theme persists. In 1968, Drunina was still writing of the war as the time when she was youthful and vigorous.

The verses of Bulat Okudzhava, set to music and sung with guitar accompaniment, have made him, in a way, the most popular contemporary Soviet poet. Among the broad public he is known chiefly as a balladeer whose songs have circulated through private tape recordings. His public performances have been periodically restricted by the authorities: this has lent an illicit quality to his songs and has served to increase their popularity.

Okudzhava himself thinks of his ballads primarily as "verses" and has insisted that "the words and intonation are more important than the music." It is true that as he performs them in a warm but small, untrained voice, his simple tunes in minor keys have little musical value. But it is also true that, as they appear on the printed page, many – although by no means all – of his verses seem to lack poetic density and to require the added color of melody and musical intonation. Clearly the poet and the balladeer are mutually reinforcing and often in close interdependence. But the fame of Okudzhava's songs has somewhat obscured the fact that he is indeed an accomplished poet.

Because Okudzhava's poems so frequently have the quality of song lyrics – an occasional lexical vagueness, the use of sentimental clichés such as "laughing and crying" and "forgive and forget" and of capitalized abstract words such as "Love," "Hope" and "Faith" – it is often inappropriate to judge them by canonical standards. His reliance on everyday locutions, slang, and popular turns of phrase, his manipulation and repetition of ordinary, prosaic words to endow them with special significance, and his frequent breaking of meters – seemingly crude but surely intentional – prevent his verse from being classically perfect. But much of his apparent carelessness and lack of elegance is calculated. His use of simple tropes and repetition of vulgar expressions (as in one poem featuring the slangy diminutive "*do-svidanitsa*") comes from a striving to find extra meaning in the vernacular by drawing attention to it. Okudzhava is in fact a versatile poet, and although his versification occasionally seems slipshod he is also capable of great subtlety. One of his great strengths is a gift for ironic understatement, the ability to crystallize a feeling or attitude through the use of apparently petty details: in one war poem, the recalled sensation of crunching hardtack becomes an image reflecting a whole range of unpleasant and even tragic emotions.

Okudzhava's use of the popular ballad is partly rooted in Russian literary tradition, for many poets of the past – including Lermontov, Blok, and Esenin – wrote verse-songs (*"romansy"*) amenable to musical interpretation. There is also an element of folklore in his manner of incorporating historical figures (the Emperor Paul), legendary characters (Til Eulenspiegel), and mythological personages of his own creation (Len'ka the King) into his verses. His use of the ballad genre also has its source in the sad songs that emerged during World War II in response to popular need. Many of his verses, like these songs, are direct, lyrical evocations of people, places, scenes, and sentiments. What Okudzhava frequently adds, however, is an allegorical element of political and social satire.

Okudzhava was born in Moscow in 1924 and received most of his education there. It would appear that he has also spent considerable time in Georgia; he is partly of Georgian origin and has translated much Georgian poetry into Russian. At age eighteen he volunteered for army service, and he was wounded several times. After the war he finished a university education, and then became a village schoolteacher for six years. Back in Moscow he did editorial work, and he first performed his songs in public in 1960. Although he has been subjected to periodic harassment by the authorities, he was allowed to travel to Scandinavia and Eastern Europe in 1966, and he has performed in Germany, France, and Poland on a subsequent trip. In recent years his literary efforts have involved prose fiction and scenarios as well as poetry.

War is Okudzhava's single most prominent theme. It is central to many of his poems and is alluded to in so many others that at times it seems almost obsessive. He comes close to a position of absolute pacifism, although he has also indicated a reluctant belief that some wars are just. Clearly he is an irritant to conservative ideologists in this respect. In 1968 he was quoted by a Polish journalist as saying: "I believe that young soldiers should be taught to hate their potential or hypothetical enemy. They should be told about love and flowers so that they will want to defend the world they love." And in 1969 he was criticized for suggesting that Christian brotherly love is a means of averting wars. The poems themselves render particularly vividly the physical sensations of life in the trenches, the atmosphere of battle, the omnipresent fear of death. Much more than other poets of his war generation, Okudzhava concentrates on the psychology of the combat soldier, such as the infantryman who awaits the order for a bayonet charge fatalistically, but concludes:

> all the same, brother,
>
> I don't want
>
> to die. [42]

Or the thoughts of a youth before his first military action:

> I want to live!
> I want to live!
> When will this end?
>
> I'm young . . .
> only not to die . . . [43]

In other poems Okudzhava writes of boyhood friends killed in the war, the destruction of families, the gross insult war brings to little people. There is a poem recounting a constant nightmare in which he is attacked by a black Messerschmitt. Another poem glimpses a soldier kissing his girl during an air raid, "stealing minutes from the war." Nature abhors war: the forests do a silent lament; the trees behave like exhausted soldiers; how ironical it is that the infantry goes off to war when spring is in full bloom! War is also the enemy of poetry. He writes, "a hundred times I have pressed the trigger of a rifle, and only nightingales have flown out." Fiercely sarcastic about the politicians who make wars, Okudzhava also makes a direct plea to the earth:

> Ah you, blue ball,
> sad planet!
> What are we doing to you?
> What is all this for?
> We all wallow in blood,
> And we could have . . .
>
> Rivers, full of love,
> Would have flowed about you. [44]

Okudzhava has repeatedly been accused by conservative critics of attempting to foster "bourgeois" sentiments in the public and, by being a singer of gloom and passivity, of morally disarming the citizenry and instilling in them moods of individualism and defeatism. What disturbs these critics most, one suspects, is that he is an ironist and satirist who subtly masks his social commentary. The allegorical and fablelike quality of many of his verses makes his messages difficult to define, because the listener or reader is free to make of them what he will. One of his most famous songs, "The Black Cat," is popularly interpreted as a masked portrait of Stalin:

> He hides a grin in his moustaches,
> Darkness is like a shield to him,
> All the other cats sing and wail,
> Only the black one is silent.
> . . . .
> He doesn't utter a sound,
> He only eats and drinks,
> He touches the stairway with his claws,
> As one would scrape a throat.[45]

He also frequently lashes out at pomposity, pretense and, in general, people who push other people around. His very ambiguity as to the targets of his indictments is undoubtedly disconcerting to the individuals to whom they most apply. Likewise, his habit of writing about freedom in the abstract is particularly challenging in the Soviet context.

One of the most humane of contemporary Soviet poets, Okudzhava writes of mankind not as a political or philosophical abstraction but as separate individuals who aspire to, and merit, love, mutual understanding, tenderness, beauty, and the freedom to communicate with each other without restraint. He writes of workers and artisans, examining an occupation closely and deriving special symbolic significance from it. With no "proletarian" axe to grind, he writes of combine operators, a shoemaker, house painters, a washerwoman seeking a mysterious "treasure" at the bottom of her tub. As if trying to draw one's attention to one's neighbor, who is one's brother, he celebrates, but without condescension, the calling of the "little man." One of his most moving poems features the image of Moscow workers coming home at night with bunches of lilies-of-the-valley, which they have bought on the street for their tired wives. At the same time he is sharply aware of the absurdity of the human race:

> It happens, it happens:
> a five-kopek piece lies in the street,
> barely noticeable
> a simple copper disc.

But a man . . . Yes, a man!
suddenly stops running
and bends to the ground,
as if breaking in two.[46]

Although Okudzhava is not, strictly speaking, a nature poet, much of
his imagery is taken from nature – flowers, birds, forests, the seasons. He
frequently blends images of nature with images of people, as in "Leningrad Elegy," in which he describes the moon shining over the city:

Beneath her reposed in the night the expanse of the Neva,
and there was audible only the roll-call

of the empty squares . . .
And I sensed something feminine

through the sharp
confluence of her thick brows.
Like a dying lantern,

she rocked in the blue chasm,
here and there

skidding above Petropavlovka . . .
But in her very light

my friends
seemed to me
even more faithful and even more beautiful.[47]

Okudzhava is a poet of the city. As can be seen from the lines just quoted,
he portrays Leningrad, the city of tsars and revolution, as a majestic,
awesome, historical monument. Moscow he portrays intimately, not in
terms of its magnitude and complexity but of its individual streets and
courtyards, particularly those of his native Arbat, and of the people who
live there, going about their unspectacular, familiar routines. He finds a
complex joy in urban life. On a Moscow corner in April, one poem recounts, a passing taxi splashes him with slush, and his momentary anger
turns to glad forgiveness as he realizes the humor of the episode in an atmosphere of human warmth and the hope of spring. The city can also be a
place of desolation and loneliness. In "Midnight Trolleybus" the passengers are portrayed with lyric sympathy as a fellowship of outcasts, and the
bus as a refuge for those whom society has forgotten.

There are frequent moods of sadness, moroseness, and loneliness in
Okudzhava, which stop just this side of despondency and morbidity. Life
is confusing, and often painful and dreary. The sense of decency and jus-

tice, and the aspiration to freedom, are repeatedly frustrated. One is often
at a loss to find the purpose and direction of existence. Nevertheless, time
passes relentlessly, and there is no turning back. Okudzhava seems to urge
an intelligent, unblinking awareness of this bewildering tragedy, and he
faces his own extinction resolutely:

> And so, I'll grow old . . .
> Is it possible that I'll grow old,
> wind a scarf round my neck,
> buy high galoshes,
> and fall out of love with you,
>
> and in sight of passers-by
> shall sit on the Sunday boulevard,
> chilled numb in stifling heat,
> and the young will feel cramped
> beside me?
>
> Will this really happen?
> The fire won't last a lifetime.
> But birds don't grow old . . .
> Teach me,
>
> to sing, sing, sing,
> climbing steeply
> till the last minute . . .
> And then to fall
> and vanish! [48]

He tries to exorcise his gloom and bitterness by concentrating on love
and beauty. (His love poems are genuinely romantic, with an almost
courtly worship of "woman.") There are compensations in human kindness, tenderness, and integrity, in the wonders of nature, in the simple
pleasures of life. The very act of striving to understand existence, to bear
it without self-deception, has a value of its own. And, Okudzhava insists,
there is always hope; the motif of Hope ("*Nadezhda*") is the most important
counterbalancing theme in his poetry. Hope does not, of course, preclude
irony, nor does it provide a guarantee of ultimate justice. But it does offer
a foundation for moral standards and a reason for endurance:

> I do not believe in God and fate.
> I pray to the beautiful and
> higher calling,

which placed me in the wide world . . .

Devils are conceited, Lucifer vicious, God is incompetent –
　　　　　　　　　　　　he's not feeling well.
Oh, if thoughts were only pure!
　　　　　　　　　The rest will all straighten out.

I whirl like a squirrel in a wheel,
　　　　　　　　　with my hopes in my bosom
cursing like a mechanic,
　　　　　　　　now hurrying, but then lagging behind.

While the god of war slumbers –
　　　　　　　　　the baker bakes pies.
Oh, if skies were only clear!
　　　　　　　　　The rest will all straighten out.

I pray that there be no disaster,
　　　　　　　　　and to the mill I pray,
　　　　　　　　　　　and to the soap dish,
to pure water when it shoots out from the golden faucet,
I pray that there be no more partings,
　　　　　　　　　ruin,
that there be no more anxiety.

Oh, if hands were only clean!
　　　　　　　　　The rest will all straighten out.[49]

None of the poets in the present chapter is notable for stylistic innovation. Their technical level is generally high, but they tend to be conservative in matters of prosody. Only Okudzhava among them departs to a significant degree from traditional standards of versification, but he moves in
the direction of yet another well-established tradition – that of the popular song.

But these poets have been innovative in other respects. Perhaps a better
term would be renovative. For there is about them a soldierly pragmatism,
a hatred for that which is pretentious and philistine, that makes them shun
the hollow rhetoric and conventional generalities that characterized Stalinist poetry and still continue in much contemporary verse. In a modest
manner these poets have attempted to restore the clarity of the poet's
vision by sweeping away an accumulation of stale, ponderous banalities,
making it possible to replace vapid oversimplification with concrete, honest complexity.

They have contributed to the rediscovery of the personality and of the value of frank, spontaneous expression of sincere feeling. The extraordinarily arduous experience of gaining and proving their maturity in the war gave them a special confidence and authority in distinguishing between formal, often spurious, morality and genuinely humane thought and behavior. It is significant that these poets also never speak directly of civic virtue.

All of them are now approaching, or have reached, middle age. For many of them the war is now a field for private reminiscences and contemplation, a part of one's biography about which it has become pointless to generalize. For others the theme of war seems to have been exhausted and replaced by themes taken from everyday life – modest topics that either represent a retreat into small, safe areas of poetic discourse, or that can be used as points of departure for the treatment of more important, more timeless interests. In taking this tack, these poets have joined, and have helped to form, one of the major currents of contemporary Soviet poetry – that which talks, at least ostensibly, about "little things." It should be emphasized, however, that they attempt to use mundane subjects as a means of plunging *beneath* the surface of the everyday, to reach hidden spiritual and intellectual essences.

Now separated from their fading war experiences by a quarter century, these poets have become deeper. But, as they have matured, aspects of the war that seemed fleeting at the time, or that were stored in the unconscious, or impressions that, for political reasons, had to be suppressed over the years, emerged in their later poetry. In new contexts the war became a source of metaphor, profoundly relevant to the later life experience of the poet and the moral and spiritual burden of his verse.

5

The younger generation of poets

In 1968 the poet Mikhail Isakovsky complained that the Writers' Union had fostered an "inflation" in poetry. He estimated that between 1,700 and 2,400 books of poetry were published annually in the USSR, one-third or one-fourth by new authors. The trouble was, Isakovsky concluded, that the Union admitted too many poets; in 1967 there were 2,185 of them. Hundreds of these poets are members of the generation that will be described in the present chapter. Only eight of them have been selected for discussion, and this has meant the exclusion of several who, in other contexts, would indeed merit serious consideration. Among these are Robert Rozhdestvensky, Oleg Chukhontsev, German Plisetsky, Stanislav Kunyaev, Rimma Kazakova, Maya Borisova, and Yunna Morits. Not included, also, are a number of gifted young "underground" poets, many of them presently or recently incarcerated, of whom perhaps the most prominent are Natalya Gorbanevskaya and Yuri Galanskov. (Both of these poets are quoted in Chapter 13.) No doubt there are many other promising poets who have not been brought to general attention, either because they are relative beginners or because, under present Soviet circumstances, they cannot be published.

All of those to be mentioned in this chapter came to maturity well after the war. Although some of them recalled their wartime childhood painfully and vividly, its scars seemed relatively mild. Nor did they experience, as deeply as their elders, the paralyzing trauma of the postwar Stalinist repression. Their youthful temperaments enabled them to respond to liberalization with fewer inhibitions, with more exuberance and greater daring. By and large, they were more assertive, individualistic, and candid than their elders, defied authority more readily and, as a consequence of their comparative indiscreetness, were somewhat more controversial and subject to political vicissitudes.

On the other hand, they had much in common with their older contemporaries, many of whom were their close friends and mentors. There was no distinct division between these young poets and the full generation – Akhmatova, Aseev, Pasternak, Kirsanov, Martynov – who preceded them, much less the semigeneration of Vinokurov, Slutsky, and Okudzhava. Subject to similar aesthetic influences, they shared the same enemies as their elders, fought the same battles against ideological prescriptiveness and aesthetic triteness, and joined in the same aspiration to broaden the scope of Soviet poetry and deepen its significance. What does set them apart is their youthful verve, their greater willingness to experiment and to go to extremes.

Experimentation among these younger poets was largely the result of a strong feeling of necessity to develop their own individual styles. Their striving to be new and different was largely in the realm of poetic language and form. But also the new comparative freedom for the poet to be himself, to develop his own lyrical voice, encouraged them to engage in psychic self-discovery and to explain their own emotions candidly. Their explorations were also motivated by a desire to revive the color and variety that Russian poetry had enjoyed from 1900 to 1930, and they assiduously, even eclectically, studied the poets – such as Khlebnikov and Tsvetaeva – who represented that period.

Self-conscious about being young themselves, these poets often strove to be "modern" and "fresh" so as to appeal to their youthful contemporaries, to express their restlessness and thirst for novelty. Not only were they aesthetically audacious; they were also politically daring in their pleas for a more libertarian and humane society. However, these young poets, like all Soviet writers, were acutely aware of the acceptable limits of boldness, and even the most brash of those published were careful, as a rule, to avoid literary activity that would silence or possibly imprison them. On occasion, however, the political indiscretions of several of them have brought them periods of exile to the hinterland.

In the early 1960s several of these poets became stage performers, reciting their verses before audiences of thousands. This practice developed in them a strong histrionic consciousness and, no doubt, tended to accentuate the oral qualities of their poetry. As a consequence, critics in the midsixties began increasingly to complain against "noisy" verse, and argued that the new circus atmosphere surrounding the young poets had become detrimental to their talents. To some extent the critics' objections may have been dutiful reflections of official policy, for large public poetry readings by young liberals became rallying points for political dissent, and the alarmed authorities soon curbed them. Nevertheless, the poets themselves seemed to realize that the role of "poet-actor" had a somewhat shallowing effect on their verse. Moreover, the effectiveness of the poet-tribune in mobilizing mass sympathies was limited. The virtual cessation of public readings toward the end of the sixties was, no doubt, a result of official banning, but also of the poets' despair and their turning to more private, sophisticated, and intellectual verse.

In 1961 two Soviet critics remarked that a "nomadic period" in Soviet poetry had arrived, and added that "in the very tone of our poetry, in its searchings and aspirations, there is felt a readiness to take off on a long journey – not only in the literal but also in the figurative aesthetic sense."[1] For the young poets this meant, among other things, that the obligation to serve as spokesmen for their generation implied a need to see new things and to absorb a variety of experiences, as their contemporaries would like to do. With official encouragement the young poets traveled widely in outlying parts of the USSR, describing the beauties of the taiga and tundra and romanticizing the difficult lives of pioneers in virgin areas. Travel in the Soviet Union, however, was often merely a surrogate for wider explorations. There was a strong urge to see the world, particularly the West, and some of these poets engaged in considerable globe-trotting.

The new freedom to travel was selective and arbitrarily revokable, and toward the end of the sixties it had virtually disappeared. But while it lasted the young poets eagerly displayed the fruits of their junkets. Many became openly proud of their foreign associations, and their verses were laden with references to foreign places – Hyde Park, New York's Chelsea Hotel, Place Pigalle – and to modern art and popular Western styles in dress, music, and dancing. There was also a heavy incorporation of foreign words into their vocabularies. Sometimes the effects were droll: the word "bugi-vugi" fits well into Russian poetry, and Bella Akhmadulina successfully lights a "Kent" in one of her lines, but Evtushenko's "tineidzher" (teenager) is doubtful.

In its figurative sense, the long journey on which the young poets embarked was a search for formal innovation in an attempt to develop a new, "contemporary" style. First of all, this meant new and original kinds of imagery, greater extremes of metaphor, and freer, more elastic associations of ideas, all of which would contribute a new intellectual dynamism to Russian verse.

In the area of phonetics, it meant increased freedom of sound play and a relaxed and expanded concept of rhyming. Classical Russian rhyme calls for a fairly exact correspondence of all sounds that follow the final stressed vowel in rhyming lines. The young poets deviated from this standard in several ways, chiefly by the extensive use of approximate, inexact, or assonant rhymes. This involved not only a lessening in sound correspondence at line end, but also an increase in the correspondence of sounds that come before the stress – pretonic rhyme. The vaguest of similarities in the general construction of rhyming words became permissible – for example, the rhyming of words of unequal syllables. Also, the increased use of assonance encouraged multisyllabled rhyming. Hyperdactylic rhymes became popular, and poets often tried to end lines with words that rhyme in their entirety. Rhyme moved deeper into the line: many young poets rhymed words in the middle of lines, or even near the beginning, setting up parallelisms between the first five or six syllables in each line.

The increased flexibility of rhyming standards was closely related to renewed metrical experimentation. In the early part of this century, Russian poets had experimented extensively with tonic verse, whose governing principle is a fixed number of stressed syllables with a variable number of unstressed syllables in a line, and no strictly measured alternation between the two. This departure from the canonical Russian line became the basis of further experimentation in which the young poets of the sixties cultivated irregular meters, partly as a reaction against the formal conservatism of the Stalin period, and partly in an attempt to facilitate the use of more conversational language in verse. A new, constantly evolving kind of line began to appear, based on rhythmic and intonational variety rather than a symmetrical arrangement of poetic feet. Meter and stanza form were reduced to the least perceptible minimum. Meanwhile, the young continued to rely heavily on the "staircase" arrangement of intonational units developed by Mayakovsky, and to experiment with other graphic means, such as combining several typefaces in a single poem.

It should be emphasized that among the most talented young poets there were many who did not pursue a "contemporary style" through this kind of formal experimentation in rhyme and meter. Likewise, many of the experimenters simultaneously wrote perfectly competent verse of a more traditional sort. Finally, it has already been pointed out that most of the practices described above were not a monopoly of the young (e.g. Martynov and Kirsanov), nor were they new to Russian poetry. In fact, the poets of the early part of the century – such as Bely, Blok, and Mayakovsky – had been much more innovative and daring. What was new, however, was the relative freedom and intensity with which the young poets tried to revive the standards and practices of the Silver Age.

The magnetic warmth and openness of Evgeny Evtushenko (1933–), his air of sincerity and apparent freedom from inhibition, and his ability to identify himself with idealistic, impatient youth, have made him the most popular poet of his generation. With his love of travel, thirst for color and new experience, and fondness for sports, new fashions, jazz and modern art, he expressed the natural aspirations of young Russians of his time. This young Russian indeed *saw* Hemingway, became friends with Fidel Castro, had talks with Maria Schell and Robert Kennedy, spoke up to Khrushchev. At one and the same time an authentic Russian and a self-styled citizen of the world, he became in his own person a kind of romantic hero.

Evtushenko is a genuinely sensitive lyric poet and a man of great kindness and wide sympathies. Although he is capable of writing quite subjectively, there is about him a disarming air of friendly extroversion, of total personal disclosure that makes his individual interests seem inseparable from those of society. He is simultaneously an autobiographer with strong lyric impulses and a fully engaged civic poet. More candidly than most of his contemporaries, Evtushenko aspires to be a spokesman of the age. At times he seems too self-consciously aware of the tradition in which he writes, bent on inheriting too many mantles. He is Pushkin in exile; then he becomes the Populist Nekrasov, then the successor to the young poets of romantic Leninist times. He seems to think of himself as the heir of both Mayakovsky, the expansive, fiercely democratic urban poet and of Esenin, the village poet lost in the complex evil of the city.

Evtushenko's tendency to pose and parade is somewhat naive and unbecoming because he assumes too much about the level of his talent and accomplishments. Can he really be serious in speaking of his debt to T. S. Eliot? When he says, in "Baby Yar," "It seems to me that I am a Jew," we accept the identification as a statement of tragic compassion. But when, touring the Colosseum, he becomes a gladiator and, visiting Ghana, proclaims "I am African," he is merely comically egocentric. There is also something pretentious about such lines as the following:

> I am various –
> > I am industrious
> > > and idle,

```
I am ex-
              and inexpedient,
I am all incompatible,
                     uncomfortable,
shy and insolent,
              nasty and kind.²
```

Although these lines are undoubtedly shallow, they are not quite as self-centered as they seem, for in confessing to such contradictions and vacillations the poet is fully aware that they are the common property of youth. He is, quite legitimately, talking not only about himself but also, tacitly, about his generation. Often he writes of being disoriented and dissatisfied, and castigates himself for indecisiveness. There is even a kind of adolescent desperation in his affirmation of life:

```
I sing and drink,
                  not thinking of death,
with outspread arms,
                     I fall to the grass,
and if I die in the wide world,
then I shall die from the joy that I'm alive.³
```

But this vulnerability, at least in his early years, was part of his youthful appeal.

Other sources of his appeal are his personal charm and his flair for publicity. Evtushenko is handsome and energetic, with a commanding presence and a lively wit. His understanding of what is newsworthy and his sense of timing are superb, and he has made excellent use of the media. A highly dramatic reciter of his own poetry, he became an extremely popular platform attraction in the early sixties. This particular success he has come to regret, to some extent. Replying to critics who accused him of increasingly shaping his poetry with an eye to the platform, he wrote:

```
My verse did not dissolve,
                          did not become soft,
but became coarser both in theme and
                                        trimmings.
Platform,
         you gave me scope,
but took away the secret of nuances.⁴
```

Evtushenko's language is bold and picturesque, and at the same time his poetry is, for the most part, easily accessible. His verse is perfectly suited

to his chosen mission as a cultural agitator who will influence the popular
level of taste and aspiration by making readers understand their own unar-
ticulated desires more clearly:

> Borders hamper me . . .
> > > It's uncomfortable
> not to know Buenos Aires,
> > > New York.
> I want to roam as I please about London,
> talk with everybody –
> > > even if it's in broken language.
> Like a boy,
> > > hanging on the back of a bus,
> I want to ride about Paris in the morning!
>
> I want art as various as I am.[5]

With his apparently limitless energy and curiosity, Evtushenko sometimes seems like a high-strung, exhilarated boy for whom the world is a
bewildering Disneyland. He seems eager to sound off about everything.
This attitude is complicated, however, by a strong desire to appear up-to-
date, sophisticated, and "with it," so that he indulges in name-dropping
and responds to current events – particularly those in the West – by writing off the top of his head. A poem entitled "Onion Soup," datelined
Paris, 1960, illustrates the results of such impulses. With gusto, bubbling
humor, and considerable phonetic ingenuity he describes the glories of
French cuisine, and concludes with a play on the saying that "Everything
changes in France, but her onion soup stays the same":

> At tiaras
> > > and tyrants,
> cavaliers on horseback,
> at their beautiful tirades
> the soup
> > > chuckled
> > > > in its kettles!
>
> I'm correcting that bitter phrase.
> I'll amend the judgment:
> "The folk stay the same in France!
> But, of course, also . . .
> > > the onion soup!"[6]

The poem has charm, but Evtushenko gratuitously brings in the word "striptease" for an inappropriate rhyme and, just as gratuitously, points out that Brigitte Bardot likes oysters.

Evtushenko's reputation was established by poems about his native land, which are often deeply touching in their simple sincerity of feeling and intimate humanity. He was strongly influenced by his wartime impressions as a child – communiqués, hospitals filled with wounded, evacuations, and sorrowful women in queues. In "Weddings" the poet is present, as a little boy, at the marriage of a peasant girl and a soldier who is scheduled for the front:

> Perhaps their first night
> will be their last night.

The little boy is asked to dance for the wedding party:

> The bride laments bitterly.
> Her friends stand in tears.
> I feel awful.
>   I can't dance,
> but I mustn't
>   not dance.[7]

In his concern for humble and obscure "little people," Evtushenko has been accused of wearing his heart too ostentatiously on his sleeve, of being motivated by a condescending pity, and of smothering his subjects with insulting kindness. Indeed there is a rather large show of superior sensitivity as he weeps when thinking of a department store salesgirl with puny locks and tired, clumsy hands. But in his poems about the hard-working, long-enduring women of Russia there is truly reverential tenderness. Writing in memory of Akhmatova, he reminds us that there are not two separate Russias – "The Russia of the spirit and the Russia of the hands" – and insists that an old working woman and Akhmatova are sisters of the soul.[8] His respect for the individual enables him to say surprising things. In "Old Ladies," for example, he praises two survivors of the prerevolutionary intelligentsia whose speech preserves the purity of the Russian language from former days:

> Land of superspeeds and superscience,
> superphysicists, superlyricists, superconstruction,
> Russia, Russia, you are still a land of old ladies
> perhaps, superforgiving, but stern.[9]

The poem is both an expression of sympathy for declassed victims of social upheaval and a suggestion that the Revolution destroyed precious parts of the Russian cultural heritage.

Much of Evtushenko's poetry is an appeal for a new dimension of understanding in Soviet life, for an end to the artificial simplicity and obtuse, mechanical utilitarianism of Stalinist thought. One poem pleads that the individual's right to have "secrets" be restored, and another features the refrain "We want freshness!" His liberalism also includes a large ingredient of satirical irony. The poem "Career" is directed against servile and faint-hearted intellectuals:

> A learned man of Galileo's time
> was no stupider than Galileo.
> He knew the earth revolved,
> but he had a family.
> . . . .
> And so, long live the career
> When the career is like
> those of Shakespeare and Pasteur,
> Newton and Tolstoy . . . Leo![10]

The last line includes a veiled reference to Aleksei Tolstoy, considered by many to have been an arch-prostitute among Soviet writers.

Although he is justified in considering himself a pathfinder, a man in the vanguard, and a major interpreter of his generation of Russians to the outside world, Evtushenko is a leader without being a poetic innovator or a particularly original thinker. One Soviet critic has called him a "shaper," who gives form to various thoughts and feelings that are currently in the air but contributes few of his own.[11] It is true that a great many of his poems sound more declaratory than meditative. His most ambitious long poem, *Bratsk Hydroelectric Station*, is loaded with portentous references and surface erudition, but falls of its own weight for lack of deep, analytical thought.

Evtushenko has been accused of being a clever, albeit liberal, political opportunist who times his "daring" utterances with exquisite precision and is quick to recant when his outspokenness gets him into serious trouble. It is true that he has some highly developed techniques for self-preservation. Extremely prolific, he surrounds his politically provocative poetry with reams of verse that is "safe." When he goes globe-trotting, he often writes friendly, appreciative verse about many features of the countries he visits, but pays for his passport with politically orthodox commentary on other features.

All this considered, he has to his credit some stunning accomplishments in timely, politically courageous poems. The most remarkable of them is "Baby Yar," a profoundly moving, fierce attack on official Soviet anti-Semitism, but others, such as "The Heirs of Stalin" and "Letter to Esenin," are equally brave in their way. In the latter poem, which he recited publicly in the presence of some of those whom he was specifically attacking, he indicted the Komsomol and Party leadership for its dictatorial control over literature, with pointed references to the Stalin terror, which brought death to "millions in the war against the people."[12]

Evtushenko speaks of himself as an innovator in poetic style, but there is little evidence to support his assumption. A Soviet critic has argued, in fact, that he does not have a style of his own and, to prove it, cites poems of Evtushenko written in the fashions of fourteen different Soviet poets, from Esenin to Vinokurov.[13] He has been influential, but as a reinforcer of certain revived traditions, not as an originator. His most important contribution has been a new, ringing militancy of intonation, a challenging self-assertiveness which his contemporaries have been encouraged to emulate.

The stylistic versatility of Evtushenko is based largely on the experiments of the poets of the twenties, most prominently the Futurists. He is fond of elaborate phonetic play – heavy alliteration and sound repetition. His rhyme-schemes are often designed to be arresting and unusual, and he uses inexact or "carelessly" rhymed lines, rhymes near the beginning or in the middle of lines, assonance (*stróyats'ya – strógie; úgol – úmnym*), and hyperdactylic rhymes (vstrevozhennye – vz'eroshennaya). His meters are often irregular, with an indefinite number of unstressed syllables between stresses, and he also uses the Mayakovskian "staircase" line, largely because his poetry is designed for oral performance. (For this reason he also favors anaphora and other forms of repetition. In the poem about "Freshness," eleven of the fifty-nine words are either "fresh" or "freshness.")[14] On the other hand, he also uses classical meters. In 1964 he wrote a poem in which he declared, "I want to become a little old-fashioned," and praised the "good old iamb."[15] This poem and, significantly, his verses in memory of Akhmatova, are written in iambic pentameter. There is more here than mere aesthetic caprice: Evtushenko, like increasing numbers of his contemporaries, has come to value highly the prerevolutionary Russian cultural heritage.

Evtushenko's lexicon is eclectic, although in his eagerness to be up-to-date he emphasizes slang, the language of the streets, and foreign words, especially American and French. (Sometimes his foreign locutions misfire:

his debonaire references to dancing the "tvist" make him sound like a hick.) He likes startling puns and figures of speech, but these are often awkward and lack the color and power of a Mayakovsky. One of his favorite devices is antithesis. He attempts to state the complexity of things by lining up discrepancies and contrasts ("east and west," "envy and delight"), but this often strikes one as a facile means of avoiding coming to grips with true complexity.

But Evtushenko is still growing. Despite his distressing tendency to write too much, too quickly, and on too many topics, he has not become the glib court poet that many of his admirers feared he might. In his years of worldly success he has preserved a core of lyric sensitivity – notably in his love poems and those with religious and psychological motifs – that gives promise of genuine poetic accomplishment in his middle years.

The poetry of Bella Akhmadulina (1937–) is intensely personal and idiosyncratic, concerned primarily with self-discovery and the search for beauty. She seems totally uninterested in politics or any of the standard "affirmative" themes of Soviet poetry. Her stubborn insistence on going her own way, and the allegorical ambiguity of some of her verse, have earned her rather constant criticism for having narrow, subjective poetic interests. At the same time, Akhmadulina has close associations with liberal literary circles, a fact that further irritates the cultural authorities.

Akhmadulina is an emotional, vulnerable, totally female poet who mistrusts rationality and longs to rely on her heart. She is also deeply aware that the heart misleads her; full of love, she is wounded and lonely when it is not returned. Often she is tragically uneasy, restless, and insomniac – the world is too much with her. But she can also be recklessly gay, drunk with the joy of life, impetuously kittenish, and even slightly silly (of the latter she is ironically aware). Her moods are pendular. She writes a great deal about being "unwell," depressed, lost, but she can also write, "Don't cry over me – I'll live." [16]

Her lyrics are delicate and musical, her stanzas classically pure. Despite occasional lapses into frivolous whimsicality (sections of the long poem "My Genealogy") and banality (the poem "Hemingway"), she has an excellent sense of measure. Her technique is usually subtle and unobtrusive, and at their best her lines are beautifully and tenderly melodious, rich and limpid, such as these from "My Genealogy":

Da zdravstvuet tvoi slabyi, chistyi sled
i dal'novidnyi podvig toy oshibki!
Vernyotsya cherez poltorasta let
k moim gubam priliv tvoei ulybki.[17]

Like many of her contemporaries, Akhmadulina prefers end-rhyme that involves entire words (Nastas'ya – nenast'e; steregla – starika), inverted consonants (koroleva – kavalery; snimal – sminal), and loose approximation (my dyshali – Mandel'shtame). Occasionally she uses initial rhyme:

Vdokhnoven'e – chrezmernyi, sploshnoi
vdokh mgnoven'ya dushoi nemoi.[18]

Although Akhmadulina prefers assonance to exact rhyme, she uses it appropriately and with discipline. In general her sound play is not as obtrusive as that of some of her colleagues, notably Evtushenko and Andrei Voznesensky. (In one poem she teases Voznesensky because he "blasphemously marries 'garage' and 'geranium' " – his rhyme is "garazh – geran'.")[19] But she is also capable of extreme alliteration, as in the following passage from "My Genealogy," where repetition of the syllable "pra" gives the lines a solemn, rolling, declamatory quality:

Akh, ital'yanka, devochka, *pra-pra*
pra babushka! Ne*pra*vednyi, da *pra*vyi
po*pra*vshie vse *pra*vila do*bra*,
lyubvi tvoei *pro*stupki i zabavy.[20]

Akhmadulina's tropes are modest and exact, largely limited to such discreet similes as: "the dinner service gazed from behind the glass as a fish from water"[21] and "the mirrors were empty, like snow fallen and melted."[22] Such figures of speech, like many other features of her poetry, are strongly reminiscent of Akhmatova. The poet herself also proclaims a close identification with Marina Tsvetaeva, and pays frequent homage to Pushkin and Lermontov.

She was born in Moscow to a Russian family with Tatar and Italian origins, and began publishing at the age of eighteen. After attending the Gorky Literary Institute for a period, she was reprimanded there for indifference to politics, and left the institute to travel in Central Asia, probably under compulsion. Over the years she has had considerable difficulty in appearing in print, and many of her publications have been translations, notably from Georgian poetry. Noted for her beauty, she has been married to Evtushenko and to the writers Yuri Nagibin and Gennadi Mamlin. Among other things, she is a notoriously bad driver (in one of his poems Voznesensky refers to her hair-raising qualities). Her sense of humor, and her preoccupation with her Asiatic blood, appear in these lines from "Traffic Lights":

> Traffic lights are kind, like the Slavs.
> They throw their light at my face
> and implore, as if in words,
> "Stop, don't drive!"
>
> I am grateful to them for the parallax
> of these two different colored lights,
> but in me there is a mixing
> of these two different-colored bloods.
>
> Oh, for ages it has droned and blended,
> Oh, for ages the quarrel has raged:
> this good Slavic common sense
> and slant-eyed Asiatic impetuousness.
>
> Apparently the outlet is in movement, movement,
> a head bent over the wheel,
> reckless giddiness
> on the edge of the curb.[23]

Most of Akhmadulina's self-examination is much more somber and anxious. Two complex tendencies completely at variance with each other – love and solicitude for her fellow humans, on the one hand, and a confused sense of isolation on the other – are evident, for example, in "In the Metro at 'Sokol' Station." The poem begins with the statement, "I don't know what's happened to me," and proceeds to express a confused, objectless fear, approaching terror in its intensity. In the middle of the poem, these feelings are displaced by emotions of maternal love and protectiveness for crowds she sees in the underground station, but in the end her mood of sad remoteness returns.[24] Her most extremely neurotic confession is the long poem "Chills and Fever" – a mixture of reticent hints of psychic illness, grotesque fantasies, and abstruse allegory.[25]

Poems written almost simultaneously with her "maladjusted" ones emphasize the force of life and the desire to struggle against the powers that would limit or deny it. She has a natural aversion to compulsion, is distressed by the pettiness she sees in others, and restless in the presence of stuffiness. There is much emphasis on children and their viewpoint, and a loving and solicitous concern for individuals who are neglected, vulnerable, and weak. But she is heavily dependent on love, and defenseless in the face of coarseness, insult, and injustice.

Although she has a compelling eagerness to love, she approaches the opposite sex with hurt suspicion, and sometimes with amusing irony. In one of her most charming early poems she writes:

> Fifteen boys in breaking voices
> said to me:
> "I'll never stop loving you."
> I answered them approximately thus:
> "We'll see."[26]

As a rule, however, her treatment of love is much less cool and detached. In "At Night" she writes of wanting to stand guard at the window of her loved one, to protect his sleep by putting out the street lights, stifling the noise of drops of melting snow, and ordering the approaching spring to remove all nocturnal sounds.[27] She writes of the pain of disappointed love with passion but also with dignity and delicate economy. This is how she describes the sad ending of an affair:

> And you walk along the platform,
> covering your face with your collar,
> and put out your smouldering cigarette
> with your heel in the snow.[28]

Akhmadulina has written increasingly about her search for beauty, and specifically about poetry itself. The theme is not new for her. In "The Sodawater Slot Machine" (1962) she argues that the poet can find marvels of loveliness where others miss them, and describes, with childlike wonder, the act of drawing a soft drink from an intrinsically prosaic, unlovely vending machine as something miraculously beautiful.[29] In the last few years, however, the theme of poetry has become more complex and tormenting for her. Her long poem *Fairytale about the Rain* is, in part, an allegorical treatment of the problem of coping with one's creative inspiration.[30] The poem "Night" is about her poet's block – her inability to write for fear that she cannot do justice to her muse.[31] A similar theme is in "Muteness" – words cling to the dictionary, inspiration will not come:

> I choke, and gasp, and lie,
> that I am no longer in debt
> to the beauty of trees in snow,
> about which I cannot speak.[32]

It is impossible to say whether such poems are concerned entirely with her subjective problems as artist. But Akhmadulina is such a subtle poet that she may be talking not only about herself but also about her contemporaries in the period of reaction that followed the Thaw.

From the moment of his first publication in 1958, Andrei Voznesensky (1933–) impressed Russian readers with his fervent poetic temperament and startling creative energy. He seemed intoxicated with language, possessed by a seething, uninhibited originality. Moreover, this young poet had great emotional range and commanded technical resources to support his vast imagination and inventiveness.

His verse was vehement and brisk, its tone that of an expansive individual caught up in a blaze of work and discovery, impatient to express himself. It gave a sense of unconstrained, joyful involvement in life, of cheerful thirst for activity and self-definition. There was a minority of detractors who argued that Voznesensky was too bookish, that his poetry was abstract, cold, and lacking in humanity, that he was emotionally superficial and so fascinated with his own technical ingenuity that he did not develop his themes with sufficient profundity; but no one argued that he was intellectually uninteresting. And if at times this brilliant beginner seemed a little rakish and flashy, appeared to be parading his erudition and virtuosity and putting on airs, his courageous imagination and eloquence atoned for it.

Voznesensky was trained as an architect; he was also a painter. When he decided to devote himself fully to poetry, he turned to Pasternak, who for three years worked closely with him as his mentor. Voznesensky early developed his own style, but his way of looking at things, notably his view of nature and his penchant for surprising associations of disparate images, seems to have been influenced strongly by Pasternak. The most obvious formal influence on him, although not a lingering one, has been Mayakovsky. However, he is above all eclectic, original but also well versed in all modern Russian poets, and one can find suggestions of influence from many of them – including Tsvetaeva, Khlebnikov, Zabolotsky, Kirsanov, and Aseev – as well as from the folklore tradition of popular oral poetry.

Stylistically, Voznesensky soon became identified with the extreme left wing of contemporary Soviet poetry. His verse seemed strikingly laconic and telegraphic, but at the same time colorful and richly associative. It was "difficult," governed by a kind of logic that did not make it readily accessible: the transitions between his ideas were abrupt, and his images were complex, their relationships abstruse. He was fond of unusual angles of vision, montage, and other techniques suggestive of the cinema – one group of poems, he said, "are like films shot from an elevator rushing between illuminated floors." Often his imagery combined the normal with the grotesque, and the real with the fantastic, to create an intricate phantasmagoria. An additional complication was provided by his frequently elaborate sound play. The enigmatic nature of some of his verse, his predilection for puzzles, and his keen interest in linguistic means, brought him frequent accusations of "formalism."

Voznesensky is very much a poet of sound and, like Evtushenko, has had great success on the platform. His verse is heavily alliterative, with much internal rhyme and with inexact, assonant end-rhymes in the fashion of many of his contemporaries. In his early poetry, his enthusiasm for euphony often led to artificial, excessive sound ornamentation; under the spell of his own voice he sometimes got carried away into mere pyrotechnics, and meaning was sacrificed to sound. But even as a relative beginner he showed a unique talent for phonetically reinforcing and enriching the semantic aspect of his poems. In "Goya" (1959) he achieves amazing compression, depth, and resonance through echoing vowels, consonants, and syllables, each of which aids directly in the association of his ideas. And in his more recent verse he has continued to perfect his sound imagery, while largely ridding his lines of superfluous phonetic glitter.

In the tradition of Mayakovsky, Voznesensky relies heavily on daring shock effects. He freely mixes elevated, "poetic" language with slang and with vulgar, prosaic, and even obscene words. His images, which come from a huge variety of sources, often seem to clash in audacious, grotesque juxtaposition, so that the reader's attention must switch frequently and suddenly between images of vastly disparate orders. Likewise, his similes are designed to startle: the eyes of Ivan the Terrible "slide over his face like a skidding motorcycle"; white Americans are "white as refrigerators," their waxen hands "like white lime." His metaphors are often grandiose, involving bold, large generalizations: Kennedy Airport is a "neon retort"; black Americans sing:

We are Negroes, we are poets,
>   in us the planets splash.
Thus we lie, like sacks, full of stars
>   and legends . . .

When you trample on us
You kick the firmament.
Beneath your boots
The universe yells.[33]

Voznesensky's metaphors are intended to be dynamic, and they often have multiple connotations that are difficult to decipher. Moreover, individual metaphors often seem to lack connection with one another, and even to be in conflict. In most cases, however, the ambiguity comes not from carelessness or accident, but from the poet's insistence on finding endless relationships between all things. He wants to "tear the skin from the planet," remove the covers from things that seem to be unique and unconnected and thereby to destroy the illusion that they are autonomous. Thus, he entitled a cycle of poems about America "The Triangular Pear," signalling his intention to get to the essence by reducing his subject to its basic contours. This process, of course, involved distortion and risky leaps in logic, but it was the poet's way of arriving at the truth.

In its metrical aspects Voznesensky's verse is extremely varied and flexible. The rhythmic structure of his poems is governed primarily by his structure of images – and, as we have seen, sound imagery has special importance for him. He is capable of writing strictly classical verse, but he prefers the mobility of combining different kinds of feet within a single line. One reason for this preference, no doubt, is his proclivity for showing the world in constant motion, his attempt to capture the headlong rhythms of contemporary civilization.

From the start, Voznesensky has identified himself with the life of big cities, science and technology, urban and industrial landscapes. As an architect he is fascinated with the design of modern buildings, city plans, and rapid transportation. Kennedy Airport is an expression of his own soul; he calls it "my self-portrait." His poetic aspirations are stated in the following imagery:

I go down
>   into the depths
>   of a subject
As into a subway.[34]

However, he is not an indiscriminate applauder of the achievements of technology, much less a routine glorifier of Soviet heavy industry. There is a tough underlying purpose in his technologically oriented poems – to examine the quality of life in the atomic age and to ask, as he does in one poem: "Who are we? Ciphers or great men?"[35] Self-definition in the presence of the machine and the atomic reactor is the paramount problem raised in his finest long poem, *Oza*: are we to lose our souls and become robots, and are we to destroy everything in a cataclysm of our own making?[36]

Such fears and misgivings reinforce his inclination to look upon nature and the primeval as a cleansing ideal. He is attracted to the primitive, and personifies nature in the manner of ancient folklore (in "Ballad of the Apple Tree" the tree speaks in a human voice). Often he reminds us that nature is wiser and more inventive than men, in their arrogance, can hope to be. Skyscrapers, for example, are portrayed as hanging on the belly of the globe like stalactites. In "Hunting a Rabbit" he describes, with shame, his senseless participation in killing one of nature's creatures for sport.

Sensitive to the suffering of others, Voznesensky is quick to indict cruelty and inhumanity. (The title of one of his volumes is *Achilles Heart*.) In "Someone is Beating a Woman" he protests indignantly against man's age-old, sadistic humiliation of the opposite sex. "First Ice" portrays with tenderness and pity the first shock and hurt of a girl who has been jilted. "The Monologue of Marilyn Monroe" laments the callous exploitation of the actress and her suicide. These are not isolated, sentimental flights. Voznesensky writes frequently about various forms of oppression of the soul and pleads for an ennobling, self-sacrificing love among humans.

Voznesensky is erudite and well informed, and the scope of his references in the fields of literature, history, science, and art is large. The knowledge he displays is seldom mere show; each item of information is intended to *mean* something, to fit organically into the poem's system. His historical allusions, for example, move freely over the whole scale of time, and in a single poem he can cut back and forth between past and present with sometimes bewildering abandon. He engages in deliberate anachronisms, as in "Master Craftsmen," a poem on the construction of the Cathedral of St. Basil under Ivan the Terrible, where he thrusts such names as Moab and Michurin into a sixteenth-century setting. In "Ballad of Work" he juxtaposes Peter the Great, Rubens, and himself to show the spiritual kinship between "artists" of all times. He lends color to his ideas, and illuminates the contemporary scene, by finding unusual historical parallels in such disparate materials.

The curiosity and profound concern of Voznesensky with contemporary problems stands out vividly in his poems about America. To judge from them, American culture both fascinates and repels him. His travels in the United States have produced deeply critical, often viciously satirical verse. On the other hand, he clearly admires the tempo and variety of American life and enjoys exploring its subtleties. His basic open-mindedness and goodwill in this respect have brought on criticism from Soviet conservatives. In some of the stupidest lines ever written, the late Alexander Prokofiev reminded Voznesensky that over thirty years previously Vladimir Mayakovsky had visited America and had said all there was to say about it:

> I discovered America
> Through Mayakovsky.
> On this I stand.[37]

Voznesensky expresses both enthusiasm and tragic anxiety over the future of mankind. Excited by the constructive potential of science and technology, he is also gravely sobered not only by the threat of atomic destruction but also by the prospect of spiritual decay under the increasing dominance of the machine. In "Oza" he addresses a cyclotron:

> Damn you, you blasted pile
> Of programmed animals;
> Let me be damned for passing, too,
> As the poet of your particles.
>
> The world is not junk up for auction.
> I am Andrei, not just anyone.
> All progress is retrogression
> If the process breaks man down.[38]

Closely related to Voznesensky's other values, but supreme among them, is creative freedom. One of his earliest and most persistent themes is that of the ennobling nature of work, mastery, skill – creativity is the only thing that justifies human existence. In "Ballad of Work" he argues that creative labor makes all men great, and is the main thing that makes them equals. In "Master Craftsmen" he divides the world into Artists (those who create) and Barbarians (those who destroy). Throughout his verse is featured a mortal struggle between the forces of life – labor, love, and beauty – and the forces of death – stagnation, pettiness, and ugliness.

For the human personality to fulfill itself in creativity, absolute freedom is needed; many of his poems are devoted to the essential, painful battle for this freedom. "Parabolic Ballad" urges men to defy establishments and conventions – true inventiveness cannot occur in conditions of slavish conformity. In "Lament for Two Unborn Poems" he speaks with disgust and bitter sarcasm of having buried poems before finishing them, and condemns himself and his contemporaries for tolerating the condition of unfreedom that requires such behavior.

Voznesensky's passionate devotion to the cause of creative freedom is a major source of his wide popularity among the Soviet intelligentsia. He is notably a favorite with scientists and technical workers. However, his eloquent advocacy of man's right to unhampered inventiveness and originality in all spheres comes ultimately from his concern for the integrity of the arts. A great deal of his poetry is devoted to art in all its forms – especially architecture, music, and painting, and he is clearly wounded by and indignant over the humiliation suffered by the arts at the hands of Soviet cultural authorities. He has protested, furiously and often, against their callousness and dishonesty, and has himself been the victim of their arbitrary policies and bullying tactics. To this extent he has been a figure in Soviet literary politics. But Voznesensky is, above all, an aesthete and a true poet.

Viktor Sosnora (1937–   ) writes like a younger brother of Voznesensky, but one more whimsical, less disciplined. His interests are in many respects similar to those of Voznesensky: he likes extravagant sound play, fantasy bordering on the surreal, and unusual and arresting imagery. He uses history in somewhat the same fashion, celebrates labor and the rhythms of the urban industrial age, and uses nature as a moral reference point. His poetry seems as energetic and effervescent as that of Voznesensky, but it also has a narrower emotional and intellectual range.

His verse is largely descriptive, based on first-hand impressions of the things he has seen and done. (As a boy Sosnora experienced the Leningrad blockade, evacuation to the Crimea and partisan warfare during its German occupation, and schooling as a postwar itinerant in a variety of places. After a three-year period of army service he settled in Leningrad, where he has made his living as a metalworker.) But his poetry has also been strongly influenced by his interest in ancient Russian history, literature, and culture and, more recently, by his discovery of the creative potential of seemingly unbridled fantasy. A striving for originality even at the expense of clarity and a fondness for impressionistic logic appear to be among his main motivating forces.

A poet of the ear, Sosnora uses all the phonetic devices currently fashionable among young Soviet poets but develops them to an extreme. His lines are heavily alliterative, saturated with echoing vowels, decorated with staccato consonants. A poem about lathe operators, for example, is laden with clicking sounds:

> My ovladevaem
> > tokami
> i molotkami stukaem . . .
> No razve my tol'ko tokari,
> tokuyushchie
> > nad vtulkami? [39]

The concentration on sound effects, however, is not always salutary, because his images are sometimes connected phonetically but not semantically, so that the verse becomes purely descriptive and superficial. The same can be said of his daring and "far-out" rhyme, which often involves the beginnings of lines, the middles of words (*bagrov – bugrom*), the greater part of entire words (*peresudy – parashuty; polegli – piligrim*), or merely vague consonance (*po karte – blokade*). The ingenuity of such rhymes is pleasant to behold, but their significance is too elusive.

Sound is a major source of Sosnora's earthy, hyperbolic humor. In his poems based on Russia's earliest chronicles and on the ancient "Tale of the Host of Igor" he refers to Novgorod's "pimpled merchants, battling all their lives with bumptious bedbugs" and writes such lines as:

> He sees
> the pub unbuttoning,
> drains the bubbling bucket. [40]

His use of ancient and historical settings is "irreverent" and imaginative. The poems in these cycles retain the archaic flavor of their archetypes in many respects, but they are written in modern conversational language and style, with numerous satirical touches and interpretations that make them clearly anachronistic. They are artificial and, perhaps, do violence to history, but they are highly original and interesting adaptations of traditional materials.

Sosnora's metaphors are lavish and unrestrained, and can be even more arresting than those of Voznesensky, perhaps because they are less disciplined. He describes Georgian fishermen drinking in this manner:

> Moustaches – half-garlands,
> violet cheekbones,
> noses like the fins
> of sharks.
>
> In the teahouse chomping,
> gnashing of an onion!
> We drink wine from a teapot,
> as from a hatch! [41]

He compares a foundry to a harvest field, so that the sparks of metal become yellow wasps, smoke flies from the smokestacks like ducks flying south, metal shavings are damp blue hay, and the workers in their canvas clothing and caps look like mushrooms. His own house he pictures in this· way:

> The house stood at a crossing,
> tense and muscular,
> in goggles,
>   like a motorcycle champion
> before a race. [42]

Although Sosnora seems to be concerned more, thus far, with the exterior, decorative side of life than with its deeper meanings, and appears to be preoccupied with the search for new forms in which to treat conventional materials, he is a serious thinker with much to say. His verbal experiments, in the spirit of Khlebnikov, Mayakovsky, and the early Aseev, have more than mere formal significance. For one thing, his "production poems" glorifying industrial labor in bizarre and even surrealistic imagery, are a far cry from the hackneyed, standardized, official poetry of affirmation. And he has shown, as in the allegorical poem "Cactus" – a testimony to the tenaciousness and survival qualities of a flowering plant in conditions of neglect and abuse – that he has deep moral attachment to creativity.

Novella Matveeva (1934–   ) is a pensive, alert, marvelously imaginative poet of "little things." She writes about eggplants and cabbages, a stump, a jug, downspouts, paper trash – to create a lyrical fusion of reality and fantasy. In her modest, low-keyed verse she has a way of "poeticizing" routine, mundane details, of finding unusual connections between ordinary objects and transforming them into images of heightened aesthetic, moral, and even social significance. For example, her sonnet "Rhyme":

> Invisible is a nail in the sole of a shoe:
> It is busy guarding its invisibility.
> But walking is easy only when
> The nails don't crawl out and show themselves.
>
> But when nails visibly protrude,
> The step hides, the gait disappears;
> And when a rhyme too much astounds,
> The whole line dies of shock.
>
> No special talent is needed
> Merely to tie a bow of rhyme;
> Any dress can live without ribbon,
> A shoe cannot live without a nail.
>
> And firmness of poetic pace
> Comes not from ribbon, but the sole.[43]

She is romantic in temperament, and has an extraordinary sense of the fullness and brightness of life. A common red pepper evokes sunny climes:

> Could you imagine a dark canopy,
> And a vendor with dangling ear-rings,
> Without sheaves of peppers hanging by the door
> Like bunches of keys
>   To passionate southern hearts!

But also the pepper moves her to gay, although not entirely jocular, observations on the Russian character:

> It's true, we're a wintry breed,
> But we like hot stuff,
> And on occasion we too can
> Make it hot for ourselves and others.

> There's surely some reason that in January fields
> The Russian frost smells of pepper?!
> Surely there's some reason why a Russian joke
> Brings tears more than a pepper?!

She continues:

> I celebrate peppercorns and pepper ground,
> All sorts: black – in crimson borshch,
> (Like an imp in scarlet cloak),
> Fiery-red – in a bon mot.[44]

Her nature poetry is delicately perceptive, although at times (as in "Slow Spring") it is so refined as to appear attenuated. On the other hand, there is a Pasternakian freedom in her similes: rotting trees crumble like halvah; a swiftly jumping monkey is like a handful of cocoa strewn from a branch; a parrot is like ten flags in the wind, or a drunken torch, and the parrot's glance is like that of a malingerer in a doctor's presence. Such uninhibited comparisons are particularly natural to Matveeva because of the peculiar quality of her world. She was ill during much of her childhood, and physical disability still makes it impossible for her to travel. Early she learned to live in her imagination, as an armchair traveler to exotic places, many of them of her own invention. In "Land of Childhood" she refers to those places as "there":

> "There" is a palm, a mystery, a Buddhist temple.
> A paradise of sharply otherworldly
> Blue seas . . .[45]

The world of her poetry is still, in many respects, a childlike mixture of actuality and daydreams, for her imagination frequently wanders beyond the horizon in search of a never-never land of beauty, justice, and nobility.

Underneath her disarming, childlike exterior, however, Matveeva is a mature and wise woman. And she is perfectly capable of defending herself:

> They tell me: discard your dreams, draw reality,
> Write it like it is: a boot, a horseshoe, a pear . . .
> But reality also has a semblance.
> And beneath the semblance, I seek the soul.[46]

Although soft-spoken and indirect, she has a shrewd and firm moral sense, and she can write incisively about abstract values. Matveeva can also be quietly but shrewdly ironical, masking her satirical comments in figurative language that is perfectly clear to her liberal readers. In "Hypnosis" a silent and inscrutable snake terrorizes and petrifies the other jungle creatures by the very ominousness of his presence. Suddenly a rambunctious parrot loudly scolds the snake, the spell is broken, and the snake slinks away.

Matveeva has written many songs, which she sings to her own guitar accompaniment. Although she very seldom performs in public, the songs are widely popular, particularly with Soviet youth. In one of them she tells of drainpipes on city houses that threaten to turn themselves into lips, to blab secrets to the passing poet. But she doesn't want either to hear secrets or to proclaim them, for "knowing secrets, it's hard to dream and love." A very important part of her poetic credo is to respect the integrity of the individual and the free imagination. It is for this reason that, unlike many of her contemporaries, she refuses to speak for her generation or to utter ringing pronouncements in its name. Poetry, she clearly believes, is a highly moral vocation, involving self-discipline, painstaking craftsmanship and, above all, honesty and originality. Her own verse, strict and traditional in form but unique in content, is devoted to the task of cleansing Soviet poetry of worn-out words and ossified concepts, for, as she says:

> It's not the Devil I fear, but the stereotype:
> It is stupid, ridiculous, but in it is the world's demise.[47]

Among the prominent younger poets the most modulated voice, and perhaps the clearest and most disciplined, is that of Aleksandr Kushner (1936–). A Leningrad schoolteacher, he writes finely wrought miniatures, each governed by a single discrete idea. Sparing in his use of metaphor, he writes modestly about "little things," as observed by an attentive, contemplative individual who is concerned with the quality of his life and of his immediate surroundings. Kushner seems to speak only for himself, and his remarks have little overt social significance. His judgments are few and reticent (he uses question marks frequently), and his firmest opinions are about poetry itself.

When his first volume came out in 1962, Soviet critics, on too little evidence, typed Kushner as an "indoor" poet. Because he referred frequently to books and wrote of such things as decanters, telephones, antiques, and tape recorders, they concluded that his world was largely confined within four walls. It is true that his poetry was, and remains, intimate, but Kushner's curiosity extends far beyond his study, and his point of view is sufficiently objective to project his verse far into the realm of general human experience.

Each of Kushner's three volumes is a kind of open diary consisting of short meditations on everyday things in his life – objects (a doorbell) so ordinary that they usually go unnoticed. He writes as a quiet and observant city dweller, noticing the way people behave in the streets, changes in the weather, the shapes of buildings, the atmosphere of a symphony concert. Although he obviously treasures time spent alone in his room with his thoughts and books, he seems reasonably sociable; he writes engagingly about love and has a subtle, ironic wit and healthy sense of humor about himself and others. The tone of his lyrics is restrained, and he seems determined to avoid any kind of expansive or heroic posture. Rather, he prefers to examine intently, and with an awareness of his own limitations, the phenomena within his ken, and to write as deeply as possible about them. As he has a vigorous and restless intellect, his short philosophical musings have involved a constantly increasing variety of themes.

Kushner's material comes largely from the realms of literature and history and is prominently associated with Russian culture of the eighteenth century. He writes of Radishchev and of Derzhavin's saltcellar, examined in a museum. Many of his poems about his native Leningrad deal simultaneously with its present visage and its imperial past. The literary allusions in his poetry are mainly Russian – to Pushkin, Tyutchev, Fet, Blok, Pasternak, and Akhmatova. Increasingly he has alluded to art – Titian, El Greco, Van Gogh – and his second volume is entitled *Night Watch*, after Rembrandt. (His cultural orientation is primarily Western.) An interest in modern science is also evident in his speculative poem "Astrobotany." He has a philologist's interest in words: some poems are devoted to searching examinations of the makeup and various shades of meaning of an individual word.

His verse is economical and classically precise and, although so individualized as to be unmistakably his own, seems to have been influenced by the clarity, order, and concreteness of the Acmeist poets Akhmatova and Mandelstam. The striving for exactness and harmony of poetic form is in keeping with his worship of the purity and intensity of poetic thought and expression. For him poetry is both an aesthetic and a moral ideal, a means of finding proportion and unity within the disorder and chaos of life:

I have seen baseness and misfortune.
But verse is so wonderfully organized,
That I am merry and calm,
As if in a large garden.

I'll rub out accidental lines,
Treble my attentiveness.
What does poetry teach us? Order.
More exactly – harmony. Good.

Among the noisy half-shadow, it
Seems a brilliant instrument
Of high precision, with which
To collate distances and angles.

We'll not quicken our pace
And cover faces with hands.
Isn't it better alertly to discern
The distant clearing beyond the branches?

And know that evil is like a bad dream,
Good is prompted by the whole course
Of a line, by meter, by a dance
Of oaks behind your back.[48]

Kushner has learned, however, that evil and darkness cannot be avoided by remaining in one's room or be exorcized by poetry alone. The poet's commitment is an agonizing one; his victory is not assured, but he can only try. In one poem he leaves his "domestic warmth" on a December morning for a walk in the frost. Everything is covered with ice and snow, and people on the streets are cramped and suffering from the oppressive cold:

And I, with usual effort
Try to restore the beauty
To the houses, to the indifferent squares,
And to the pedestrian on the bridge.
And I let my bus pass by,
And freeze, covered with snow,
But live, until I get this trick
Right, I cannot.[49]

Now past forty, Kushner no longer finds satisfaction and solace in the compactness and refinement of poetic form alone. He writes more and more about the complexity of the world, human tragedy, and his own need for "spaciousness" and "freedom." Also he seems more genial and expansive, less a chamber poet. He still prefers brief, aphoristic utterances, but his poems are gaining in emotional and intellectual richness.

Vladimir Tsybin (1932–) grew up in a peasant village and also worked as a miner in his youth. His poetry is largely concerned with capturing the atmosphere and spirit of rural Russia, and with interpreting his own feelings as a person who has undergone its influence. He writes as a complex individual, keenly sensitive to the natural and social environment, who wants to relate his own psychological and spiritual conflicts to the more generalized conflicts within contemporary Russia. At the same time he has a pronounced historical awareness (his ancestors were Cossacks), and his lyrics are imbued with a strong sense of the poet's obligation to serve as a recorder of the culture of his time.

Tsybin's early poetry depicts the customs, popular speech, traditions, and exotic features of the village, emphasizing the colorful and earthy details of a way of life that is gradually disappearing as Russia becomes more urban. Although he shows a powerful emotional attachment to his native soil, his verse did not, at first, attempt to evaluate the quality or historical significance of the rural experience. Soon, however, his treatment of the landscape and people of the steppes increased in profundity. One of his finest early poems tells, in simple, respectful detail, of the quiet, dignified death of a lonely old peasant who has outlived his time. With great economy, using interior monologue with a wealth of psychological shadings, the poet reconstructs the hard life of the old man, his spiritual grandeur and his calmness of soul. A recent poem states directly the poet's feeling for his soil:

> And we have come
> from that simple land,
> where there is silence, where the blizzard strews sparks
> on yellow straw roofs,
> and where snows stand,
> like ships,
> where the damp rustle of birches is so easy to understand,

and the faded smoke
of the chilled sky,
from that land, where simply and earnestly
life goes on for the sake of children
and bread.[50]

A prominent theme of Tsybin is his childhood in wartime – ill-clothed and hungry, in a village without men, surrounded by widows and orphans, all facing the specter of famine. There is a touching poem, "Holidays," in which he recalls that such events, so precious for children, took on a cruelly distorted meaning during the war. But he also writes about an even greater trauma, which antedated the war but continued beyond it:

I remember, in long-ago, bitter days
Mother reproached me:
                    "Don't babble
In front of others about your superiors.
Or about the Authority,
                         or about anything at all.
For this, little son –
                    it's Vorkuta!"
I didn't listen to her grumbling,
Saw only one thing – how in her eyes
Her terror
              rose upright.
It shrouded her eyes in tears . . .
Perhaps I have adopted
                    her terror?[51]

Tsybin treats the war and Stalinism as national catastrophes involving the folk, and himself as a representative of them. When he writes about terror, his tone is not political. The self-questioning hero of his poems is a separate personality with strong fears and inhibitions and a conscience that demands he show uprightness and courage. But in dramatizing the conflicts within his own psyche, this hero reflects the moral sufferings and aspirations of the Russian people as a whole.

For "village poetry" Tsybin's verse is surprisingly modern, colorful, and daring in its formal qualities. The rhymes are often barely approximate and are sometimes achieved through the introduction of a rare dialect word or a neologism. The rhythms are energetic, pulsating, and changeable, in much the same fashion as those of Voznesensky. There is little attempt to achieve a pastoral elegance in versification, and sometimes the lines seem intentionally awkward and harsh. Lexically, Tsybin's poetry is a mixture of contemporary standard Russian, archaisms, and rural dialect; the grammar is emphatically coarse and clumsy in places, but authentic in keeping with subject matter. Recently, however, Tsybin's verse has become more conventional in style, as in these lines on the traditional dwelling place of the Russian peasant:

> What sort of soul has a peasant hut?
> When it has scarcely been born,
> right away, tactfully, not breathing,
> it has hidden itself in pine corners.
> It doesn't sleep, a peasant hut's soul,
> and listens from every crack,
> to the clocks merrily ticking
> all day on the walls,
> to the birch in full leaf
> knocking on the window sill.
> The soul of a peasant hut remembers everything,
> it preserves everything carefully.
> The green crackle of a besom
> over the floorboards, still new,
> and a widow's bitter longing
> for her man, a new dress.
> What sort of soul has a peasant hut?
> All the same it has to hear,
> constantly hear, not breathing,
> the joyful racket of kids,
> a martin's swoop over the roof,
> in winter the soft tinkle of an icicle,
> as from a little whistle, –
> such is the soul of a peasant hut!
> A peasant hut's soul, it is radiant
> and it awaits you, without growing old at all.
> The stork has long since returned –
> so why is it sad, this soul? . .[52]

In other poems, Tsybin emphasizes the remoteness and somber silence of the peasant village, its ambivalent but increasingly dependent relationship to the city, and the subtle mixture of continuity and change in the rhythm of its present life. The dramatic interest of his verse consists in the troubled combination of sensitivity to nature, nostalgia, alarm, and folk pride with which he interprets this changing rhythm.

Although Joseph Brodsky (1940–) has been publishing poetry for over a decade, very little of it has appeared in the Soviet Union. For this reason Soviet criticism has paid no attention to him, and he remains outside the accepted sphere of Soviet literature. At the same time he is considered by many abroad as the most promising poet writing in Russian today. A more profound, cultured, and versatile poet than most of his contemporaries, he seizes upon larger segments of experience and ruminates more deeply about them. There is more evident intellection and, along with it, a greater element of mystery.

Brodsky seems to respond to current events with indifference. He is surely alert to his times and much better informed on modern cultural currents than most young Russians, but as a poet he spends most of his time brooding, in depth, on the eternal questions – death, loneliness, love, suffering, and other enigmas of existence. For him, poetry is an intense exertion of the imagination without "purpose," hard thought in what must be ultimately a resigned attempt to cope with the ineffable. He broods without illusion, without real hope of discovering answers to the riddles he so complexly states. His is the kind of metaphysical meditation that cannot but irritate any proponent of topical or socially useful art.

While Brodsky is apolitical in the sense that he seems completely uninterested in immediate social issues and finds the notion of historical progress to be meaningless, many of his poems have broad historical significance and contemporary relevance. In the title poem of his volume, *A Stop in the Wilderness*, for example, he contemplates the destruction of a Greek church in Leningrad to make way for a concert hall, and speculates:

> In Leningrad few Greeks are now remaining.
> In general – outside of Greece – their number
> Is small. Too few, at least, to well preserve
> The basic fabric of their own religion.
> That they believe in what we are constructing
> Is something no one will demand of them.
> To baptize any nation with a cross
> Is one thing, but to bear a cross, another.

He notes that Christianity has not triumphed in Russia, and these thoughts lead to more general speculations on the current direction and destiny of Soviet civilization:

As I look out the window on this night,
I cannot help but think, what have we come to?
I wonder, have we moved farther away
From Orthodoxy or from Hellenism?
What are we nearing? And what lies ahead?
Does there await us now another era?
And if so, where does our main duty lie?
What are the sacrifices we must offer?[53]

Brodsky's long poem "Gorbunov and Gorchakov" is a dialogue, or possibly an ambivalent monologue, set in a Soviet insane asylum. A treatment of general human anguish, it nevertheless features ideological and moral conflicts that are integral to present day Soviet society. One of the two main voices is that of a religious believer, a philosophical idealist with a "non-Party view of things and events"; the other voice is that of a materialist who believes, as a proper Marxist, that "existence determines consciousness." The whole situation is ominously contemporary: the doctors behave like political interrogators, and it is evident that one voice represents a man who has been locked up in the asylum only because his philosophy is politically unorthodox.

Brodsky left school when he was fifteen and is largely self-educated. His learning is quite evidently enormous, including a knowledge of English, Polish, and Serbo-Croatian, and a wide knowledge of classical and modern literatures, especially English and American. Until he left the Soviet Union in 1972, he supported himself as a translator – notably a volume of English metaphysical poetry, although he has also dabbled in such exotic items as the verse of Muhammad Ali and the Beatles' "Yellow Submarine." Although his poems appeared in Soviet underground publications, he was not, strictly speaking, an "underground poet," as he published abroad apparently without hindrance from the Soviet authorities. However, his expulsion from the Soviet Union in 1972 and his subsequent articles in the American press have made clear the mutual antipathy between Brodsky and the Soviet regime.

Although Brodsky is not showy, his style is versatile. Generally speaking, he prefers nouns and verbs and avoids relying on other parts of speech for his nuances. As a consequence, his verse at times can be extremely laconic – impressionistic lists of words that the reader must associate for himself with little aid in the form of grammatical and syntactic connections. On the other hand, he often relies heavily on repetition (he uses anaphora extensively) and can slip into overstatement. He also writes free verse, combining lines of strikingly unequal lengths. For the most part, however, his style is conservative, using classically rhymed iambic lines without the pronounced assonance or other sound play that have been popular among the younger poets.

Brodsky is delicately sensitive to the physical world, and he writes of shapes, reflections, and shadows with precision. His poetry is dense in the sense that the imagery is abundant and complex – so much so in the long poems that it not infrequently becomes diffuse and confusing. This is particularly true of "Gorbunov and Gorchakov," which is so packed with images and allusions that many passages are verbose and opaque. Brodsky's imagination, it should be added, is daring to the extent that his imagery sometimes approaches the surreal.

Inventive and fanciful, Brodsky has a well-developed sense of the bizarre. Some of his poems have the surface aspect of games, in which he clothes serious thoughts in disarmingly playful garb. The poem "Verbs," for example, combines heavy, intentionally comic alliteration and pedantic, formal grammatical terminology to examine, quite earnestly, the moral aspects of language. A section of "Gorbunov and Gorchakov" is devoted to the phrase "he said" (and variations of it) employed as a *noun*, in a baffling but stimulating essay on the problem of direct and indirect discourse in Russian dialogue, which may also be a commentary on the practice of police interrogation and informing. Brodsky's wit and irony also make him an effective satirist. In 1964 he was sentenced to five years of forced labor in the Arkhangelsk region on a trumped-up charge of "parasitism" – living without a permanent job. (The sentence was commuted after a year and a half.) In the following lines, written in his northern exile, he refers to himself and the sentencing judge:

> On being released from prison,
> now that the winter's in the rearguard,
> he mends in some woodland village
> barrels in the spring season,
> and in the oval of a tub
> beholds the face of Judge
> Savelieva, and with his hammer
> furtively taps on her forehead.[54]

As a rule, however, Brodsky writes with much less levity. His most constant theme is death, whose utter desolation and horrible totality he personifies in one poem as a black horse (the word "black" or its derivatives appear sixteen times in thirty-five lines):

> He was black, impervious to shadows.
> So black, he could have grown no blacker.
> As black he was as darkest midnight.
> As black as the inside of a needle.
> As black as the trees before us.
> As that place in the chest between the ribs.
> As a hole in the ground, where lies a seed.
> I think it must be black inside us.[55]

Images of autumnal wandering and the pain of waiting for death abound in Brodsky's verse. At times he seems to think fearfully of death; at others he accepts it with dispassionate irony as a fact. In "Verses on the Death of T. S. Eliot" he emphasizes the impartiality and blindness of death's greed: it takes poets like everyone else. Furthermore, "It was not God, but only time, mere time that called him."[56] However, in this and other poems, notably the splendid "Elegy for John Donne," he insists on the death-lessness of art – the creativity of the poet's lifetime is his promise of a kind of immortality.[57]

Not only does Brodsky find a form of religious consolation in creativity; he also finds creativity a moral need. He wonders why men, who are presumably higher on the evolutionary ladder than birds, "do not sing when we're up a tree in the thick of winter," and asks:

> Have we not fallen then too far behind
> those who are said "to lag behind us"?[58]

Repeatedly he argues that although life appears to lead nowhere, the journey need not be one of despair. The world is full of beauty, man is hardy and curious, and the very striving to know, although it may be ultimately pointless, is a source of joy and even of rapture.

But Brodsky is not fundamentally a poet of affirmation. Moods of melancholy isolation and alienation, nervous night thoughts, and themes of parting, loneliness, and suffering predominate in his verse. He writes often of the strangeness of the world, deserted rooms, and people who are forlorn, defeated, and devastated. However, he is capable of separating his emotions as an earthly being, subject to dread and anguish, from the rational processes through which he poses metaphysical problems. He is, moreover, too modest and controlled to present himself as a prophet or latter-day Symbolist seer, or to claim special mystical insight into the mysteries he witnesses. As a philosopher he is cool, orderly, and concrete.

Consequently there is no easy religious consolation in Brodsky's poetry.

He affirms that the soul is independent of the body, and in several passages he seems to be stating an absolute belief in the existence of God. But he is not on familiar terms with Him, and is clearly skeptical and ambivalent. Brodsky's inability to make a total commitment can take the form of impish humor:

> In villages God does not live only
> in icon corners, as the scoffers claim,
> but plainly, everywhere. He sanctifies
> each roof and pan, divides each double door.
> In villages God acts abundantly –
> cooks lentils in iron pots on Saturdays,
> dances a lazy jig in flickering flames,
> and winks at me, witness to all of this.
> He plants a hedge, and gives away a bride
> (the groom's a forester), and, for a joke,
> he makes it certain that the game warden
> will never hit the duck he's shooting at.
>
> The chance to know and witness all of this,
> amidst the whistling of the autumn mist,
> is, I would say, the only touch of bliss
> that's open to a village atheist.[59]

Or his skepticism can take the form of intelligent, puzzled humility:

> There is a mystic lore; faith; and the Lord.
> They differ and yet have some points in common.
> The flesh saved some men; others it destroyed.
> Men who lack faith are both blind and inhuman.
>
> God, then, looks down. And men look up. But each
> has a peculiar interest of his own.
> While God's being is natural, mere man
> has limitations which, I trust, are plain.[60]

Although the cast of Brodsky's thought is indeed religious, and although biblical influences and religious imagery are extremely prominent in his poetry, his outlook at times is startlingly dispassionate. This brilliant poet, still in his thirties, views the world and his life with his own peculiar mixture of tragic concern and ironic detachment.

Most of the young poets with whom this chapter has been concerned are now approaching middle age, and all of them are well past thirty. There may still be surprises from many of them because their talents are still growing, but they no longer represent an exciting and unpredictable wave of the future in the same degree as they did a decade ago. And in retrospect they do not seem, as a group, to have been as original or iconoclastic, either as artists or as thinkers, as they hoped to be or as their warmest admirers thought them to be. It is questionable whether any of them, with the possible exception of Brodsky, will achieve the stature of Akhmatova, Pasternak, or Zabolotsky.

They came into prominence at a time when the liberal intelligentsia, eager for release after long years of cultural repression and stagnation, hoped fervently for a renaissance. The climate was relatively receptive to expressions of youthful exuberance, irreverence, idealism, and individuality – qualities that many of their older colleagues welcomed and nurtured in them. In their writings and platform performances they spoke both for their own generation and for their more frustrated and inhibited elders. Both the militant Mayakovskian tone of Evtushenko and Voznesensky and the private, subjective vision of Akhmadulina, Matveeva, and Kushner can be attributed not only to a youthful striving for self-assertive originality but also to a sense of mission in overcoming the Stalinist heritage of uniformity. But the things they were saying and the ways in which they were saying them were not remarkably unique: what made them stand out from their elders was the degree of intensity and daring in their utterances.

To a great extent the subject matter of these young poets was dramatically contemporary. However, most of that which seemed stylistically innovative was merely a revival of devices that had long ago been introduced by such poets as Khlebnikov, Tsvetaeva, and Pasternak. Against the background of the poetic techniques of the last fifteen or twenty years of Stalin's rule, the productions of such poets as Voznesensky, Matveeva, and Sosnora stood out clearly as something *different*, in the sense that the devices they employed had not been evident in the recent past. But many of the technical elements that are found in these poets did exist in the poetry of the first quarter of the twentieth century.

The chief technical contribution of these younger poets was in reinforcing the post-Stalin trend toward a relaxed, conversational diction and lexical style, an expansion of poetic language to include more elements of intimate, popular speech, and a purging of stale formulas from verse. Another contribution, although it was not markedly original, was in the area of phonetics. The poems of Voznesensky, Evtushenko, and Sosnora were often saturated with echoing vowels and heavily decorated with consonant repetition. When it did not become an end in itself, sound play was a rich source of melody, imagery, and semantic complexity. And sound repetition frequently became an effective agent of exuberant, hyperbolic humor. On the other hand, the young poets often became intoxicated by their experimentation and tended to create images that were based solely on the sound similarity of words. Vinokurov complained of this sacrifice of meaning to sound among his younger colleagues and added that he sometimes wondered whether "the combination of sounds, of spectacular words," represented " a psychological, a poetic, or simply a *phonetic* phenomenon." But there was also a counter-movement toward a more conservative style. In their contemplative, philosophical poems, such poets as Kushner, Matveeva, and Brodsky often used strictly classical forms, and many of them, like their older contemporaries, wrote sonnets.

The younger poets benefited from and, in turn, contributed to, the fragmentation of Soviet poetry, its division into many separate, autonomous, mutually exclusive sectors. Individual perceptions, expressing the personality of the poet and his own understanding of life, and reality as filtered through his own unique personality, became increasingly valued and practised. Not as accountable in an ideological sense as poets formerly were, those of this group took it for granted that the poet has the right to cultivate his own garden. The fantastic, sometimes childlike world of Matveeva, the miniatures of Kushner – each of them individualistic to a degree that would have been considered prohibitively eccentric a few years before – were tolerated, allowed to flourish, and even encouraged. More and more, poetry became concerned with the private personality, with attempts to define the nature of man, and with the discovery of one's own identity by following a path of free meditation totally divorced from anything resembling dialectical materialism. The narrator could be naive or confused and the poet could now become involved in previously unacceptable types of exploration into the disorderly depths of his own mind and soul. Often the young poets, such as Sosnora and Akhmadulina, seemed to be conducting these explorations under special conditions – heightened nervousness, hallucination, alienation – that until recently would have been deemed so unhealthy that their verse would be branded antisocial. The young poets were now free to write as if they were deeply neurotic, and they often did so.

By increasing the autobiographical quotient, expressing more directly and in their own voices that which they had personally experienced, the young poets were able to bring lyric and civic elements closer together.

Mistrusting the official version of things, readers could find a new source of authenticity in the relative freedom with which the young poets related events in their private lives to large social issues. The most eloquent in this respect was Evtushenko, who had an impressive facility for projecting his personal feelings and experiences on a broad social plane, and for publicly displaying his youthful idealism. But each of these poets, in his own way, was preoccupied with a fundamental moral problem that had the widest social implications: truthfulness.

Most of them wrote poems about poetry. The urge to do this is age-old, but the particular prominence of the theme among these young poets came, no doubt, from their realization that since some of the preconditions for the development of genuine art had been achieved, it was now necessary to reexamine the role and purpose of poetry. Also, poems about poetry became a way of examining not only the problem of truth in art but of truth in general. The young poets pleaded for boldness and honesty in art and, with great persistency, for sincerity and rectitude in all things. The necessity to hammer away at a principle that, in freer societies, is axiomatic and trite, was evidence that the struggle for this basic right had by no means been won.

Another moral concern of the young poets is evident in their interest in "little things" and the "little fellow." The trend toward scrutinizing the everyday details of existence and the lives of ordinary people involved a repudiation of the easy, pompous, dogmatic, poetic generalization that papered over the stains and fissures in Soviet society. There was much insistence on the necessity for kindness, on the fact that the simple man is in fact a complex individual and not merely a working part of the social machinery. Poetry of this sort represented a new wave of normal, youthful, philanthropic sentiment, and a recognition of the need for a broad cultural awakening.

Together with a new respect for the individual, the young poets developed subtle new variations on the orthodox glorification of the dignity of labor. In writing about work, Voznesensky and Sosnora, particularly, stressed the element of unfettered creativity that should be associated with it. This emphasis contained an implicit insistence on the general need for increased freedom.

Among these young poets there is a new, less condescending attitude toward the reader's intelligence and degree of cultural awareness. They seem to be making more generous assumptions about the reader's sophistication – his knowledge of art, science, man, the world and its history – than poets did during the Stalin years, when the hypothetical reader was a believer in mass action, the supreme wisdom of the Leader, and the virtue of not asking difficult questions. The chance for the poet to show his skill and learning without risking the paralyzing charge of being incomprehensible and "formalistic" did result, at times, in displays of undigested erudition. But the young poets, by and large, were intellectually much more graceful and stimulating than any similar age group had been in the four previous decades.

A major source of richness in their poetry was the use of historical materials. The obligatory touchstone, of course, was the October Revolution; Evtushenko and Voznesensky frequently paid their respects to it, and there is no reason to doubt their sincerity in doing so. But more interesting is the way in which all the young poets leapfrogged back over October in search of a deeper, more meaningful past. To a great extent, they did this simply in the consciousness that Russian culture did not begin in 1917 and that in order to know their language, their people, their heritage, and themselves they must burrow among the treasures and tragedies of many centuries. But they were also using the thematic device of the implicit historical analogy through which the poet can comment indirectly on the present by describing the past or employ history as a means of questioning the accuracy of the ideological blueprint of the future. (The fact that poetry can thus be utilized as a veiled form of social protest explains in some measure its present ascendency over prose in Russia.)

Among the younger poets there was also a marked increase in the use of religious material. This does not necessarily indicate greater faith, and may simply be a result of increased freedom to make religious references. To a certain extent religious imagery and conceits are a convention, much like the use of imagery and names taken from classical mythology. Much of it is simply a labor-saving device in the poet's arsenal, implying no real belief on the part of the poet and requiring none from the reader. It is interesting that Brodsky, the one poet among them for whom religious material has distinctly profound significance, is not published in the Soviet Union.

With the exception of Voznesensky and Evtushenko, these young poets seem less interested in modern science than might have been expected. All of them, it is true, have expressed anxiety over nuclear warfare and, in varying degrees, voiced their concern over the fate of the individual personality in a technological culture. But none of them seems to have been intellectually absorbed by scientific concepts in the manner of Zabolotsky and Martynov. Their main interest is in the psyche, poetry itself, the world as perceived by the senses, and the destiny of society.

6

The rise of short fiction

The Russian novel today is in decline. Huge, majestic explorations and evaluations of life, inherited from nineteenth-century Russia and cultivated in the Soviet period by such novelists as Sholokhov, Leonov, and Fedin, are still attempted but, except for Solzhenitsyn, the best writers favor the short story, or at most the short novel (*povest'*). Nearly all of the large novels of the past twenty years have been stodgy, formula-ridden, and ponderous. And those who write both large novels and shorter works – such as Daniil Granin, Vladimir Tendryakov, and Vladimir Soloukhin – are more successful with the latter.

Soviet critics are inclined to attribute the recent reaction against the novel to a residual distaste for the large forms that represent the legacy of Stalinist culture. Like the wedding-cake architecture of the time, novels became spurious and showy displays of the splendid superiority of Soviet man and all his works – monuments to the wisdom, humanity, and glory of the Communist Party and its Leader. The novel under Stalin suffered from the obligation to affirm a priori truths and frozen propositions, in which scenes from "everyday life," detailed descriptions of production and technology, and contrived depictions of the meetings of local Party organizations became a boring surrogate for genuine conflict. Prohibited from telling the truth, novelists had resorted to masses of colorless "local color" in an effort to create the *illusion* of truth.

But even since the death of Stalin, there have been continuing reasons for writers to eschew exhaustive investigations of the moral, social, and ideological problems that beset contemporary Soviet civilization. It is difficult and dangerous, in uncertain and rapidly changing times, for a democratically inclined writer to give his views the full exposure that a large novel requires. The very terseness of many of the best writers, and their preference for short forms, are not only a result of their urge to avoid the ponderous, pompous falsity of the recent past but also of their realization that under present circumstances the price of survival is to write suggestively rather than explicitly, and impressionistically rather than exhaustively.

Short prose forms tend to emerge in times of accelerated social or cultural change, when new attitudes toward human relations, morals, and social behavior are breaking forth but have not yet become universally recognized. The short story can pose questions, suggest dissatisfaction and doubts, and, in general, present problems without proposing solutions. Because it concentrates on isolated, limited – although often extremely evocative – themes and situations, the short story is ideally suited for use in periods of transition, when new social and cultural tendencies are discernible but not yet established.

In recent years, when partial de-Stalinization has introduced a somewhat increased variety and mobility into the lives of Soviet citizens, and has permitted the reevaluation of some beliefs and standards of behavior while still prohibiting the reexamination of others, the short story is a particularly appropriate form of literary expression. In a moral atmosphere that has been partly renewed, the short story can focus on single episodes in a variety of concrete situations without resolving them, leaving it up to the reader to draw his own ethical conclusions. It can make discrete moral points and raise limited ethical questions without seeming to threaten the prevailing ideology as a whole. At the same time, the short story is effective in narrative situations that emphasize "seeing things with new eyes." And the burden of a great many stories of the last twenty years has been either "things are not what they seem," or "things are not now what they have heretofore seemed to be" or, more subtly, "things are not now what 'they' would like us to think they are."

To put this situation in perspective, however, let us turn for a moment to earlier periods of Soviet literary history. In the 1920s, the Russian short story was colorful and motley, embracing a wide spectrum of themes, attitudes, situations, and character types – all reflecting the social turbulence, ideological confusion, psychological bewilderment, and moral doubts that attended a period of profound cultural upheaval. The grotesque and the absurd were prominent, and many stories – those of Isaac Babel, Boris Pilnyak, and Vsevolod Ivanov, for example – featured the exotic, the primitive, and the violent. Negative or at best neutral portrayals of human nature predominated. Satire was extreme in range and degree, and many short story writers, such as Evgeny Zamyatin and Mikhail Zoshchenko, were preoccupied with irrationality and human stupidity, and emphasized a sense of purposelessness, pessimism, alienation, and tragedy. There was little insistence on the dignity of the human race.

The best writing in the twenties tended to be subjective, lyrical, ironic, and free of moral didacticism. Although Zamyatin and other prominent short story writers dealt in stylized caricatures, with little interest in refined psychology, many others, such as Yuri Olesha, engaged in close exploration of psychological states, with liberal use of dreams, the unconscious, and stream-of-consciousness techniques.

In an attempt to stretch the conventional limits of the short story, writers in the twenties experimented extensively with narrative structures, freely mixing and juxtaposing a wide variety of narrative elements and styles. There was a tendency to combine multiple points of view and angles of vision within a single story, and as a result the works of such writers as Babel, Zamyatin, Olesha, and Pilnyak often seem – at least on first reading – to be illogical and chaotic, episodic and fragmented.

The language of stories in the twenties tended to be heavily figurative, and loaded with startling, arresting imagery. There was much linguistic experimentation in the form of word play, neologisms, distorted syntax, and invented speech derived from the regional dialects of peasants and the slang of semiliterate urban dwellers. At the same time there was a massive intrusion of poetic devices into prose – the so-called ornamentalism that had been inherited from the decade immediately preceding the Revolution. "Ornamentalism" was the search for a special artistic language in which words have independent aesthetic value, as opposed to "practical" value. Primarily lyrical, ornamental prose strives not so much for accurate depiction of the objective world as for adequate transmission of the writer's emotional perceptions, based on principles of association, analogy, and contrast. As a result, language tends to become an object in itself, an intrinsically self-justifying element, and the prose text is characterized by rhythmic devices, difficult syntax, sound play, and extended systems of tropes and leitmotifs.

The narrator in the stories of the twenties tended to be highly subjective, with a distinct personality indicated not only by an individualized point of view but also by his use of markedly colloquial language, frequent lyrical digressions, and rhetorical questions and exclamations. Further individualization and intimacy were achieved through the extensive use of unattributed direct discourse in a variety of forms, expressing in interior monologue the subjective views of separate characters or, at times, those of a distinct collective or social element. Similar to these narrative methods in its intimacy, but linguistically different, was the extensively cultivated technique of *skaz*. In form, *skaz* is an artistic imitation of oral monologue that serves to characterize the narrator, whose voice is not that of the author, but rather that of a person psychologically, and often socially, culturally, and morally distinct from him. The author may or may not be sympathetic toward his *skaz* narrator. In the twenties, as a rule, he was not. *Skaz* thus became a method by which an author, without directly disclosing his own views, could force his narrator-monologist to reveal himself with comic, satiric, ironic, and sometimes tragic effect. The two most successful practitioners of *skaz* were Babel and Zoshchenko.

The array of narrative devices in vogue in the twenties provided authors with a number of masks behind which they could express themselves satirically, lyrically, ironically, and ambiguously. This situation changed radically around 1930. From then until the middle fifties the short story, like the rest of Soviet literature, was forced to take on the narrow obligation of illustrating official theses. A more "positive" view of human nature was propagated; the writer was expected to show a more generous view of the human race and its potential for good. Primitive, instinctive, irrational, and perverse aspects of human nature were deemphasized and there was a new stress on morality, with a pronounced social focus – a new didactic emphasis on correct behavior, on duty. Forbidden to explore subjective avenues to truth, writers concentrated on awed and reverential accounts of the exploits of enthusiastic builders of socialism. There were exceptions, but as a rule the short story became publicistic in nature and psychologically shallow.

Narrative structures became simpler, more logical, and the individual story became more classical in the sense of being monothematic and discrete. Prose became more inhibited and "prosaic," less colorful and metaphoric. There was less attention to language as such: ornamentalism disappeared and, although characters continued to speak in colloquial language, the language of narration itself settled into a form of standard Russian with a heavily journalistic flavor.

The writer from 1930 to the middle fifties was obligated, above all, to make his position absolutely clear. Various types of narration such as *skaz*, based on the language and point of view of someone other than the author himself, which had been a major source of subtlety and irony, were now forced out of use. They were replaced by more direct and unambiguous forms of third-person and first-person objective narration, in which the author and his narrator are closely identified, and in which there are sharp lines of demarcation between the point of view of the author and those of his characters.

Short fiction written since the beginning of the Thaw in the middle fifties has displayed a peculiar combination of traits inherited from Stalinist times, on the one hand, and, on the other, of characteristics that represent a revival of or variation on the attitudes and creative practices that were prominent in the twenties. The positive, generous view of human nature continues to dominate, but a new and fairly strong ingredient of skepticism is now permissible. Many Stalinist taboos are still in force; writers must still refrain from being overly explicit in their treatment of sex, and such things as downright misanthropy and violence for its own sake are still discouraged. But the authorities now permit writers to feature negative, unattractive, individual heroes, as well as collectives. Attitudes of purposelessness, alienation, and pessimism, unchallenged and uncorrected by authorial interference, are now permitted.

Irrationality, the grotesque, and the surrealistic, features of the twenties that are once again prominent in Soviet *poetry* and are fairly conspicuous in *underground* prose, have just barely returned to the officially authorized short story. Although writers continue to show an interest in questions of morality – duty and correct behavior – as established in the thirties, and still often center their stories on the exemplary, socially useful exploit, they are less didactic about the matter, and many stories are carefully, pointedly "pointless" in this respect. It is above all this quality of "pointlessness" that represents a repudiation of the schemes and clichés of Stalinist literature. Characters are no longer apprehended primarily in terms of their attitudes toward the work they perform, their degree of social dedication or of the extent to which they have absorbed official dogma and patterns of conduct. The writers of short stories in recent years have, in fact, been conducting a subtle form of guerilla warfare against officially prescribed morality. Whereas in the thirties, forties, and early fifties authorial language borrowed extensively from the formulas, slogans, bureaucratic ideological jargon, and moralistic patterns of official newspaper style, such language now is not that of the author but of characters who are depicted satirically. An example is the young hero of I. Grekova's "Ladies' Hairdresser," whose use of the stilted ideological jargon he has picked up in school and from the media is the author's delicate way of showing her hero's obtuseness, intellectual deprivation, and somewhat retarded emotional growth.[1]

Conflict is still the heart of the Soviet short story. Although most contemporary stories are based on the antagonism between the social and the antisocial, there has been growing latitude for the use of internal conflicts within the individual that have little immediate social relevance. The best writers usually succeed in intertwining both kinds of conflict in a single work. However, there are distinct gradations among writers in two major respects – the degree of the writer's commitment to resolve the conflicts that he presents, and the degree of the writer's intimacy with and sympathy for the protagonists in his conflicts.

Contemporary Soviet writers tend to avoid placing an explicit moral at the ends of their stories – largely, no doubt, because the device is considered archaic, but also because it renders them more vulnerable to censorship. One of the traditional demands of socialist realism, however, is that the author take sides, that he be willing to serve as the arbiter of his conflicts. A great many writers still do this, openly intruding into the narrative with direct observations and evaluations, or by setting up a narrator who obviously expresses the author's bias. Sergei Antonov and Yuri Nagibin, for example, usually bring their protagonists to definite decisions concerning their conflicts, and even younger writers such as Vasili Aksenov, Vladimir Voinovich, and Anatoli Gladilin, whom conservative critics often accuse of being amoral and irresolute, usually manage to steer their characters at least somewhere near a resolution of their conflicts, a resolution giving a clear indication of what is right and what is wrong. But the tendency, particularly among younger writers, is to do this as subtly and indirectly as possible. This infuriates critics of a conservative bent, who accuse the young writers of moral ambiguity.

The bone of contention here is the preference of many present-day writers for muffling or disguising the voice of the author. The writer's motive for doing this, it would seem, is at least twofold. First, writing in the Soviet Union is still a politically dangerous game, and it is safer to speak in an assumed voice than in one's own. Second, writers in the past twenty years have had an opportunity to become less schematic, less civically blatant, more humane, and more intimate. In third-person narration, the author's voice has been replaced by interior monologue, which serves the dual function not only of conveying the author's views indirectly and in disguise but also of providing a sense of closeness to, and psychic intimacy with, the protagonist. Even greater opportunities for this approach are provided by narration in first person. Here the sense of intimacy is supplied by a diaristic, confessional, lyrical, or conversational intonation. It is one of the paradoxes of Soviet literary criticism that it is precisely this intimate, often ironical, delicate, and sensitive kind of first-person narration that is frequently accused of being "objectivistic," neutral, "unheroic," devoid of meaningful conflict and lacking in moral commitment.

Many writers resort extensively to unattributed direct discourse, in which impersonal sentences express psychic and physical conditions, subconscious impulses, emotions, and spontaneous mental reactions of which their possessors are unaware. Intimacy is also achieved by the fact that, in contrast to the often pompous and artificial, official language of the Stalin period, the contemporary language of standard authorial narration is relaxed and conversational. The chief source of intimacy, however, is the psychological presence of the author in his own story. Many writers take the narrative position of participant or eyewitness. By relying on personal experience, or the aura of it, they can create the impression of unvarnished truth, by providing a kind of autobiographical verification to their writing. Even though he may be closely identified with the author, however, an eyewitness or participant can be merely an *objective* narrator. What distinguishes the writing of recent years from that of the Stalin period is the presence of a *subjective* narrator who is close to the writer. The narrator serves as a kind of double of the author, both in his outlook on the world and in his manner of speaking.

The *skaz* method of narration, which went into sharp decline during the Stalin period, has been prominently restored in recent years, but with a difference. As employed by Zoshchenko and others, *skaz* was chiefly a device to satirize eccentric, usually negative characters. The *skaz* narrator was often someone remote from the author, and the satiric or ironic effect of the story came from the lack of correspondence between the views of the narrator and the implied views of the author. Nowadays, however, *skaz* is used mainly as a *sympathetic* device, in which the narrator is not an alien individual disparaged by the author, but rather a surrogate for him, speaking, perhaps, in an eccentric voice, but expressing subjective views very close to those of the author.

In the 1960s Soviet literary critics were fond of classifying contemporary short story writers into two groups – the "archaists," such as Yuri Kazakov and Yuri Kuranov, and the "innovators," such as Aksenov, Gladilin, Andrei Bitov, and Viktor Konetsky. However, the "innovations" of the innovators would scarcely startle a reader acquainted with modern Western writing, and the archaists, whose writing seems traditional in *form*, are making important contributions to the renewal of the literary atmosphere. What is perhaps most important about both the archaists and the innovators is that the two groups revere and take their inspiration from Chekhov. The brevity, compactness, and restraint of Chekhov, his trust in the imagination of the reader, and his ability to suggest large truths in small forms seem to have set the standard for a large number of contemporary Soviet short story writers.

When in 1962 a number of young Soviet prose writers were asked to name the authors for whom they felt a special affinity, the authors most prominently mentioned were Tolstoy and Chekhov. But a large number of those questioned also named such writers as Hemingway, Erich Maria Remarque, Heinrich Böll, and J. D. Salinger.[2] Clearly the urge to be "modern" and up-to-date is a strong one. The extreme interest in dialogue, and to a certain extent interior monologue as well, is partly attibutable to Western influence. Writers who use documentary techniques are frequently said to be imitating Dos Passos. The striving for compactness, terseness, and dynamism, and the cultivation of the short sentence, particularly noticeable in the works of younger writers, are all evidence of Western influence. Although there is much unpleasant grumbling from reactionary critics about the "so-called Western style," some of the experimentation that is tagged as Western in orientation takes its inspiration and many of its models from Russian writers of the twenties and early thirties, such as Babel and Zoshchenko, who were driven out of literature during the Stalin period.

The most notable feature of the Soviet short story in recent years has been its increasingly wide range of topics. Of course, many subjects are still forbidden, and even permissible topics must be handled with care. Nevertheless, the breadth, depth, and subtlety of themes have grown markedly. There is a new interest in private lives and purely personal problems – the choice of occupation, a mate, finding a place to live, divorce, broken families, or loveless marriages. Sexual infidelity and the eternal triangle, long considered frivolous and even harmful topics for Soviet literature, are accepted as intrinsically interesting and self-justifying. More and more, short story writers have been digging beneath the surface of routine existence, dismissing the external signs of vulgar felicity, and examining the *quality* of life at the individual level. The traditional search for exemplary social behavior has been deemphasized, and there is a tendency to prefer characters apprehended in isolation, outside the collective.

Psychological problems can now be depicted in detail, provided they are not apprehended in total divorcement from the social context. Formerly a person's occupation, his "line of work," was his most significant characteristic. Now the individual is worthy of attention not only because he has a function in society but also because he has a soul. There is a more tolerant interest in human error and inadequacy, and a greater freedom to portray maladjustment, neurosis, and personal conflicts without making moral judgments or coming up with pat solutions. For example, the conflict between parents and children – a favorite theme in recent years – can now be depicted not only as a product of social change but also as something inherent in the human psyche.

With greater opportunities for psychological subtlety and complexity, some writers of short fiction have undertaken increasingly complicated plots. The urge to make fuller statements and to explore situations more deeply has caused narratives to expand beyond the strictest limits of the short story. As a consequence, the boundary line between the short story (*rasskaz*) and the short novel (*povest'*) – always a vague one – has approached obliteration in recent years.

Like all the other genres, the short story became a vehicle for sharper social criticism. With writers such as Antonov, Solzhenitsyn, Vladimir Tendryakov, and Daniil Granin, moral problems – problems of conscience, honest conduct, of groping with the temptation to compromise with a lie – are given a strongly social cast, and questions of ethics are explicitly related to the public interest. But issues of trust, honor, decency, justice, and loyalty are also placed at a more personal level. As writers have displayed an increased interest in human beings, not as they should be but as they are, morally negative characters have taken on increased subtlety and a greater variety of shadings. Moral questions are posed, of course, in varying degrees of clarity. At one extreme is Tendryakov, whose ideas are always presented with Tolstoyan distinctness and are easily grasped. At the other is Grekova, many of whose stories seem, at first glance, to be practically devoid of moral commitment. Significantly, more and more short story writers prefer to delineate moral problems without suggesting their resolution, to ask trenchant questions without answering them. And the questions asked are often timeless ones, with no particular ties to the specific conditions of Soviet life.

Urban topics – involving problems of living in the rapidly growing and increasingly complex city, with its housing shortages, impersonalism, crime, and nervous career building in the harsh, bustling collective – continue to interest the writers of short stories. But there is also a strong trend toward "decentralization" – depiction of the collective-farm village, its mores and conflicts, of minor ethnic groups, and the people of remote regions in the Far North, Central Asia, and the Far East. A massive examination of folk values and traditions, and of the spiritual gulf between the city and the countryside, is taking place, with an often strongly implied advocacy of spiritual return to the soil. The short story is paying close attention not only to the customs, speech, and psychology of Soviet citizens but also to their natural environment. The lyrical treatment of nature is particularly prominent.

In the past two decades the Soviet short story has offered a wider range of characters than it did in the Stalin years. This has come about largely because of its increased concern for the individual, its respect for eccentricity, and its search not as much for heroic figures as for representatives of all stations and walks of life. The enlarged cast of characters has helped short story writers to show that even in a planned society life can be colorful, difficult, complicated, and mysterious.

Yuri Nagibin, born in Moscow in 1920, is a prolific author of short stories who also writes extensively for films, produces hunting sketches and articles on conservation themes, and has written numerous accounts of his travels in the USSR, Eastern Europe, and North Africa. His early stories, based largely on his front-line experiences in World War II, display strong powers of observation but are marred by awkward arrangement of detail and a tendency for trite socialist-realist heroics. His mature work, beginning in the mid-1950s, is psychologically sensitive and disciplined in the manner of Chekhov and Bunin, with clear, uncomplicated moral values tempered by a sense of irony and compassion. Although he is generally identified with the liberal wing of Soviet letters, his stories are not notably concerned with political issues.

Nagibin writes of love among people of all ages, but most often of love between mature adults – emphasizing, as a rule, not its romance but its psychology and its complications – joy, misunderstanding, disappointment, and suffering. He also writes copiously, and often autobiographically, about childhood. In such stories as "Komarov," "Making Snowmen," and "Winter Oak" he deals with the spiritual life of children, their confusions and frustrations in an adult world, their imaginings and the awakening of understanding. Perhaps his best story about children is "The Echo," an episode in the lives of a pre-adolescent boy and girl, which conveys the enchantment of a child's world combined with sober perception of a child's capacity for selfish and callous behavior.

The cast of characters in Nagibin is diverse and widely representative. He favors people of ordinary occupations and average aspirations – peasants, truck drivers, soldiers, hunters, and petty bureaucrats – engaged in activities that are not of a conspicuously public nature. They are shown not in terms of a preconceived ideology but in terms of their own, usually strongly individualistic, personal values. Their strengths, weaknesses, and idiosyncrasies are frequently emotional in origin, and although they can be strong-willed and courageous, they are often frustrated and unable to communicate. Often they seem driven or tormented by deep psychic wounds.

"A Man and a Road" is a story of a young truck driver who has been disappointed in the only love of his life and who, although hardworking and energetic, has become a kind of hardened wastrel, wandering about the Soviet Union doing various strenuous jobs. On a dangerous truck run, he picks up a young woman hitchhiker, who haughtily rejects his advances. Tamed by her coldness, he confides to her the story of his life and disappointment. She falls asleep and, over steep and slippery roads, he brings the truck to its destination. Discovering that the girl has been totally untouched by his confidences and has listened only to keep him from pawing her, he angrily dismisses her and decides to get drunk as usual. At the last minute, however, he changes his mind. Although the girl is gone, the experience of telling his story to a woman has restored his tenderness and given him a new faith in life.

The story illustrates both the shortcomings and the virtues of Nagibin. Its ending is a bit sentimental and insufficiently motivated. On the other hand, although the narration is muscular rather than delicate, it has grace and subtlety. The opening of the story is swift: the action begins immediately, character and atmosphere are established deftly and rapidly. The language of narration is vigorous but unobtrusive, occasionally metaphorical but largely free of decoration, and the dialogue is lean and convincing. There is vivid suggestiveness and dramatic intensity in the description of the truck as its headlights cut through the black night: its isolation underlies the story's motif of human isolation. Nagibin is particularly good at creating the atmosphere of rugged, violent action, and his depiction of the motion of the truck is strikingly tangible. Although the story gives a strong sense of environment, local color is not presented for its own sake. Like most of Nagibin's stories, "A Man and a Road" is not especially rich in purely external signs of the times; rather, the times are indicated in the characters, their way of thinking and the peculiarities of their speech.

Nagibin is more interested in psychological than in moral and social problems, and when he deals with the latter they are not notably tied to Soviet conditions. But he does occasionally examine socially conditioned evil. Two stories published in 1956, "A Light in the Window" and "The Khazar Ornament," criticize, respectively, the material privileges reserved for high Party officials, and the backwardness and neglect of rural areas and the spoilation of their natural resources. One of his best stories, "The Chase," combines the author's conservationist concerns with a portrait of a stupid and malicious latter-day Stalinist petty bureaucrat.

"The Chase" features a one-legged duck-hunting guide who, in a self-imposed test of courage and stamina, pursues an armed poacher through marshes and dense forest and finally captures him. Somewhat suggestive of Hemingway's "Old Man and the Sea," the story portrays a man alone in the natural element he loves, struggling against extreme adversity for a goal that has great spiritual significance for him. Nagibin has a partiality for examining characters in lonely situations where, near the limit of their endurance and almost at the breaking point, they must prove themselves. In this story, the hero's feat of determination, through his refusal to remain down despite his constant tripping, stumbling, and falling in the thick underbrush, becomes, ironically, the cause of his ruin. His accomplishment arouses the jealousy of his superior, who fires him. Injustice prevails, and the story becomes a pessimistic testimony to the impotence of a good man in conflict with a corrupt bureaucracy.

In Nagibin's hunting stories, usually set in the wild Meschera region of central Russia, the author not only espouses a strict sportsman's code of respect for living creatures and a strong concern for preserving the environment but also a sensitivity to nature akin to worship. He describes nature's beauty for its own sake, but he also gives nature an active role in his narratives, endowing it with a vividness of movement and personality equal to that of his characters. There is a unity of plot and setting, so that the psychological and spiritual states of his characters are perceived in close interaction with the rhythms of natural surroundings.

There is an extremely close relationship between natural phenomena and human psychology in Nagibin. The depiction of men's physical sensations while undergoing natural hardship, strain, and suffering, is an essential element in his narrative strategy. He often focuses on internal crises in individual lives, and discloses human psychology through the effects on mind and body of danger, pain, and stress. His favorite method of doing this is to place a character in isolation against hostile natural forces. And although sympathy between man and nature tends to be more frequent in his stories than understanding between men, nature often serves as a harsh monitor over men's thoughts and actions.

The setting of "Chetunov, Son of Chetunov" is a geological field station in the deserts of Central Asia. Its hero is a vain, self-centered young man whose ambition is to emulate as quickly as possible the fame of his father, a renowned geologist. His opportunity to perform an outstanding feat comes when he volunteers to get specimens from a remote salt marsh. Flown to the site, he scrambles down the craggy cliffs of a deep crater and finds himself trapped and utterly alone in the blazing white marsh. In a struggling climb of several hours over hot boulders, fighting thirst, fatigue, confusion, and delirium, he manages to save himself from failure, humiliation, and the stark probability of baking to death. He brings back the specimens and achieves his glory, but he has made painful and humbling discoveries about his own inadequacies.

The story is vivid and suspenseful, and its intimate account of the workings of fear and self-pity in the mind of an arrogant youth has great psychological strength and subtlety. Nature, once again, is used as a medium for testing and exposing human character. In this instance, an individual's lonely battle with an unyielding natural environment reveals the gap between his idealized vision of himself and his real, unheroic essence.

The short stories of Yuri Kazakov, possibly the best that were written in Russia in the fifties and sixties, represent a revival of the artistic tradition of such classical writers as Turgenev and Chekhov. The beauty and concrete precision of his language, his stylistic economy and sense of measure, and the emotional profundity and poetic suggestiveness of his narratives seemed new and refreshing in the Soviet context, but also seemed to herald the restoration of precious Russian literary values.

Kazakov was born in Moscow in 1927. He early became a musician, but he also began publishing stories in 1952 and completed the Gorky Literary Institute in 1958. Most of his works are set in rural areas of central Russia and the far north, where he has traveled extensively. In recent years he has published little but children's stories, and there are indications that he may have undergone a creative crisis. Certainly his life as a writer has not been easy. In the late fifties and early sixties his writings were attacked repeatedly for insufficient contemporary social content, for pessimism and morbidity, and for featuring passive, estranged, and otherwise negative heroes spiritually unworthy of emulation by Soviet citizens.

Prominent among his major male characters are a number of isolates whose most distinguishing traits are misanthropy, self-absorption, or poisonous cynicism. Even his sympathetic characters tend to be antiheroes, brooding, taciturn loners groping in solitude for the solution to personal and intimate problems. At times these problems gain poignancy by the very fact of being undefined. The hero of the "The Outsider" is a nocturnal creature, wasting his life on a simple job as a buoytender along a river because he has repudiated society for some mysterious reason. "An Easy Life" presents a rootless, wandering worker who avoids responsibility and is vaguely troubled over his own spiritual emptiness. In "Adam and Eve," perhaps Kazakov's finest story, the central figure is an artist whose career is stalled, partly because he is at odds with the Moscow establishment, but mainly because he has slipped into a profoundly self-destructive funk.

Not all of Kazakov's major characters are thus alienated. Some are merely unfortunate – possibly only temporarily disappointed in their search for happiness and fulfillment. Such are the seventeen-year-old heroine of "Manka," bewildered and ambivalent in her first encounter with a sexually aroused man, and the heroine of "Unattractive," a plain young woman whose first timid attempt at a liaison meets with callous indifference from the lout on whom she pins her hopes. Although most of Kazakov's characters are young adults, he is capable of great diversity. "Pomorka" is the portrait of a ninety-year-old peasant woman, "Going to Town" features a brutal and stupid peasant of fifty-five, and there are several stories about children. Two of his best works are about animals: "Arktur – Hunting Dog" recounts the story of a dog whose indomitable instinct triumphs over his blindness, and "Teddy" is the account of a trained bear who escapes from a circus and returns to life in the wilds. In his treatment of young or old, men or animals, Kazakov writes always with impressive psychological understanding and great sympathy for the unfortunate.

The moral and social values in Kazakov are firm but not doctrinaire. Like Chekhov, he seems to prize decency, honesty, kindness, and sensitivity above all among humans, but he does not flinch at showing their opposites. He is seldom scolding or indignant, but it is silly to accuse him, as hostile Soviet critics have, of moral and social neutrality. Often his stories are open-ended, and finish on a note of gloom, without a clear-cut resolution that would serve as a guide to conduct. This is not because the author is irresolute, but because he senses the excruciating complexity of the individual psyche and the pressures of society.

Although purely social questions do not play a prominent role in Kazakov, the social context is frequently important. Many of his stories are located in provincial settlements and peasant villages, where the behavior of individuals is closely conditioned by local customs, mores, and living conditions. He is alert to picturesque ethnic nuances, regional speech peculiarities, and the exact details of rural culture. Much of the charm of such stories as "Nikishkin's Secrets," "Pomorka," "But We Are Not Strangers," and "Nestor and Kir" is in their colorful depiction of the social rituals of northern fishing villages. On the darker side, the swinish conduct of men in such stories as "Unattractive," "The Old Men," and "Going to Town" is plainly attributable, if only in part, to the coarseness and poverty of their social surroundings.

Like many Soviet writers, Kazakov deals with the spiritual gulf between the countryside and the modern Soviet city. In "At the Station," we get a brief glimpse of the parting between a country girl and her village sweetheart, who has suddenly become harsh and insensitive in his impatience to catch the train and start a new life in the big city. "The Smell of Bread" tells of the visit of a hardened city dweller to her native village, where her mother died several months before. Indifferent to her loss, she has come merely to settle her mother's meager estate. Momentarily the smell of bread awakens in her a sincere sense of bereavement, but she quickly recovers, finishes her business, and returns to the city, callous and self-satisfied. Broken forever is the tenuous thread of humane values that had tied her to her birthplace.

Ultimately Kazakov's interests are not sociological, but moral and psychological. Often his stories are based on a failure to communicate or misunderstanding between individuals, and missed opportunities to help and love one another occasioned by preoccupation and insensitivity. The hero of "There Goes a Dog," leaving the city on a night bus for a fishing trip to a remote spot, discovers that the attractive young woman seated next to him is troubled, lonely, and desperate for companionship. In his eagerness to get away from it all, he ignores her quiet cry for help and leaves the girl and bus at his destination. Only after three soul-satisfying days of perfect fishing does it dawn on him that he may have acted selfishly in refusing responsible contact with another human being. The beauty of the story is not only in its delicate moral perceptions but also in its deft description of the joys of a sportsman, a man alone in intimate communion with nature.

Nature is a major reference point in most of Kazakov's stories. He writes lyrically of its loveliness and magic, and implicitly argues its superiority over the noisy and agitated world organized by men. Many of his characters seek solace in nature and find in it a stimulus to thought and reflection, a help in solving their most important problems. The redeeming feature of the dropout hero of "The Outsider" is his responsiveness to nature's quiet poetry; through this he has maintained the integrity of his soul. But Kazakov does not offer up nature as an easy palliative for men's woes. Contact with nature may clarify, or even temporarily soften the social, moral, and emotional questions his characters bring to it, but it does not remove them.

Kazakov is fond of narrative situations in which a man has isolated himself in a natural setting, either alone or with a woman. The character has sought this solitude as a refuge from society, a place to think more creatively and clearly, to rediscover and purify himself, or to recover from some disappointment or emotional trauma. Nature thus represents a kind of escape from the trials of contemporary daily existence, a chance to find happiness, freedom, and harmony outside the rat race. His heroes seem bent on simplifying their lives and at the same time intensifying and enriching them through the pleasures of art or sport, or through the delights of love in a sequestered natural setting. The theme of flight from society is thus often united with the theme of love. The stories "Autumn in the Oak Woods," "Two in December," and "Adam and Eve" all involve couples who have temporarily repudiated the responsibilities and conflicts of their normal life routines in the pursuit of emotional fulfillment in unfamiliar and idyllic surroundings. In all three stories, however, it is made clear that such happiness, even if attained, is fleeting, and an insubstantial defense against stern reality. As a consequence there are melancholy, even tragic overtones in all Kazakov's stories about men and women.

At the heart of Kazakov's stories is the unspoken question: "What is happiness?" Usually there is no answer, and if there is one it is conditional. His characters often ponder about happiness, and dwell on its incompleteness, or its loss. In its very presence there is the disturbing awareness that it is bound to end, that it may soon be transformed into its opposite. Moreover, happiness is so elusive that it is usually not found where his characters look for it. In "On the Island" a reasonably happily married man, searching for a perpetual state of romantic love, has a brief, idyllic affair with an unmarried girl, knowing all along that his quest is impossible. In several stories there is the suggestion that happiness is in the tragic acceptance of life's mixture of beauty and pain, its ineffable mystery. The hero of "The Outsider" finds a periodic morose felicity in sitting on the riverbank with his mistress at sunset, using his magnificent voice to sing ancient, sad duets with her.

Kazakov's most subtle and complex story is "Adam and Eve," the account of a disastrous rendezvous between a bitterly alienated artist and the Moscow girl he has invited to join him at a northern lake. She arrives expecting love, but discovers that he is so absorbed in self-doubt, self-pity, and justified anger at the art world from which he has retreated that he refuses to communicate, much less make love to her. A combination of her own psychological ineptitude and his vain, perverse rudeness sets up a wall of estrangement between them, and after a day and night of bewildered humiliation she goes back to Moscow. Kazakov is unsparing in his depiction of the emotional immaturity of the artist, but he is also sympathetic in showing the torments of a sensitive and talented man whose spiritual life has become painfully confused. The hero is an independent man, dedicated to his art in a hostile world, and the reader is implicitly invited to understand his impossible conduct, conditioned at least in part by his struggle to retain his creative integrity.

The characterizations in "Adam and Eve" are fuller than they usually are in Kazakov. As a rule, he deals with discrete states of mind and single emotions, with only subtle overtones of more complex feeling. The details of his characters' lives are seldom spelled out, and their backgrounds are merely hinted at. The story is typical of much of Kazakov, however, in its objective third-person narration, in which feeling is conveyed not through the author's identification with his characters but through dialogue and interior monologue. This is not to say that Kazakov is devoid of lyricism: his first-person narratives often express, in intimate, confessional tones, emotions that are obviously those of the author.

Kazakov's language is colloquial and easy, musical without being elaborate. His descriptive detail, although colorful and evocative, is kept at a minimum, and although his prose is rich in sensory impressions it is precise and economical. He avoids tropes for the most part, and relies heavily on adjectives to convey exact meaning and to particularize his vision of things. Essentially, Kazakov's narrative method is impressionistic and indirect. He seldom formulates a firm and simple thesis but relies, rather, on tonality and the repetition of motifs. He favors understatement and, although his plots are compact, he avoids neat conclusions and usually ends his stories on a questioning note.

The open-endedness and uncertainty of Kazakov's conclusions come largely from his insistent awareness of the mystery of life. It is insufficient, he seems to imply, for humans simply to experience the sorrows and joys of existence. They must understand, in addition, that also natural to life is wonder at the strange and inexplicable forces surrounding it. In many of his stories there are passages that gently suggest the unfamiliarity of the atmosphere, the ambiguity and oddness of things. He is fond of writing about fog, twilight, and darkness, and frequently plays on the contrast of light and shadow.

His humorous story, "Kabiasy," concerns the young director of a village club whose duties include antireligious propaganda. Walking along a country road one night, he comes upon, and teases, an old crackpot who fancies it his job to guard the local orchard against nocturnal devils who haunt the place. As he proceeds along the road, the young man gradually becomes terrified of the night sounds and shadows, panics, and only comes to his senses when a friend arrives on a bicycle. But before this happens, our militant atheist has managed to cross himself to ward off evil spirits.

Sergei Antonov writes chiefly about the personal problems of ordinary Soviet individuals, with occasional excursions into social criticism of a rather orthodox variety. His writing is not as vigorous as that of Nagibin, nor as emotionally intense as that of Kazakov. Calmer, more restrained than either, he still shares the same Chekhovian tradition – economy of means, careful selection of detail, suggestiveness rather than assertion.

Antonov was born in Petrograd in 1915, was a civil engineer, and fought in both the Soviet–Finnish War and World War II. Prominent and active in the Writers' Union, he is also a screenwriter, and several of his stories have been filmed. In addition he has written extensively on the theory and practice of the short story. Unlike most of his war-veteran contemporaries, Antonov has restricted himself to postwar, civilian themes. His early works, dating from 1947, dwelt with obligatory sunniness and optimism on the standard topics of the Stalin period – production stories and accounts of life on collective farms. Although he eschewed the more egregious practices of "varnishing reality" then in vogue and handled the canonical themes with considerable originality, he was essentially a mild and dutiful writer who avoided offending the authorities by concentrating on sympathetic characters, patently resolvable conflicts, and local color in pastel shades.

In the mid-1950s his writing became somewhat more dramatic in manner and his social criticism sharper. He continued to concentrate on private lives. "The New Office Worker" (1954) tells of a District Party Secretary, distressed and disillusioned by his wife's increasingly middle-class tastes and love of privilege, who becomes infatuated with a charming girl in his office. Ironically, he is obliged at the same time to break up the extramarital affair of one of his party subordinates. Both situations are resolved virtuously; duty and decency triumph. The story ends, however, on a muted note of melancholy – the tension between middle-aged temptation and the sense of obligation is a sad and painful thing. There is sterner social criticism in "The Application Form" (1956) – the portrait of a rigid, lying bureaucrat with an obsession for routine and order and a timidity that comes from an indoctrinated fear of higher-ups. His longer story, "The Penkovo Affair" (1956), speaks candidly of a number of defects on collective farms – poor discipline, inefficient management, backward farming methods, window dressing and low morale. The characters, although somewhat typed, are lively and vivid, including a skillful but impetuous young tractor driver whose wild, insubordinate, and hooligan behavior brings him a two-year prison sentence. There is considerable robust humor, as in the account of a tug-of-war between tractors, which wrecks both machines, and an all-out drunken village wedding celebration, as seen through the amazed eyes of a city girl. It is typical of Antonov that the central situation is a love triangle. Unfortunately, it is also typical of this author, who has difficulty in managing plots, that the point of view shifts awkwardly between individuals and that the triangle is resolved by a sudden, implausible change of character by one of the principals, the jealous wife.

Antonov himself has correctly described the period from 1956 to 1960 as a stagnant one in his literary career. Around 1960, however, his writing gained firmness and versatility. Despite lapses into strident melodrama, there is a new strength, directness, delicacy, and psychological profundity in such works as "Running Empty" (1960), in which a young journalist stumbles upon corruption at a Siberian logging site, and "The Torn Ruble" (1965), which is concerned, once again, with collective-farm problems.

Antonov's virtues are best illustrated in his fine story, "Alyonka" (1960), the account of a journey in an open truck across 150 miles of barren Siberian steppe, by a bright, engaging nine-year-old girl whose parents are sending her from the remote state farm where she lives, to board a train for a city where she can go to school. Her fellow passengers in the truck, all adults, are a motley group, beautifully individualized, and each of them has an arresting, and often a touching, life story. All of them are perceived from the point of view of little Alyonka, who performs the connecting role of observer and listener. The story is rich in episodes, warmly humane, and leavened, much in the manner of Chekhov's "Steppe," with a poetic treatment of the dynamic presence of nature.

A charming phenomenon of the 1960s was the literary debut of I. Grekova, a woman of mature years with a distinct and unusual voice. I. Grekova is the pen name of Elena Sergeevna Ventzel', a mathematician who has been a professor at the Moscow Air Force Academy for over thirty years. Writing is apparently only her avocation, a hobby pursued chiefly during holidays. It is all the more impressive, therefore, that she writes not only with great originality but also with professional sophistication and polish.

Nearly all of Grekova's stories feature a dramatized narrator whose highly individualized personality, point of view, and way of saying things contribute importantly to the tone and flavor of the story. In some works this narrator becomes a major character in her own right. The masks vary in their details from story to story; the biographies of the separate narrators are not literally consistent with one another. Still, one cannot escape the conclusion that Grekova's narrators are basically autobiographical.

The composite narrative voice, then, is that of a woman somewhere between fifty and sixty, the mother of one or two grown-up children. She is a widow (probably a war widow) or a divorcée, and has never remarried. The special harshness of the Soviet period, with its extraordinary demands on women, has left a strong imprint on her. She has suffered and endured, without a mate, the burdens of wartime evacuation and total family responsibility – rearing her children while working full time to support them. Now that she has reached middle age and her children are grown, she has fleeting thoughts of resting, of changing her life by giving up her job and, possibly, remarrying. This will probably not happen: responsibility is a habit, and she likes her work. She could never have been happy by neglecting either, and she cannot now.

Each of Grekova's narrators has her own idiosyncrasies, and there are also varying degrees of psychological distance between the individual story and its teller. But their composite voice is that of a woman who realizes that despite twinges of middle-aged restlessness and the wistful feeling that much has passed her by, her difficult life has been honorable and rewarding. She can be irritable, but she has balanced emotions and a keen, healthy sense of humor; she is critical of others but just as critical of herself. She is receptive, intelligent, and still willing to learn. Her point of view is entirely feminine, and her attitude toward the younger generation is maternal, sensitive, and sympathetic without being sentimental. Because she has a genuine sense of self-irony and honestly understands her own failings, she is an exceptionally reliable witness. Finally, she invariably speaks of the practical world with a special authority, because her employment is responsible and professional.

Grekova's first published story, "Beyond the Entryway" (1962), describes, through the fictional form of a highly personalized sketch, a contemporary scientific reasearch laboratory and the individuals who work in it. The story is essentially a group of deft, sympathetic, humorous, and sometimes satirical character portraits, as subjectively perceived by one of the woman scientists. The "hero" is the laboratory itself, considered as a human collective with an atmosphere, rhythm, and personality of its own. In addition, two independent but complementary themes run through the story. By having separate characters use contrasting language in describing one and the same phenomenon, Grekova underscores the opposition between the scientific interpretation of things – the view of "physicists" – and the artistic interpretation – that of "lyricists." Through these different kinds of language she not only creates psychological characterizations but also dramatizes the opposition between the two prevailing contemporary modes of perception. The story's second theme is a polemic against the stale and empty formulas and jargon that Soviet newspapers use in describing scientific work. A journalist comes to do an article about the laboratory. One of the scientists teases him by answering his questions, not substantively, but in the inflated and meaningless terms in which he knows the article will be written. The contrast between the journalist's eventual cliché-ridden and absurdly false description of the laboratory and the accurate way in which the workers themselves describe it is sharply satirical and very funny.

A remarkable feature of Grekova's writing, especially for a person of her generation, is her mastery of the inventive narrative language and clever dialogue that otherwise seems to be the exclusive property of much younger writers, such as Vasily Aksenov and Vladimir Voinovich. Her ear is excellent, alert to the speech characteristics of the city dwellers of whom she chiefly writes. Like Zoshchenko, she plays ironically with semieducated urban language, such as that of the garrulous, gossipy Polya of "Summer in the City," whose vulgar chatter, even in its specifically linguistic qualities, marks her as a petty philistine. Grekova's close attention to language is evident in her discriminating mixture of the various lexical levels of the everyday speech of the 1960s and her sensitivity to the contrast between city and rural language.

Abundant, spontaneous dialogue is Grekova's chief means of characterization. It is always effective, and when it takes on a bantering, sarcastic, or quarrelsome quality it is highly entertaining. In characterizing her narrators, however, she relies heavily on interior monologue, so that the narrator achieves an easy and intimate relationship with the reader by sharing confidences with him. The narrator's language, although tart and sometimes arrestingly metaphorical, is conversational and relaxed. Constructed as apparently loose groupings of everyday episodes, the stories feature no single event and lack a final resolution. The effect is of course intentional, for Grekova seems above all to be a writer who wants to show life, not shape it.

Grekova's best story, "Ladies' Hairdresser," is told by a middle-aged widow who is an administrator in a cybernetics institute, and portrays in an accumulation of episodes, a young man named Vitaly, who is her hairdresser. The story begins when she becomes his client and ends when, frustrated by the state bureaucracy that runs the hairdressing trade, Vitaly quits in disgust and goes to work in a factory. Out of this material, unpromising and even ludicrous in terms of the traditional demands of socialist realism, Grekova has constructed a humorous, subtly poignant, and deeply humane tale.

We gradually learn that Vitaly, whose manner is abrupt, businesslike, and humorless, is a complex young man. He is a perfectionist, fanatically dedicated to hairdressing, which for him is a highly creative art, and he is very good at it. We also discover that he is remarkably ambitious, a tireless worker with spartan habits, no friends, and a single-minded, almost pathetic drive to make something of himself. One of the paradoxes about Vitaly is that in his determination to become a cultured and useful Soviet citizen he has stunted his own emotional and intellectual growth. His rigid plan of self-development precludes an early marriage (the housing shortage also contributes to this); therefore he avoids involvement with girls. To educate himself about literature he is reading not literature itself but, instead, the complete collected works of Vissarion Belinsky! His ultimate ambition is to become an expert on dialectical materialism – he impractically believes that this will ensure his success in Soviet society.

It becomes evident that Vitaly, for all his admirable qualities, is a kind of social casualty, an innocent parody of several elements in Soviet culture. He is indeed an artist (in addition to his flair for hairdressing, he has latent musical talent), but his standards are so high that, rather than compromise with the corrupt and unimaginative authorities who administer his trade, he is willing to repudiate it altogether. At the same time he is singularly devoid of grace and imagination in vital areas of thought and behavior. He stuffily accepts an invitation to a social evening and dance at the narrator's cybernetics institute on the grounds that it will be useful for him to "study various strata." He spends long hours trying out coiffures on a girl whose hair especially interests him, and then breaks her heart by dropping her when he has "exhausted the possibilities of her head." Underneath the apparent insensitivity and obtuseness of this excessively sober young man, however, there is idealism, stubborn honesty, and a touching vulnerability. Much of his boyhood was spent in a children's home. Too early in life he experienced emotional insecurity and the need to fend for himself in the world, and the scars are deep.

But Vitaly's peculiar utterances and attitudes are not solely the result of his lonely and bewildered childhood. In addition, he is only semieducated, the victim of undigested or poorly integrated official dogma. His half-baked notions, couched in jargon he has picked up in school and from the official press and other propaganda media, are the product of real cultural deprivation. His longing to find a meaning in life, complicated by his worldly ambition and earnest gullibility, has caused him to strike out in awkward directions, and his unconsciously comic use of the Russian language readily at hand produces a deadly parody of Soviet success patterns.

Vitaly is, at one and the same time, an entirely plausible character and a subtle grotesque. On the other hand, there is nothing bizarre about the narrator, who develops a mildly motherly relationship to Vitaly and serves as witness and controlling intelligence. She is very engaging in her own right as we hear her amusing quarrels with her two sons, see her relations with her colleagues and her not-too-bright secretary, and share her wry observations about herself and her amazement at Vitaly's pronouncements. It is through her eyes and ears, also, that we perceive a multitude of fascinating detail about Soviet urban life. We witness, for example, the gossip, bickering, and infighting of Vitaly's clients as they maneuver for priority on his waiting list.

In the controversy that followed the publication of "Ladies' Hairdresser," Grekova was accused of being "objectivistic," "neutral," interested merely in showing the "stream of life," and of having written a story that was devoid of meaningful conflict and lacking in moral commitment. It is true that she did not seek to solve a problem, draw a moral, teach the reader, or perform a judgment. However, there is indeed a strong moral foundation in this, as in all other stories by this author. It consists in her intelligent and ingenious social satire, her honesty and humanity, and her deep concern over problems of personal integrity.

Yuri Trifonov (born 1927) established his reputation in the Stalin years with the novel *Students* (*Studenty*, 1956), a cautious, politically orthodox treatment of university life in the dogmatic spirit of the times. His second long work, *The Quenching of Thirst* (*Utolenie zhazhdy*, 1963), is a rather traditional construction novel reminiscent of those of the 1930s, but with a fashionable anti-Stalinist slant. The setting is a huge irrigation project in Turkmenia in 1957–8, and the novel deals with long-established themes: the romantic enthusiasm and spiritual uplift of the mass effort to conquer nature (in this case, the Central Asian desert); self-sacrificing devotion to the collective versus the striving for personal advancement; the problem of creative individual initiative at the risk of criminal prosecution for violating present plans. The novel's title refers not only to the need for water to make the desert bloom but also to man's thirst for justice. Sections of the narrative take the form of the diary of a young journalist who is obsessed by the injustice done to his father, destroyed in the purges of 1937.

Trifonov's numerous short stories, and especially his recent ones, are better, on the whole, than his novels. A cycle of stories of indifferent quality, written in the fifties and early sixties, is set in Central Asia. Another cycle, written in the sixties, consists predominantly of travel sketches set in Western Europe. In the late sixties Trifonov concentrated on a cycle of urban stories, and it is these that display his talents most favorably. Concerned primarily with the private lives of the Moscow intelligentsia, they investigate the psychology and moral climate not only of individual households and families but of a whole stratum of Soviet society, with its shifting pecking order, intrigues, and intellectual fashions and frauds. In several respects there is a startling resemblance between Trifonov's Moscow and the cosmopolitan cultural centers of the modern Western world. Heterosexual mores seem as liberal as those of London, Paris, or New York, perhaps more so, although homosexuality is not mentioned. The same kind of status seeking prevails, together with essentially the same bourgeois tastes and aspirations. Even the hectic rhythm of jostling city life seems similar: the author recreates vividly and tangibly both the details and the general atmosphere of contemporary Moscow existence. There is also a prominent historical dimension, as Trifonov seems especially concerned with omnipresent processes of change – for example, the way in which urban sprawl is altering the quality of life, engulfing and destroying the ring of suburban villages around Moscow.

Trifonov's greatest strength, however, is in the creation of character, and the main focus of these urban stories is on individuals, usually husbands and wives. The heroes of the trilogy "The Exchange," "Preliminary Conclusions," and "A Long Goodbye" are all disappointed Moscow intellectuals – semifailures whose career problems are compounded by family difficulties. "The Exchange" centers on the bickering, lusterless, loveless relationship of a weak, mother-fixated man of thirty-seven and his mean-spirited, social-climbing, boorish wife. Their quiet hell is complicated by the intrigues of her materialistic, opportunistic parents, who aggravate the couple's hopeless incompatibility. There is comic relief of a rather sardonic nature in the couple's infighting, and in the shrewish exchanges between the wife and other female characters. And there is a special social dimension in the depiction of the in-law problem, the histories of both sides of the family and the hostile relationship between them. Psychologically subtle and grimly realistic, the story ends on a dispirited, defeated note.

"Preliminary Conclusions" is the first-person narrative of a neurotic, 48-year-old free-lance translator of verse who is living temporarily in the mild climate of springtime Turkmenia because of a heart condition. His dilettante wife has been attracted by more glamorous and successful men; his semidelinquent teenage son has drawn away from him; and, in a huff, he has left them both in Moscow. In a leisurely, discursive monologue that combines self-pity, self-knowledge, and irony, he reviews his life with regret and resignation, gives vent to middle-aged feelings of frustration, disappointment, and loneliness, and expresses self-doubts and fear of death. Although he is weak and dispirited, he is intelligent and has a good sense of humor. He thinks of his marriage:

> We shouldn't have lived together twenty years. *Also sprach Zarath-ustra:* it's too long. Twenty years is no joke! In twenty years forests thin out, soil gets poor. The very best house needs repair. Turbines stop working. And what gigantic successes science achieves in twenty years, it's terrible to think! Transformations take place in all branches of science. Cities are rebuilt. October Square, where we once lived, has completely changed its face. To say nothing of the fact that new African states have emerged.[3]

The story ends with the hero's return to Moscow, reconciled with his family and his mediocre lot in life.

"A Long Goodbye" is a similar treatment of private lives and emotional problems within Moscow literary and theatrical circles. Marred by structural defects and soap opera tinges, it is nevertheless a revealing study of contemporary manners and morals. Like the majority of Trifonov's urban stories, it seems refreshingly authentic.

In January 1976 Trifonov published "The House on the Embankment," a long story focusing on the cowardice and opportunism of a university student in the early postwar years who allows himself to be used in a conspiracy to destroy one of his professors – who also happens to be the father of his fiancée. Like all of Trifonov's best writing, the story is rich in detail about Soviet urban life. (The narrative shifts back and forth among the immediate prewar and postwar years, and also the years 1972 and 1974.) Although the story is retrospective in its portrayal of the iniquity of Stalin's time and of a generation that is now well into middle age, the evils it portrays are still very much a part of the Soviet scene. Its publication in 1976 seemed a happy anomaly.

Trofim is a local fisheries inspector, universally hated because of his single-minded, malevolent zeal as a law enforcer. Rigid and vicious, he constantly mumbles to himself that "the public is trash" and "the people are filth." Misanthropy so dominates him that even his wife and son, whom he loves, are cold to him. One day he chances upon a newborn baby, abandoned by its mother in a remote shack in the woods. He tries to save the baby's life, fails and, with the little body in his arms, makes his way back to civilization through dangerous forests and swamps, an exploit that almost costs him his life. His motive is "duty," to find and punish the person who abandoned the child.

It turns out that Trofim's inability to refrain from trying to save the baby's life has aroused in him long-dormant humane impulses, a sense of measure, and a degree of moral flexibility. He reports the affair to his cynical superior, and is astounded by the latter's callous and indifferent response. When Trofim finds the guilty mother he is touched by her plight and decides not to turn her in to the authorities. But the resolution of the story is melancholy and inconclusive. Trofim is still isolated, bitter, and lonely. Although a process of rehumanization may have begun, it is altogether possible that misanthropy has permanently poisoned his soul.

Chance has precipitated a moral crisis in Trofim, has brought about a dramatic test of his fibre, and caused him to examine frozen values. He may have learned something, but a dark, sad cloud remains over his spirit. In the course of the story we discover that much of his sourness comes from the fact that he is a dispossessed victim of collectivization of agriculture and also that his behavior is conditioned by harsh Soviet laws and bureaucratic practices unresponsive to genuine social needs. These, presumably, are accidents of historical development – it is within the power of human enlightenment to prevent their recurrence. But the story leaves an aftertaste of deep pathos, perhaps tragedy – fate has weighed down the human race with perverse and destructive impulses that are beyond understanding or control.

The story of Trofim is "The Windfall," by Vladimir Tendryakov, and it is treated with the author's typical exhaustive, brooding intensity. Tendryakov usually writes of loss, defeat, and personal tragedy, of situations in which positive human values are clearly affirmed but in which brave and honorable conduct gives no assurance of positive solutions. His characters are well individualized, not, it would seem, because colorful personalities are intrinsically interesting to the author but because he is seeking moral essences behind their surface behavior. And although the conflicts he features and the questions he raises are usually direct outgrowths of specifically Soviet social problems, they are designed to have a relevance far beyond the realm of immediate social criticism.

The stories of Tendryakov are heavily laden with complex questions of ends and means, personal moral obligation and civic responsibility, guilt and evil. He explores their psychological aspects in depth and detail. At times he seems so worried over the question of who is to blame that his uncovering of its multiple layers, for all its compassion, becomes tedious.

But the great merit of Tendryakov is that he avoids easy answers, that he finds no pat socialist-realist remedies for human error and weakness, and that he faces squarely the problem of unexplained evil.

Born in 1923 in a village in the Vologda region, Tendryakov completed ten-year school and entered the army in 1941. He fought in the Battle of Stalingrad and was wounded near Kharkov in 1943, experiences that enriched the accounts of military action in his novel *A Rendezvous with Nefertiti (Svidanie s Nefertiti,* 1964). From 1944 to 1946 he served as a Komsomol secretary in a remote village in Kirov Province, and joined the Communist Party in 1948. He entered the Gorky Literary Institute in 1946 and graduated in 1951. Identified with the Party's liberal wing and officially reprimanded from time to time for unorthodox writings, he nevertheless appears to have been spared virulent attacks.

Tendryakov's early writing consisted of sketches and stories about collective-farm life, and although he has written war stories, science fiction, and stories with a city environment, he has continued to favor rural settings. He is sensitive to the Russian landscape; nature and the elements serve both as a backdrop and an active dramatic force in his stories. Rural settings also enable him to assemble casts of characters from among the common people, to deal directly with social, ethical, and emotional problems in a relatively pristine form.

His story "Potholes" (1956) is typical in this respect. The truck driver Dergachev, delivering smoked fish on a bad road between two villages, picks up a random load of paying passengers – a practice that is common because it is often the only means of transportation for ordinary people in remote areas – but illegal. The truck tips over, and a passenger is gravely injured. Another passenger, Knyazhev, who happens to be the director of a machine and tractor station in the next village, organizes a rescue attempt, and the driver and some of the passengers arduously carry the injured man there on an improvised litter. When they arrive it becomes evident that the injured man needs expert medical attention, which can only be found by hitching a tractor to a cart and taking him back to the first village. Heretofore concerned and cooperative, Knyazhev refuses to release a tractor on bureaucratic grounds. The injured passenger is placed in a horse cart, which sets off in the rain. Finally, another passenger, a young army lieutenant, bullies the local authorities into providing a tractor, but it is too late; because of the delay, the injured man dies on the way. The story ends in complete gloom: a man is dead because of the intransigence of a bureaucrat; Dergachev, who worked feverishly in the rescue attempt, faces a sure prison sentence.

Tendryakov individualizes nearly everyone in the truckload of passen-

gers, and numerous incidental characters as well. Their function, however, is collectively to represent the ordinary Soviet people, and they
mobilize themselves purposefully in this emergency. Dergachev is one of
them; Knyazhev, when he begins acting as an official, ceases to belong and
in fact becomes, indirectly, a murderer. This rather daring indictment of
officialdom is characteristic of Tendryakov, but also typical are the over-
done, maladroit passages of rhetorical dialogue between Dergachev and
Knyazhev, designed to hammer home the author's ethical and social message.

Other works of Tendryakov criticize more specifically the conditions of
life in rural areas and deal with problems of inefficient management, authoritarianism, and corruption on collective farms, as in the long story
"Tight Knot" and in "The Mayfly – A Short Life," the story of a girl who
gains celebrity as a pig raiser by falsifying records. In "Short Circuit" he
examines the city as a social organism under stress. On New Year's Eve a
short circuit in a main power line disrupts numerous lives and forces
rapid, far-reaching administrative decisions. At stake is the problem of
lives interrelated by a centralized technology and bureaucracy, and the
necessity for initiative within a complex administrative hierarchy whose
scapegoat mentality has taught it to fear individual responsibility. In
these, as well as in many other stories of Tendryakov, there are clear anti-
Stalinistic implications, but for the most part these implications seem incidental to the search for more universal human truths.

Ultimately, Tendryakov's reputation will probably depend less on his
effectiveness as a liberal propagandist than on his success as a moral pro-
ber. There is Tolstoyan persistence in his attempts to anatomize questions
of right and wrong. Two of his best stories – "Three, Seven, Ace" and
"The Trial" – culminate in acts of moral cowardice on the part of otherwise good men. In the former, a professional gambler poisons the morale
of a logging camp and physically attacks the foreman, who is forced to kill
him in self-defense. The one man who knows what happened – an innocent who nevertheless fears criminal implication – withholds the evidence that might have saved the foreman from prosecution. In "The
Trial," the truth about a hunting accident is similarly withheld by a
witness who fears the personal complications his honest testimony would
involve.

Tendryakov eschews most of the platitudes of socialist realism. It is true
that, like many socialist-realists, he is sometimes excessively attentive to
documentary detail, for example in "Short Circuit," which is overly laden
with technological description. On the other hand, his use of landscape

and natural detail – as in "The Windfall," "Potholes," and "The Trial" – is exceptionally rich, powerful, and dramatic. It is also true that he shares with his more orthodox contemporaries a tendency to overexplicitness, an apparent fear that his readers will miss the point. He is a vivid writer but not a deft one; he distinctly prefers thoroughness to economy, and as a consequence his stories tend to move slowly and often approach novel length.

Language in Tendryakov is exact and strong, although occasionally prolix. The speech of his characters is precisely differentiated, and flavored with regional, occupational, and psychological traits. He uses figurative language aptly and in moderation, and is also capable of ironic and parodistic use of officialese, as in "Mayfly – A Short Life," where the newspapers trumpet the glory of the pathetic girl swineherd, a fraudulent champion, as a "distinguished pig tender" and "the proud banner of the collective farm."

One of the most dramatic of present-day writers, Tendryakov organizes his plots, as we have seen, around extraordinary, often violent, situations and events, which put his characters under great strain and tension. In this respect he is similar to Nagibin. He differs from Nagibin and most other contemporary Soviet writers, however, in his extensive probing into the roots of the crises he depicts, their psychological consequences, and their moral implications.

With the exception of Tendryakov and Trifonov, the writers thus far discussed in this chapter specialize in short fiction exclusively. There are, however, a number of novelists who have made significant contributions to the short story. Foremost among them is Solzhenitsyn, whose stories are discussed in the chapter devoted to him. Mikhail Sholokhov, whose fame is based on his epic novels, has always written short stories, and in 1957 published "The Fate of a Man," the powerful, harrowing story of a pathetic veteran, wounded in battle, tortured for two years as a prisoner of the Germans, and devastated by the loss of his wife and children, all killed in the war. The story is heartbreaking, made all the more poignant by the presence of a little boy, orphaned by the war, whom the hero has adopted and with whom he roams the countryside.

The novelist Viktor Nekrasov (see pp. 270–1, 280, 289–90) is another whose short stories are largely concerned with the war and its spiritual aftermath. Even in the sixties he continued reverting to the Battle of Stalingrad for plots and settings. Nekrasov has always been primarily interested in showing how the character of ordinary soldiers manifests itself on the battlefield. In the story "Senka" (1950) he examined the cowardice of a young soldier in his first engagement, its psychological origins, and its cure. "Private Lyutikov" (1950) tells of an apparently weak, malingering, useless soldier who astounds his comrades by volunteering for a suicidal mission and dies a hero. In "Sudak" (1958) a diffident, unsoldierly lieutenant – a former ichthyologist who appears to be an untrainable misfit – leads an immensely successful night sortie against the Germans and displays extraordinary initiative, bravery, and resourcefulness. The narrative tone of these stories is dispassionate and objective, the authorial presence at a minimum.

In the sixties, the war became a vehicle for changed, expanded, and more subjective interests in Nekrasov's stories – questions of the relationship between war and the artist, between his own attitude toward the war and that of the younger generation, and the problem of chronology in the artist's imagination. "The New Recruit" (1963) tells of a writer who, incognito, joins a detachment of sappers, endears himself to them with his warmth and wisdom, and proves himself as a soldier. When his identity is revealed, however, his comrades become confused, respectful, and remote – the very fact that he is a writer has opened up a psychic distance between the artist and his subjects. Another story of the sixties, "The Dugout," speaks of the unbridgeable psychic gap between those who fought in the war and the younger generation that, although sympathetic, has only heard about it. As Nekrasov grows older, he seems to realize more and more profoundly the impress of the moral and spiritual values he absorbed in the war. But the relevance of this story, and of "The New Recruit" as well, is not only moral and spiritual but also, more importantly, psychological and aesthetic. The relationships between the past and the present, between subjective and objective knowledge, and between art and reality, have become increasingly the burden of Nekrasov's stories.

All of these themes are united in the fantastic story, "An Incident at Mamai's Burial Mound" (1965). On an excursion to Volgograd (formerly Stalingrad) the author visits a basement that was his command post during the Battle of Stalingrad, and served as a setting in his novel *In the Trenches of Stalingrad*. Suddenly time is displaced, and he finds himself once again a young officer, in the company of soldiers and officers, some of whom he had known in actuality, others of whom had been characters in his novel – either pure inventions or composites of persons then living. Among those present is the hero of his novel – not, however, exactly as Nekrasov had originally drawn him but as the famous actor Smoktunovsky portrayed him in the film version of the novel. The Battle of Stalingrad is raging. Everything is as it was twenty-three years before, except that the author has the disturbing knowledge of hindsight – he knows who will be killed, how and when, he knows when the battle will end. He knows, further, all the history of the coming twenty-three years – the defeat of the Germans, the death of Stalin, and the subsequent changes in Soviet life. His psychological dilemma is emphasized when one of the officers gives him a drink of cognac: "I had drunk cognac like this, or approximately like this, in Italy, but this was five years ago, or, on the contrary, fifteen years later."

He wants to warn some characters not to do the things they did in his novel that cost them their lives, but finds that he cannot. He tries to tell his hero about the outcome of the war and postwar developments, but the latter is not interested: "Consider me an ostrich if you want . . . but I'm not sure I should know all this. One must learn everything for himself, from life." The author has an eerie feeling, as if he were participating in a film. He realizes he is involved in a fantasy; with his knowledge he should be able to control the action, but he cannot, and he is not sure that he wants to.

The story is an objective treatment of the most subjective kind of speculations, a delicately haunting fantasy. Nekrasov is examining not only the sources of his own art and the tenuous relationship between art, memory, and reality but also the very nature of artistic perception and impulse. He continues these meditations, slightly tongue-in-cheek, in "A Story Strange to the Highest Degree." The author tells in this story of helping to edit a documentary candid-camera film on Italy, for which he studied each of the very brief scenes dozens of times. In one episode a beautiful woman, walking along the sidewalk away from the camera, passes a young man coming toward her. He looks back at her, and passes on toward the camera. But at the premiere of the film, the author is horrified to see the young man turn, overtake the woman, and walk off in conversation with her. The author is so bemused and tormented that he avoids the film until one day he sees it again by accident. This time, however, the couple has disappeared from the film completely. What would have happened, he wonders, if everyone in the film, whose lives had been captured and suspended for a fleeting moment, had similarly refused to cooperate, gone about his business, and walked out of the picture? Once again, this fantastic story leads to disturbing speculations on the intangible and unstable relationship between art and life.

Two works by the novelist Emmanuil Kazakevich suggest that, had he lived beyond 1962, his contribution to the contemporary short story would have been a major one. "By the Light of Day" (1961) and "A Father Visits His Son" (1962) are both distinguished by an abundance of masterfully developed psychological detail, a relentlessly unsentimental treatment of human nature and, at the same time, a remarkable understanding of the human heart. In "By the Light of Day" a one-armed, demobilized soldier, shortly after the war, travels from his peasant village in Siberia to Moscow to pay his respects to the widow of a beloved officer who had died in his arms two years before. As he tells her about her late husband's devotion to her, and his warmth, courage, and nobility as an officer, she gradually realizes how gravely she had underestimated, and often overlooked, his splendid qualities. In turn, the soldier discovers, to his horror, that she remarried shortly after her husband's death and has made a new, happy life. Insensitive, she offers to pay his train fare, and he leaves, angry and mortified. The only thing left to all concerned – the soldier, the woman, and her new husband – is bewildered remorse.

"A Father Visits His Son" is distinguished by a similar combination of authorial tough-mindedness and compassion. A successful Magnitogorsk worker and Party member, who was pushed out of his home at a tender age to make way for his father's second wife and family, has nevertheless been generously supporting them all for twenty-five years. He also has a wife and family of his own. In all this time he has not seen his father, and so he invites the old peasant to Magnitogorsk for a reunion. The event seems to be a great success, the old man is lionized and leaves laden with presents, for which the son has gone heavily into debt. After several weeks with no word from the old man, the son is summoned before a local judge, who tells him his father has filed a complaint against him for insufficient support. In their sentimental enthusiasm, no one had seen the stupid and greedy old peasant for what he was. The story is not only ironical, but also rich in social and psychological insight.

One of the literary sensations of 1956 was Daniil Granin's story "One's Own Opinion," which features a middle-aged bureaucrat who has made a career by compromising with a corrupt and dictatorial hierarchy. At various stages in his life he has postponed acting according to his conscience in the hope of gaining a position of influence through which he could at last do what he knows is right. As the story closes, however, he realizes that the very process of compromise has atrophied his will forever and that, no matter how high he rises, he will remain in this same moral trap. An examination of the question of ends and means, the story has an obvious universality, but it was read by many as a devastating criticism of

Soviet society, and it created a furor that lasted for more than a year. It is an excellent example of the appropriateness of the short story form for making a single moral point and its effectiveness in periods of social and cultural transition. In his novels, Granin has frequently dealt with the same problem, but nowhere has he attained such concentrated power as in this short story.

The novelist and playwright Leonid Leonov was also one of the finest short story writers of the twenties, and he has continued to write stories from time to time. The spirit of the Thaw seems to have come to him belatedly, however, and it was not until 1963 that he published a story that took advantage of the new, relative liberalism. This was "Evgenia Ivanovna," on which he had been working for twenty-five years. In his customary involuted, allusive prose, Leonov tells of a young Russian woman who fled during the Revolution to Constantinople with her husband, who deserted her there. Making her way to Paris, she marries a British archaeologist, travels with him to Asia Minor, and plans to join him on a trip to her native soil. En route, they stop in Georgia, where her former husband turns up as an Intourist guide. He has shed his old identity, and now professes enthusiasm for bolshevism. Her bitterness toward him now becomes compounded with revulsion at his hypocrisy, self-pity, and parasitism. For her he becomes the image of a Russia she never wants to see again, and from Tiflis she goes directly to England, where she dies in childbirth a few months later. The story can be interpreted variously, but its consistent sympathy for the expatriate heroine and its clear disparagement of her ex-husband, a shabby, compromising fellow-traveling opportunist, provide a kind of social criticism that, although retrospective, is strong indeed.

The novels of Vera Panova are discussed elsewhere. She was also, however, one of the most gifted of contemporary short story writers, with an unmistakable personal style. Writing in third person, she achieved intimacy by using a narrative language that is very close to that of the characters she is depicting. The narrator conveys the thought processes and perspective of her characters, but at the same time maintains a more objective, understanding, almost grandmotherly attitude to them. At times this attitude seems a bit too wise and condescending, lending a slightly cloying tone. But for the most part the tone is ingratiating and sensitive, that of a sympathetic, keen-eyed observer.

Panova's extraordinary talent for writing about children was established in the short novel "Seryozha" (1955), in which the world is seen through the alert eyes of a little boy. Probably Panova's masterpiece in this genre,

"Seryozha" shows, in a variety of amusing, heart-warming, and occasionally sobering episodes, the early process of character formation in a youngster who is distinctly an individual but also recognizable the world over.

The story "Valya" is set in wartime Leningrad. Its first part takes place mainly in the railroad station and depicts the departure of the girl Valya and her little sister, who are being evacuated in anticipation of the blockade. The dramatic atmosphere of this time of crisis is conveyed in rapid, impressionistic narration, in which we are alternately shown the reactions of Valya, her little sister, her mother, and her father to the same phenomena. There are also episodic characters, whose brief appearances further contribute a number of nuances and shadings to the panorama. The second part of the story depicts the return of Valya and her sister three years later, from the children's home where they have spent the war. In the interim both parents have been killed and the family house destroyed. Valya, who is old enough to remember everything, wants to visit her mother's grave and their former neighborhood; her younger sister, who remembers little, is uninterested. Throughout the story, Panova shows a precise understanding of the quality of feeling and comprehension of which individuals are capable at different ages.

The companion story to "Valya" is "Volodya," which features a sixteen-year-old boy who appeared briefly in "Valya." In a sense this story fills in the three-year hiatus between the two parts of "Valya," because it tells of its young hero's hard life in evacuation, burdened with a weak-willed and stupid mother and forced to grow up virtually on his own. In portraying Volodya's return to Leningrad after the war to patch up his life and establish his identity, Panova creates an admiring but convincing image of a young person whom the war has forced to become a prematurely responsible adult. In both stories, Panova not only presents sensitive treatments of youthful psychology but also relates it specifically and inextricably to the national circumstances in which it develops.

In the next two chapters further aspects of the contemporary short story will be discussed – with emphasis on its ironical and satirical features and on the prominence of rural and folk themes. From what has been said thus far, however, it is evident that the writing of the past twenty years represents, to a great extent, a revival of the traditional narrative methods and candid moral and psychological explorations of Russian literature, as exemplified by such writers as Tolstoy and Chekhov. The pretense of moral and ideological assuredness, together with obligatory optimism, no longer predominates. There is a revived intimacy and individuality in the techniques of the best short story writers, and there is increased latitude for ambiguity and open-endedness, for the tacit admission that the human condition is mysterious and ultimately unfathomable.

But the revival is by no means complete. In nearly all of the writers discussed thus far one senses a reserve, an inability to be freely and widely allusive. When a writer such as Kazakov artfully leaves things unsaid or deals in suggestions rather than in specifics, this may not be the result of free aesthetic choice, but rather a matter of making a virtue of necessity. We can be sure that if the contemporary Soviet short story were completely uncensored it would be much richer than it is.

7

The youth movement in short fiction

In the early 1960s it seemed that nearly every young Soviet writer of short stories was preoccupied with the conflict between his own generation and that of his parents. To some extent they were simply writing about a familiar psychological phenomenon that was by no means limited to this particular time and place – the feeling of young people that their parents represent an establishment that is trying to rob them of their individuality, to buy them out with communal protections. One of the teenagers in Vasili Aksenov's *A Starry Ticket*, talking to his older brother, puts it this way:

> Your life, Victor, was devised by Papa and Mama when you were still in the cradle. A star in school, a star in college, graduate student, junior scientific worker, M.A., senior scientific worker, Ph.D., Member of the Academy, and then . . . a dead man, respected by all. Never once in your life have you made a truly important decision, never once taken a risk. To hell with it! We are scarcely born when everything has already been thought out for us, our future already decided. Not on your life! It's better to be a tramp and fail than to be a boy all your life, carrying out the decisions of others.

The "conflict between the generations," however, also had more local and immediate aspects of both a moral and ideological nature. Living in the aftermath of Stalinism, young people realized that their parents had allowed themselves to be duped, cowed, and to some extent shaped by a regime that was now declared to have been badly tainted. The new generation felt it had been betrayed and misled by loving but compromised parents, who had given them a false and morally unstable upbringing by lying to them in an effort to protect them. The realization caused not scorn and resentment but puzzlement, compassion, and respect for their parents' sufferings, and redoubled hatred of an ossified authoritarianism that they had ceased to respect. Ultimately the tension between fathers and sons centered on the conservatism of the elders, their tired lack of interest in social idealism, their preference for playing it cosy, and their desire to find snug berths for their children in a planned society. As the hero of Anatoli Gladilin's story "First Day of the New Year" says to his father:

> You don't repair the consequences of the cult of the personality by limiting yourself to the removal of portraits and the renaming of cities.
>
> The cult of the personality is sluggishness of thought, it is fear to think for oneself, it is a dream of tranquility and hatred for the new.

Although references to the conflict between generations have been prominent in Soviet literature of the past twenty years, the fashion of explicitly framing social problems in terms of the opposition of fathers and sons reached a peak in the early sixties and then died down. However, the traditional literary stream of which this theme was a tributary – the "education of a young man" – continued in full force. As a rule the protagonists were young persons of urban origin, reluctant, at least for the moment, to enter the paths that society had charted for them and trying to work out ethical standards to replace outworn or suspect ones. Frequently the central figure was a person troubled by moral doubts, uncertain of his role in life, puzzled and concerned about the future, socially disoriented and, in some degree, psychologically bemused. Older heroes among them, usually in their twenties or early thirties, appeared as wanderers and drifters, dislocated and lonely, lacking permanent ties and unwilling to make a firm and stable life commitment.

A few writers – notably Andrei Bitov – preferred to concentrate on the psychological process of growing up *per se*. The major problems of their young heroes were universal ones related to late adolescence – self-doubts, frustrated idealism, ungainly behavior – and the social context seemed incidental. However, the dominant mood of this writing about the development of young persons was polemical, militating against simplified notions of man, and especially against the well-established inclination to measure the worth of an individual in terms of the degree to which he conforms to a rigid social and ideological pattern, rather than in terms of the richness and uniqueness of his personality. The Thaw had made it possible for writers to deal more candidly with human emotions than before, to examine immediate, authentic experience more closely, and to concentrate more fully and precisely on the private problems and interests of the individual. The spirit of this writing was one of moral exploration and discovery, of increasing realization that there are multiple and various legitimate avenues to the truth about human existence, and that no single system of belief is final and immutable.

Writing about young people often involved either a direct or an implied repudiation of the dogmas of the recent past and a questioning attitude toward the words, phrases, and formulas in which these dogmas were couched. The very restraint of many writers bespoke a mistrust of previous values, an unwillingness to indulge in verbal speculation for fear of becoming trapped in the clichés that had recently prevailed and, at times, a need for leaving things unsaid. Their compactness and brevity conveyed on the part of their heroes a mood sometimes of skepticism and sometimes of resigned indifference, all as if motivated by the unspoken question: "What are they going to do to me next?" The attitude seemed to stem from a sense of being hemmed in, of conscious submission to the necessity of having one's life assigned, and a feeling that one must simply "make do" because circumstances conspire to make it impossible to have one's choices really respected.

Sometimes the dominant tone was one of suppressed rage. Among the younger writers a minor convention developed: at least once in the course of a story the hero gets wildly drunk, insults and scandalizes everyone about him, and flails blindly at a malevolent world before he passes out. It is the explosion of a frustrated idealist, whose habit of tight-lipped awareness and direct responses has been temporarily conquered by despair. The world is a congenial place for phonies and bastards: one must learn how to spot them and fight them without losing one's head, but occasionally it is just too much.

To ingratiate these new protagonists with the reader and ensure them a sympathetic hearing it was necessary not only to establish their worth and admirability as human beings but also to make them authentic and plausible. Often writers did this by gently ridiculing their troubled, questioning young heroes, bestowing on them a kind of ironic affection, as in the following passage from Ilya Zverev's story "Dima," which gives a glimpse of the daydreams of an ambitious young repairer of electric razors:

> The evening paper announced the forthcoming arrival of German Titov in the city, and this notice promised much. Very

likely the hero of the cosmos would break his electric razor and come into the shop. They would exchange a few words and understand each other. Dima feared only one thing: that in his recent American trip the hero had bought himself a foreign razor – for example a "Phillips"? And then he couldn't fix it and would be disgraced. But no, Dima hoped that Cosmonaut No. 2, as a patriot, shaved with a fatherland razor. Let's say a "Neva," which, as everybody knows, is not inferior to the best foreign models.

In third-person narration, a flexible relationship was established between narrator and protagonist, so that sometimes their subjective spheres, their voices, were distinct, but at others indistinguishable. Intimacy was achieved through interior monologue, constructed so as not only to convey ideas but also to suggest thought processes themselves. This form of narration permitted the author to come extremely close to his protagonists, and at times almost to become one of them, but it also enabled him to remain above them and, while maintaining a generally sympathetic attitude toward them, to engage in skeptical or ironic evaluations of their words and acts. Despite a certain ironic distance, the affection of the author for his hero was so evident that the latter often seemed an emotional and intellectual double of the former, a surrogate for him.

The chief means of achieving a sense of authenticity in protagonists was first-person narration. The narrator was dramatized, speaking in individualized, often highly emotional language – sometimes tense, laconic, and troubled, at others slangy, sarcastic, and self-deprecatory. Whatever their age or configuration of character, these first-person narrators had one thing in common – a wry, ironical attitude toward themselves. The narrator's awareness of his own shortcomings and foibles, and his display of self-knowledge and humorous self-criticism, served both to heighten his apparent intelligence and to bestow on him an aura of impartiality and trustworthiness. This intimately self-disparaging attitude served to disarm and ingratiate the reader, to make him receptive to the hero's reflections and complaints.

Occasionally, writers experimented with multiple first-person narrators, repeating individual episodes as seen through different eyes and told in different voices. In "Oranges from Morocco" Aksenov uses five such characters. The thoughts of one of them, a young woman working on a construction site in the Soviet Far East, are thus transcribed:

> At the edge of the square, blackened posts stick up out of the snow. They say these posts used to hold up a watch-tower. They

say that once long ago, during the time of Stalin, where our set-
tlement is now, there was a prison camp. It is simply hard to
imagine that here, where we are now working, dancing, going to
the movies, laughing and howling at one another, there was once
a prison camp. I try not to think of those times, those times are already very incomprehensible to me.

The point is, of course, that those times *were* comprehensible to the author
and many of his readers. Through such a narrator he could comment on
the moral atmosphere much more candidly and convincingly than he
could by other means.

Writers also seemed particularly concerned with developing techniques
for giving the reader a sense of close psychological proximity to the narrative. Thus, in first person the individualized speech of the narrator not
only served as a characterizing device but also promoted intimacy. Passages in second person, a time-honored vehicle for psychological intimacy
in Russian literature, were employed extensively. Manipulation of tenses
to achieve temporal immediacy was widespread. Sudden shifts to present
tense within a past-tense context brought the reader closer to the emotions
a character was experiencing, and shifts to future tense enabled the reader
to participate more intimately in a character's subjective ruminations and
speculations – his daydreams and wishful thinking – as illustrated in the
passage from Zverev quoted above.

For these young writers, dialogue became the main vehicle through
which protagonists expressed and tested their unsettled, developing views
and attitudes, voiced their doubts and objections, and commented on
moral and emotional problems of both a private and a social nature. The
writer aspired to capture the exact rhythms of actual thought and discourse in its spontaneous, disorganized essence. Often dialogues were extremely disputatious and turbulent, involving contention among the increased number of controversial ideas currently circulating. The "topics of
conversation" changed rapidly without overt motivation, and remarks
often seemed illogical, random or accidental. Just as often, however, dialogues were quieter than this, disclosing with candor and subtlety the in-
tricacies of the human heart. "Information" often became less important
than *feeling,* and dialogues were so constructed that the factual content of a
spoken remark was important only insofar as it served to express a corre-
sponding emotion. On the whole, the young writers' increased attention
to the aesthetic potential of dialogue enabled them to say much more
about what their contemporaries were thinking and feeling than writers
had in previous periods.

The use of a special kind of reported dialogue – tense, rapid, and influenced by the ironic intonation of the first-person narrator, was very extensive. It tended to be choppy and elliptical, with little auxiliary support in the form of narrative commentary. Some passages of dialogue consisted entirely of questions. The terseness and reticence of many dialogues indicated that characters were reluctant to meditate aloud and openly, because they abhorred the lofty abstractions that had been misused for many years and were now discredited.

The fragmentary, seemingly disjointed nature of dialogue also came from the fact that it was often closely related to the lyrical digressions and interior monologue of the narrator. In situations, which were frequent, where the narrator reported a dialogue that took place between himself and another person, his own remarks were not related to those of the person he was conversing with, but rather to the thoughts and emotions he had expressed *outside* the context of the dialogue. A rather frequent phenomenon was dialogue in which one of the "speakers" does not participate, or, as in the following example from Aksenov's *A Starry Ticket*, ceases to participate:

> "Tell Papa and Mama there . . ." I say.
> "I'll tell them," he says.
> "Write them, old man," he says.
> "For sure," I say.
> "Well, I've had a rest," he says.
> "Too bad it turned out this way," he says.
> "O.K., old man," he says.
> "Chin up," he says.
> "So long," he says.

Another variation of this phenomenon is dialogue in which the words of one character find their response in the stream-of-consciousness of another. There are also dialogues in which no words are uttered aloud – rather, the characters "speak" to each other in the mutterings of their respective interior monologues. All of these phenomena represent a maximally "natural," psychologically verisimilar depiction of communication in its most intimate form.

Emphasis on psychological accuracy was usually accompanied by an effort to approximate as closely as possible the rhythms and tone of contemporary colloquial speech. The young writers attempted to transmit authentically the living vernacular of their contemporaries, and the foundation of their dialogue was this. On the other hand, dialogue was frequently a mixture of ordinary conversational speech and "artificial" elements designed to give it a startling, ironic flavor. Many young writers made no pretense of hiding the fact that their dialogue had been "constructed" to give it special emphasis and heightened significance. The result was a combination of popular speech – including slang, urban jargon, and dialect elements – and abnormal phraseology consisting of elements borrowed, for ironic purposes, from bureaucratese, foreign languages, the newspapers, underworld argot, literature, and other sources. The language also tended to be permeated with puns, aphorisms, poeticisms, various periphrastic devices, and playful distortions of normal conversational usage. All of these elements lent the dialogue a sarcastic, whimsical flavor, but underneath the surface bantering and fencing, serious and often very subtle things were said.

The "artificial" ingredient in the language of these young writers consisted primarily in its alternation between standard literary lexicon and style, on the one hand, and traditionally subliterary or blatantly antiliterary elements on the other. The poetic and the vulgar, the high and the low, the abstract and the concrete, were freely united, so that the stylistic coloration of the text was in constant flux. Young authors of short fiction were paying much more attention to *language* than did writers of the Stalin period. Their comic and satirical use of bureaucratic jargon and scientific terminology, and their ironical combination of solemn "big" words and phrases with vulgar colloquialisms, often in the same sentence, were evidence of a new and unusual degree of linguistic experimentation. The high incidence in their writing of antiphrasis, associative repetition, and telegraphic effects in which normal connections of words are broken for extra semantic emphasis, suggest that these young writers were the most enthusiastic participants in the partial revival of ornamentalism.

To a great extent these stylistic practices were part of the general pattern of liberation of literary forms, the removal of traditional inhibitions, characteristic of this period. They represented a kind of experimentation encouraged by the opportunity to reassess and, if desirable, to revise literary norms established in previous decades – a concomitant of the generally renewed intellectual climate of the times. Many stylistic tricks and much of the verbal inventiveness were obviously in the spirit of pure comedy and artistic whimsy. Often there was exuberant extravagance in the new language permeated with puns, comic aphorisms, sarcastic poeticisms, and fanciful parody, and in the use of such visual devices as bizarre indentations, changing type faces, and diagrams. On the whole, however, the new stylistic developments contained a strong ingredient of artistic play that was calculated and serious.

Indirection, circumlocution, and the intentional use of "inappropriate" language became major characteristics of the contemporary satirical style. Things were not given their common, expected names, but rather were designated by periphrastic terms – scientific, for example – that did not belong in the context in which the young writers employed them. Gladilin made comically out-of-place usage of the language of literary criticism and irreverently abused the exalted word "life," while Fazil Iskander did the same with the Soviet language of political polemics. Aksenov, Iskander, and Bitov made tongue-in-cheek displays of stylistic awkwardness (e.g. Bitov: "Apparently she has been thinking about what I have been thinking, I think").

Very frequently the young authors engaged in this kind of writing for strategic reasons that had little to do with stylistic experimentation in and for itself, for the spirit behind their various devices was predominantly one of irony. One aspect of this spirit, no doubt, was an impudent desire to show off, to dazzle the reader and, indeed, to tease, startle, and shock him. But more important, the ironic manner represented a revolt against the moral and intellectual complacency that hid behind linguistic purism, stale locutions, and the official cliché. In the thirties, forties, and fifties, for example, official bureaucratic language and newspaper formulas were seldom used ironically in prose fiction. Now, however, they were lampooned abundantly and became an integral ingredient in the ironic style. Aksenov, Voinovich, and Iskander, for example, became fond of sarcastically referring to writers with a cliché from the thirties: "engineers of human souls." For the key device in this style was to emphasize the ridiculousness of such language and formulas by using them in "inappropriate" contexts.

The most disciplined and economical of these young writers, with a special gift for tight and swift narration, pungent dialogue, humorous episode, and deft irony, is Vladimir Voinovich (born in 1932). Only five of his stories, published between 1961 and 1967, have appeared in the Soviet Union, and his reputation is correspondingly modest. Yet Voinovich embodies, in many respects, the best qualities of the "young prose" of this period. He is a realist who deals in everyday happenings and ordinary characters, but who manages to infuse them with heightened interest and significance through picturesque speech, lean but vivid detail, a sure grasp of individual psychology, and an authentic sense of the mood of his times.

We Live Here (1961) is a long story set in a small, remote collective-farm village in the virgin lands of Kazakhstan. Its characters are mostly young Russians, frustrated by their culturally barren life in the sticks and envious of their urban contemporaries. Although their environment is backward – attempts to enliven local cultural activities are often ridiculous failures, improvements in living conditions come painfully slowly, inefficiency and corruption abound – these young people manage to cope with it through sheer pragmatism and resilience. Critics accused Voinovich of having written a "naturalistic" libel of Soviet life. Others, however, defended it as a polemic against works that romanticize and oversimplify the exploit of cultivating virgin land areas.

What prevents the story from being simply a depressing portrayal of rustic benightedness are the verve and honesty of Goshka, its hero, the dogged pride with which several characters defend their rural life and, above all, the vigorous humor that dominates the narrative. Part of this humor is based on the ironic discrepancy between word and deed. (The girls complain of the absence of glamorous men, but they are stubbornly enterprising in their attempts to snare what is available.) Brisk, rapid changes of scene permit an abundance of comic details and incident. The chief source of humor, however, is the terse, vividly witty dialogue, whose wryness closely harmonizes with the third-person narrator's own ironical intonation.

A more sober story is "I Want to Be Honest" (1963), whose central figure is a construction supervisor, dispirited in the knowledge that the work going on about him is shoddy, graft-ridden, and ill-conceived, and who is powerless to correct the situation. Under pressure from his superiors to certify the completion of an apartment house in time to win honors for his organization (although everyone concerned knows that the building is unfinished and unsafe), he refuses. His own honor is saved, but he is hounded off the project.

The story has obvious civic import as a condemnation of cynicism, inertia and criminal dishonesty in housing construction. Its most interesting aspect, however, is the character of its hero. Although well-trained and highly competent, he is a middle-aged drifter who moves about the country from job to job, maintaining his integrity by refusing promotions to positions of responsibility that might involve a moral compromise. His life is further complicated by a pregnant mistress; although he is bored with her, he resolves to marry her to save her from a possibly fatal abortion. As first-person narrator, the hero is attractive not only for his honesty but also for his humorously disparaging view of himself and his justifiably ironical outlook on many of his associates. For the most part, the narrative tone is lightly satirical; the story is often funny, but there are frequent bitter notes that disclose the hero's full burden of frustration.

The only unrelievedly gloomy story of Voinovich is "A Distance of Half-a-Kilometer" (1963) – a bleak account of the death and funeral of a village no-good, in which the local peasants are portrayed as ignorant, narrow, and shiftless. By contrast, his story "In the Sleeper" (1965) is pure humor. Voinovich writes of traveling by overnight train from Moscow to Leningrad in a double compartment whose other occupant, by the random chance of Soviet ticket arrangements, is a young woman. Aggressively prim and terrified for her virtue, she instantly bares her claws and sits frozen the whole trip, insisting that her harmless and bewildered fellow passenger keep the compartment door open and the light on all night. But she wildly misjudges his disgusted fantasies:

> And I continued to think of what it would be like if this neighbor of mine were made the mistress of all our lives. She could do a lot to rearrange the order of things between men and women. Now we have separate baths, toilets and dormitories. This division could be extended, for a starter, to movie houses, stores and public transportation. On one streetcar, let's say, there would be "Men" and on another "Women." Also separate stops, divided by thin partitions . . . Cities and towns could be separated into Men's and Women's. In mastering outer space we could solve this question once and for all by settling the different sexes on separate planets. With this devilry I fell asleep. And I dreamed of the universe and a multitude of round planets. Some were marked with a "W," others with an "M."

The author's most engaging story is "Two Comrades" (1967), which looks at the world through the eyes of Valeri Vazhenin, the son of divorced parents, who lives with his mother (an economist) and grandmother, and who occasionally goes across town to visit his father, a pathetic writer of copy for circus acts who is now married to a taunting harridan. Valeri loves his mother, although her protectiveness annoys him, and he has a pitying affection for his father; he cannot understand how two such good people can have separated. His narrative covers a period beginning a few months before his induction into the army and ending when he is a full-fledged soldier. The heart of the story, however, is a cluster of episodes in the course of which Valeri, wandering about town in a state of mildly rebellious indecision, begins to grow up. He tries to fail the entrance examination for the pedagogical institute his mother wants him to attend, only to learn that he has passed with flying colors because an examiner discovers extraordinary writing talent in him. He finds himself alone with a girl of easy virtue and nearly loses his own.

The central episode is one in which he discovers a major moral flaw in his boyhood friend, Tolik. Late one night the two of them are accosted on the street by a gang of hoodlums. After a one-sided struggle, they pinion Valeri's arms and force Tolik to pound his face to a pulp. A few days later, Valeri and Tolik meet at the induction station:

> "Valeri," began Tolik, agitated and hunting for words, "you're probably sore at me, but in my place . . ."
>
> All these days I had been thinking how I would have acted in Tolik's place, whether I could have acted otherwise. And in the end I understood that I could have. And not because I'm so brave, but because I couldn't have done what Tolik did.
>
> "You understand," he said, "they forced me."
>
> "Yes, but you really let me have it," I said.
>
> "But they would have beaten up both you *and* me."
>
> "OK," I said, "We'll talk about it some other time."
>
> What could I have explained to him?

Months later they meet again, and Valeri discovers that Tolik is now a general's orderly and has taken to publishing poetry in praise of his top-sergeant. (He is well paid for his sycophantic doggerel – one of the author's many references to literary prostitution.) Tolik again brings up the subject of the beating:

> "I've thought a lot about that thing that happened near the Palace . . . Of course I feel bad about it, but that's how it turned out . . ."
>
> "Yes, it's tough," I agreed.
>
> "Yes, a little," said Tolik. "But for you it was better that way."
>
> "Interesting!" I was sincerely surprised. "And just why?"
>
> "They would have hit you harder," he said, looking me straight in the eye.
>
> This was philosophy already. Later I met up with it in other circumstances, heard approximately the same words from other persons who hastened to do what anybody else would have done in their place.

The episode of the beating is thus raised to a symbolic level. It has a universal moral meaning, of course, but it has a special significance in a society burdened with a history of debilitating rationalizations, and in which the individual has all too frequently signed over his ethical responsibilities to the collective.

But the story is not as gloomy as these quoted passages might indicate. Valeri, the narrator, is a bright, energetic, idealistic boy who is trying to stand on his own two feet. For all his irony and frequent irreverence, his manner is not flip. His is the charming sarcasm of a young person who understands the limitations of his own knowledge but who is smarter and more observant, and morally more sensitive, than most of the people around him. He is attractive and good-natured, and he has a marvelous sense of fun. His grandmother read the New Testament to him as a boy. Somehow he is reminded of this as he takes his first ride in a small airplane:

> I had long since ceased to believe in God, but the fact that everything relating to God was written there in capital letters still pleased me. On occasion I wanted to write about myself in similar style. For example, when they seated me in the airplane: "And they took Him by His Hand, placed Him in the cockpit. And His Shoulders and His Stomach and all His Body they fastened with straps."

As the story of two childhood friends who develop in opposite moral directions during postadolescence, "Two Comrades" does not have a happy ending: Tolik is thriving, and there will be a place for his kind in the world. All the same, Valeri, with his honesty, intelligence, and sense of humor, has an equal chance to survive.

The stories of Voinovich are rich in incident and detail, and provide fascinating, although often satirically colored, glimpses of Soviet life. His narrative language (in third and first person it is often nearly identical) relies heavily on contemporary vernacular, is frequently figurative, and is larded with slang and parodies of slogans and jargon. Especially humorous is his use of "inappropriate" language to create an incongruity between an event and the speech used to describe it – as in "Two Comrades," where Valeri uses the solemn terminology of physics to tell how his body bounces in the bed of a speeding, lurching truck. Voinovich is deft at understatement, and particularly his dialogue (which is extraordinarily lively, and which carries much of the burden of his narration) employs much reticent, deadpan sarcasm. At the same time, both his language and the actions he describes are often hyperbolic, although quite evidently presented tongue-in-cheek and not to be taken literally. In general, Voinovich is master of many of the narrative resources of his more prominent colleague, Vasili Aksenov, without the latter's verbal excesses.

The stories of Andrei Bitov almost invariably concentrate on a single character, apprehended at a time of psychological or moral crisis. As a rule, the circumstances of the crisis lack the external trappings of more conventional Soviet stories of this sort: there is no explicitly related social issue, the sources of the crisis are to be found not so much in external reality as in the psyche of the protagonist, the element of pain and suffering is not pointedly dramatized, and the outcome of the crisis is unclear and indecisive. Bitov is probably the most subtle psychologist among writers of his generation and most closely resembles his Western contemporaries in the deftness with which he portrays private emotions.

On the surface the episodes through which Bitov relates the subjective experiences of his protagonists are everyday and unremarkable. An infatuated adolescent lingers in a hallway, waiting in vain for a glimpse of the woman who is deceiving him ("The Door"). An office worker, killing three hours at a movie, strikes up a conversation with a rather frowzy young woman, agrees to help her find a job, and then takes fright and ditches her ("Penelope"). A writer, caught up in a fallow period, spends a month of self-torment at a *dacha* with his wife and baby son ("Country Place"). In such episodes the interest lies in the precise, intimate tracing of the mental processes of the protagonist. The reader becomes both a close observer of these processes and a near-participant, because he is usually allowed to see the world only through the eyes of the hero. A special quality of many of Bitov's heroes, however, is their ability to express their subjective feelings and, at the same time, to examine them objectively. They are not engaged in mere lyrical outpouring; rather, they constantly weigh their feelings and impressions, striving for a rational self-understanding.

Some Soviet critics have argued that Bitov is capable of writing only about himself, and it is true that many of his stories have an autobiographical ring. His intensity of feeling, sense of emotional nuance, and concern for unconscious motivation do seem to be the products of careful self-observation. But he is also capable of creating characters who do not remotely resemble the author. Moreover, his depiction of the shadings of relationship and interaction between individuals suggests an unusual sensitivity to the world outside himself. Whether he is writing about children, adolescents, young adults, or oldsters, Bitov displays a vivid and sure sense of the ways in which the human psyche develops and manifests itself in the various stages of life.

Born in Leningrad in 1937 and educated as a mining engineer, Bitov began publishing stories in 1958. His first volume, *The Big Balloon* (*Bol'shoi shar*, 1963), was a collection largely devoted to vignettes of children and youths – the awakening of their awareness to the mysteries of death, love, beauty, and human irrationality. A large section of the book is devoted to anecdotes and small essays about the discoveries of a young man on a trip to Central Asia. (Bitov is a traveler and amateur ethnographer; his account of a "sentimental journey" to Armenia was published in 1969.)

The stories in *The Big Balloon* are distinguished by a Chekhovian modesty and reticence and show a preference for small insights over ambitious generalizations. At the same time they give the cumulative impression of being the sketchbook of a writer who is preparing for larger things. An example is the story "The Wife's Not at Home," the account of a few wasted hours in the life of an alienated young man, married to an actress who supports him. He wanders aimlessly about the city, has trivial and meaningless encounters with a few chance acquaintances, does a bit of drinking, goes home and waits jealously for his wife, quarrels with her, and goes to bed. The narrative is disjointed, jerky, apparently governed only by a purely chronological sequence of accidental events in which there is no inherent logic. But the story's structure is obviously designed to reflect the chaotic state of the hero, whose dominant mood is his longing for a meaningful path of conduct. Intimacy in this story is achieved through laconic, staccato first-person narration, but the story is too fragmentary and impressionistic and, in view of the fullness of Bitov's later stories, it is the étude of a talented beginner.

A more ambitious work is the short novel *Such a Long Childhood* (*Takoe dolgoe detstvo*, 1965), in which Bitov traces the psychological growth of a boy crossing the threshold of manhood. Kirill Kapustin has been expelled from a mining institute for poor grades. Following an impulse, and without consulting his parents, he joins a group of his former classmates who go to a mining town in the far north for their required summer of practical experience. When he arrives Kirill writes to his parents and tells them what he has done.

> Mama answered him immediately, and he read that she was not angry with him, that they all were very sorry for him, but nevertheless he himself had acted pitilessly in relation to his father, who was so worried about him and was such a sick man, that your things, Kiryusha, I have already collected and will send off tomorrow, and have already sent money by telegram, that at home all are well, that he measure his sleeve length and waist,

because she is going to knit him a sweater, because it is very cold in the Polar region, but if he will try, perhaps they will reinstate him, but if nothing works out, don't be upset, because she loves him very much just the same and waits for him, her only son, of her blood, and he should return soon, and she gives him a big, big kiss – mama.

Soon after mama's he received a letter from father, that he is a pup and a greenhorn, and a complete milksop, and let him now try to find out what life is really like, and how he didn't appreciate what they all had done for him, that he was a heartless slob and makes his mother suffer and torment herself, she who is so very sick, that he should expiate his guilt by work and show that he does not bear for nothing the name of the Kapustins, all of whom were very honest working people, but he should nevertheless take care of himself, dress warmly, be careful when he's swimming and watch out for accidents when he's working, that he sent him money and he's given mother a good fishing rod and tackle to send along with his things, there, they say, they have remarkable fishing, he himself would be glad to come fishing, but he's swamped with work, well, Kirill, behave yourself, I squeeze your hand – papa.

It should be noted that Bitov does not reproduce the letters verbatim, but rather as filtered through the consciousness of the boy who reads them, in an ingenious variation of interior monologue. Through this and related means, Bitov maintains a sympathetic proximity between the omniscient third-person narrator and his hero, but at the same time sustains a tone of ironic objectivity.

At the mine Kirill becomes an ordinary worker and is gradually estranged from his former classmates; they are going back to school, but he is in the world for good. As a miner he accomplishes nothing in particular. He has an affair – his first – with a local girl, and will presumably marry her. This must wait, however, because he gets drafted. The novel ends as Kirill, with shaven head, marches off in a company of recruits. Experience has matured him somewhat, but the narrator has this to say about his hero:

Nothing has yet been attained. And there are no guarantees that, having merged himself in the group, he will calm down and distinguish himself from the others – no. And it is also not known whether the moment of parting from childhood – which should have happened many years before and which was moved back and postponed because of circumstances independent of Kirill – is joyful. It remains for those who love him to believe in him, and for others to hope.

The inconclusive ending is typical of Bitov: a stage in the growth of an individual has been described in affectionate but objective detail; the story asks for no other justification. As Bitov has matured, however, he has shown an increasing proclivity to combine psychological observation with moral exploration. Such is the case in the story "Penelope." In running away from his temporarily assumed obligation to help a fellow human, the hero has not done much real harm. The obligation was slight; the girl, who is evidently quite worldly, will quickly shake off her disappointment. What really matters, however, is that the hero is suddenly stricken with shame over his selfish, cowardly, nasty little trick. He realizes, in a moment of revelation, that his everyday life is made up of such petty moral evasions. There is no promise that this instant of heightened moral awareness will effect a change in his routine behavior, but such a conclusion would be unnecessary and irrelevant. The story exists simply for the purpose of this flash of moral and psychological understanding.

There is a different combination of psychological and moral concerns in "Journey to a Childhood Friend," in which a first-person narrator gradually reveals his complex attitude toward a friend who has become a celebrity through his feats as an explorer of live volcanoes. The narrator views his friend with a mixture of love and admiration, on the one hand, and envy and hatred on the other. There is also a strong element of scorn: much of the "vulconaut's" fame comes from the inflated need of the official press to create popular heroes. The story deals, simultaneously, with three interlocking topics: the ambivalent attitudes of the narrator – a "little man" – as he debunks his friend – a "big man"; a polemic against spurious, myth-making Soviet journalistic writing (the story is constructed as a commentary on newspaper stories, which are quoted extensively); and a close critical examination of the concept of the "feat" or "exploit" (the Russian world is *podvig*) – as contrasted to ordinary, decent, unrewarded behavior – on which much of this journalistic practice is centered.

Bitov is a versatile stylist who writes with an easy, natural grace. His language is colloquial, with a texture, diction, and rhythm designed to reflect closely the varied thought processes of his protagonists. At times he uses the clipped, laconic speech of ironic understatement, and at others the complex, involved language of analytical mental exploration. The language is always precise, intimate, and lively – carefully appropriate to his individual characters and their states of mind. A consequence of his primary concern for capturing the fragmentary, loosely associative quality of natural, unconstrained thought is the subordination of plot to other narrative elements in his stories. Most of them seem singularly plotless. On the other hand, they are carefully structured, and the paragraphs that convey the seemingly effortless flow of his narration are subtly organized, balanced, and integrated.

The most mature and generally the finest story of Bitov to date is "Country Place," the account of a young writer in the throes of an identity crisis – to use the currently fashionable American term. His work is not going well. Although he has reached adulthood – with a loving wife, a baby son, and an amiable father with whom he is on reasonably good terms – he is restless, dissatisfied, and disoriented, tormented by the realization that he still has some growing up to do. A complex of interlocking questions beset him – intellectual, aesthetic, moral, emotional, behavioral – all governed by his lonely awareness that despite the cushions, allies, and hostages he has accumulated, he is and will always be on his own. He is intelligent, ambitious, sensitive (both to people and to natural beauty), rational, and he has a powerful conscience. At the same time he is given to fantasy, evasion (he keeps running into the city on trumped-up errands to keep from facing his writing) and, occasionally, quite infantile conduct.

The most tangibly meaningful experience in his month in the country is his first close observation of his son and the vicarious thrill of sharing the child's discovery of the natural world. His rediscovery of the power of naive astonishment inspires him to reexamine his own ossified, routine view of things, to find new spiritual value in the strangeness and mystery of existence. This does not provide, however, an easy solution – there is no liberation – but rather a deepening of experience and a motivation for further difficult, perhaps more constructive, introspection.

The great merit of this beautifully written, delicately detailed, and richly evocative story is in its unobtrusively adroit weaving of disparate but complementary themes. It can be read as an account of the normal anxieties of a young, adult, urban, male professional. Likewise it can be viewed as a more special treatment of the psychology of creativity, of problems of aesthetics (several are brought up, directly or indirectly), and of the artist's inevitable loneliness. Throughout the story, also, are arresting speculations on the relationship between subjective and objective knowledge, imagination and reality, and time – which sporadically either ceases to exist for the narrator or seems to rush with blinding speed. Although the story is charmingly lyrical in places, it is always soberly controlled by the clarity of rational insight.

Vasili Aksenov (born 1933) is now in mid career, but he appears still to be the most energetically developing writer of his generation. His prose is neither as refined and psychologically subtle as that of Bitov nor as lean and precise as that of Voinovich. No contemporary Soviet writer, however, surpasses him in terms of formal inventiveness and exploratory daring.

Brisk, racy dialogue is a main feature of Aksenov's style. Much of his abundant humor and satire and a great deal of his narrative development center on dialogue. The tension and conflict in his stories is frequently based on the ironic incongruity between remarks and the replies they elicit, on the hints behind incomplete utterances, and on things left unsaid. Very often Aksenov uses *reported* dialogue, in which the first-person narrator has been involved either as a participant or as an interested observer – a method that lends intimacy, warmth, and an especially opinionated flavor to the writing. Even monologue in Aksenov is often presented as dialogue: a character holds conversations with himself, or with someone who is absent.

Until recently, Aksenov's narrative manner has been fundamentally a subjective one, with extensive use of interior monologue and frequent lyrical digressions. In the early story "Oranges from Morocco" he mingled five narrators, each addressing the reader in first person. As a rule, his narrators are extremely candid in reporting their own feelings, and a startling emotional authenticity shines through their joking, skeptical, off-beat language. Their attitude is ironic or flippantly perverse, and they have a habit of masking their feelings behind witty, empty phrases intentionally devoid of sentiment. One of the reasons Aksenov's characters speak as they do is that they are profoundly dissatisfied with the hypocritical, hollow vocabulary that was foisted on the public during a quarter-century of Stalinism and, despite some reforms, continues to plague Soviet life.

Much of Aksenov's language is figurative, and is particularly rich in bold and sprightly metaphors. Interjections and wry rhetorical questions are abundant. He has often been accused of unnecessary vulgarity in his use of the salty, swinging language of modern urban youth, the jargon of the streets. More often than not, however, it is an artificial language, a literary transformation of popular oral speech, compounded of clichés, puns, bookish phraseology, inventions, circumlocutions, and parodies of a wide variety of the conventions in contemporary Soviet verbal culture. In the following passage from "The Overstocked Tare of Barrels" ("Zatovarennaya bochkotara," 1968) for example, he introduces a pretty young schoolmarm:

> The teacher of incomplete middle school, the teacher of the geography of the whole planet Irina Valentinovna Selezneva, was going on vacation to the zone of the Black Sea subtropics. Her original decision to go to the banks of the short but deep Neva, which flows into the Gulf of Finland of the Baltic Sea, to the city-museum Leningrad, had been changed by thoughts about a southern tan covering an astounding figure, by the cardinal thought – "do not bury, Irina, your treasures."

Aksenov early cultivated a vein of terse, laconic description and exposition based largely on verbs and nouns. He likes to describe movement, both of people and of things. He is fascinated by the jet age and awed by speed, and the world of his stories and novels is full of cars, helicopters, and airplanes. His style, however, is more than just a mixture of colorful dialogue and telegraphic authorial statement, for it is full of all kinds of tricks and surprises. Some of these, such as his occasional bizarre experiments with typography, are merely amusing and he often seems interested only in stylistic play. As a rule, however, his devices have a satirical function. He parodies the clichés of newspapers and classroom, the cozy advice of parents, and the smug admonitions of the collective. He cites snatches of songs, current slogans and catchwords, the names of sports greats and movie stars. And his prose is so crammed with topical references that his works constitute a small, though slanted, encyclopedia of contemporary Soviet life.

In all of Aksenov's works the traces of his individual style are clear, but his tone, moods and topics, and his literary stance in general, have undergone a complicated evolution. Trained as a physician (he graduated from Leningrad Medical Institute in 1956, and served as a doctor in the Arctic, Karelia, and in Leningrad until he became a full-time writer in 1960), he first published rather orthodox fiction based heavily on his own immediate experience. His first novel, *Colleagues* (1960), often reads like a study in socialist realism. It is the story of how three friends, just out of medical school, pass the initial tests of their ability, moral fibre, and stamina. While two of them are marking time in the port of Leningrad awaiting assignment as ship's doctors, their Komsomol vigilance helps to break up a ring of embezzlers. The third, assigned to a rural dispensary in Karelia, becomes a kind of Dr. Kildare of the wilderness and proves his mettle in a series of rugged adventures.

The work that brought Aksenov to prominence was his second novel, *A Starry Ticket* (*Zvyozdny Bilet*, 1961), which featured an engagingly irreverent and rebellious group of Soviet teenagers, rock-and-rolling runaways from the discipline of both parents and society, whose pungent, flip language was loaded with foreignisms (especially Americanisms) and whose skeptical, wry view of the Soviet middle-class success pattern earned their creator, for a time, the title of the Russian Salinger. Aksenov's "starry boys," as hostile critics came to call them, met with bitter disapproval from those who not only resented their hip lingo (a mixture of foreign borrowings, pure invention, Soviet underworld argot, and jargon from the concentration camps) but, even more seriously, were shocked by their open, though adolescent, mockery of Soviet sacred cows.

Although conservative critics viewed Aksenov's heroes of this period as dangerously iconoclastic, the author had taken pains to distinguish them from antisocial parasites. It is true that they are reticent and prefer silence or at best a cryptic response to challenges that are supposed to produce ringing communist answers. One of their major traits is their passion for seeing things simply and clearly, without the encumbrance of ideological preconceptions. They abhor lofty words, are seeking independent answers to the questions they ask of life, because they are weary of prefabricated solutions. Hence the irony with which they refer to practically everything that is orthodox and established, the relish with which they pronounce new words, and the eagerness with which they embrace things that are foreign and off-beat.

These early characters are dissatisfied with many things, but they are really not cynical at all. (They are also "healthy." Although their tastes are mildly decadent – they are intrigued by rhythms, and collect jazz tapes and dance steps – they love sports and play them well, are handy with their fists and quick to resort to them.) They are wary of emotional and intellectual commitments, but underneath their skepticism and occasional surface callousness there is an idealism of a rather pristine type. With few exceptions, these early characters observe a clear, if unspoken moral code that emphasizes simple honor and decency, faithfulness in love and friendship, the dignity of conscientious effort, and efficiency and trustworthiness in one's work. As a rule, they experience some sort of saving revelation in accordance with the principles of socialist realism, or at least there are indications that their problems are beginning to straighten out. And despite their attempts to cultivate the flippant sneer and a certain premature, world-weary acidity, they are ultimately warm and engaging.

In the next few years Aksenov's cast of characters became more diversified, but the majority of them still had a number of things in common. They tend to be ordinary persons in their twenties and thirties, trying to get along in the world without too much discomfort, and largely unconcerned with the fate of society at large. They do not have impressive intellectual and moral stature and, aside from the fact that they get along passably well with their fellow men, there is little to recommend them as exemplars of constructive thought and demeanor in any society. They are ideologically passive, and only minimally aware, if at all, of participating in the building of communism. As a rule, they are shown away from their work and, in contast to Aksenov's earliest stories, there is a pointed avoidance of the traditional socialist-realist correlation between constructive labor and the spiritual welfare of the individual.

In selecting such protagonists, Aksenov seemed to have lost his youthful confidence (or the pretense of it) that the answers to life's questions are simple and unambiguous. Many of these stories center on universal problems of maturation and emotional adjustment – finding and keeping a mate, discovering the fact of inevitable death and somehow digesting it, selecting one's life work and qualifying for it, and reconciling one's ideals with an imperfect world. His heroes brood, drift from job to job, disappoint and sometimes insult one another. They wander about the country puzzled, frustrated, and dissatisfied, and often they act more like victims of a social order than builders of one. They flounder, waste time and talent, and engage in aggressive or self-destructive behavior. By and large, however, they are never more than mildly neurotic, and they approach their problems with a minimum of self-deception, with energy, and with courage. Their ability to see the funny side of things and to ridicule themselves does prevent them from seeming simply sour and lugubrious.

Despite his increased concern with the darker and more painful issues in private lives, Aksenov has continued to write as if he believes that the human situation is good and its maladjustments curable. "Papa, What Does That Spell?" concerns a sports-loving young lathe operator who is taking care of his six-year-old daughter on a Sunday afternoon while his wife, who is well on her way to a doctor's degree, is presumably studying somewhere. Father and daughter stroll to a park, where he has a beer with some old soccer buddies. Suddenly he realizes that his wife, who has surpassed him in life, is not studying but having a rendezvous. The discovery that part of his world is about to cave in produces a momentary panic. As he looks at his daughter, however, he feels a new sense of responsibility and purpose in life: taking care of her is ample reason for living. At last, after too long a delay, the hero has been shocked into full adulthood.

One of Aksenov's greatest strengths is his sense of fun. He purposely lets things get out of hand. At times his taste for the extravagant and the improbable get him involved in huge, farcical situations that can best be described as a kind of rollicking panic. In "Oranges from Morocco" (1963) a ship laden with oranges arrives in the dead of winter at a remote port on the island of Sakhalin. The locals, many of whom have never seen an orange, rush in from every outlying village and work site, clogging the roads and plowing through the snow on tractors, dump trucks, motor- cycles, road graders, bulldozers, cars, and buses. Nanaian tribesmen on dogsleds join the crush. A steamy bacchanale ensues as the entire popu- lace, punctuating its revelry with fistfights, gorges on oranges.

The episode in "Oranges from Morocco" is possible but most improb- able, heightened, somehow larger than life. Very early Aksenov showed a disdain for consistent plausibility and an occasional preference for the ex- travagant and fabulous. In "Halfway to the Moon" (1963), Kirpichenko, a roughneck tractor driver in the Soviet Far East, begins his vacation with a three-day binge, then boards a jet for Moscow. On the plane he is fatally dazzled by the beautiful stewardess Tanya. Tamed and bemused, he spends the rest of his vacation, and all his money, flying back and forth, back and forth, on the 4,000-mile Moscow–Khabarovsk run, hoping for another glimpse of Tanya. When he finally sees her again in the airport, it is too late: he must go back to work. But it is clear that he did not really want to find the girl; her gift to him is a newly found vision of the unat- tainable, an understanding of the spiritual beauty of fantasy.

Increasingly Aksenov has featured characters who flee everyday reality and the practical to find spiritual fulfillment in the realm of imagination. And as this tendency has developed, his stories have become mixtures of the real and the fantastic, with a growing proportion of the latter. At the same time, his characters have tended to become abstractions, caricatures, vivid but arbitrary collections of attributes, and often outright grotesques. Together with this, the stories have become prominently allegorical.

The story "The Strange One" (1964) concerns the nostalgic visit of an old man to the village of his birth, after a lifetime of state service that in- cluded eighteen years' imprisonment and exile under Stalin. There he finds a boyhood acquaintance whose nickname is Dikoi (The Strange One). Fifty years before, the narrator, with a group of other boys, had

smashed a weird, Rube Goldberg machine that Dikoi had been building in
a deserted bathhouse. They talk of their lives and, as the visitor is about to
leave, his host takes him to a locked shed in back of his hut.

> I saw the same intricate machine which we had broken in the
> bathhouse. It was built along the same lines, only more compli-
> cated, more majestic. The machine was moving, wheels rotated,
> big and small, the spokes and levers moved silently, the belt-drive
> slid quietly over the pulleys, and there was the weak click of a
> little board, a little board, a little board . . .
>
> "Remember?" Dikoi whispered.
>
> "I remember," I also whispered.
>
> The little board clicked, as if ticking off the years of our lives to
> the end, and even beyond the end, back and forth, and we didn't
> even know where these noises were rolling to . . .
>
> I felt sick.
>
> "An amusing gadget," I said in a sarcastic voice, to give myself
> courage. "What's it for? Eh, Dikoi?"
>
> I called him Dikoi for the first time.
>
> "Simply, Pavlusha, for motion," he answered again in a whis-
> per, still looking at the wheels.
>
> "And when did you start it up?" I again asked sarcastically.
>
> "When? I don't know, don't remember. Long, very long ago.
> You see, it doesn't stop."
>
> "What is it – perpetual motion or something?"
>
> He turned to me and his eyes gleamed madly, no longer in the
> electric light but in the light of the early moon.
>
> "It seems so," he whispered with a sickly smile, "but perhaps
> not. So . . . let's take another look . . ."

The story is an intentionally puzzling one. The reader is free to dismiss
Dikoi as a lunatic, to admire him for his lonely, staunch pursuit of an impractical ideal, or to compare him favorably or unfavorably with the narrator, who has lived just as staunchly in the service of a different ideal.
The reader can also either exult in or deplore the fact that good human
beings can live spiritually poles apart without communicating – one in the
real world and the other in dreams. The story is subject to other allegorical interpretations as well.

In two recent stories, "The Overstocked Tare of Barrels" and "Rendezvous" (1971), Aksenov's use of the grotesque and the fantastic is extreme.
Both stories are grounded in reality, but quickly take off into the realm of

hyperbole and the surreal. The first ostensibly recounts the journey of a small but motley group of Soviet citizens, in a truckload of standing, empty barrels, from a village to a railroad station. Each passenger is sharply and comically individualized, but each is more of a mask than a flesh-and-blood character. Both their interactions and their subjective musings (through stream-of-consciousness) are heavily, satirically stylized, and it soon becomes clear that each one is not an individual but a type, and that collectively they are meant to suggest the Russian community in the abstract. As the journey progresses, each of them has a series of dreams that reveal both his character and his aspirations. Gradually the dreams of each penetrate and blend with the dreams of the others, until finally they all converge, at the end of the journey, into a common vision of the Good Man. The story is packed with colorful, amusing, and sometimes mystifying episodes, but at its heart is the ennobling spiritual transformation that takes place in each of the passengers. As a parable it seems to symbolize the necessity – or more optimistically, the possibility – for the breaking down of barriers between humans and the growth of brotherhood.

"Rendezvous" is the account of a moment of crucial, bitter truth in the life of a fantastic Soviet Renaissance Man, a jet-setter who knows everybody and can do everything. Like the poet Evtushenko (who is not named, but whose resemblance is implied), he is well connected throughout the world. Not only is he on first-name terms with the most famous intellectuals, sportsmen, and artists of all nations; he is a facile poet and musician, a champion hockey and chess player, and a virtuoso with the ladies. The Soviet public adores him. His flaw, aside from the obvious ones of insincerity and vanity, is in his self-appointed role as emblem and spokesman for the Soviet generation. He gets his come-uppance in the course of an evening in which he is made to realize that he is aging, has lost his charm, and is on the verge of becoming a laughingstock. The evening culminates in a weird confrontation with his Nemesis in the form of a ghastly, supernatural hag who offers her love to him. Dumbfounded and chastened, he goes home to his faithful wife, who has spent that evening reading Stavrogin's confession. The story is in large measure a farcical spoof, but it also has elements of deadly satire. As a parable it is directed against vanity and arrogance, superficial worldliness, and opportunistic attachment to ephemeral values.

In recent years Aksenov's extensive excursions into fantasy and the grotesque and his love of verbal pyrotechnics place him unmistakably in the Gogolian tradition of Russian literature. In this respect it is worthy of note that "Rendezvous" has prominent points of similarity to Mikhail Bulgakov's *The Master and Margarita*. Attempts to define such a dynamically developing writer as Aksenov, however, can only be tentative. Often his fondness for verbal experimentation and narrative tricks suggests that he is primarily concerned with amusing himself and his readers through formal devices and anecdotes. (This is particularly true of his longer stories; the shorter works tend to be more serious and psychologically richer.) On the other hand, Aksenov obviously has deep moral and social concerns, and his recently increased use of allegory and parable is another move in the direction of moral interests.

Although Aksenov occasionally leaves his stories unresolved, he is more prone to supplying them with happy endings than are most of his contemporaries. There is often an artificial sunniness about his conclusions, which suggests an unwillingness or inability to follow the logic of his darker observations on the world he sees about him. In resorting to the fantastic and to parable, he is in a sense arbitrarily reducing the complexity of his environment, engaging in a kind of wish fulfillment that vitiates his effectiveness as a social critic. But even his most "unrealistic" fantasies are crammed with details taken from the life about him and allusions to its problems. By choosing a course of grotesque abstraction and indirection, Aksenov could ultimately prove himself to be a truly profound and eloquent interpreter of his era.

The stories of Anatoli Gladilin (born 1935) are similar to those of Aksenov in many respects, but they are cruder and less polished. Gladilin has not been published in the Soviet Union since 1965, and his latest work, the novel *Forecast for Tomorrow* (*Prognoz na zavtra*, published abroad in 1972), seems to indicate that, unlike Aksenov, he has failed to grow as an artist. In the early 1960s, however, he was one of the most vigorous and candid spokesmen of the young Soviet generation.

His heroes are urbanites on the awkward and painful threshold of adulthood, searching for personal values, suspicious of the prevailing moral and social standards, and groping for a sense of the meaning of life. Underlying their maladjustment is a profound unease over the spiritual instability of the times and the lack of historically proven, firm guides to behavior. Their immediate concerns are ordinary ones – love, family, career. But there is a special emphasis on their striving for individuality, identity, and self-expression, born of their determination to avoid sinking into the acquiescent conformity of the Stalin generation.

In Gladilin's "First Day of the New Year" (1963), a young woman innocently asks the hero to tell her about himself. He replies:

> "I understand. Questionnaire. Feoktist Filimonovich Fildepersov. 1936. No. Male. Served in White Armies, member Cadet Party. Was in left and right opposition. Lived in occupied territory. At present a spy for Paraguayan intelligence. Underground name – Felix. Everything in order?"

This ironical parody of the *anketa*, or personnel questionnaire, is characteristic of Gladilin's bantering first-person narrators. Their speech is clever, breezy and sarcastic, and full of humorous circumlocution. In this same story, the hero describes his approaching emotional involvement with the young woman in this manner:

> I put the bill in front of me and said that probably it would start to rain, and what a pity it was, and what a good evening it had been. Ira agreed and expressed a readiness to discuss the weather of all latitudes. We had just clarified the subtleties of the rainy season in the republic of Mali when the waitress stopped circling the table and stood beside it . . .

The narrators are often querulous and given to hyperbole. Later in the story, the girl faces the hero with a moral choice, and he becomes desperate:

> "Do you love your wife?" she asked.
> "I very much love my wife, my daughter, my mama, the capital of our motherland – Moscow, our country, our earth, all nine planets of our solar system, our Milky Way and even that neighboring galaxy that peeps out in the constellation of Cassiopeia . . ."

Gladilin seems particularly anxious to authenticate his stories by packing them with documentary data. Often, as in the questionnaire quoted above, the documentation is parodistic, and one finds footnotes, lists and inventories, transcriptions of play-by-play sports broadcasts, snatches of news stories, and excerpts from diaries – all clearly derived from the Soviet milieu but, as a rule, satirically slanted. His parodies of the mass media, to show how they distort reality, are particularly effective. Although such devices usually enhance the social criticism in Gladilin's stories, they are often obtrusively mannered and clumsy. There is frequently a slapdash quality in Gladilin's writing, and it begs for a stern and tasteful editor.

Moral concerns have always been most prominent in Gladilin. The story "Smoke in the Eyes" (1959), an account of the rise, fall, and redemption of a spectacularly egotistical soccer star, frequently resorts to allegory in its treatment of questions of good and evil. In his other stories the heroes constantly observe themselves, testing the purity of their own motives and agonizing over questions of right and wrong. But Gladilin's greatest strength is in his talent for social criticism and his ability to record and dramatize the frustrations and aspirations of his generation.

The hero of "First Day of the New Year" – his best story – is a young artist with two problems: his relationship to his dying father, and his duty, on the one hand, to his wife and child and, on the other, to the girl with whom he is having an affair. Gladilin infuses the latter problem – love versus family responsibility – with more than routine interest, but the story's main appeal is in its portrayal of the estrangement between father and son, who love each other but are unable to communicate across the barrier that separates the Stalin generation from its progeny. The two of them tell their stories in alternating subjective monologues. Sadly and wistfully the father laments his incapacity for implanting his feelings of social dedication and sense of purpose to his son, and his inability to provide a convincing justification for the moral compromises, in the name of an ideal, that his generation's tolerance of Stalinism entailed. In turn, the son, despite his respect for his father's suffering, cannot accept the latter's rationalizations and faith in authority. Gladilin's delineation of the psychological and ideological differences between these two generations is vivid and explicit, and the story is perhaps the frankest and most factual statement of this theme to appear in the 1960s.

The stories of Fazil Iskander (born 1929) are nearly always set in his native Abkhazia and, although written in Russian, abound in loving and colorful descriptions of the people and customs of this southern region nestled between the Black Sea and the Caucasus. Most of the stories have an autobiographical framework. In "Grandfather" a young boy accompanies his grandfather who goes to cut brush on a mountain slope on a hot summer's day. The child's boredom and irritation at the thorny old peasant are periodically relieved by the fascination of the grandfather's accounts of the past. Iskander does not, however, cast his childhood self in the role of a passive listener. Throughout the story the boy's mind and psyche are at work and developing, and he has a complicated emotional involvement with the old man – a mixture of love, exasperation, respect, and disrespect ("I feel that we are at equal distances from the middle of life, although we are on different sides of it"). He also finds the grandfather a useful but somewhat disillusioning informant, a corrective to his boyishly romantic notions about the past.

Iskander's first books were collections of poetry, and he continues to publish his verse. His prominence, however, is based mainly on stories of his childhood and youth. In the Russian tradition of Tolstoy, Chekhov, and Gorky, he writes often of serious, fundamental, adult matters as they are seen from the perspective of an intelligent child. Iskander has observed that "perhaps the most touching and profound characteristic of childhood is the unconscious belief in the necessity of common sense." His young hero, although not precocious, is sensitive and morally alert and, despite his normal misconceptions and mistakes, is frequently able to see cruelty, stupidity, and irrationality more clearly than his elders. Nevertheless, Iskander does not use a child's point of view as a device for scolding or preaching – there is nothing harsh or blatantly didactic about his writing. Rather, the author seems concerned with the progress of a developing awareness, as stimulated by small, ordinary events and the emotional lessons they teach. The mood of such stories is warm and often humorous, and the young hero is presented in a confiding manner that is sometimes ironical but always affectionate. In "The Letter," for example, Iskander traces the chain of wishful thinking that leads his hero to believe that his love for a girl classmate is requited, and his confusion, embarrassment, and wounded pride when he discovers that he has fooled himself.

Iskander's style is graceful, relaxed, and unpretentious. His plots are simple but marked by frequent easy digressions in which the narrator confidentially ruminates with the reader, tells anecdotes, or lightly philosophizes. Unlike many of his contemporaries, Iskander does not write *skaz* or otherwise attempt to distort or disguise the author's voice. His manner is direct, assured, and genially conversational, but at the same time it can be marvelously witty, barbed, and aphoristic. Above all, his style is so informal and his humor so warm and ingratiating that they are apt to disarm the reader and leave him unprepared for the serious satirical ingredient of Iskander's stories.

In "On a Summer Day" the narrator is sunning himself at a waterfront cafe in Sukhumi. He overhears snatches of the absurd conversation of an old pensioner, whose misinformation and narrow view of the world are comic and, at the same time, subtly disturbing. The old man's smug and stupid prejudices seem to be not so much a product of senility as of environment. The main incident in the story, however, is the narrator's conversation with a cultured, highly intelligent German tourist, who tells in detail of how, during World War II, the Gestapo had used familiar methods of bullying and bribing in an unsuccessful attempt to recruit him as an informer against his colleagues in a scientific institute. There ensues a fascinating and trenchant discussion between the two concerning a decent individual's moral obligations and alternatives under conditions of this kind.

Iskander's finest work to date is *The Goatibex Constellation* (*Sozvezdie Kozlotura*, 1966), the long, adroitly rambling account of a bureaucratic attempt to propagate a new animal, a cross between an ordinary goat and a mountain wild ox. The goatibex is purported to be woolier, meatier, milkier, and more fecund than its parent species, and its very existence is an affirmation of the Michurinist genetic theories then in official favor. Not only will this hybrid solve problems in Soviet production of food, wool, and hides: its successful propagation will put its provincial place of origin on the map, boost national morale, and bolster bureaucratic and journalistic careers up and down the line. The idea swiftly snowballs in a nationwide orgy of self-deception. Rapturous official slogans proliferate, poets compete in dithyrambs to the new animal, chorales sing its praises, fierce ideological quarrels arise over whether it should be called goatibex or ibexgoat (*kozlotur* or *turokoz*), a competition with the State of Iowa in production of the beast is proposed. Inevitably the snowball is shattered, amidst general confusion and recrimination. The bureaucrats simply run for cover, however, and apparently no one learns his lesson. Built on an extended hyperbole like Gogol's *Dead Souls*, the story is a rollicking, widely ramifying satire which, for all its playfulness, penetrates deep.

Iskander writes the story in the first person, as a young journalist who observes the events he recounts, for the most part, with an amused detachment. The journalist has a similar, mildly ironic view of himself. At one juncture he writes a letter that "in my opinion, sustained a calm tone with a light touch of wise condescension." Another time he notes, "I felt cheerful and sensed in my soul an inexhaustible supply of reportorial perspicacity." He loses his watch: "It seemed to me that the bitterness of the loss of my watch would infuse into my article a mysterious lyricism, and this to a certain degree consoled me."

At the same time the narrator is unabashedly engrossed in his writing and proud of his skill. There are passages of playfully heavy alliteration and, occasionally, long, unnecessarily involved comic sentences, just for the sheer fun of it. The narrative is frequently broken by graceful, lyrical passages devoted to the Abkhazian landscape, Gogolian flights of fancy, jokes and anecdotes large and small, and the narrator's own love story. Although all of these digressions lead the reader temporarily away from Iskander's central themes, they do not detract from them. Rather, the digressions are ingratiating, and increase the reader's confidence in the narrator and his satirical point of view.

Although this story's satirical objects are numerous and range from the specific (the grandiose "hare-brained" schemes of Khrushchev and the Michurinism of Lysenko) to the general (not only the Soviet, but the universal proclivities for fads, opportunism, and credulous attachment to anything that promises to make a big splash), Iskander's main focus is on the bureaucracy and the press that serves it. The window dressing, arbitrariness, and petty tyranny of local officials are frequently lampooned. Throughout there are parodies of Soviet polemical jargon, hollow sloganeering, and journalese, sometimes in the form of newspaper headlines ("The Goatibex – Weapon of Antireligious Propaganda"), but usually through the narrator's sly insertion of wooden official language into his own speech. It is not surprising that *The Goatibex Constellation* was twice nominated for a Lenin Prize; nor is it surprising that it did not receive it.

The heroes of Viktor Konetsky are brooders, burdened with grief, disappointment, or feelings of guilt. They are responsible, mature men of proven courage, but they are also alienated, lonely, and troubled. The hero of the story "Mooring Path" (1958) is a hardened old boatswain, endlessly devoted to his work, for whom life has lost all meaning and purpose because he realizes that when he dies there will be no one to lament his passing. In "Above the White Crossroads" (1962), a colonel visits the grave of an officer whose death he had caused years before through momentary cowardice. Although the colonel has subsequently atoned for this by numerous acts of bravery and devotion, he still cannot conquer his guilty, sorrowful emptiness.

Konetsky was born in Leningrad in 1929 and educated at the Higher Naval College. Before becoming a full-time writer he worked on fishing boats in northern waters and served on sea-rescue vessels in the Arctic. Many of his early writings, and some of his most recent ones, are concerned with life at sea. The traditional heroics of maritime adventure interest him less, however, than the inner struggles of individuals with problems of duty and conscience. His characters live rugged, dangerous lives, but their internal conflicts are the main source of interest. For example, the seiner captain in "Tomorrow's Cares" (1961) is so laden with bitter memories and the sense of failure that he seems to work only to keep from thinking. He argues that "ours is a time of deeds, not philosophy" – but this is a purposeful evasion. His reluctance to think is the product of his disillusionment with the manipulated ideology of Stalinist times, and it takes the form of a reaction against all ideological approaches to life. For him, as for other Konetsky heroes, the sea is a refuge for strong but mortally wounded men, who feel unsettled and out of place in the complexities of a changing world.

Konetsky's narrative style is unpretentious, calm, and not as original as those of such contemporaries as Iskander, Bitov, and Aksenov. He has cultivated, however, the intimate approach to character – mainly through extensive interior monologue – that is typical of this generation. His plots are compact and distinct, designed to illuminate character through dramatic episodes of trial and tension. Thus, in "More About the War" (1962), a nurse, after a three-year absence from her beloved husband who is serving at the front, commits a momentary romantic indiscretion and suffers a retribution whose severity is incommensurate with her guilt.

The book *Some Look at the Clouds* (*Kto smotrit na oblaka*, 1967) is an experiment in combining short narratives to give a panoramic portrait of an era. Each of the ten chapters is a separate novella, dated somewhere between 1942 and 1966, and concerned with a separate character – the fifteen-year-old Tamara as she makes her painful way about Leningrad during the blockade, or Pavel Basargin, the middle-aged captain of a training ship whose weakness and self-betrayal show the dispiriting effects of the Stalin regime in the year 1950. Occasionally the path of a character pictured in one novella will cross that of a character from another. The main unifying element, however, is the flow of time, as shown not only by the dated chapters but also by selected details indicating changes in Soviet life and attitudes over the years.

Konetsky's best story is "A Tale About Radio Operator Kamushkin" (1961). A disabled war veteran who sailed for many years as a ship's radioman has retired because of heart trouble. On doctor's orders he has just renounced his only contact with the outside world – his nighttime hobby of ham radio. Much of the narrative takes the form of the hero's night thoughts about episodes in his past, such as his father's arrest during the terror of the 1930s. Although innocent, the father had tried to protect his son by insisting on his guilt and ordering the boy to renounce him forever. The ethical dilemma of misleading a loved one to preserve him from sharing one's own fate, however, is merely one of the problems on which the hero meditates. He is burdened by a sister who has been victimized by many men and has had several abortions. The story is rich in minor characters and in social and psychological detail. Problems of love, personal obligation and honor, religion and public life become interwoven as the hero scans the events of his own life. He feels a subtle, suffocating pressure at work against him, partly from his illness and partly from his lonely isolation and the frustration of his need to communicate with humanity. In the story's climax, he partly satisfies this need by catching and reporting the signal of a space rocket, after which he collapses from overstrain. Far from being a melodramatic resolution of his situation, this episode emphasizes its poignancy and unites the various threads of the story in a single image of human aspiration and courage.

Most contemporary Soviet writers from time to time include in their stories characters who drift about the country without personal or family ties, changing jobs frequently, driven by a wanderlust whose motivation is not clearly specified. Some are suffering from psychic wounds, others have shadowy pasts involving periods of incarceration, and still others seem simply unwilling to commit themselves to the disciplined and orderly careers that society expects of them. Although such characters sometimes occupy central positions in stories, they are usually peripheral, and in any event the impression of aimlessness and alienation they make is countered, as a rule, either by a change in their own attitudes or by the presence of more purposeful and resolute characters in the same story.

The most prominent exception to this principle is to be found in the works of Vladimir Maksimov, many of whose heroes are not just drifters but actual outlaws, rejected by society and dominated by a virulent hatred of it. Maksimov's first major success was the long story *A Man Survives* (*Zhiv chelovek*, 1962), whose hero is a runaway from a Siberian labor camp. Abandoned by a fellow escapee, he has been found half frozen in the forest and brought, unidentified, to a rural hospital where he awaits a probable leg amputation. The narrative, in first person, switches back and forth between the hero's dazed observation of his rescuers' spontaneous kindness and his recollections of his past life. As a boy he was ostracized because of his father's political imprisonment, became a petty thief and drifter, and later worked in a smuggling ring. Arrested, he spent two years in forced labor, then was commandeered to the front in World War II, rearrested on his return for having been captured by the Germans, and recommitted to the camp from which he has just escaped. Life has turned him into a brute and misanthrope, for whom criminal activity is the only means of self-expression. At the story's end, however, he has been so touched by the self-sacrifice of those who are saving his life that he reveals to them his identity – an act of atonement that will surely return him to prison.

The burden of this and other stories of Maksimov is that the human soul can remain alive in even the most wolfish existence, that the good in man is primordial and indestructible. On the other hand, the main interest of these stories is in their exploration of the psychology of the outcast and the delineation of the environmental circumstances that have contributed to his attitudes. Maksimov does not sentimentalize his criminals or soften their guilt. But he does show that society's abuse of the unprotected and vulnerable individual is the major source of spiritual casualties.

Some of Maksimov's works are quite orthodox in the sense that they conclude with the moral rehabilitation of antisocial characters or portray the uplifting effect of a dedicated individual on the collective. Maksimov's interest in the psychology of the outcast, however, and his concern over social neglect and inhumanity, often lead to a more pessimistic treatment of issues of good and evil. In the story "Sashka," for example, a Tatar foundling, tormented and abused in a Russian children's home, runs away, falls in with criminals and, after a series of harrowing experiences, commits suicide. Similarly, most of Maksimov's major characters are rebels, pariahs, lonely wanderers on the fringes of society. What is most important, however, is that they are portrayed not merely as a social category but as individuals in a moral context, engaged in solitary struggles for freedom from a society they find oppressive. Criminality among them is not a matter of hardened cynicism, low mentality, or insensitivity to humans, but is rather the product of desperation, of rejection by a humanity of which they long to be a part. Guilt, remorse, and a compelling urge for atonement are prominent in their psychology.

The language in which Maksimov conducts his searches among disturbed spirits is difficult, sometimes clumsy and tortuous. Much of it is subjective, brooding interior monologue, in which characters express their thoughts in the form of complaints and questions, couched in earthy vernacular and dialect. Although the prose is largely devoid of grace and plasticity, it is vivid and notably rich in its allusions to Russian folk culture, and its tormented quality is in keeping with the painful confusion of his heroes.

The darkness of Maksimov's view of the world seems to have come to a great extent from the author's personal experience. He was born in Leningrad in 1932, reared in a series of children's homes, and early introduced to the life of an itinerant, traveling as a construction worker over much of Russia and Siberia. He began writing in 1952, published a volume of poetry in 1956 and his first story in 1961. Quite surprisingly for one of his evident sympathies, he served on the editorial board of the reactionary magazine *Oktyabr'* – but was dismissed in 1967. At one time, for reasons unclear, he was committed to a psychiatric hospital, and later was under severe pressure from the authorities to repudiate his first long novel.

Such demands are not surprising. The offending work, *The Seven Days of Creation* (*Sem dnei tvoreniya*, 1971), has not been published in the Soviet Union but was printed abroad under émigré sponsorship. It is one of the most powerful and thoroughly despairing fictional portraits of Soviet life ever written. The work consists of six long stories, comprising a chronicle of the Lashkov family that embraces nearly the entire Soviet period. Each story features a separate member of the family, but all of the stories interlock thematically and through family associations. The sum total of the Lashkovs' experiences, and those of numerous subsidiary characters, is one of disillusionment, of hopeless, distorted, and broken lives. Alcoholism, suicide, brutality, and the multiple pressures of the callous state authority are ubiquitous. Although there is an abundance of ugly naturalistic detail, *The Seven Days of Creation* is by no means cold or clinical in manner. Maksimov writes with respect for human aspiration and compassion for human inadequacy. Moreover, he presents the Lashkovs' experience as a profoundly *Russian* one, a product not only of the Soviet era but of the national culture that preceded and to a great extent survived it. Vividly revolting behavior, suffering, cruelty, remorse, and kindness are present on all sides. The Lashkovs themselves are varied and, taken together, offer a wide spectrum of strengths and weaknesses, unselfish love and self-centered anxiety. What they have in common is a bitter sense of family destiny and, as they grow older, a wistful compulsion to search for a meaning in their suffering. The only consolation available to them is tragic acceptance, mitigated somewhat by a last resort to religion. For religion, which is presented throughout the stories as a prominent and enduring element in the popular culture, is the only institution that is not totally discredited in *The Seven Days of Creation*.

Maksimov, a leading Soviet dissenter, emigrated in 1974 and now lives in Paris, where he edits the journal *Kontinent*. His novel *Karantin* is discussed in Chapter 13.

The young writers discussed in this chapter display in common a skeptical and questioning attitude toward the quality of life in their society and a special sensitivity to the changes that have taken place in it. Not all of them could be classified specifically as "social critics." Bitov in particular often seems much more concerned with the individual psyche than with the social environment. Most of them deal with issues so universal in human experience that their stories frequently transcend the bounds of time and place. Yet all write with an unmistakable awareness of the unsettled aspects of Soviet life and of the need for reexamining its essence.

More sombre than the others, both Konetsky and Maksimov emphasize the pain and frustration of existence with stark realism and tragic overtones reminiscent of Dostoevsky and Gorky. In certain features, both writers appear to be fairly conventional products of socialist realism – Konetsky in his preoccupation with heroism and Maksimov in the emphasis of a few of his stories on the positive influence an exemplary individual can exert on a collective. (In both writers, however, heroic behavior is dogged, despairing, and lacking in the confident sense of high purpose that is demanded of socialist realism.) Neither of them, moreover, is a lively or innovative stylist. They share with the other young writers a new boldness in showing the darker sides of the Soviet scene and exceed the others in their degree of gloomy candor. But their writing is traditional in form, and it testifies to the fact that many writers of this new generation are essentially content with the established models of nineteenth- and twentieth-century Russian realism.

Clearly, however, there is a demand for other models. The young writers, together with a few of their most enterprising elders, launched a campaign against the simplistic representation of human nature in literature, a campaign to restore the cultural richness and resonance of Soviet writing. A major result of these efforts was the introduction of a new kind of protagonist into works of short fiction, either by adding new dimensions to the traditional "positive hero" or, less frequently, by entirely discarding the traditional mold. The general characteristics of these protagonists (not all of them, of course, possessed these traits in equal proportions) were a degree of restlessness and bewilderment, a lack of self-confidence, disappointment over the prosaic and sometimes immoral quality of life about them, uncertainty and apprehension about the future, doubts and reservations about certain prevailing social standards and modes of behavior, and an aversion to ideological generalizations and pronouncements and to the conventional phrases developed to express them. In such protagonists these qualities were usually tempered by innate feelings of personal pride, a healthy humility, occasionally playful, mischievous exuberance, and a habit of ironic self-expression. The portrayal of such protagonists required a high degree of psychological subtlety and precision, as well as narrative devices that would show the complexity of their emotions and attitudes. At the same time, these devices must reflect the reticence of many of the protagonists, their reluctance to commit themselves fully, and the puzzled, tentative quality of their thought. There was also a need for a model of irreverent, satirical expression that would convey the whimsical, iconoclastic attitudes of many of these protagonists, their penchant for saying things by indirection, and their inclination to ridicule things that they disapprove of but cannot change.

The social climate in the Soviet Union had become such that both the need and the opportunity for expressions of irony had become more prominent than before. A confluence of forces – social and purely literary – encouraged the reemergence of the ironical manner in Soviet Russian writing. The literary influence came from two streams: Soviet literature of the twenties and early thirties and twentieth-century Western literature.

Writers of the 1920s such as Ilf and Petrov, Isaak Babel, and Mikhail Zoshchenko, who had been proscribed during the last years of Stalin, began to be republished in the mid-1950s. The reappearance of their works provided sanction for contemporary writers to adopt their attitudes and methods. These writers were not dependent solely, of course, on the example of the twenties for the ironic devices they employed. A great many of them were developed in the Russian literature of the nineteenth and early twentieth centuries. We can be sure, for example, that such writers as Aksenov and Iskander have studied not only Zoshchenko but Gogol as well. On the other hand, the special quality of satirical irreverence, the ultracontemporary nature of the oral speech employed, the pointedly topical application of parodistic devices, and the intensity of reliance on linguistic incongruities in these authors, all are based mainly on the example of the twenties.

Contemporary Western literature, a large part of which had been banned in the Soviet Union for many years, was now being translated into Russian in increasing quantities and variety. The susceptibility of Soviet writers to Western influence increased correspondingly, but their receptivity was highly selective, based on the need to develop specific forms of literary expression. Writers were not engaging in formal experimentation for its own sake but were searching for means of expressing moods and attitudes that they themselves felt and whose presence they sensed in the society about which they were writing.

The quality and extent of Western influence on these young writers needs to be thoroughly investigated. Probably dozens of twentieth-century European, British, and American writers are involved, but for the moment one can mention with assurance two Americans: Ernest Hemingway and J. D. Salinger. The lean dialogues of Aksenov, Bitov, and Voinovich, in which the distinguishing features are close imitation of the rhythms and language of popular speech, a paucity of supplemental narrative commentary, and the abruptness and reticence of the speakers themselves, are all typical of the Hemingway manner. In this dialogue there is a studied primitiveness, an avoidance of emotionally or ideologically laden locutions, and a preference for understatement and the simple, direct, "neutral" word that all suggest the influence of Hemingway. Furthermore, there are evident echoes of Hemingway in the brooding, ironic interior monologue of Aksenov, Voinovich, Gladilin, and Bitov, who use deceptively simple language to convey intimate moods of loneliness, frustration, disappointment, and suppressed rage.

The young narrators of Voinovich and Aksenov think and talk like Salinger's Holden Caulfield. Their ingratiatingly quizzical, self-mocking accounts of their experience and their wry, ironical outlook on the world they have inherited are closely akin to those of Salinger's hero. Moreover, their inventive use of authentic, contemporary language to express these attitudes closely resembles that of their American counterpart. There is clearly a spiritual affinity, a similarity of moral and psychological attitude between Salinger's hero and the narrator – protagonists in these Russian stories. It is not accidental that in Voinovich's "Two Comrades" the following dialogue takes place:

> "And what did you do yesterday?" asks Tolik.
> "Nothing. Lay down, read a book."
> "What kind of book?"
> *"The Catcher in the Rye."*
> "About espionage?"
> "No, about life."

The literary trends discussed in the present chapter became prominent in the latter half of the 1950s, attained their most extensive development in the years 1962 and 1963, and diminished in the latter half of the 1960s. Their diminution is attributable partly to a natural exhaustion of literary fashions and the writers' normal change of interests as they moved from their thirties into their forties. Probably the most important cause of the change, however, was the regime's decreasing tolerance of the satirical and ironical manner of these writers – which implicitly called into question too many of the fundamental assumptions about how Soviet life should be lived – and its correspondingly increased intolerance of the sharper and more direct social criticism of a Maksimov. In this respect it is significant that recent works of Gladilin, Voinovich, and Maksimov have been published not in the USSR but abroad.

8

The village writers

Literature about peasant life has always been prominent in the Soviet Union, and some of the most interesting writers – such as Boris Pilnyak, Leonid Leonov, Mikhail Sholokhov, Andrei Platonov, and Aleksandr Tvardovsky – have devoted themselves to countryside themes. Under Stalin, however, both the aesthetic value and the social integrity of village literature were largely vitiated by the demands of socialist realism. There were exceptions, notably the first volume of Sholokhov's novel about the forced collectivization of agriculture, *Virgin Soil Upturned* (1931). But by the beginning of the 1950s village literature had been almost completely reduced to state propaganda.

In the decade following World War II, writing on rural themes tended to be hortatory, designed to promote discipline and enthusiasm for the painful sacrifices involved in restoring agriculture after the war's devastation. At the same time, it painted an artificially rosy picture of the countryside. The narrator of Kazakov's story "Nestor and Kir" sarcastically recalls:

> dozens of novels and stories about the village, magnificent in their time – how wonderful everything was there! In the village – according to these books – there were electricity, radio, hotels, sanatoriums, highly-paid work days, fabulous harvests, television and God knows what else. There was everything you could imagine and even more, and consequently there was happiness and abundance, socialism had been built, vestiges of capitalist mentality didn't exist. Moreover, once someone got things started, socialism was not enough, the village was proceeding to communism, and those peasants who still stupidly clung to a satisfied,

calm life, to decrepit socialism, were proclaimed backward, and in the struggle of the excellent with the good, that is, of communism with socialism, there was built a *conflict!* What a competition then went on among writers, how they feared being reputed to have torn themselves away from the life of the people, and how they wrote about that life in brighter and brighter colors!

The liberalization that accompanied the Twentieth Party Congress enabled writers to portray the countryside with relative candor, disclosing an actuality that, of course, was far grimmer than these idyllic pictures. An era of unprecedented frankness in rural literature began. In opening up the countryside to genuine criticism, the authorities took a utilitarian view because, according to *Pravda*, such writing "helps the Party to mobilize and form public opinion, to solve the most important social and public problems." But the authorities got much more than they bargained for. In airing the problems of the village, many writers engaged in quite a profound examination of many other issues that were troubling the national spirit.

The best rural writing in this period was either semifictional or fictional and tended to be documentary in method. At the outset the favorite genre was the *ocherk*, or sketch, which combined a stylized form of reportage with the author's invention and analysis – a scheme permitting a union of art and journalism, of the lyrical and the practical. Later in this period the rural *ocherk* was largely displaced by the short story and the novel.

Both the sketch and works of pure fiction usually focused on everyday situations – mowing, woodcutting, the household routine, personal problems, and problems of farm management – and tended to eschew dramatic incident in favor of the rhythms of rural existence. The best writers avoided indulging in the picturesque or artificial "folkishness." Although all of them, in varying degrees, found romance and spiritual inspiration in farm labor, few of them sentimentalized it. The favorite narrative tone was calm and even, with an avoidance of extreme feeling or obtrusive stylistic effects. The language of village writers ranged from standard literary Russian, larded on occasion with folk expressions, to dialogue and interior monologue in which folk speech was an organic element of characterization and atmosphere. Through moderation, scrupulous honesty, and the avoidance of gratuitous local color, these writers strove to give an accurate and sympathetic portrayal of contemporary peasant culture.

To a great extent the increasingly serious attention to the countryside as a literary subject represented a search for stable national values, a turning to the peasant as a source of moral renewal. Portraying deprivation and discontent in the village with a fidelity that often approached naturalism, writers also emphasized the stubborn endurance of peasant psychology and culture and revealed a Russian character little touched by the Revolution. The writers of rural literature all felt that the cultural and moral values of the Russian countryside must be considered a major factor in solving modern Soviet problems, and they argued the absolute necessity of preserving folk traditions.

They insisted that the peasant should retain his special psychological identity, and many expressed the fear that the increasing mechanization and centralized management of agriculture would transform the peasantry into an amorphous mass of semiproletarians. In investigating the peasant "soul," writers were motivated by sympathy for the underdog, unfairly treated and exploited. In this sense, they participated in Soviet literature's rediscovery of the importance of the individual, his innate qualities, his appetites, skills and desires, and his true beliefs as contrasted to those that the mythology of official propaganda had attributed to him. But they also tended to view the peasant as a last repository of precious traits of the national character: individualism and self-reliance. Their main concern was to show that the peasant should not be forced and driven but should be allowed to be productive on his own initiative. A corollary of this concern was the feeling that the peasant should be encouraged to maintain the traditions associated with his best trait: his closeness to the soil.

For some writers, emphasis on the moral importance of the peasant's intimate contact with the land became strongly tinged with a kind of wistful idealization of Russian rural existence. This tendency was particularly evident among neo-Slavophile writers and literary critics (sometimes known as *Rusity*, or Russites), who proclaimed a sentimental, almost religious trust in the innate wisdom of the Russian peasant masses. This blind faith may have been to some extent a desperate product of the gap in communications between the Soviet intelligentsia and the peasantry. It also represented, one suspects, a kind of wishful thinking, a form of lame nationalistic utopianism.

Rural writing was closely connected at many points with the contemporary interest in Russia's national origins. The countryside was the richest source of folk traditions and ancient cultural monuments, which, in the cities, had been largely obliterated. It is probable that many writers who traveled to ancient towns and villages, collected peasant artifacts and folklore, and visited old monasteries, battlefields, palaces and secular shrines such as Yasnaya Polyana, were simply rejecting – whether consciously or unconsciously – the twentieth century, motivated by a feeling that precious traditional values were being lost in an epoch of rapid cultural transition. But in hunting and describing the traces of a vanishing antiquity in folk customs and songs, and in praising medieval icon painting and church architecture, writers were also engaged in a search for historical continuity through the rehabilitation of pristine Russian culture. Thus, the interest of village writers in the way of life and personality of the peasant, and the often expressed "back-to-the-roots" affection for the soil, were directly related to a nationalistic quest for the ultimate sources of the Russian spirit.

The nationalist element in village writing requires at least a few more words of explanation. If not explicitly a repudiation of the October Revolution, it nevertheless represented a reaction against many developments that the Revolution helped to bring about – urbanization, technology, and the modern industrial, bureaucratic society. There was also alarm over the disruption of the natural environment, and Russian conservationist writers frequently couched their protests in nationalistic terms. Above all, a substitute was needed for the corrupt and discredited Stalinist ideology and moral values. Something was required, moreover, to counteract a widespread growth of general skepticism and cynicism – the notorious "nihilism" of which Party propagandists frequently complained. There was a mounting, although usually unspecified, popular demand for sober thinking about ends and means, about decent and realistic social goals. To reject socialism as such was patently unthinkable and, as neo-Stalinism set in during the 1960s, the latitude for variation within the framework of socialist ideology itself began to narrow. Consequently, some Russian writers turned to various forms of nationalism for an explanation of their historical circumstances and for something that would give meaning to their existence. To some extent nationalist thought came to them by default; it became increasingly dangerous to advocate "decadent" Western values, and many Russian intellectuals, no doubt, resolved to make the best of what was left to them. Others were inclined simply to reflect a traditional feeling of Russia's spiritual superiority over the West. Still others adopted a subtly fatalistic, even somewhat masochistically consoling nationalism, based on the feeling that "it's always been this way, and only the strength of a Russian peasant makes it possible to endure it."

The theme of the dichotomy between the city and the countryside has been constant in Russian literature since the Revolution – one need only recall the melancholy verse of Esenin. More recently, however, the appeal for moral return to the natural wholesomeness of the village, for renewed spiritual contact with the land, has come from the fact that the continuing migration of peasants to the cities has produced a large class of Russians who are neither peasants nor townspeople, but something in between. They are culturally and psychologically confused, without clearly established urban or rural values. Such is the hero of Kazakov's story "An Easy Life," a young, rootless itinerant whose visit to his mother in his native village gives him an uneasy feeling of emptiness and purposelessness. Often, as in Kazakov's "The Smell of Bread" and Nikolai Zhdanov's "A Trip Home," citified characters return to the village and prove to have been irreparably corrupted by callous urban ways. More often, however, such works focus on feelings of puzzled nostalgia: the city dweller longs to return to the village but knows that such a return is psychologically impossible. At one ideological extreme in this respect are the Russites who argue that "land" is good while "asphalt" is bad. More sober writers recognize that urbanization has brought cultural advances that should not be denied to peasants, and put forth suggestions for combining the best of both worlds.

The cumulative picture of contemporary Russian peasant life that emerges from rural writing is not a pretty one. Plainly democratic in sentiment, it is the frankest and most penetrating body of social criticism that has been allowed publication in recent years. It is critical realism, an examination and affirmation of the roots of Russian culture, which at the same time expresses grave concern over the indications of incipient decay. In this picture, peasants stand out as victims of the social order, exploited and humiliated, their anguish either ignored or, at best, misrepresented. All too frequently they are not farmers responsible for the earth they till, but rootless workers with little real stake in the enterprises to which they have been attached. From them as a class the state has extracted the highest price for existence.

In exploring the village, recent writing has emphasized not so much the changes that have been wrought by socialism, as the continuing harshness of peasant life. The peasant's feeling of proprietary responsibility for the soil is in deep jeopardy. Often he appears demoralized – apathetic, ignorant, and incapable of initiative. He lives in poverty, his home and village in disrepair, deprived of the goods and services that city dwellers take for granted. His pay is uncertain and inevitably low. Because of central mismanagement and the resulting poor productivity, low farm prices, and meager collective-farm income, he must cultivate his private plot intensively and raise his own livestock. These operations are so heavily taxed that they must often be curtailed or abandoned.

Perhaps the most pervasive evil portrayed in literature about the countryside is the bureaucratic atmosphere that pervades agricultural management. Rural literature abounds in examples of brutal arbitrariness in the enforcement of rigid and wildly impractical central plans or in the pursuit of impressive statistics. Meddlesome advisory and inspection commissions fan out from the cities to waste the peasants' time. Under such circumstances, peasants and local farm administrators develop crafty, and often illegal, methods of getting things done. The moral cost of such a necessity is obviously very heavy. Palliative measures undertaken in the last decade have alleviated the peasant's lot somewhat, but the system remains fundamentally unchanged from that of the Stalin era.

The first important work of critical realism in postwar village literature appeared in 1952. This was *District Weekdays* (*Raionnye budni*), by Valentin Ovechkin, who initiated a vogue of militant sketches indicting the government's methods of administering agriculture. The publication of a work that frankly and boldly deplored social and economic conditions in the countryside, and clearly blamed the government apparatus, was an act of great courage – particularly as Stalin was still alive at the time. The appearance of *District Weekdays* and Ovechkin's later collections of sketches – *At the Front Line* (*Na perednem krae*, 1953), *In the Same District* (*V tom zhe raione*, 1954), *With One's Own Hands* (*Svoimi rukami*, 1954), and *A Difficult Spring* (*Trudnaya vesna*, 1956) – heartened numerous other writers who aspired to explore the countryside candidly.

Ovechkin had already been writing for many years. Born in Taganrog in 1904, he worked in his youth as a shoemaker and teacher in schools for illiterate peasants. Later he served as secretary of a Party bureau and chairman of a collective farm. He published his first stories in the late twenties while still in the Komsomol, and his first collection came out in 1935. In World War II he was a front-line correspondent. He became prominent in the literary establishment in the fifties, and subsequently served on the board of the Writers' Union.

Although Ovechkin's career as a critic of the countryside was assisted by the demise of Stalin and the Party's ensuing reformist attitude, his courage and outspokenness later caused him grave difficulty. In 1962, as a member of the Kursk District Party Committee, he became a leader of the opposition to Khrushchev's "adventurism" in agricultural matters. Failing to gain decisive support, and under heavy political pressure, he attempted suicide by shooting himself. Although his life was saved, he lost an eye.

The authorities tried to conceal the tragedy. He was later sent to a mental hospital for a time and finally retired to Tashkent, where he died in 1968.

The damning implications of Ovechkin's sketches reached the top of the Soviet managerial hierarchy, but the sketches themselves were confined to the problems of kolkhoz chairmen and rural officials at the local level. The ultimate focus was the peasant himself – his aspirations, interests, psychology and motivation (or lack of it) in performing farm work, and on those factors that impelled him to neglect his kolkhoz obligations, work badly, spend too much time on his private plot, or desert the land altogether for work in the city. Not the least of these factors were the tensions, rivalries, and infighting within the local Party organization, which produced widespread uncertainty, confusion, and ultimately inefficiency. Ovechkin's immediate focus, however, was on the problem of leadership as exemplified in the Party District Secretary. His strategy was to dramatize the problem by examining the behavior of secretaries good and bad.

Ovechkin's chief villian is Borzov, initially the First Secretary of the district committee, a martinet and lover of red tape who on first acquaintance gives the impression of being a zealous public servant but who soon proves to be merely a stupid bully and careerist concerned only with window dressing and with carrying out government orders to the letter. In direct contrast to Borzov is his antagonist Martynov, who starts out as Second Secretary under Borzov and soon replaces him. Martynov, a wise man and a humanitarian, respects the collective farmers, understands their psychology, and identifies himself with their daily lives and difficulties. He realizes that the peasant works best and most enthusiastically when he is not ordered about in arbitrary fashion but is given a prominent voice in the affairs that concern him and provided with incentive in the form of a clear personal, material interest in the kolkhoz. The character Borzov eventually leaves the scene of Ovechkin's sketches, and Martynov dominates the stage. As negative and positive images of rural Party officials, both characters have made a lasting mark in Soviet literature.

Ovechkin's sketches resemble short stories in many respects. Their characters are fictitious. Action and episodes are arranged in simple plots, centering on the everyday activities of Martynov as he travels about, has business meetings and conversations, and muses on his various professional problems. The tone of narration is leisurely, objective, and dispassionate. At the same time the author makes no attempt to hide his own sentiments. Martynov is his hero; the author is arguing for a liberalized attitude toward kolkhoz management and wants to set forth his views with maximum clarity. Hence the sketches are organized as arguments designed to compel the reader to think logically and practically, on the basis of concrete evidence, and to come to specific conclusions on the problems of the peasantry.

The author's chief device for stimulating the reader to think about these problems is to engage his characters in long conversations and occasional disputes. Although the device is rhetorically powerful, it is often aesthetically defective when the characters are reduced to mouthpieces for ideas – their remarks merely lengthy polemical monologues lacking in personal flavor. Moreover, the arguments that Ovechkin favors, for all their practical humanity, are largely limited to the question of good leadership and organization on the collective farms, and they slight or ignore many fundamental questions of peasant personality, life and culture.

Nearly all of those who wrote critically about the countryside included at least some satirical shadings, but the first village writer to specialize in satire in this period was Gavriil Troepolsky. Born in 1905, Troepolsky has been publishing short stories and novels since 1938. His knowledge of the rural scene is based on his experience as a practicing agronomist, and his best-known series of writings, beginning in 1953, are entitled *Notes of An Agronomist (Zapiski agronoma)*. Troepolsky's works remain a landmark in the postwar use of the device of sharp ridicule to point out the darker sides of village life.

Troepolsky's narrator is a professional, interested in efficient, scientific agriculture, who travels about collective farms observing peasants and their work, recording his thoughts and feelings, and sometimes expressing ironic bitterness because of his own impotence in the presence of the prevailing backwardness. The chief targets of his satire are bureaucratic ineptitude, senseless "reforms" designed to cover up sloth and lack of genuine enterprise, and various kinds of local demagoguery. Attention centers on personages who embody, in the fashion of a Russian neoclassical or possibly a Gogolian caricature, specific negative traits of the peasantry.

Notes of An Agronomist presents a colorful gallery of types – natural, earthy, comic, expressing themselves in their own peasant language. There is Prokhor Samovarov, known among the kolkhozniks as Prokhor the Seventeenth because this is his seventeenth position in as many years and also because he is the seventeenth in a procession of unsuccessful chairmen at this kolkhoz. Samovarov is a self-assured idler and ignoramus who, despite his series of dismissals for malfeasance and bungling, has always managed to survive through the protection of the equally stupid chairman of the regional executive committee, one Nedoshlepkin. Samovarov is particularly adept at the techniques of *perestrakhovka* ("playing-it-safe"), of obsequiousness toward his superiors, and of the saving, tearful, "self-critical" confession after he has made a mess of things.

Another character is Nikishka Boltushok, the village obfuscator, a no-good babbler who has a compulsion to "debate" all issues, including the tiniest matters of day-to-day kolkhoz business, boring his neighbors with vulgar political jargon and wasting everyone's time. Grishka Khvat, a compulsive thief and pilferer, appropriates pieces of the collective-farm machinery for his own use and steals grain and hay from the collective fields and barns. Grishka is both brazen and ingenious, a master of pettifoggery who always knows his "rights" under the law. Not everyone in Troepolsky's fictional village is a fool or scoundrel, but the author avoids the socialist-realist convention of offsetting his negative characters with positive ones. Aside from humor, the major element that relieves the gloom is loving and sensitive nature description, a warm affirmation of the essential goodness of the countryside.

Troepolsky's first-person narrator is often lyrical, acutely receptive to the flavor of village life, opinionated and ironical. Although he ridicules, he does not moralize or preach. The episodes in his sketches are plotted in the fashion of the short story, with alternating passages of local color, humor, nature description, and subjective musings. The speech of his villagers is rural and comic, and their suggestive names (in addition to the ones mentioned above, there are such characters as Pashka-Pomidor – round and pink as a tomato – and Tugodum – a man with slow responses) provide additional evidence of the tradition in which Troepolsky writes – that of eighteenth-century Russian comedy, later of Gogol, and especially of Gogol's harsher successors as social critics such as Saltykov-Shchedrin.

Efim Dorosh (born 1908) is the writer of sketches who seemed best able to see things through the eyes of a peasant and at the same time to convey a sense of the complex historical, social, geographical, and psychological factors that conditioned the countryside. An acute observer of the details of village life, with a strong practical understanding of how Russian agriculture operates and should operate, Dorosh also showed a poetic appreciation of the beauties of the countryside and a deep concern for the preservation of the Russian national character. Obviously a democrat with strong liberal convictions and a deeply respectful solicitude for the Russian peasant and his culture, Dorosh combined critical realism with a tone of pragmatism and reasoned persuasiveness. At the same time, he showed a more pronounced interest in Russia's cultural antiquity than most village writers.

Although Dorosh has been writing about village life since the thirties, his rise to prominence began in 1954 with a sketch of Ivan Fedoseevich, the collective-farm chairman who became the central figure in a series of separate works, published from 1954 to 1970, known under the general title *A Village Diary (Derevenskii dnevnik)*. The locale of the sketches is a small farming community in central Russia, which Dorosh calls Raigorod – a name with both archaic and pastoral overtones. Dorosh writes as a frequent visitor who knows intimately and loves the natural setting of Raigorod, its people, customs, history, and the rhythm of its life, and is sympathetic to its problems.

The style of *A Village Diary* is modest and restrained, calmer and more subtle than that of Ovechkin or Troepolsky. The narration and description are full and leisurely; the tone of exposition and argumentation is gentle and meditative. Dorosh does not dwell on the picturesque or indulge in exotic decoration. Although his narrator has a distinct personality, his manner is epic rather than lyrical, and he is given to careful, intelligent pondering over concrete facts, motivated by a practical concern for the welfare of the village. At the same time, there are often delicately poetic passages – landscapes and miniature essays on such topics as the ancient beauty of hay mowing. The language of Dorosh is pure literary Russian, with a sparse and judicious admixture of folk elements.

A Village Diary was published over a period of fifteen years, and the individual works that comprise it provided a running commentary on current developments in Soviet farm administration. The criticisms that Dorosh made in any given year were not necessarily applicable in succeeding years, and the author scrupulously noted positive changes, of which there were several, as well as chronic evils. His most prominent and constant target was senseless bureaucratic management of agriculture – ambitious regional Party workers, kolkhoz chairmen, and agronomists who, regardless of crop conditions, always strive to be the first to sow and harvest so that they can read about themselves in the newspapers; the wholesale planting of corn without preparatory research, on orders from high up, which results in extensive crop failures; the arbitrary gobbling up of a kolkhoz by a huge state farm, the balance of the kolkhoz's funds being spent on band instruments the peasants don't want. It often seems that only the peasant intelligence of Ivan Fedoseevich prevents his kolkhoz from being utterly ruined by officious outsiders, and the things he does to make it run successfully render him "almost always guilty before the authorities." The oblast Party Secretary accuses him of speaking "in an alien voice, sounding like the BBC."

Under such circumstances, the peasant can only rely on his private plot. Dorosh describes so great a production of onions in this fashion that it seemed there were not "private plots attached to the kolkhoz but a kolkhoz attached to private plots." He is distressed over the situation of peasant women – often the main support of their households, beleaguered by myriad chores, old at forty – and he notes that kolkhoz work for men is largely mechanized, whereas women use pitchforks and scythes. Villagers are culturally deprived – one reason why they leave for the cities. He describes a village club decorated in verbose hortatory slogans that meet with utter indifference, and a kolkhoz meeting at which the chairman drones out information that everyone has long before known from radio and newspapers.

Nature for Dorosh is no mere pastoral backdrop or aesthetic appurtenance. When he comments on the vegetables that grow best in his region or the harmony of the ruins of the ancient Raigorod kremlin in their natural context, he is thinking first of all of the primordial, creative link between men and their environment. He notes "how closely were intertwined the natural, economic and moral categories in that complicated world which from time immemorial and customarily has been called the village." His interest in folk customs, the design of rural houses, dress, and implements is based on his deep feeling of the importance and value of tradition. It is this concern, for example, that leads him to bring up an incident in which peasants on a newly created state farm, forbidden to pasture their private cows, sell the animals to buy washing machines and television sets. These, he argues, cannot give them the same native delight and satisfaction as the simple purchase of a cow. Coming from Dorosh, observations such as this are not sentimental or patronizing, for they are based on respectful admiration for peasant psychology and tradition.

The most vivid emblem of popular tradition for Dorosh is the ancient village church. He describes a wooden structure built in 1687 as "festive" and "soulful," with "the simplicity of a peasant hut," and refers to another as "a magical monument of our ancient architecture, akin, it seems to me, to the fantastic and merry fairy tales, heroic *byliny*, clever tales and sayings coined from time immemorial." He notes that the local church is always the most imposing, well-placed, and beautifully decorated building in a village, and feels that the disappearance of village churches is impoverishing the landscape. They should at least be preserved, he argues, by converting them into village clubs.

Although Dorosh disavows any personal religious beliefs, his attitude toward religion is tolerant and even sympathetic. He sees the religious tradition as satisfying an essential folk need, both spiritual and aesthetic. Describing a Russian religious commune that existed 600 years ago and the monk who founded it, he comments: "even though this ideal seems naive today, the devotion with which he served it cannot but call forth feelings of rapture." The building of village churches, he argues, was inspired not by Christian asceticism but by "living life, a conception of the beautiful born of surrounding reality," and he adds that in such churches "there is significantly more habitation, domesticity, than in any village club!" The religious impulse is integral to the Russian national character: he describes a group of women – "the old and the elderly, bereaved mothers and early widowed wives" – descending the decorated steps of a wooden church and asks, "are these not the folk!"

Dorosh notes the *lack* of religion in many peasants who, for example, refuse to work on church holidays not because they are believers but because their working lives are boring and they need rest and diversion. But he also attacks the haughty condescension of much of the Soviet public toward religion, and argues that this callous attitude comes from habitual, routine atheism that gives no thought to the spiritual, psychological, and ethical significance of religious belief. Ultimately, he feels, the peasant goes to church not so much from superstition, fear of death, or motives of guilt, as from a search for consolation.

Better than any other writer of countryside sketches, Dorosh combines an understanding of Russian peasants as a class with a profound respect for them as individuals, each with his own personality, desires, and ambitions. He finds them more interesting and wholesome than city dwellers. In their traditional qualities, which he attributes to intimate relationship with the soil, he sees the hope of Soviet society. Chief among these qualities are circumspection (*osmotritel'nost'*) and thrift (*raschetlivost'*), as exemplified in Ivan Fedoseevich. A totally devoted collective-farm chairman, Ivan Fedoseevich makes the economic welfare of his own local community the measure of his actions. He is careful to see that every individual gets his just share of the farm's income, and he is willing to challenge or circumvent the regional bosses if need be. Thus, in one lean year he procured seed grain from the authorities, ground it and distributed the flour to his hungry kolkhozniks, and sowed his fields on time with seed he had stored on the sly – an offense for which he could have gone to prison.

A Village Diary is frequently punctuated with quietly reasonable suggestions for the improvement of village life. Although Dorosh stresses age-old peasant values, he is by no means a reactionary, and his suggestions seek to combine tradition with innovations that will not violate what he considers to be the special peasant genius. For one thing, he insists on the inviolability of the peasant's right, his *moral* right, to own a cow and cultivate his private plot, because "here everything depends on his own initiative, his own knowledge, his own capabilities, his own labor. The fact that he himself decides how he is to use the land and how to dispose of the products of his labor." Dorosh quarrels with the word "culture" (*kul'-tura*) as it is frequently applied to the village – meaning amusements in the village club, with amateur plays, dances, and movies. For him culture means the natural activities of peasants free of compulsion – for example it is they, and not specialists in the cities, who should decide how often to milk their cows.

Dorosh suggests that collective farms should be allowed more freedom to trade their own produce in the market and that collective-farm chairmen should have greater latitude to violate centrally established plans, thus utilizing the native wisdom and practicality of the Russian peasant. He insists that the peasant should retain his psychological identity: "A peasant should remain a peasant regardless of whether he rides a horse or an automobile, tills the land with a hand plow or a tractor, milks cows and shears sheep by hand or electrically." In order to do this, the peasant must have a *proprietary* interest in the land. He must feel, however, that he earns his living on the kolkhoz, and not on his private plot. To sustain a proprietary feeling while devoting himself to the collective with his full energy and creative initiative, he must have a sense of complete, democratic participation in the decisions that govern farm policy and management. It is impossible, and probably unthinkable, for a Soviet writer to advocate a return to the private ownership of land. Therefore Dorosh arrives at a compromise that, he thinks, combines the virtues of proprietorship with those of collectivity.

Because he feels that an intimate relationship of peasant and land is essential for the preservation of the national culture, Dorosh opposes the recent Soviet trend toward "agro-cities" – mammoth farms on which the agricultural workers are gathered together in towns. These, he feels, run counter to the national spirit, for "the land, and only the land, must decide where [the peasant] is to live." This opposition to centralization is based on his faith in rural tradition: "A village should be a village. A farmer should have some animals, a garden, so when he steps out of the house, the earth is right there." Furthermore Dorosh senses, no doubt, that the organization of huge farms is yet another implicit government admission of lack of confidence in the Russian peasant. He argues repeatedly against the practice of *commanding* the peasant, because it causes both economic and *human* losses: "injury to the faith of the rural worker in his strength, in his land." "I think that the collective farmers should be trusted more, their common sense, their experience," he says.

Dorosh recognizes that urbanization has brought advances that should not be denied the peasant. His suggestions for combining the best of both worlds are the following:

> I think that if the existing villages were contoured, given paved roads and protected against the ravages of subsoil water, and if this were done immediately, and then, after that, model plans that take the terrain into account were designed and modern houses were built in the villages with plumbing and running water, electricity, gas, central heating and telephones – after all the country homes around Moscow have all this, but for some reason or other the villages nearby do not, although there the people do not live only temporarily, during vacations, but permanently, for work – I think that if the owner of such a three or four room one-family house were able to buy a sturdy inexpensive automobile or motorcycle, which in our technological age could serve the great majority of the population not only as a means of transportation, but also as a source of pleasure, then there would be as many people living in the villages as are necessary for efficient farming.
>
> As for central and household services in such comparatively small modern villages, it would be no trouble at all for the car owner to drive 10 or 15 kilometers along a good road that is kept cleared in the winter to the center, where he could shop, order a tailor-made suit, go to a movie, see a doctor, sit in a cafe or restaurant, be seen. After all, residents of the big cities travel as far for the same purposes. And the children would be taken to and from school by special buses.

The poetry of Aleksandr Yashin has been discussed in Chapter 3. He became prominent as a prose writer in 1956, with the publication of the story "Levers," one of the most notable early works of anti-Stalinist rural fiction. Four peasants sit around a table in a smoky room at a collective-farm headquarters, griping casually but vehemently about local conditions. Regional officials do not trust the farmers or understand their problems, but merely issue uninformed orders without seeking their advice. The district Party Secretary is domineering, other officials are more interested in statistics than in actuality. The four peasants find themselves to be mere "levers" in the heartless machinery of government.

Presently, however, these four normal Soviet villagers are convened as the meeting of the local Party nucleus, whereupon they change into docile robots. Their complaints abruptly cease and they talk subserviently, using the same trite bureaucratic language as the presiding District Secretary. When the meeting closes, however, they step out of their Party roles and become once again warm and honest humans. Yashin's work is a dramatization, in the form of a short story written in third person, of precisely the kinds of rural problems and conflicts treated by Ovechkin, Troepolsky, and Dorosh in the form of sketches by a first-person narrator. In this sense Yashin's story is an early precursor of the fictional genres that largely replaced the countryside sketch in the sixties. In addition, it is a story of vigorous protest, which, among other things, portrays a segment of the Communist Party in an extremely critical light, and for this it was severely censured in the press.

In 1962 appeared two even harsher works of critical realism by Yashin – the long story "The Orphan" and the sketch "Vologda Wedding." The former is a study of the contradictory characters of two brother orphans raised in a village. The elder, Pavel, a lazy, glib opportunist who early masters a "command of the correct official phrases," is sent to the city for an education and becomes a worthless parasite. Shurka, the younger brother, who is bright, energetic and devoted, remains in the village and becomes an excellent worker, although his stubborn integrity earns him a reputation with local officials as a "troublemaker." The story's ending is depressing: Shurka, finally exasperated by Pavel's rottenness, gives his brother a thrashing; their native hut, symbol of a way of life, is broken up and Pavel takes his share of the lumber back to the city. Much of the supplementary thematic material in the story – illustrating the estrangement between rural and urban life, petty tyranny and bungling in farm management, and the distortions in a society that induces it to coddle and nurture a Pavel – is similar in emphasis and detail to that of Dorosh.

Yashin was excoriated for writing "Vologda Wedding," a particularly negative and depressing portrayal of the decline of peasant culture and morale. The setting is a remote northern village, the occasion a wedding, which the narrator witnesses unobtrusively from the background. What is most shocking is the misery and brutality of the populace, which is so de-moralized that wives compete with one another in boasting of their husbands' swinishness and police records. The sketch is rich in ethnic detail and, although its tone is unsentimental and even harsh at times (it is reminiscent in this respect of Chekhov's *Muzhiki*), its basic note is elegiac. The wedding itself becomes a device through which the narrator examines the status of peasant traditions, and he finds that they are fading, cor-rupted by the counterforces of change. Women and girls, for example, have either partially forgotten or have never learned the ritual songs, chants, and laments that have traditionally accompanied the ceremony, and the wedding parties of the bride and groom, which used to travel in gay troikas, are now delivered in trucks. The sketch is built on this sort of explicit and implicit contrast between the old and the new, and leaves the impression of a sorrow that is sometimes bitter and indignant, sometimes resigned.

In the April 1954 issue of *Novy mir* there appeared a remarkably frank crit-ical survey of postwar prose about the countryside, which accused Soviet writers specifically and in general of having falsified village life by glossing over its real problems and making it much prettier than it was in actual-ity.[1] The author was Fyodor Abramov, a young critic and teacher at Leningrad University who had written his dissertation on Sholokhov's *Virgin Soil Upturned*. The outspoken article in *Novy mir* earned him cen-sure from the presidium of the Writers' Union and, although he had been a Party member since 1945, established Abramov as a difficult person in the eyes of the authorities. Neverthless, he went on to serve as head of the department of Soviet literature at Leningrad from 1956 to 1960, when he abandoned his university career for full-time writing. Meanwhile his first novel, *Brothers and Sisters* (*Brat'ya i sestry*), had appeared in 1958.

Abramov's most controversial work was the story "Around and About" (1963), an unsparing treatment of a variety of rural deficiencies and evils. The story was denounced as anti-Soviet (it had an "incorrect ideological basis" and bore "the stamp of despondency, sorrow, hopelessness"),[2] and the Party organized in *Izvestia* a campaign of letters from farm workers protesting it. As a result, Abramov almost totally disappeared from publi-cation until the sequel to *Brothers and Sisters*, the novel *Two Winters and Three Summers* (*Dve zimy i tri leta*), ended his forced silence in 1968.

The important social content of Abramov's fiction has, particularly in the West, somewhat obscured the fact that he is an excellent writer. He was born and raised in a village deep in the Arkhangelsk forests, and all his fiction is based on his first-hand knowledge of the hard life on northern farms. His prose is lean and precise, packed with vividly tangible, concrete details of ordinary village existence. Although his themes are closely bound to the folk character and rural social currents, he avoids decorating his narrative with superfluous local color. Abramov lovingly and intimately sustains the point of view of the peasants about whom he writes. He maintains a close psychological proximity to his characters through extensive use of interior monologue and quasi-direct discourse. The language of his third-person narrator, as well as that of his characters, is richly infused with local dialect, which imparts a poetic aura and a sense of community to the whole.

A number of Abramov's short stories about Northern peasants are simply affectionate studies of a people and their culture and are not concerned with immediate social issues. Such is "To St. Petersburg for a Sarafan," in which an 83-year-old *babushka* recalls her lone journey as a young girl to the capital – a distance of 1,500 kilometers – to buy a bit of finery. Her adventure has become a local legend. Entirely different is "Around and About," in which a kolkhoz chairman makes the rounds of his village trying to recruit people for extra work to get in the hay in an emergency. He meets with universal foot dragging and outright refusal until he inadvertently makes a drunken promise to increase the year's dividend by an amount that will enable the farm members to keep private cows. On the strength of this slip, the whole village shows up early the next morning and swiftly brings in the harvest. This ending adds ironic emphasis to Abramov's depiction of general malaise on a collective farm, whose symptoms are indolence, absenteeism, procrastination, malingering, and drunkenness. There are chronic departures to work in the timber industry or government service, and the majority of peasants spend most of their time in private enterprises – building houses for themselves and tending private plots. Although the story is unsparing in its treatment of the moral deficiencies of the peasants, it is humane in disclosing the source of their low morale and discontent – a malfunctioning Party and government.

Brothers and Sisters is a novel of the village in World War II. The hamlet of Pekashino in the Arkhangelsk region is remote from the front, but the quiet suffering and self-sacrifice of its inhabitants are herioc nevertheless. Particularly arduous is the lot of women, who must sustain the village virtually by themselves. The novel is a compassionate and proud account of the moral resources that held the village together under harrowingly difficult conditions. Its sequel, *Two Winters and Three Summers*, carries on the story of Pekashino in the early postwar years.

If *Two Winters and Three Summers* had been written by Aleksandr Solzhenitsyn, it would have immediately been translated in the West and proclaimed a masterpiece on the order of "Matryona's Home." The novel has the same mixture of tragic compassion and indignation as Solzhenitsyn's story, no less narrative grace and power, and a much more intimate feeling of identification with the peasant spirit. It is a work that simultaneously depresses and inspires: a combination of fate and governmental callousness places people in a hopeless situation; they endure it only through amazing strength of will and devotion. Its publication in 1968 can only have been possible because the story and the indictments it makes are fairly remote in time, safely tucked away in the Stalinist past.

Pekashino is devoid of men. Those who did not die in the war are away working in the forests or on timber rafts. The poverty is total: the village has exhausted most of its food and property in the war. There are no lamps and no matches; what little grain there is has to be ground by hand, and many are shoeless. Often the only thing that keeps a family from going under is their cow. Isolated and backward, the farm has been given no tractors, and even a motorcycle is a sensation.

An unscrupulous government, which promised better times, is exploiting the peasants by demanding even harder work and greater sacrifices. Power and pressure put on local Party officials from above have made most of them callous. Their function is to falsify figures, to make things look good to their superiors. They have no need to consider their inferiors, who may be subjected to heartbreaking, impossible production goals and betrayed at will. For the village the regional center is a source of evil – crippling demands and corruption. Those few local Party members who do assume leadership and responsibility do so only out of an earthy, parochial feeling for their community, and they are otherwise ideologically passive and indifferent. The only genuine source of moral support for the village is the sense of solidarity that comes from having lived, worked, and suffered together, speaking the same dialect and thinking the same thoughts. Abramov portrays this age-old feeling of mutual dependence and confidence especially beautifully at the family level.

Undramatic in manner, the novel is built on an accumulation of everyday situations – wood felling, the death of a cow, haggling over scraps of meat at the local market. The scenes of incessant, arduous labor (often without shoes!) on poor and unproductive soil are particularly poignant –

even such labor offers no hope of escape from the drab and cheerless poverty. Occasionally the characters pause to admire nature, but for the most part Abramov uses the quiet beauty of the setting to emphasize the unnaturalness of their anguish. One views them with both admiration and pity: such noble people, on such a lovely earth, should not be forced to suffer so.

Abramov has populated Pekashino with a large number of interesting and carefully individualized characters. The point of view alternates among a few of them, chiefly Mikhail Pryaslin, who is a youth of eighteen at the novel's beginning and a man of twenty at the end. The war has robbed Mikhail of a childhood: his father died at the front, and from the age of fourteen Mikhail has done a man's share of farm labor and has been the main support of his mother and her numerous smaller children. Despite his terribly hard work, premature responsibilities, and constant anxiety (he often worries at night over what he will eat the next day), Mikhail has not lost his youthful sensitivity and imagination. He is responsive to nature (most of the nature descriptions are from his point of view), and he dreams of making a life for himself.

He could do this by abandoning the village, rejecting farm labor for easier and more profitable work. This would break up his family, however, and sever his ties to the soil and his native environment. Despite his frustration, Mikhail makes an almost instinctive moral decision to resist the allurement of a "better" life and remains true to his family obligations and his peasant destiny. He makes another, hauntingly similar moral decision when he angrily and sorrowfully accedes to the marriage of his sister Liza to his renegade friend Egorshka. Having found a soft job in the regional center, Egorshka in effect buys Liza by offering to sell his motorcycle for money to purchase a family cow the Pryaslins desperately need.

Mikhail is a unique and formidable hero. His situation is pathetic because he is completely tied down and because society provides him no honorable opportunity to realize his potential. Honest, devoted, and strong, he is mature beyond his years because of the enormous responsibility that has been thrust upon him. He differs from the usual Soviet positive hero because he lacks the standard ideological stamp: he simply does bravely what he *has* to do. Because of his uniqueness, nationalistically inclined critics have claimed something especially and outstandingly *Russian* in his character. The assumption is that no other people in the world have his qualities, at least in such abundance. ("Faithfulness like this, of course, is the very deepest riddle of the Russian character for foreigners.")[3] Such critics tend to ignore the intent of the novel, which is to protest against the kind of governmental abuse and neglect that force a Mikhail to suffer as he does.

There are other victims. An Old Believer, an illiterate but valuable member of the village, is hounded and exiled on a spurious charge of spreading religious, antistate propaganda. (Like many village writers, Abramov implicitly urges respect, if not for organized religion, then at least for the religious impulse.) A victim in another sense is Egorshka, whose role is that of Mikhail's chief foil and antipode. Resourceful, enterprising, and charming, he is also an opportunist who becomes an exemplary Komsomolets, is heaped with honors from the district center, and rapidly decays both morally and ideologically.

Vladimir Soloukhin (born 1924) is both poet and prose writer, well placed in the Soviet literary establishment, and extremely prolific. He often writes, in one and the same context, about antiquity, the magical beauty of the countryside, and urgent social and agricultural matters. He has traveled extensively outside the Soviet Union as well as within it and, although he is clearly identified with the nationalist or Russite stream in contemporary literature, his cultural interests are broad. It is perhaps his intellectual eclecticism and literary versatility that make it difficult to define precisely his positions on many matters. He can be viewed as both a reactionary and a liberal, a narrow chauvinist and an enlightened nationalist, a writer of countryside protest and one who glosses over village problems. Above all, he is a very energetic writer and often a masterful one.

Soloukhin was born of a peasant family in a village in the Vladimir region, graduated as an instrument maker from the Vladimir Engineering Technicum in 1942, and served in the army from 1942 to 1945. He attended the Gorky Literary Institute from 1945 to 1951 and then became a magazine feature writer. Although he originally gained prominence as a poet and continues to be one, he has devoted increasing attention in the past twenty years to essays and fiction. His best-known work is *Vladimir Country Roads* (*Vladimirskiye proselki*, 1957), a collection of sketches based on a summer's walking tour with his wife through his native region. A related collection of sketches, *The Dewdrop* (*Kaplya rosy*), was published in 1960. His partly autobiographical novel, *Coltsfoot* (*Mat'-Machekha*) came out in 1964, and 1966 saw the magazine publication of *Letters from the Russian Museum*, a work so controversial that it was heavily cut by censorship when it appeared in book form in 1967. His *Black Boards* (*Chernye doski*), a group of personal essays about icon collecting, was published in 1969. All along, he has published numerous short stories, essays, and travel notes as well as poems, and has been active as an official of the Writers' Union.

Nature is the theme of most of Soloukhin's verse, and the best passages in his prose are about nature. It is lyrical prose, the confession of a closely attentive and sensitive observer who is in love with the Russian countryside and wants the whole world to share his joy and delight in its charm. Often, as in *Vladimir Country Roads*, it has the flavor of rediscovery: the narrator, who has become urbanized, returns to his native region and perceives its beauty with a new and special intensity. Soloukhin has acknowledged a debt to Turgenev and, like Turgenev, knows the precise names of all living things, is alert to their exact color and aroma, and creates landscapes that combine the talents of the naturalist, the ethnographer, and the poet. But in celebrating the countryside, Soloukhin is also searching (sometimes nostalgically or even elegiacally, as in parts of *The Dewdrop*) for some primordial source. The poet hero of *Coltsfoot*, for example, is saved from suicide only by roaming the fields and woods and contemplating the eternal, elemental dignity and beauty of the Russian land. And when Soloukhin argues the superiority of the Russian white birch over the palm tree, his discrimination of flora has an ideological ring.

Soloukhin's reverence for Russian folk culture is similar to that of the village writers previously discussed. Throughout his prose there are appeals for the preservation, and often the restoration, of precious traditional national values. He regrets the decline of folk arts in the village. He harps on the practical and especially the spiritual importance to a peasant family of milk cows, and rhapsodizes on the wonderful smell of their manure. For him the most essential peasant qualities are a taste for the land and a love of working it. Mowing is arduous, but it is also the most friendly and communal work in the village. The author asks himself:

> what is hidden in it, in the age-old work of the farmer, which is the very hardest and not the most rewarding, but so attracts a man that even with one foot in the grave he takes that very same scythe with which he mowed in his youth, and goes forth and mows and even cries for joy.

Soloukhin carefully avoids idealizing the peasant in his bucolic surroundings, and he candidly reports on apathy and slovenliness where he finds it. He writes that when the authorities order that crops be sown that the kolkhoznik knows to be unsuitable, his reaction is: "Well, all right, I'll do it – it's not my worry." Also Soloukhin observes farm machinery rusting in the fields all winter and milking sheds so dirty that the milk is brown with manure. His description of a village club in *Coltsfoot* is bitterly satirical, and in *The Dewdrop* he argues the pitiful need for educated, talented people to head such clubs. He complains of the barbaric noise in village streets and the bloody fist-fights and drunken brawls that happen there. At times he rivals Troepolsky in the irony and sarcasm with which he points out the shortcomings of peasant behavior.

There are accounts of administrative corruption and injustice. Village stores are woefully understocked compared to those in the cities. The kolkhoz must give its produce to the government "practically free," and the peasant must buy flour at the stores for thirty times the price he received for his wheat. As for this price, "it would be better if it were entirely free; then it would be clear to the kolkhoznik that he has to give it over to the government – period." Much of the peasant's difficulty comes from centralized mismanagement. Because of rigid planning from above, planting orders come, without consultation or discussion, in the form of unalterable directives. With no voice in the matter, the kolkhoznik loses interest and incentive. The result is low productivity and low pay, which in turn drives the peasant to his private plot and livestock. But even these do not save him:

> They collected a tax on every apple and cherry tree, and the trees were dug up by the roots so that they wouldn't have to pay for them. Whole orchards disappeared from the face of the earth. They collected a tax on cows, and the cows disappeared, so that the village herd consisted mostly of goats.

Despite the sharpness of his criticism, Soloukhin's position is not a radical one. He is quick to note that various reforms have made the village more spruce and prosperous, and he does not propose any fundamental changes in the agricultural system. He lightly passes over the historical background of horror in the collectivization drive of the 1930s, and subtly ignores several aspects of the more recent rural scene. He argues, in the face of much of his own evidence, that true democracy exists in the village. Such inconsistency is characteristic of his political-literary conduct in general. The novel *Coltsfoot* is distinctly and explicitly anti-Stalinist throughout, and is a startlingly bold, often wickedly satirical indictment of a wide variety of authoritarian, police-state attitudes and institutions. *Letters from the Russian Museum* has several equally arresting passages of daringly unorthodox opinion. Yet Soloukhin was active in the persecution of Pasternak after the latter was awarded the Nobel Prize, and quarreled with Evtushenko's liberal, "Western" views in the 1960s. Soloukhin would seem to be ruggedly independent, a writer with an unusual combination of attractive and repulsive opinions.

Soloukhin is the most prominent contemporary writer of nationalist orientation, but he carefully dissociates himself from extreme reactionary positions and cultivates a tone that combines reason, outspokenness, and common sense. Although his writings are occasionally somewhat daring in their affectionate backward glance at controversial aspects of the Russian past, he represents in general an officially tolerated nationalism. He waxes indignant over the mindless Soviet obliteration or distortion of the historical record. In *Letters from the Russian Museum* he writes that:

> in 1961 on an illustrious day there did not appear in a single newspaper of our country a single line that would have reminded us that a hundred years had passed since the days of the abolition of serfdom. An event of enormous historic importance. It is as if we were not glad that the horrible, barbaric serfdom was finally abolished.

He sarcastically notes that Obiralovka, the station where Tolstoy's Anna Karenina ended her life by throwing herself under a train, "has been renamed, given a very fresh and original name – Railroad." At times he can be abusively defensive on behalf of his cultural heritage. Deploring the fact that a Leningrad exhibit of contemporary American architecture, organized by the U.S. State Department, received considerable fanfare, whereas the museum of old Russian art in the same city is given, he feels, meager publicity, he writes:

> I ask: why can we permit the conducting in Leningrad of organized, well-planned propaganda for an architectural style alien to us (and to man in general), while we fear to popularize ancient Russian art even a thousandth as much? The American exhibit turned up here in the role of a self-satisfied, well-fed, sleek, but in general rather vulgar daughter, and our native art in the role of a shabby Cinderella.

Soloukhin frankly avoids attempting a scientific or scholarly definition of a "nation" or a "people" and writes that "for me, personally, a people [*narod*] is that which they have created and accomplished in the course of many-centuried history." Feelings of national consciousness are essential to any people, he argues, for without them:

> no mechanical agglomeration of people will be capable of an historical action; either to defend its independence by winning a war

or to accomplish a revolution, or to build a new society, or, more-over, to create and hand down to descendants a system of ethical and moral ideals, without which the full-blooded life of any soci-ety is impossible.

By way of illustration, he offers long, rhetorical catalogues of Russian attainments from antiquity to the present, listing the building of cities an-cient and modern, military heroes and victories, monuments of folklore and literature, famous Russian dissidents and rebels, and dozens of writers, poets, artists, composers, scholars, scientists, and musical and theatrical performers. He also lists numerous items of Russian national art and custom: types of utensils, furniture, dwellings, dress and decoration, songs and dances, and various kinds of oral folklore, such as the epos, riddles, and proverbs. His chief interest, however, is in medieval Russian architecture.

Soloukhin is strongly opposed to the notion of an international culture. He feels, in fact, that the chief danger threatening contemporary Russian art is denationalization. Tacitly defending himself against the possible ac-cusation of being an aesthetic isolationist, he argues that "a writer can be interesting to other peoples, can be international, only to the degree that he expresses the soul and character of his own people." He further insists that aesthetic *innovation* not based upon national cultural tradition is fruit-less.

These views contrast with those of Dorosh, whose interest in Russian culture and antiquity run parallel to those of Soloukhin. Dorosh objects to those who scorn contemporary foreign architecture, "thinking it indis-pensable to return to national architecture, naively supposing that any sort of style that has departed into history, upon being counterfeited, will take on the force of living art." Dorosh writes:

> Art, of course, is always national, but it is also always contempo-rary, in other words it is connected to the spirit of the times, with the dominant ideas of the epoch, and only on those occasions when a people, to its misfortune, is for some reason excluded from the culture that is being created by all humanity, its art becomes exotic, even though it may be respectable academism.

The comments of Dorosh, I suspect, are a veiled protest against neo-Stalinist exclusiveness and isolationism in contemporary Soviet practice. They were made, however, in a more deeply historical context. Like Soloukhin an admirer of medieval Russian architecture, Dorosh has pointed out that the ancient Russian churches were designed under a strong Byzantine influence. In all of Dorosh's writings there is a quiet but firm appeal to Russians to respect other cultures and interact with them. He speculates, for example, on the beneficial effects of Greek and Mongol influences on the Russian national character and culture and points out, further, that "the culture of Ancient Rus was part of the great pan-European culture" of the time. But Dorosh is by no means an extreme internationalist. He differs from Soloukhin mainly in degree and direction of emphasis: Soloukhin stresses the national, Dorosh the international *within* the national.

Soloukhin is an insistent, and most articulate, propagandist for the preservation of historic monuments. He is indignant at the sight of old bell towers being torn down for bricks with which to build factories, deplores the razing in the Kremlin of the first stone building in Moscow, and observes sorrowfully that more than 400 architectural monuments in Moscow alone have been senselessly obliterated. Although Moscow was once "the most original, unique city on earth," he prefers Leningrad, a much younger city that has nevertheless been allowed to retain much of its originality. He lashes out against the postrevolutionary practice of renaming old cities, squares, and streets after Russian and Soviet heroes, notes sarcastically that "Florence was not renamed Dantegrad," and proposes that the original place names be immediately restored.

Like Dorosh, Soloukhin is particularly fond of Russia's ancient churches. He writes that those in the Arkhangelsk and Vologda regions are "wooden fairy tales" and "stone songs," observes that "the ancient masters in a surprising way knew how to bring the creations of their hands into harmony with the surrounding locality," and concludes wistfully that "with the disappearance of the village churches the Russian landscape becomes somewhat poorer." "In my view," he adds, "it would be better to achieve a cessation of services in all churches but preserve them as architectural monuments than, in our struggle with religion, to permit all the ancient churches that are not operating to fall to pieces."

His views on religion itself seem ambiguous. On the one hand, he believes that religious art should be viewed historically, in terms of aesthetic qualities that have a purely human measurement and significance. On the other hand, he argues that icons are "simply prayers" and that "what is depicted on the board corresponds completely to the mood, the spiritual condition of the man who is praying." The religious essence of an icon is a special something, which eludes art historians who rely only on the analysis of line, color, composition, and subject. Soloukhin comments sarcastically that "the fact that religion is ignorance and darkness should have been suggested to the artists when they painted, or even before they painted." Such an argument sounds like an implicit defense of religion, for at the very least it conveys a tolerant respect for religious inspiration. It is typical of Soloukhin, however, that on such a sensitive subject as religion he should appear inconsistent and evasive.

It is of course possible for a writer to be close to the soil and to maintain an affectionate interest in the people of the countryside without feeling an obligation to purvey a social message. Such is Evgeny Nosov, who was born (1925) in Central Russia and still lives in Kursk. A war veteran, Nosov has also written a number of stories about the military. "The Red Wine of Victory" is set in a hospital on VE Day, where the narrator is recovering from wounds, and simply and touchingly examines the reactions of a ward of maimed soldiers to the news of victory.

Nosov's greatest strength is in the portrayal of people in the out-of-doors, at work in the fields or otherwise in an intimate relationship with nature. "Var'ka" is the charmingly sensitive story of a teenage girl who tends ducks on a kolkhoz, as she experiences a first mysterious transport of romantic eroticism. She goes swimming at night, has a simple supper of luscious tomatoes beside the pond, wanders through the night to a camp-fire where a young gypsy herdsman dances for her, then impulsively gallops away on one of his horses, is chased by him, and finally runs back to her village. The story is a delightful, unpretentious, but psychologically refined portrayal of the innocent awakening of the desire for sexual expression in a youthful spirit. Nosov's rendering of the natural setting and the power it exerts on the girl is closely observed, delicately haunting, and reminiscent of Turgenev in its evocation of the wonder and poetry of life.

Nosov's plots have an open-ended, almost accidental quality, consisting of events that in themselves, as a rule, have no unusual importance. What infuses them with meaning is the evident authenticity of his characters and his language (both narrative and dialogue are flavored with local speech), and his gift for precise emotional detail. He features kind and simple people. The milkmaid Anisya goes to a fair in a nearby city to show her three cows. Timid, dazed by the urban crowds, she is taken to a fancy restaurant and sees there a waitress who had been one of Anisya's fellow milkmaids but had been expelled from the kolkhoz for cheating. Later, they reminisce and discuss changes in the village, after which the selfless, devoted Anisya goes contentedly home. However, there are elements of sober nostalgia in Nosov, governed by an unsentimental realization that the patriarchal way of life of the village is gone forever. In "Beyond the Dales, Beyond the Forests" the narrator visits a tiny, remote village and finds, to his sorrow, that its inhabitants have lost their traditional arts and crafts (even an old babushka is fooled by a fake icon), and that the church has ceased to be the village social center.

Yuri Kuranov (born 1931) specializes in gemlike miniature sketches of nature, persons and customs of the countryside past and present. He is lyrical and meditative, and prefers to concentrate briefly and intensely on discrete phenomena, capturing their essence, trenchantly suggesting their significance, and then passing on. Few of his sketches are more than two pages in length, and many are no more than four or five lines. His language is compressed and poetic, but easy and graceful. Unsentimental and disciplined, he is nevertheless a loving writer with a deep respect for his subjects.

Kuranov merely hints at the large social, ideological, and cultural issues of the countryside. Clearly he is not aloof from them, but he is more inclined toward affectionate appraisal of what *is* than toward polemics over what should be. He celebrates northern nightingales, modestly details the feelings their singing arouses in him, and tells what distinguishes them from nightingales in other regions. Two swallows build a nest in the attic where the author has his room, and he watches their antics with amused admiration. Rain, storm clouds, birch trees, and the smells and rustling of the seasons are described in precise emotional shadings. Here, in its entirety, is a piece entitled "Autumn Hum":

> I have heard it many times. In fact it is not even a hum. Suddenly it begins to seem that a movement arises over the whole forest: someone is leaping, bursting through a thicket. And then it is all transformed into thin distant sounds. Now it is barking dogs racing through a fir grove, now the distant ringing of bells. They ring as in ancient cities, when ships sail up with tall and elegant sails.
>
> The wind rises, the forest trembles from top to bottom, and the sounds blend again into a distant hum, recalling the sound of long sea waves scattering over the sand.

For several years Kuranov lived in Siberia, and the group of sketches entitled "On Steep Slopes" records his impressions of the Siberian atmosphere, way of life, and traditions, and of the qualities of human nature that are nurtured there. More recently he has lived in and written about northern parts of European Russia, where he often wanders on foot for a close-up and detailed view of things. He describes the standard village loudspeaker as it sounds at different times, compares newly built village log houses to ships at anchor, laconically and observantly sketches interesting people he notices. In "A Man on a Road" he writes of an elderly landscape artist who can often be seen walking to a nearby village to get cardboard for his painting. The alert old man has walked this road a thousand times, but it always has something new for him.

Kuranov is not as successful with short stories as he is with miniatures. The commitment to a conflict involving imaginary characters, to developing a plot, and to curbing his own personal lyricism, seems to thin out his perceptions. But when he writes a story in which he subjectively identifies with his surroundings and concentrates on a single mood, it can be subtly moving. "High Water" is a tale of a man stranded alone in flood time. In the silence various birds and animals come and go. A wolf floats by on a raft. A cutter hauling a barge appears, but the narrator does not ask to be "saved." His loneliness gives him a strange peace, a haunting enjoyment.

The single agrarian novel most talked about in the sixties was Vasily Belov's *That's How It Is* (*Privychnoe delo*, 1966). It became a touchstone for the expression of various critics' views on contemporary countryside fiction and on the peasant experience in general. Belov was born in 1933, in a village in the Vologda region, worked as a joiner and a mechanic on electric motors, served in the army, had experience as a newspaper writer and regional Komsomol secretary, and attended the Gorky Literary Institute from 1961 to 1963. His first volume was a book of poems in 1961, and he has continued to publish poems occasionally in regional newspapers. However, he is best known for his several volumes of prose fiction that have appeared from 1963 to the present.

All of the topics previously mentioned in this chapter that have come to be associated with countryside literature can be found in Belov's stories. What is notable in his treatment of them is the tragic and yet affirmative light he casts on them. He concentrates intensively on the moral structure of the village, its difficult life, and the injustices that individual peasants seem fated to endure. But in their very endurance he finds a conquering nobility that transcends the bitterness of their destinies.

In the story "Spring" the world of the peasant Ivan Timofeevich collapses. Shortly before the war's end his third and last son is killed, and his wife dies of grief. His meager household is finally wiped out when the family cow and mare die of starvation. He tries to hang himself, but the milkmaid Polina, herself a war widow, finds him and frees the noose. The two of them weep as they hear a spring stream gurgling behind the barn – "and the land quietly breathed, awaiting human hands." Ivan Timofee-vich softly says to himself: "You have to live." A less painful version of the same thought is in the story "Former Years." An old peasant of the Mur-mansk district goes to a neighboring village to trade a cow and discovers that the widow he is to deal with is his former fiancée, whom he has not seen in thirty years. They reminisce and learn that both have had hard lives, have lost children in the war, and are tired and lonely. Although their love had long been forgotten, they wish each other well and are affec-tionate. Their chance meeting has been bittersweet, the summing up and nearly the final punctuation mark in two similarly arduous lives, and they accept their fates as a matter of fact, with quiet dignity.

Belov finds an essential good in the leisurely rhythms of peasant exis-tence: planting and harvesting; love, marriage, and children; the cares of daily life and the quiet acceptance of death. Like most village writers, he stresses the value of stable traditions and, especially, of labor in intimate relationship to the soil. The natural setting, as it interacts with men, is a fundamental and integral part of this system of good. As a beginning writer Belov did not escape the temptation to sentimentalize and idealize this bucolic routine. His mature works, however, show a sober critical awareness of rural backwardness and stagnation and of the governmental abuse that has made village life a hell for many. The narrator of "A Car-penter's Stories" (1968) is a 35-year-old engineer who left his village as a youth so angry and frustrated with the local bureaucracy that he hated his very birthplace.

As the years passed, the engineer's attitude mellowed, and he more often remembered the good things he had left behind. His return to his native haunts on a vacation visit frames "A Carpenter's Stories." (Such visits have now become a convention in countryside literature.) The mo-tive for his return is a combination of nostalgia, curiosity, and the psycho-logical need to find an alternative to the urban style of life, which also dis-turbs him. It is not, however, a pendular reaction against the city – he simply finds something spiritually lacking in his present existence and hopes to find a moral supplement for it in the calm and simplicity of the village. He is not disappointed – the good things of the countryside are as he remembered them. But he finds that he himself has become so citified that he often feels clumsy and inept in village social situations and is ill equipped with the practical, manual skills and knowhow that are second nature to the self-reliant peasant. Furthermore, he learns from observing and listening to two old men (who embody much of the history of the Soviet countryside and personify the peasant's good and bad qualities) that the price of survival in the village is either an opportunistic, selfish cunning, which he finds repulsive, or a patience and resignation which, although admirable in itself, seems out of place in the latter half of the twentieth century. He concludes that a good way of life, with its precious traditions, is doomed, and he views the uncertain future with foreboding.

Belov is more concerned with capturing the village character and atmosphere through full and detailed accounts of ordinary persons and their activities than he is in dramatic episodes or pointed conflicts. As a consequence, his stories appear loosely structured and digressive, with a minimum of plot. The narration is oriented to the natural harmony of peasant life, conceived as a broad stream, and it tends to be inclusive and tangibly circumstantial. The tone is calm and measured, in subtle correspondence to the deliberate tempo of rural existence, and the point of view is close to that of the peasant himself. This he achieves by approximating his narrator's language to that of his characters, and through extensive interior monologue. Also he lets his country folk speak for themselves, by standing aside as much as possible and simply listening to them. The narrator's language, as well as the dialogue and interior monologue, is based on the colorful vernacular of the Vologda region – not as an ethnographic display by the author but as a means of achieving a maximally intimate and authentic intonation.

Characters in Belov's stories are also presented in a fashion that corresponds to the kind of society they live in. We know them, except for a few intimate and subjective details, just as their neighbors do, on the basis of close, daily acquaintance in one small community. This kind of comprehension makes it natural and easy to understand the sources of their conduct and to avoid quick and categorical judgments about them. Such a perspective is particularly important in viewing Belov's most famous and controversial character, Ivan Afrikanovich of *That's How It Is*.

A war veteran, devoted to but trapped by a large family and heavily dependent on his extremely hardworking and selfless wife Katerina, Ivan Afrikanovich works indefatigably in the fields all day and then secretly mows hay in the forest at night for the all-important family cow. The hay is discovered in his loft and confiscated, and he is threatened with criminal prosecution. This misfortune, an accumulation of injustices he has suffered, and the threat of starvation for his family, drive him to a desperate acceptance of his brother-in-law's proposition that the two of them go to the city of Murmansk to look for work. His attempt to break out of the vicious circle of grinding collective-farm poverty proves futile, and he soon returns to the village, only to learn that his Katerina has died. After burying her, he wanders into the forest in a suicidal mood, and only the experience of being lost in the woods, the elemental challenge of finding his way out, and ultimately the terror of death, convince him that "It is better to have been born than not to have been." He has lived through the war, terrible postwar privation and discouragement, and heartbreaking loss, and as the novel ends he has resolved simply to endure without the slightest hope of improving his lot or that of his many children.

The novel can be and has been interpreted variously, but it is certainly something more than the lugubrious and philanthropic account of a peasant's misfortune. Perhaps it is primarily a story of love – the steadfast devotion of Katerina, whose faith kept the family together and whose example in death gives Ivan the courage to continue. Continuity, in fact, is a major theme of the novel – the endless renewal of life that comes from the soil. Ivan's return from Murmansk is the correction of a peasant's aberration, a literal but also a symbolic return to the soil.

The traits of character in Ivan Afrikanovich have been the subject of considerable disputation among Soviet critics. Belov has been taken to task for making him too "timid" and "socially passive." Certainly Ivan is ignorant and almost completely devoid of civic awareness – indifferent to anything that takes place beyond the outskirts of his village. As a man of the soil, he clearly gets spiritual enjoyment from his labor, but in fact he is industrious because he has no alternative. Ivan is no saint: he gets involved in a reckless and destructive drunken spree with his brother-in-law, and has not been entirely faithful to Katerina. But his strength is in the power of his love for his wife and children, his quiet patience, and his devotion to personal duty. And for all his faults he has a natural spiritual delicacy and great humanity.

Interpretations of the character of Belov's hero form an interesting nationalistic spectrum – from those who find his image an insult to Soviet Russian dignity to those who, like Dorosh, found that "all his good qualities are rooted in the occupation which he inherited from his ancestors – in peasant labor, in a way of life conditioned by this labor."[4] One enthusiast called the novel "a patriotic hymn to the millions of sowers and preservers of the Russian land."[5] Objecting to this messianic interpretation, another critic wrote that "it does not summon us to 'save' and 'be saved,' it teaches us to remember what exists."[6] One hopes that Belov himself is unmoved by such polemics, which are basically irrelevant to the evaluation of what is, regardless of ideological interpretations, a very moving work of art.

Viktor Likhonosov (born 1937) is of Siberian descent, and his stories, which began to appear in 1963, frequently have a Siberian village setting. As one of the youngest countryside writers, he also represents a recent tendency to use rural materials to focus on problems that are eternal and universal, and not intrinsically indigenous to the village. He writes of young love, the cares of a widowed mother, marital difficulties, the relations between adults and their aging parents. The social background is important, but private lives are the center of attention.

At the same time Likhonosov frequently reminds his reader that it is *Russians* who are experiencing these problems, and his works are prominently concerned with the folk spirit. His manner of emphasizing the peculiarly national cast of the psychology and moral values of his characters has irritated some critics, who find his persistent use of such terms as "common people's" (*prostonarodnyi*), "simple" (*prostoi*), "time-honored" (*starinnyi*) and "ancient" (*drevnii*) is merely an easy and rather pretentious shorthand. Likhonosov seems to feel, one of them argued, that to a noun such as "woman" it is merely necessary to add "the all-powerful epithet '*Russian*' to give it a lofty, extraordinary meaning." The suggestion of superficiality is unfair. Likhonosov is a serious and talented writer, deeply concerned with and poetically sensitive to the peculiarities of his national culture.

Likhonosov's narrator is typically a young man who lives in the city but has strong village ties. He visits his old haunts, talks with his relatives and other people, and observes their way of life with a sympathetic but apprehensive eye. Often the narrator's function is that of a listener who records the stories and reminiscences of villagers, chiefly oldsters. What interests him most is the tension between countryside tradition and the forces of change; the vision is affectionate, tinged with sadness. The narrator thinks of himself as a connecting link between the rural culture of the past and the urban one of the present and future. Although he accepts the inevitability of a cultural transition, he hopes that the best of the old – the resilience and moral strength embodied in the peasantry – can somehow be preserved. His own function is as a kind of scribe who will perpetuate the memory of a dear but vanishing Russian mode of existence before it is too late. His style is quiet and conservative but warm and lyrical; the narrator's emotions and opinions, which are expressed frequently and freely, are those of the author.

The stories "Folks from Bryansk" (*Bryanskie*, 1963) and "Relatives" (*Rodnye*, 1967) are in this vein. More tragic is the short novel *On the Broad Street* (*Na ulitse shirokoi*, 1968), a portrait of the narrator's mother – a soldier's widow whose hard life was devoted to the single purpose of bringing up her son. She subordinated everything to this aim, bustling about in a state of undernourishment, going without sleep, marrying a second time and taking care of her husband's son for the sake of her own. She is both admirable and pitiful – worn out, prematurely aged, and finally made dull and apathetic by her self-sacrifice.

As the writing of Likhonosov suggests, the younger generation of village writers seems to have turned away from urgent social issues – maladministration and injustice on the collective farms and various forms of discrimination against and exploitation of the peasantry – and taken up somewhat broader cultural problems that obviously could not be solved by means of governmental remedies and reforms. The curtailment of immediate and direct social protest by village writers was no doubt largely the result of the increased conservatism of the literary atmosphere in the latter half of the sixties. But a mellower, less militant attitude in the use of village materials seems to have evolved gradually as well, and writers appeared to be more interested in telling stories and examining peasant character than in producing exposés.

An attractive and promising young writer of this inclination is Valentin Rasputin, a Siberian born in Irkutsk in 1937. Rasputin is an excellent storyteller, with a gift for combining interesting plots with psychological insight and trenchant rural detail. Like the best village writers, he has an accurate command of peasant speech and uses it extensively. In contrast to Likhonosov, he keeps his stories free of lyricism and authorial speculation on the significance of the situations he writes about. He makes no special plea for the virtues of the rural life he describes, and his narrator remains always in the background.

The story that brought Rasputin to prominence was "Money for Maria" (1967), whose hero is Kuzma, a kolkhoz chauffeur. Kuzma's wife, Maria, manager of the village store, is faced with a 1,000-ruble shortage at inventory time. The whole village knows that the couple are honest, and no one, including the inspector who made the inventory, thinks that Maria has stolen. Nevertheless the shortage exists, and Maria is given five days in which to find money to cover it, or face a five-year jail sentence. The story is mainly an account of Kuzma's efforts to round up the needed sum.

The kolkhoz is poor, and 1,000 rubles is a huge amount. Also, Kuzma is proud, and reluctant to ask money from his impoverished neighbors, though he does get a bit from them. The kolkhoz chairman helps by adroitly persuading every member to pledge a month's pay as collateral for a loan he is prepared to give Kuzma. But even this is insufficient, and Kuzma must go to the city to try to get the balance from his brother, with whom he has been out of contact for years. One of the finest parts of the story is his train trip: he must go first class because all other places are taken, and as a peasant he meets with scorn and condescension from other first-class passengers. The story ends abruptly as Kuzma is about to knock on his brother's door: we will never know whether or not Maria had to leave her husband and four young children and go to jail.

"Money for Maria" is written with unassuming compassion, leavened with humor and irony, and gives an impression of great social and cultural authenticity. In Kuzma's talks with his village friends and their reactions to his predicament, Rasputin deftly creates a series of incisive, realistic portraits of representative peasants. The same is true, though to a lesser extent, of the portraits of Kuzma's fellow passengers on the train. The psychology of Kuzma, a peasant in trouble, is sympathetically and vividly shown in his attitudes toward money, his wife, his family, and the community. In the circumstance of the village store itself – everyone is traditionally afraid to be its manager because of the possible dire consequences – there is a strong, though implicit, protest against the harshness of Soviet law.

In the past two decades the literature of the Russian countryside has been voluminous and varied, but two major and closely related preoccupations have been present in it with great consistency. The first of these is a concern for the economic and social welfare of the village, as shown in detailed accounts of the organization and day-to-day operations of farming, close study of the psychology and aspirations of the peasantry, and protest, either implied or direct, against the conditions under which the agrarian sector has been forced to exist. The second general area of concern has been cultural and broadly historical, involving an intensive examination, and usually a celebration, of folk traditions, values, and customs, and of Russian antiquity and cultural monuments. This latter preoccupation, largely nationalistic in orientation, represents to a great extent a search for values to replace those of a Marxist–Leninist ideology that quite obviously does not satisfy many fundamental spiritual needs.

The ramifications of countryside literature thus go far beyond the village itself. Nearly every specific issue it has raised and explored is directly related to broader problems of Soviet society. From 1954 to 1964, moreover, village literature achieved its new penetration and candor through the sufferance and even the encouragement of the Communist Party, which viewed it as a medium for the public discussion of ways and means to increase the productivity of agriculture. What the Party leaders perhaps did not realize at the outset was the power of suggestion inherent in this literature, the wider implications of its humane content.

By the early sixties, when it became clear that literature about agrarian discontent was alarming not only in its picture of the countryside itself but also in its suggestion of a much wider malaise in Soviet society, the authorities began to curb such literature. All along, writers such as Ovechkin, Yashin, and Abramov had been disciplined for overstepping permissible bounds. Now even Dorosh, clearly identified as a liberal but apparently never before harassed, had to wait for several years before the publication of the last sections of *A Village Diary*. One can be almost certain, moreover, that the only reason works such as Abramov's *Two Winters and Three Summers* and Boris Mozhaev's bitterly critical story, "The Life of Fyodor Kuzkin," could have been published in the late sixties was that they were set in the Stalin period and dealt with iniquities that were, presumably, past history. Many of the most critical works of village literature are set safely in the past – but the reader is free to draw his own conclusions as to how much of what is said applies to the present as well.

The present chapter has mentioned only the most prominent and representative members of a fraternity of village writers that is, in fact, huge. For reasons of economy such writers as Sergei Krutilin, Elizar Maltsev, Mikhail Zhestev, and many others have been ignored. In addition there are numerous authors – such as Tendryakov, Kazakov, Solzhenitsyn, Chingis Aitmatov, and Sergei Zalygin – who do not write exclusively about the village and will be dealt with elsewhere.

9

Literature reexamines the past

The death of Stalin and the ensuing Thaw provided an opportunity for revisions in Soviet citizens' conceptions of the past. Not only were writers given permission to make available new facts about and interpretations of the Stalin years; they were, for a time, mandated to do so. The authorities' immediate aim was to destroy the "cult of personality," to release creative energies that had been pent up during the decades of one-man rule, and to attribute the mass suffering and injustice of those decades to Stalin himself.

Several unplanned and unexpected developments resulted. Some writers, for example, chose not to write about the Stalin years but about previous periods of Russian history in the light of more flexible interpretations than those previously permitted. At times, these recastings of historical trends, personalities, and events simply provided cultural enrichment by adding new facts and attacking myths, and at others they made implicit or allegorical reference to the present. In addition, many authors, while ostensibly writing about the period of the "cult," were obviously aware, without mentioning the fact, that they were depicting evils still endemic, and even organic, to contemporary Soviet society. The new literature about the past, then, became to a great extent a literature of *pretending*, in which candor about the present was thinly covered by a veil of retrospection.

A composite plot summary of the typical novel in this vein would go something like this: the young hero, who entered the army as a mere boy and grew up under combat conditions in World War II, is either still at the front or recently demobilized. He soon discovers that the Stalinist peacetime world is unjust and corrupt, and under conditions of oppression and falsity he must test his values and chart a life course. He finds a girl who, as a rule, helps him to make an adjustment, but not before he has severely clashed with, and been temporarily defeated by, venal authorities in the bureaucracy or Party or both. The novel ends on the day Stalin dies (in some variants, with the opening of the Twentieth Party Congress) with the question: what use will the hero make of the new horizons?

Soviet authorities, however, have been reluctant to allow writers to dwell for long on the injustices of the past. Not only might this practice cultivate a dangerously large and depressing sense of national guilt; it might also uncover too many embarrassing skeletons. Moreover, brooding at length over the past might reveal that conditions have not improved as much as they are purported to have done. Writers have therefore been urged to feature the glories of the present and the promise of the future. But in the years of greatest liberalism (roughly 1956–66), the spirit of candor about the past among writers had developed to such proportions that it became extremely difficult to control. In consequence, writers such as Solzhenitsyn and several of those with whom the present chapter is concerned resorted to publication in *samizdat* or abroad.

An outpouring of reminiscences by writers who had witnessed nearly the entire twentieth century took place in the 1960s. Many writers, such as Lev Nikulin, presented merely a sentimental falsification of the past, adhering rigorously to official views of literary personalities and affairs, and served mainly to perpetuate Party-inspired mythology. Others, however, have greatly enriched the Soviet reader's knowledge of the literary scene. The more honorable of them evidently felt that there was much to be gained in a candid, detailed account and appraisal of one's life and times. Their memoirs served not only to correct the record in large measure but also to encourage a thorough reevaluation of the Soviet literary experience.

Most memoirists, conscious of the epic quality of the events they had lived through, dealt with more than purely literary affairs. Thus Ilya Ehrenburg's *People, Years, Life* (*Lyudi, gody, zhizn'*, 1961–5), eight years in the writing, is a vast historical panorama involving movements, periods and personalities – East and West – over a span of more than four decades. Although Ehrenburg, in response to attacks by reactionary critics in 1962 and 1963, disclaimed an historical purpose and called his work "not a chronicle but rather a confession," the work caused a sensation among Soviet readers with its accounts of Russian artistic schools and trends and of figures – such as Babel, Meyerhold, Mandelstam, and Tsvetaeva – previously either unmentionable or denied sympathetic treatment. His literary evaluations were excellent, his artistic taste highly sophisticated. Years of residence in Western Europe, moreover, had provided him with perspective, knowledge, and a host of acquaintances unfamiliar, exotic, and fascinating to his compatriots.

Although Ehrenburg was an interesting witness, he was an unreliable one. For all his apparent daring and veneer of sincerity, he was an expert in techniques of omission and euphemism, and he felt compelled to gloss over the most poignant and tragic phenomena of the Stalin period. (The censorship, of course, accounts to a great extent for his lack of candor.) An inveterate name dropper, he often produced secondhand, biased, or superficial portraits of individuals. Moreover, as a writer who not only survived the Stalin regime but profited by it, he seemed to be motivated by an uneasy combination of reverence for fallen fellow intellectuals and the desire to justify himself.

Another large, comprehensive account of the past is Konstantin Paustovsky's *The Story of a Life* (*Povest' o zhizni*, 1945–63). Devoted largely to the years before, during and immediately following the Revolution and civil war, these memoirs make fewer explicit judgments on people, events, and political and social developments than do those of Ehrenburg, but they seem more scrupulously reliable, based on things the author had seen and people he had known at firsthand. Paustovsky writes of people in general with affection but without sentimentality and, although he portrays literary persons he has known – notably Babel, Ilf, Bagritsky, and Bulgakov – he seems less impressed than Ehrenburg by his contacts with notables. Meditative, sensitive to the quality of existence at its everyday level, Paustovsky records the social change brought about by the Revolution but also subtly conveys a feeling of the continuity of a Russian way of life largely independent of historical events. He is a lyrical writer, digressive and romantic, with a special concern for nature. The value of his memoirs is their wealth of picturesque scenes.

More pointedly aesthetic in orientation than those of Ehrenburg or Paustovsky, the memoirs of Viktor Shklovsky, *Once Upon a Time* (*Zhili-byli*, 1962), offer a reconsideration of literary values and at least a partial refutation of the distortions in orthodox literary histories. Although his standards seem more specifically cultural than ethical, and although he avoids a discussion of the Stalinist years, Shklovsky's work is valuable in his emphasis on Russian literary accomplishments that had long been neglected. He writes of the 1910s and 1920s, stressing the richness and diversity in the literary activity of the two decades surrounding the Revolution. His first-hand reminiscences of critical schools (*Opoyaz*) and literary groupings (the Serapion Brothers), his detailed portraits of individual writers (Mayakovsky), and his uncompromising attempts at rehabilitating such abused figures as Khlebnikov and Eisenstein, all constitute a powerful argument for a widespread reassessment of the past.

Another memoirist who dwelt on the early years of the century was the genial and graceful Kornei Chukovsky, whose reminiscences took the form of portraits of individual literary figures he had known during his long life. Loaded with interesting personal anecdotes and sensitive critical appreciations, these portraits often extend beyond the individual to form commentaries on the literary situation of the time in general. Chukovsky is warm, expansive and engaging, with strong opinions and an evident, if indirect, compassion for the victims of oppression. In his portraits of Mikhail Zoshchenko and Anna Akhmatova, for example, Chukovsky discreetly omits the ugly facts of these writers' official persecution, but his perceptive and sympathetic tributes to their artistry mark him as their humane champion and the enemy of their enemies.

Less comprehensive and more fragmentary than most memoirs are Valentin Kataev's *The Holy Well* (*Svyatoi kolodets*, 1966) and *The Grass of Oblivion* (*Trava zabven'ya*, 1967) – highly mannered blends of fact, fiction, and semifiction governed by an intentionally jumbled chronology in a subjective attempt to recapture and understand past time. Both works are experimental in style and intensely personal, and in many respects they do not qualify precisely as memoirs. There is nevertheless a substantial foundation of actual experience in both books and an evident concern with the heritage of twentieth-century Russian literature. Kataev does not attempt to break new historical ground or to challenge the standard version of literary and social developments in the Soviet period. But in *The Grass of Oblivion* he juxtaposes portraits of the two writers he considers to have been most important for his formative years – Mayakovsky and Bunin – in a way that constitutes a plea for recognition of Bunin's literary importance despite his bitter opposition to the Revolution. However, Kataev could obviously have done much more to correct the record had he chosen to. It is even possible that, consciously or unconsciously, he selected a semifictional narrative posture to avoid the unpleasant challenge of complete candor.

The memoirs of Olga Berggolts, *Daytime Stars* (*Dnevnye zvezdy*, 1959), are somewhat similar in construction to those of Kataev, but they are less showily experimental, more passionate, and more trustworthy and convincing. Her narrative covers the period from her childhood through the siege of Leningrad in World War II. Neither chronological nor "logical" in structure, the work at times appears to be a loosely connected collection of notes, but it is unified by poetic association and by the strong, dignified spirit of the author. She sees her individual fate as a part of the common Russian destiny, so that in writing of herself as an enthusiastic Komsomolka in the 1920s, adorer of Lenin and Lermontov, activist poet and journalist, survivor of personal tragedies, and intimate witness of the terrible but heroic war years, she speaks at one and the same time for Olga Berggolts and for the Russian people. The work is rich in poignant scenes and episodes, such as her icy walk to visit her father through a hungry, frozen, and exhausted city of Leningrad, meeting starving fellow staggerers and corpses. Much of her own suffering over the years – the deaths of her children and husbands, political persecution that destroyed loved ones and imprisoned her for a period – is merely hinted at or touched upon. Pride, patriotism and, no doubt, the censorship prevent her from protesting. Nevertheless, *Daytime Stars*, a unique lyrical fusion of the private and the public, remains one of the most authentic, moving, and revealing recent books of memoirs.

The brief memoirs of Boris Pasternak, *I Remember* (1959), are subjective and cautious, and serve more as a commentary on himself than on his time and his contemporaries. Delicately perceptive in places, humane and sensitively reflective, they are essentially turned inward, a chronicle that perceives all life in terms of its effects on the author's self. The social turmoil and suffering, the intellectual repression that constituted the harsh truth of his generation, are subordinated to his meditations on his role as an artist. His comments on other writers are often laudatory and generous, but he is circumspect in dealing with crude realities. Of the fate of Marina Tsvetaeva, for example, he writes merely that "the general tragedy of the family exceeded my fears." For Pasternak a much more effective medium for evaluation of the past was the fiction of *Doctor Zhivago*.

It is evident that memoirists of this period, despite their concern for uncovering the truth and for rehabilitating not only individual writers but also a whole literary heritage, were inhibited by a combination of self-censorship and external, official censorship. This is true not only of the writers already mentioned but also of numerous others, such as Munblit, Slonimsky, Lidin, Rozhdestvensky, Kaverin, Marshak, Isbakh, Tikhonov, Selvinsky, and Shchipachev. Even the bravest memoirists taking pains to portray writers of the past (such as Khlebnikov and Babel) who had either been destroyed or placed under some form of interdict, stopped far short of telling the whole story.

Most memoirists were no doubt motivated in some measure by their feelings of guilt as survivors of Stalinism and wrote as a means of expiation. This may be true least of all of Nadezhda Mandelstam, who shared the sufferings of her poet husband until his final arrest and death, and who seems to have survived for almost the sole purpose of preserving his poetry and his memory and telling the story of his contemporaries. Her works are marked by a staunch ethical approach to life and by a fierce determination to convey the atmosphere of her times by telling the absolute truth. Utterly fearless and uninhibited by any hope of publishing her memoirs in the USSR, she is free of other memoirists' proclivities for ignoring, camouflaging, or softening the brutal aspects of Soviet reality. She has been the first to tell, thoroughly and in depth, the story of the literary intelligentsia (and, by implication, the *entire* intelligentsia) in utterly candid, harrowing detail.

The first volume, *Hope Against Hope* (*Vospominaniya*, 1970), mainly concerns her life with Mandelstam, including a cumulative portrait of the poet himself, comments on his poetry and views (compared and contrasted with those of his contemporaries), and an account of his fatal persecution. There is also much commentary on literary schools and personalities, social developments, and the gradual imposition of government control over intellectual life. The second volume, *Hope Abandoned* (*Vtoraya kniga*, 1972), is less concerned with her husband (although there is much about his poetry) and more with the author herself in the various stages of her life. This volume, too, contains a wealth of profound and fascinating observations on Soviet cultural history, literary groups, periods and trends, and numerous portraits of individuals – from famous writers to ordinary working people, for whom she has the deepest respect.

The dimensions of Nadezhda Mandelstam's memoirs are so great, and their ramifications so wide and deep, that they can only be viewed as many stories in one. A remarkable feature is the lucidity and comprehensiveness of her memory, which has retained and organized thousands of detailed impressions, unaided by diaries or other documentation that would have incriminated her during her decades in the semi-underground of flight, isolation, and exile. (It should nevertheless be noted that her memory, and her opinions as well, have been challenged in various quarters.) Her most persistent and probably most important story is of the decline and capitulation of the Soviet intelligentsia, which she dates in the time of Lenin shortly after the Revolution, in contrast to the prevailing opinion, which associates the decline with the consolidation of Stalin's power. Her explanation of Soviet intellectuals' failure successfully to resist their oppressors is detailed and intricate, but in sum it is an accusation of gradual moral compromise in which naked survival became the primary goal, with all other human values subordinate to it. She writes that "we all became slightly unbalanced mentally – not exactly ill, but not normal either: suspicious, mendacious, confused and inhibited in our speech" and adds that "leading a double life was an absolute fact of our age and nobody was exempt."

The story of the Mandelstams – man and wife and then wife alone – at first spiritually alienated from and then forcibly isolated from the literary establishment and respectable Soviet society, is bitterly told. Imbued with a firm and lofty conception of culture, she is viscerally indignant at those who threaten it. Her personal allegiance is to Acmeism – by which she means, in fact, everything her husband believed in – and her opinions, usually vehement, are governed by those beliefs. There are numerous descriptions and evaluations of schools, writers, and poets. The most prominent and intimate portrait, after that of Mandelstam himself, is of Anna Akhmatova, whom she pictures as proud, strong, passionate, vain, impetuous, and brave. Without intending it, however, Nadezhda Mandelstam has also created the vivid self-portrait of a woman who has loved with enormous courage and extraordinary constancy, who is truly cultured and literate in her own right (she is an extremely perceptive critic), and whom the direst, most persistent adversity could not break. Her memoirs are a truly great literary event, and they rank with the highest achievements of twentieth-century Russian literature.

Fictional treatments of the October Revolution and the events surrounding it have been a traditional preoccupation of Soviet literature. The Revolution has been central in the works of many of the most prominent writers, such as Mikhail Sholokhov, Konstantin Fedin, and Aleksei Tolstoy, as well as dozens of others over the years. As a rule such works have been written to indoctrinate and exhort, to remind readers of the epic significance of the upheaval. The historical inevitability of the Revolution and the moral and tactical correctness of the means used to achieve it have not been questioned. Recent historical novels about the Revolution and Civil War, however, while affirming the heroic cause, have featured characters and raised issues that cast doubt on the morality of revolutionary means. Often such characters and issues become a kind of critical metaphor in which the past can shed light on the present. Sergei Zalygin's novel *Salt Valley* (*Solyonnaya pad'*, 1968) examines a revolutionary leader who is dogmatic, suspicious, and dictatorial, and whose preference for dealing with political waverers through punitive measures rather than persuasion provides a powerful, though indirect, commentary on practices that survive to this day.

A more profound treatment of similar problems is Pavel Nilin's novel *Cruelty (Zhestokost'*, 1958 – published in English in 1959 under the title *Comrade Venka*). Set in 1922, it recounts events leading up to the suicide of Venka Malyshev, a young Cheka officer. Assigned the job of investigating a band of counter-revolutionary guerrillas, Venka develops sympathy for, and wins the confidence of, one of their leaders. Through careful persuasion, Venka brings his man to the verge of political rehabilitation and induces him to turn himself in. Venka's world is shattered when his superior officer callously betrays him by entrapping and arresting his man as a common political criminal. Venka, a highly moral idealist, has been the unwitting instrument of a colossally evil trick performed in what he has believed to be the cause of social justice. His fate is so poignant that it casts doubt on the inevitable rightness of the revolutionary process. With its sharp focus on a single moral issue – the issue of ends and means – the novel, although set in what is now a remote period, resounds to the present, unpoisoned by the false optimism and specious justifications that are typical of the literature of socialist realism. The story is the material of universal tragedy – by no means limited to a Soviet environment – but Venka's dilemma echoes loudly the Soviet Union today.

The most famous recent novel of the Revolution is Pasternak's *Doctor Zhivago*. The author submitted it for publication in *Novy mir* in 1956, was refused, and sent it to Italy, where it first appeared in translation in 1957. By 1958 the novel was so well known, in Russian and numerous other languages, that it won Pasternak the Nobel Prize, which the Soviet government forced him to reject. It is appropriate to discuss *Doctor Zhivago* in the present context because one of its most prominent aspects is its evaluation of the past. The evaluation is of a special kind – a very personal, lyrical statement about the entire complex of issues – historical, cultural, aesthetic, moral, ideological, and emotional – that interested the poet over his entire lifetime. It attempts to combine an historical epic with an intimate confession, uniting various layers of experience and belief. One of its distinguishing features is the depth of its cultural background and the author's extraordinary awareness and sensitivity to all things. The novel therefore transcends the bounds of the immediate and is much more than a documentation and interpretation of an historical era. Rather, it is an appreciation of the flow of life itself, both an interpretation of twentieth-century Russian history and a treatment of life that transcends history.

In rejecting *Doctor Zhivago* for publication, the editors of *Novy mir* wrote to the author that "the spirit of your novel is the spirit of nonacceptance of the socialist revolution." This statement is only partly true. The novel has very little to say about socialism as such, but the Revolution itself gradually assumes the quality of an evil force, directed against the rhythm of nature and stifling to the individual. It is also a strong polemic against a number of the tenets of Soviet ideology – the emphasis on rationality as the motivator of human behavior, the belief that the end justifies the means, and the demand that Soviet citizens sacrifice themselves for the sake of future generations. (Yuri Zhivago remarks that "man is born to live, and not to prepare for life.") Christian in its orientation, the novel argues both implicitly and explicitly against the Soviet Marxist illusion of omniscience and infallibility, against the arrogance of man when he thinks he is the maker of history.

The editors of *Novy mir* also wrote to Pasternak: "The pathos of your novel is the pathos of the assertion that the October Revolution and Civil War and the social changes that followed them brought the people nothing but suffering and destroyed the Russian intelligentsia either physically or morally."[1] Again the assertion is only true in part – the part that refers to the intelligentsia. All of the major characters, and most of the minor ones, come from the intelligentsia and experience either destruction or some form of decline. The most notable of those who survive to the novel's end are Yuri's boyhood friends Dudorov and Gordon, portrayed as obedient intellectuals who have endured persecution only by complying with the humiliating demands of the Soviet authorities. Pasternak's characterization of these two can be seen as a sad, sweeping indictment of a capitulated intelligentsia. The most prominent representative of this class, however, is the hero himself.

The doctor-poet, whose moods, vision, intuitions, and feeling for life (as seen in nature, art, and love) dominate the novel, is also a human failure in many respects. Despite their exaggerations, *Novy mir*'s editors were essentially correct in telling Pasternak that "there is not the slightest hint of Christianity about Doctor Zhivago's dismal path because he is concerned least of all about mankind and most of all about himself."[2] As a social being, Yuri is indeed weak and selfish. After welcoming the Revolution he flees it when the going is hardest, and the rest of his life is essentially a fugitive, seedy underground existence. A gifted doctor, he abandons medicine precisely at the time when his talents are most needed. His behavior toward wives and children is irresponsible. Indeed, Yuri Zhivago is the absolute negation of the traditional Soviet "positive hero." He is not, however, callously antisocial; rather, he is a Hamlet whose response to historical developments in Russia is posited as the only one possible for a poet who desires above all to remain intellectually alive, to preserve his inner freedom, and to remain true to himself.

With the exception of Zhivago himself, the characters in the novel are two-dimensional in the sense that they are largely lacking in psychological motivation. They are presented, rather, through poetic and intellectual association: each of them "stands for something" in the novel's moral and ideological structure. Lara is not only Zhivago's beloved mistress; she is also the spirit of freedom, life, and creativity and, in her role as a Magdalene, she is Russia – ravished, betrayed, beaten, but enduringly beautiful. Pavel Antipov (Strelnikov), the charming, idealistic youth turned stern commissar-executioner, represents the colossal ineptitude of the revolutionary as he attempts to serve Russia (Lara). Evgraf, Zhivago's mysterious Eurasian half-brother, is the hero's guardian angel, and also possibly a symbol of the élitist, authoritarian power that has always controlled Russia's destiny. Sets of values can likewise be assigned to numerous other characters, whose functions in the novel are similarly loosely evocative.

The interlocking themes of *Doctor Zhivago* are so numerous that most of them can here be given only a passing mention. The novel is indeed an examination of the course of Russia in the twentieth century, but it is also a poetic credo, a hymn to life, and a compendium of Russian culture – literary culture in particular. Much of the very structure of the book (its numerous coincidences) is governed by Pasternak's notion of predestination, or conditioned by his theme of death and resurrection. Nature – vivid, alive, and interacting with human events – is present on every page. Art in nearly all its forms is constantly mentioned, and is the substance of the novel's concluding section – the poems of Yuri Zhivago. Finally, the theme which embraces all others is love – love of nature, art, man and woman, and humanity.

As we have seen, the Revolution has been used as a kind of critical metaphor in recent Soviet prose, but the more remote past has also been employed for much the same purpose. The leaders of the Decembrist uprising of 1825 have been officially canonized in the Soviet Union as authentic revolutionary heroes, and it has always been permissible to praise them as an historically progressive force. But contemporary Soviet writers have been making increasing use of Decembrist materials. This has been most manifest in poetry, both published and underground, which alludes to the Decembrists in such a way as to suggest that present-day Russians might well emulate their idealism and rebelliousness. *Poor Avrosimov (Bednyi Avrosimov*, 1970), a novel by Bulat Okudzhava (who, after making his name as a poet and balladeer, has written a book for children, several plays, scenarios, and short prose works), belongs to this literary trend which, in the cloak of ideological legitimacy, expresses implicit, wistful libertarian aspirations and makes allegorical reference to the present.

Poor Avrosimov centers on events purportedly related to the investigations that culminated in the execution of the leading Decembrist conspirator, Colonel Pavel Pestel. Its hero is a young, minor country squire who by chance becomes a clerk with the commission investigating the uprising. The main development in the story is the gradual transformation in the hero's attitude toward Pestel – from his initial assumption that the prisoner is a scoundrel, to bewildered admiration for the accused to, finally, overwhelming sympathy that leads the hero to dream up an inept plan for Pestel's escape from the Fortress of Peter and Paul. In the course of this development Pestel's character and ideas are cast in an increasingly positive light. His career is presented as a source of inspiration: libertarian revolts may fail, but their cumulative example makes for revolutionary progress.

The novel's implicit references to the present are neither heavy nor pointed, but there are unmistakable correspondences between the Russia of early 1826, as Okudzhava portrays it, and the Soviet Union. Pestel was convicted of *intending* to commit regicide – although there was no actual regicide or even any proof of his intent. The cast of characters includes informers, recanters, and betrayers of the Decembrists, with their inevitable "denunciations." But *Poor Avrosimov* is also a historical novel with distinct peculiarities. First, the highly idiosyncratic narrator (a man supposedly writing in the 1860s) is both omniscient and uncertain, witty and obtuse, exact and careless. He is often garrulous and given to pompous, windy, platitudinous asides to the reader, and to little digressive essays on this and that. Second, there is the hero, whom the capricious narrator regards affectionately but whom he constantly makes fun of as an almost impossibly stupid dolt. Avrosimov is a psychologically profound comic hero – a good-hearted, naive bungler combining traits of Candide, Oblomov, and Don Quixote – who lives in a world of romantic fantasies of all kinds. The third peculiarity is the novel's grotesque and phantasmagoric quality. Part of this comes from the hero's inability to distinguish between dream and reality, and between the real and fancied adventures to which his peculiar turn of mind leads him. But it also results from Okudzhava's evocation of an eerie St. Petersburg in the tradition of Gogol, Dostoevsky, and Bely, governed by intangible and mysterious forces and subject to weird happenings. Okudzhava has written an arresting, funny, elusive, and stimulating novel.

In the time of Stalin it was extremely dangerous for a writer to express feelings of nostalgia about the years preceding his coming to power. This is precisely what Vera Panova did in 1958 in her *Sentimental Novel* (*Sentimental'nyi roman*). Set in the southern city of Rostov in the early 1920s, and drawing heavily on the author's own experiences as a young journalist, the novel is presented as the reminiscences of a successful writer on a visit to his native haunts after an absence of thirty years. In a bittersweet manner he recalls the events and emotions of his early manhood – a rapturous but short-lived marriage to a beautiful girl who deserted him, the ebb and flow of friendships, the heady but confused political activity of the times, and the beginnings of his writing career.

Although the narrative is focused on the 1920s, there are frequent references to the present which, in combination with the hero's own evaluations of the past, lend added perspective. The details of life and customs of the times – dress, slang, fashions in poetry, naive disputes among youthful idealists over revolutionary morals and ideology, and the generation gap accentuated by a rapidly changing scene – are presented abundantly and with affectionate irony. Particularly attractive are the young characters themselves as they strive earnestly to avoid "bourgeois" behavior, work out communist values, and ardently speculate on the communist future, and their bewildered elders, anxious to adapt themselves to new ways and keep in step with their children.

Sentimental Novel is indeed sentimental, but in a low-keyed, controlled way. Its picture of days gone by is neither lachrymose nor idealized. Life, it is true, is presented as confused but busy, amusing, and optimistic and, in comparison to the present, seems more interesting and vibrant. But the novel also shows people good and bad, generous and selfish, idealistic and cynical, behaving as they always have and always will.

Beginning in 1954, but especially after the Twentieth Party Congress in 1956, Soviet writers were allowed increased opportunities to write critically about the Stalin years. This qualified freedom waxed and waned for about a decade: at times the license to indict aspects of Stalinism had nearly the force of a mandate; at others writers could touch upon them only lightly and with extreme caution. Finally, with the fall of Khrushchev, substantial criticisms of the Stalin period became virtually outlawed and thus passed into the community of *samizdat*.

One of the grimmest of such works, which embraces the entire Soviet period but concentrates on the Stalin years, is Vasili Grossman's *Forever Flowing* (*Vsyo techyot*, 1970). The author – a successful writer of novels and short stories, a playwright and war correspondent whose works, however, had been periodically attacked by party-line critics and who had suffered during the anti-Semitic campaign against "homeless cosmopolitanism" – finished *Forever Flowing* shortly before his death in 1964. The novel, which has only been published abroad, has an intensely pessimistic flavor, based on the idea that the painful condition of the Soviet Union is the product of a centuries-long Russian historical current whose course cannot be altered. An affirmation that men eternally aspire to freedom provides the only timid note of hope.

Forever Flowing begins and ends like a novel, but it is basically a collection of essays. The chief character, who ties pieces (but by no means all) of the narrative together, is a man seen as he visits European Russia after thirty years of Siberian imprisonment, goes south and gets a job in a factory for the handicapped, and falls in love with a woman who soon dies. There are a few other characters – ephemeral types used as pegs on which to hang various accounts of the iniquities of the Stalin period, including Great Russian chauvinism, the system of police informers, anti-Semitism, the horrible famine decreed by Stalin in the campaign of "dekulakization," the purges of 1936–9, and the camps (notably a section on the cruel and bestial treatment of women there). There are many powerful indictments of the ideology and immorality of the Stalin regime. What is perhaps most notable, however, is Grossman's insistence that the root cause of the evil was Lenin and the revolutionary mentality he represented, and Grossman's emphasis on Russia's ancient subservient mentality, her "slave soul":

> In the Russian fascination with Byzantine, ascetic purity, with Christian meekness, lives the unwitting admission of the permanence of Russian slavery. The sources of this Christian meekness, and gentleness, of this Byzantine, ascetic purity, are the same as those of Leninist passion, fanaticism, and intolerance.

The most dramatic and far-reaching phenomenon of the early Stalin period was the forced collectivization of agriculture. The first volume of Mikhail Sholokhov's *Virgin Soil Upturned* (1931) has traditionally been considered the best novel on this theme. (The second volume, completed after a long delay in 1960, is considerably weaker.) In recent years several reexaminations of the period of collectivization have appeared, and the best of them – franker, more humane, more painful than Sholokhov's – is Sergei Zalygin's *On the Irtysh* (*Na Irtyshe*, 1964). Zalygin, born in a Ural village in 1913 and trained as an agricultural technician, witnessed the turmoil and tragedy of collectivization at firsthand. Later he became a hydraulic engineer, and his career has combined writing with scientific activity. He began publishing stories and sketches (*ocherki*) in 1936, and his movement toward the novel form has been gradual. *Paths of the Altai* (*Tropy Altaya*, 1962), labeled as a novel but actually a collection combining fiction, sketches, and editorials, is a work based on an expedition to map vegetation and concerns the need for far-seeing management of natural resources. Zalygin's novel about a partisan detachment in the Civil War, *Salt Valley* (see pp. 259–60), won him a Lenin Prize in 1968.

On the Irtysh, set in a small Siberian village in 1931, reappraises forced collectivization in terms of the sacrifices it exacted from the peasantry. Its main interest is in its dramatization of the moral and psychological struggle of a good peasant caught between his desire to support the Soviet system (he had fought against the Whites) and his proprietary instinct and love for his land. Stepan Chausov is a natural leader, the strongest and wisest man in his community. Kind, capable, and energetic, he also has a large streak of independence and is bold, sometimes to the point of rashness. He is willing to join the newly formed collective, but he refuses to risk starvation for his family by contributing his last ounce of wheat to the common store of seed-grain. His very qualities of uprightness, self-reliance, and a firm sense of personal responsibility – qualities badly needed in the building of the new order – are precisely the ones that antagonize the regional organizers, who insist on his blind acceptance of official decrees. Ultimately it is a simple, decent act of compassion that brings about his downfall: he and his wife shelter the innocent family of a saboteur in defiance of his ignorant and terrorized neighbors. Badgered and cheated by the local authorities, alienated from his confused and suspicious fellow peasants, he is dispossessed, ripped from his community, and exiled.

An excellent novel, *On the Irtysh* features many colorful, authentic peasant characters, an acute sense of the community (often a blind herd, without volition, and easily preyed upon), and vivid descriptions of the Siberian natural surroundings. The language of narration and dialogue contains many Siberian turns of speech, and the narrative itself is taut and dramatically concentrated.

A much sunnier novel, nostalgic and warmly humorous but also satirical and with foreboding undercurrents, is Boris Balter's *Goodbye, Boys* (*Do svidaniya, mal'chiki*, 1963). Told in retrospect by a man in his forties who was one of them, the novel concerns a group of teenagers in 1936 during the days of their graduation from secondary school. It captures the mixed feelings of young people everywhere as they prepare to leave school and enter the world, and at the same time tells of the special circumstances under which Soviet youth of the thirties lived: the language they used, their relationship to the opposite sex, parents, school, and Komsomol, their amusements (the setting is a resort town on the Black Sea, and they spend much time on the beach and in the water), their reaction to ideological indoctrination (including a discussion among them of the new Stalin Constitution), their attitude toward discipline, and their ambitions and expectations.

The narrator portrays his generation with pride and affection (these young people are vigorous, bright, witty, and enterprising) but also with a compassionate understanding of their limitations. Earnest and obedient, they diligently learn ideas and habits of mind that will confuse and betray them in future years. Looking back at himself after more than two decades, the narrator remarks:

> But now, when I'm alone with myself in the long, sleepless nights, I realize that I knew very little then. I knew all Hegel's and Kant's mistakes by heart, without having read either.
>
> The world of reason, the only world worthy of man, was for me that country where I was born and lived. All the rest of the planet was waiting to be liberated from its suffering. I believed that this liberating mission would fall to me, and to my contemporaries. I was getting myself ready, and waiting till my hour struck. I could think only within the framework of this vision of the world. I reduced the most complicated manifestations of life to this simplified notion of good and evil. I lived accepting these oversimplifications as the absolute truth.

These are, of course, largely the universal feelings of persons in their middle years, but their special, intentional relevance for the Stalin generation is unmistakable.

Goodbye, Boys is impressive in its literary resources: the use of its charming seaside setting; the tart, youthful dialogue; the tender treatment of dawning sexual love; and the abundant, often satirical use of social detail – current slogans; showy, Stakhanovite busy-work; high-flown, stereotyped political jargon. In addition to the youths themselves there are numerous colorful characters, such as the head of the local Komsomol, who got his job through an oration on gophers, which "opened our eyes to the parasitic nature of this treacherous enemy of young collective farms and of the Soviet regime in general," and the narrator's mother – a driving, leather-jacketed Party official who, among other things, had thrown out his stepfather because, she said, he was a Trotskyist.

Early in the story, the narrator and his two closest friends learn that they will soon begin training as military officers, and their mood throughout is a combination of sadness over the passing of their carefree youth, and apprehension and excitement over the coming changes in their lives. A particularly effective and sobering device is the narrator's disclosure, several pages before the novel ends, that his two buddies are destined for early deaths – one in the opening days of World War II and the other, a Jew, in prison after being arrested in connection with the infamous "doctors' plot," an anti-Semitic fabrication by Stalin in the early 1950s.

Books published in the Soviet Union have made at best fleeting references to the mass paranoia and terror of the purge years 1938–9. Thorough and detailed accounts of these phenomena can only be found in works published abroad, such as those of Solzhenitsyn. A lucky or, more likely, calculated exception to this rule is Yuri Dombrovsky's novel *The Keeper of Antiquities* (*Khranitel' drevnostei*, 1964). Narrated by an intelligent, level-headed but wryly outspoken young curator at an archaelogical museum in Alma Ata, the novel chronicles the absurdities that accompany the moral collapse of a community paralyzed by government-induced fear and suspicion in the year 1937.

The museum (located in a former cathedral) is headed by a retired military officer with no antiquarian knowledge or taste, motivated solely by a kind of Party-inspired boosterism, who produces unscientific, corny exhibits that nevertheless please the populace. His main ambition is to house his museum in a new, more impressive structure. Basically decent but stupid, he presides over a little realm that gradually becomes a microcosm of the general social madness. The museum personnel, most of whom are as benighted and provincial as their boss, become infected with an increasingly pernicious atmosphere of intrigue and informing. Their crazy maneuvering begins on the basis of the petty hatreds of the weakest and most dishonest employees and gradually spreads to the more decent ones. There is a gathering willingness, even an eagerness, to swallow the most outrageous lies that come from the media. Names are expunged from the record, pictures taken down, certain persons no longer mentioned – all on the flimsiest of pretexts. Individuals are persecuted for the most remote and tenuous association with purported "criminals" or, for example, for having received a totally innocent letter from *Germany*. The narrative mood is one of both amusement and exasperation. Ostensibly the novel is a burlesque founded on preposterous happenings and behavior, and it is indeed very funny, but it is a comedy with unmistakably grim overtones.

Two works by Lydia Chukovskaya, daughter of Kornei Chukovsky (see p. 256) and herself a leading Soviet dissident, expelled from the Writers' Union in 1974, deal powerfully with the Stalin period. The first (and better) of these, *The Deserted House* (*Opustelyi dom*), was written in 1939–40, miraculously preserved, and accepted for publication in Moscow in 1963 only to have the acceptance rescinded in 1964. It finally appeared in the West in 1966. This short novel concentrates exclusively on the atmosphere of Leningrad in 1937, as perceived by a bewildered and incredulous woman, a loyal Soviet citizen, whose son is arrested and sent to prison camp on false charges. It details the heroine's transformation from a busy, believing, well-adjusted member of society to a shunned and demented recluse, and shows the sinister transformation of the society itself in the tightening grip of Stalinist terror. Dramatic but almost documentary in its authenticity, the novel has great psychological, social, and moral depth.

Chukovskaya's second short novel, *Going Under* (*Spusk pod vodu*), written in 1949–57, was published in the West in 1972. It, too, is devoted to showing how an entire society was poisoned by Stalinist iniquity, but its special focus is on the writing community and its adoption of the official cant and stale phrases that clothe lies and oppression. The date is 1949, the setting a rest home for writers, and the heroine a widow who lost her husband in the purges. In the central plot the heroine meets a writer, a survivor of the camps, who is busy on a story in memory of one of his fallen fellow prisoners. When the story itself turns out to be a doctored and spurious version of the truth in the official spirit of socialist realism, the heroine is repelled. But on reflection she realizes that the author is morally no worse than most others who must lie in order to survive. A subplot concerns the wave of anti-Semitism in 1949 and its effects on the literary world.

The preceding discussion of fictional treatments of the Stalin period is not, of course, exhaustive. In other contexts of the present study the works of Solzhenitsyn and Vladimir Maksimov – heavily involved with the Stalin period – are considered, and many other writers have touched upon Stalinist times in greater or less degree.

Of all the national experiences of the USSR, none has been written about more extensively in the last three decades than World War II. For the Soviets the war began in 1941 with massive defeats and retreats and did not reach its turning point until the Battle of Stalingrad in 1943. The war continued furiously and with enormous cost until the Soviet armies drove the Germans back to Berlin in 1945. Soviet literature encompasses all stages of this long and bloody conflict, a source of colossal sorrow and pride, and of continuing political controversy.

During the war itself, prose fiction was intensely patriotic and hortatory, but it differed from the fiction of the prewar period in that, to some extent, ideological considerations and indoctrination in correct attitudes toward service to the state were subordinated to compassionate, proud depiction of suffering, courage, and endurance. Writers young and old rallied to the cause, but most had difficulty finding time to write, and initially they confined themselves to sketches, poems and short stories. The most popular and enduring work of the period was Alexander Tvardovsky's narrative poem *Vasili Tyorkin* (1942–5). Other prominent works were Leonid Leonov's long story *The Taking of Velikoshumsk* (*Vzyatie Velikoshumska*, 1944), Valentin Ovechkin's *Greetings from the Front* (*S frontovym privetom*, 1945), Vasili Grossman's *The People are Eternal* (*Narod bessmerten*, 1942), and Aleksandr Bek's *Volokolamsk Chausee* (*Volokolamskii Shausee*, 1944). Konstantin Simonov, who received an extraordinary leave for the purpose, wrote *Days and Nights* (*Dni i nochi*, 1943–4), a laconic, documental novel of Stalingrad, showing the stubborn bravery and determination of Soviet fighters. A chapter depicting some soldiers as indifferent about the cause and suspicious of their leaders was excised by the authorities. In general, the war literature of this period did not mention elements of defeatism that were known to exist nor did it grope with shortcomings in the military effort.

Two of the finest novels about the war – Vera Panova's *Sputniki* (translated as *The Train*) and Viktor Nekrasov's *V Okopakh Stalingrada* (translated as *Front-Line Stalingrad*) – appeared within a year of its close. Both are marked by close and loving attention to individual character, to private motivations, and to intimate feelings. *The Train*, a deceptively simple narrative about the routine life of a hospital train, is notable for the absence of heroics, preaching, or obvious propaganda. Alternating between episodes on the train and flashbacks to show the characters' prewar, civilian existence, it portrays ordinary people as they love, relate to their families, suffer, and show courage or cowardice. Nekrasov's novel tells, in a calm, everyday first-person manner that approaches a diary form, of the strengthening of morale that led to the stiffening of resistance against Hitler's forces. The narrative is so free of large generalizations and lofty rhetoric that the novel was criticized for being insufficiently ideological. Nevertheless, it won a Stalin Prize in 1947.

Panova and Nekrasov were exceptional, however, for shortly after the war the literature concerning it became, in response to official pressure, intensely political and chauvinistic. The function of war fiction became one of demonstrating the role of the Communist Party leadership and ideology in mobilizing for victory, of showing the indispensability of Stalin's leadership, and of proving that the heroic exploits that won the war could only have been accomplished by the especially endowed New Soviet Man. An example of a novel that satisfied this mandate is Mikhail Bubennov's *White Birch* (*Belaya beryoza*, 1947–52); one that failed is Aleksandr Fadeev's *The Young Guard* (*Molodaya gvardiya*, 1945, 1951), which was withdrawn from circulation and rewritten to order. Similarly, Emmanuel Kazakevich's *Two in the Steppe* (*Dvoe v Stepi*, 1948), which displays pity for a young officer sentenced to death for failure to perform a responsible mission, was removed from circulation and not restored until the early 1960s.

During the Khrushchev years Soviet authors were given the chance to write afresh about World War II (at a time when Western authors had already exhausted and abandoned the topic), and to deal with its human implications with new sensitivity and candor. Many of them used the conflict to evaluate the recent past and, by implication, the present. The novels of such writers as Vasili Bykov, Grigori Baklanov, Nekrasov, and Yuri Bondarev are often more concerned with moral explorations and questions of ends and means than with the patriotic heroics that governed most earlier fiction about World War II. In these more recent works one frequently sees the examination of ethical problems that are, on the one hand, timeless and, on the other, pointedly timely.

War literature at times took on the political function of correcting the record by criticizing the conduct of the war: to show the military unpreparedness – now attributed to Stalin's bungling and his mass purges of army officers – that permitted the initial rapid German advances deep into Russia; to demonstrate how Stalin's failure to heed advice, his cruelty, rigidity, and suspicion crippled the war effort by causing needless sacrifices of human life and resources; and to illustrate numerous other corrections of the military record. Stalin had largely divested Soviet troops of the ability to take initiative and responsibility. They had only been trained to take orders and to rely on Party members to make decisions for them. Gradually, as this literature illustrates, both troops and officers learned the necessity of making independent decisions and acting on them without specific, detailed orders from above. The new literature showed this, as well as such previously unmentioned phenomena as the patriotism of men released from concentration camps to serve in the army.

Simonov's novel *The Living and the Dead* (*Zhivye i myortvye*, 1959) frankly portrays the army's lack of preparation and the inexperience of the commanding officers who replaced those destroyed in the purges of the 1930s. His later novel *Men Are Not Born Soldiers* (*Soldatami ne rozhdayutsya*, 1963–4), goes on to deal with Stalin's penchant for ostentatious military successes in which human lives are senselessly sacrificed. Grigori Baklanov's novel *July 1941* (*Iyul' 41 goda*, 1965), in a series of flashbacks, emphasizes how MVD purges of Soviet officers created an atmosphere of suspicion and distrust in the armed forces, and Vasili Bykov's *The Dead Feel No Pain* (*Myortvym ne bol'no*, 1966) shows the cruelty and injustice in Stalinist methods of command, and the damage wrought by the caste system in the army.

The literature that began to appear in 1956 reasserted, and even expanded upon, the humane quality of literature written during the war. It became somewhat less heroic than before, often dwelling on the sheer ghastliness of war and its senseless, nightmarish qualities. There was increased emphasis on the individual human experience and its significance; the moral problems involved in command decisions; the effects of the fear and sight of death, and the loss of comrades, on the human psyche; the nature of a sense of duty, of loneliness, of self-reliance, and bravery. No longer was the activity of the individual soldier submerged in accounts of large-scale military action. The Party's role was deemphasized in favor of that of the ordinary citizen-soldier as a person relying on himself and his comrades, and not on political leadership. Vignettes of private life – love between nurses and fighting men, and soldiers' thoughts of home and family – became more prominent. Although some writers continued to paint broad, epic canvases of the war after the fashion of Simonov, many others wrote "one-hero" books, examining closely the mentality and psychology of a lone soldier or partisan. Often authors chose to feature a desperate rearguard battle in which a small, probably doomed detachment covers a general retreat. Such a situation permitted the examination and comparison of the feelings and behavior of individual soldiers under identical circumstances.

All of this was especially true of writers of the "war generation," those who had been in their teens and early twenties when they served as soldiers and junior officers. By 1956 there had been a number of developments to give their writing its own particular characteristics. Over a decade had passed since the war's end, and the distance enabled them to understand better what they had experienced and witnessed – not only self-sacrifice and bravery but also cowardice and betrayal. Moreover, writers in general had begun to assert the right to work out their own individual styles and to stress the legitimacy of a *variety* of narrative viewpoints. The possibilities of the short novel, in capturing discrete, pointed, and dramatic situations, began to be explored. In general, the emphasis on unadulterated heroism was replaced by the study of war as it is.

The writers of this generation tried to analyze the psychology of soldiers in the trenches, showing men under the cruel conditions of war but without dwelling on its horrors. They were keenly interested in moral problems, often placing their protagonists in situations where they were alone with their consciences and where their conduct depended on the strength of their conviction and sense of duty. First-person narration, close in tone to memoirs and with a strong lyrical element, became popular. In war fiction of this sort, the narration is retrospective, so that two time planes – wartime and the present – are felt simultaneously, either through direct reminders from the author or through montage effects of sharp transition between past and present. A major function of this use of time was to shed light on the Soviet people and society of the present by examining the social, moral, and psychological sources that helped shape them during the fight against fascism.

Two novels of Yuri Bondarev, *The Battalions are Asking for Fire* (*Balal'ony prosyat ognya*, 1958) and *The Last Volleys* (*Poslednie zalpy*, 1959), are fairly typical of the writing of the war generation. Bondarev, who writes from the point of view of the fighting man on the ground or in the dugout, conveys vividly and convincingly the sights, sounds, and inner sensations of combat. His portraits of soldiers and officers, and their dialogue, are deft and strong. He avoids tropes, and his color comes not from comparisons but from direct descriptions. Using a minimum of flashbacks, he provides through reminiscences in dialogue sufficient information about his major characters' civilian backgrounds to give them depth. Only his love episodes are weak and artificial. In general his characters, although perceived as military creatures whose exclusive problem is how to behave in this battlefield hell, are persons with a clearly outlined past. One desperately hopes, with them, that they also have a future.

The central situation of *The Battalions are Asking for Fire* is an action in which Soviet forces push the Germans across the Dniepr River and gain a foothold on its right bank. To mislead the enemy into thinking that the main attack is taking place elsewhere, two battalions are sacrificed. The moral center of the story is the cruel fate of these battalions, which become isolated and surrounded without the artillery support promised them, and are wiped out. Ironically, the tactic that sacrifices them proves completely successful and wins the battle. The situation is shown from several points of view: that of the bewildered soldiers in the doomed battalions; of Captain Ermakov, one of the five persons to remain alive after the disaster, whose moral indignation and sense of betrayal cause him to challenge the colonel responsible for the action; of Colonel Gulaev, who is also shocked at the horrible injustice of the situation; and of Colonel Iverzev, commander of the division, who devised the tactic and has ultimate moral responsibility. Emphasizing the excruciating cruelty of war and the necessary moral ambiguity of command decisions, Bondarev writes with great compassion for his characters, admiration of their bravery, and appreciation of the tragic nobility of their sacrifice.

Also a novel of tragic irony, *The Last Volleys* is set in the closing days of the war, when the beaten Germans are still taking a heavy toll of the victors. The Soviet personnel have all been through gruelling, endless fighting, and are weary and desperate for its conclusion. Each of them knows that the last shots can be just as fatal as the first. There is great emphasis on the knowledge of imminent and certain death and the soldiers' varying degrees of fatalistic adjustment – in fact, nearly all of them, including the hero, are killed. The hero Novikov, an artillery officer in his middle twenties, young for his rank, is a superb leader. He combines great powers of physical and moral endurance with high intelligence, much technical military experience, and self-possession. His dominant traits are his understanding of his men, his sense of responsibility to them, and his sensitivity to the demands he must make on them. When he must send them to their deaths he does so without flinching, but he deeply suffers each death. Mature beyond his years, he has earned life and happiness many times over, but war destroys him just as blindly and impersonally as the others.

The novel's point of view is mainly that of Novikov. The other characters are his men, a group with a strong sense of comradeship and responsibility for each other. Deftly sketched, they serve as foils to emphasize Novikov's qualities and show varying reactions to combat conditions: a nervous coward who finds courage in battle; a cynic who is captured, defies enemy torture, and dies heroically; a gallant, earthy, old peasant-soldier. Bondarev stresses their psychology: their nerve and morale in the violent chaos of battle, as shown in behavior and gesture, dialogue, and authorial description of their feelings. His style is laconic, but his battle-field descriptions, featuring rapidly shifting scenes, have a kind of horrible aesthetic beauty, shaped from the pain, stench, grime, and shocking ugliness of combat. By his microcosmic method of looking intently at a small group in a single incident, Bondarev produces a distinctly superior war novel.

The poignancy of a number of wartime stories is based on the extreme youth of the participants, mere boys compelled to hate and kill, and often to bear the terrible responsibilities of command. Their personalities become an abnormal compound of innocence and astounding maturity. One of the most famous such stories is Vladimir Bogomolov's "Ivan" (1958), later successfully filmed by the noted Andrei Tarkovsky, whose hero is barely in his teens. Ivan witnessed the death of his father on the first day of the war, his baby sister was killed in his arms, and he escaped a German death camp and became a partisan. Obsessed with vengeance, he becomes a hardened and valuable scout behind enemy lines, effective because he is so implausibly young and unmilitary in appearance. In the epilogue (the narrator himself is a 21-year-old battalion commander) it is learned that Ivan was captured on a mission, refused to break down under interrogation, and was shot.

Another story built on the contrast between the discipline and harshness of wartime life and the pristine idealism and purity of a youth caught up in it is Bogomolov's "Zosia." Its hero, a nineteen-year-old lieutenant devoted to poetry, falls timidly and secretly in love with a girl in the Polish village where the company he commands is billeted. So inexperienced that he cannot muster the courage to declare himself, he only learns, as his company suddenly leaves the village, that she loves him too. They will never see each other again. A starker account of the impact of military violence on the young psyche is Viktor Nekrasov's "The Second Night," in which a sensitive young soldier, realizing that a German sentry he has strangled is a boy like himself, broods over the cruelty and appalling waste of war.

A work in most ways quite separate and distinct from other literature about the war is Anatoli Kuznetsov's *Baby Yar* (1966). It is his eye-witness account of the German capture and occupation of Kiev and the Soviet retaking of the city, as seen when he was in his thirteenth and fourteenth years. The narrative is spare and stark, although documents – mostly German proclamations, newspaper stories, and leaflets – are used extensively, and there are passages of rhetoric, chiefly expressing hatred of the Germans and fascism. The heart of the book is Kuznetsov's account of mass atrocities – chiefly the sadistic and systematic slaughter of the large Jewish population.

Baby Yar has a curious and revealing history. When Kuznetsov defected to England in 1969 he brought a microfilm of his original, uncensored manuscript. This he has published in English (1971), augmented by new information and opinion, and with a typographical arrangement that indicates what the Soviet censors deleted from the original version. The differences between the Soviet version and the one Kuznetsov published abroad are impressive and, in places, shocking. In general, the censors had deleted everything that reflected even the slightest discredit on the Soviet armed forces or civilian population (including Ukrainian anti-Semitism), that indicated that much of the local population had initially welcomed the Germans as liberators, or that suggested that the NKVD was responsible for destructive acts that Soviet histories attribute to the Germans. Kuznetsov's detailed account and demonstration of how the censors bowdlerized his book about the war is sobering and unsettling, and is a reminder that all other works about the war published in the Soviet Union may have been similarly treated.

Orthodox Soviet critics have felt that in certain instances, concentration on the ugliness of military action and its effects on the individual has harmfully directed the reader's attention away from the positive goals and heroic nature of the Soviet war effort. Most often cited in this respect is Bulat Okudzhava's *Good Luck, Schoolboy!* (*Bud' zdorov, shkolyar'!*), which is accused of presenting a subjective, one-sided, and untrue impression of events. Its hero is a green recruit of eighteen in his first combat experience, whose battery is wiped out. Alone, gripped by the feeling of being trapped in a situation of senseless confusion, he is forlorn and afraid, and willing to admit it. The story itself is excellently presented – a first-person narration in soldier's vernacular with a tone of sincere, intimate confession. There is much exact battlefield detail, but the focus is on the psychology of the boy as he is introduced to the front-line routine, thinks back to his recent schooldays, frets about no letters from home, gripes sarcastically about those who buy and sell exemptions from military service and, above all, tries to imagine how he will meet his death. (Who am I? Am I a coward? I'm too young to die!) What irritates the critics is that war in the story seems devoid of positive meaning or aim, and that Okudzhava does not show his hero developing into a dedicated and effective fighting man.

The war fiction of Okudzhava has been influenced by Ernest Hemingway and the grim realism of Erich Maria Remarque, so much so that he has been accused of "Remarquism" – painting war in such dismal colors that one's work is an implicit argument against the institution of war itself. An attitude of absolute pacifism, which finds no distinction between just and unjust wars, is antithetical to official Soviet ideology. The accusation of Remarquism is therefore a serious one, and it is noteworthy that two other gifted writers of the war generation – Grigori Baklanov (born 1923) and Vasili Bykov (born 1924) – have also been subjected to it.

Baklanov's *An Inch of Ground* (*Pyad' zemli*, 1959) caused considerable debate in the Soviet press because its realistic approach was so grim as to constitute, in the opinions of some critics, an "excess of naturalism." It portrays a small detachment of soldiers isolated from the main forces. These are ordinary men, apolitical and unheroic, whose main concern is to escape alive. Baklanov does not cast doubt on the worthiness of the war aims, and thus was easily defended against the charge of Remarquism, but the insistent cruelty of battle, as seen by his simple combatants, divests it of any element of grandeur. Similarly, his *The Dead Should Not Be Shamed* (*Mertvye sramu ne imut*, 1961) centers on an episode in which the only survivor among the officers in a single detachment is an arrant coward. The greatest furor, however, was caused by Baklanov's *July, 1941* (*Jul' 1941 goda*, 1965), which tells of the first weeks of the German invasion, as seen through the eyes of the commander of a Soviet army corps. He and his colleagues are helpless as they try to stop the Nazi assault, and it is clear that the Soviet lack of preparation comes from Stalin's failure to heed their warnings. In flashbacks, the ineptitude and inexperience of the Soviet command is attributed to the purges in the late 1930s by Stalin's MVD.

In Vasili Bykov's *The Third Flare* (*Tret'ja raketa*, 1961), an antitank crew of six men finds itself in a suicidal position. After destroying many enemy tanks and numerous infantry, the crew, and the female nurse who accompanies them, perish. The only person left alive is the narrator, who shoots a flare gun in the face of the treacherous coward who is partly responsible for the crew's demise. Told subjectively in first person, usually in the present tense, the novel is both highly dramatic and convincing in its psychology and soldier dialogue. The Soviet crew is multinational, and the ethnic differences within it (one is a Tatar and another, like Bykov himself, a Byelorussian) are emphasized. Although Bykov makes clear the patriotic, antifascist purpose of the war, he makes the innovative suggestion that the Soviet Union's punishment of its own returning prisoners of war from Germany has been unjust. The same point is made in *Alpine Ballad* (*Al'piiskaya ballada*, 1964), the rather melodramatic and sentimental story of an escaping Russian POW and an Italian girl fleeing the Germans in the Austrian Alps.

The most fiercely criticized of Bykov's works is *The Dead Feel No Pain*

(*Myortvym ne bol'no*, 1966), in which a small group of German tanks causes terror and panic in a Soviet regiment. The Soviet forces are divided into two sharply defined categories: the "little people," who are brave and self-sacrificing and the military leaders, who are characterized as base, cowardly, careerist, and indifferent to the fate of the men under them. Their Stalinist methods of command suggest that injustice, cruelty, suspicion, and a caste system based on Party affiliation were rife in the army at that time. Both Bykov and the editor who printed his novel were severely attacked by Party officials.

Sotnikov (translated as *Ordeal*, 1970) is a short novel based on the contrasting moral characters of two partisans on a scouting mission who, after being sheltered briefly by peasants, are captured. Both men are tough, competent soldiers with a strong sense of mission. Under interrogation and torture, however, one holds out while the other, after wavering, opts to save his skin by informing, as a result of which his comrade, two peasants, and a Jewish girl of thirteen are hanged by the local Russian authorities in the service of the German occupiers. The narrative itself is tense and suspenseful, and the use of the natural setting (the Russian winter) to emphasize the drama is effective.

The works of Bykov, as well as those of Baklanov, Okudzhava and others, are so concerned with physical and moral anguish, with confused psychological states, and with social injustice, selfishness, and cowardice in the Soviet armed forces that – despite the authors' clear espousal of the antifascist cause and pride in the heroism of Soviet soldiers and officers – critics have speculated on their possible resemblance to the Western writers of the lost generation after World War I.[3] These Soviet writers' emphasis on the blood, filth, violence, and cruelty of the battlefield, and the gloom and sense of loss that emanates from their works, do suggest at times the kind of despair expressed by those Americans and Europeans. In defending Soviet writers against these ideological accusations, sympathetic critics point out that their fiction does not present the war as something senseless; it is a just war of defense, shown to be motivated by legitimate hatred of the enemy. Moreover, these critics assert that the lost generation wrote about war as a tragedy in the abstract, in which man was a mere victim or pawn, whereas Soviet writers present war as a social cause, in which the collective effort makes the individual an active, purposeful, and effective participant.

Many stories and novels written by the war generation employed a time span that enabled them to embrace both the war and the ensuing period up to the death of Stalin (or thereabouts). Such works usually drew a contrast between front-line morality, where individual honesty, loyalty, and cooperation among comrades are indispensable, and where the single purpose of destroying a monolithic enemy brings about a pragmatic knowledge of right and wrong, and a complex and corrupt peacetime scene, where falsity and moral compromise are a prominent feature of life. Bondarev has written two novels on this theme. In *Silence (Tishina,* 1962), Sergei Vokhmintsev, a demobilized young army captain who is now a student at a mining institute, meets up in a Moscow cafe with Uvarov, another former officer whom Sergei alone knows to have been guilty of front-line cowardice that cost the lives of several comrades. Enraged at the sight of Uvarov, Sergei beats him up. In the course of the novel, through intrigue in Party circles and with the fortuitous help of a secret-police frameup that sends Sergei's father to a concentration camp, Uvarov succeeds in engineering Sergei's expulsion from both the Party and the institute. The novel stresses the loneliness, isolation, and frustration of a young man whose wartime habits of stubborn honesty and direct confrontation of injustice do not seem applicable in a peacetime world of secret denunciations, careerism, and doublecross. In Bondarev's related novel *The Two (Dvoe,* 1964), Sergei's friend Kostya, also a veteran who is now a Moscow taxi driver, keeps a Luger – awarded to him as a souvenir at the front for bravery – as protection against thugs who prey upon taxi drivers at night. It is illegal for him to have the gun: the state, which he risked his life to defend against outside enemies, cannot now protect him against enemies within; nevertheless he has been ordered to turn in his arms. Symbolically, Kostya throws his gun into a canal shortly after he learns of the death of Stalin.

Bondarev's characters have been criticized in the press for not thinking "big thoughts," for not groping with large, significant ideological problems. In his defense it should be said that he has purposely chosen ordinary young veterans who by nature are not particularly articulate but who nevertheless have a stubborn, commonsense comprehension of what is right and wrong. Nevertheless, Bondarev is not notably adept at characterization, and he is uniformly unsuccessful with female characters.

Still, there are no false or easy solutions in his works. Evil is shown in full dimensions, the heroes in all their fallibility and vulnerability. Bondarev creates physical atmosphere and violent action well, although he often overwrites in the attempt to capture the exact feel or look of a situation or place. The plots of these two "civilian" novels are excessively episodic and melodramatic, and his attempts to create suspense are clumsily transparent. It is interesting, however, that these novels, which are artistically inferior to his earlier war novels, are the ones that gave him true prominence in the Soviet Union. The reason is that in them he was one of the first to write about the Stalinist terror.

A more able writer is Viktor Nekrasov, who earlier than Bondarev had taken up the theme of the returned veteran in *Home Town* (*V rodnom gorode*, 1954). His hero is also an average, decent, uncomplicated young fellow, an army captain and Party member attempting to remake a life that had barely started when the war came. The setting is the bombed and disrupted city of Kiev, which the author depicts with great sensitivity and sympathy (its lovely natural setting, crowded living conditions, black market, and flea market) as it tries to pull itself together. A prominent concern of the novel is the question of how those Soviet citizens who remained in the city during the long German occupation should be treated. The attitude should be one of complete respect and charity, Nekrasov argues: the main villainy comes from a Party hack who tries to frame a professor by insinuating that, in remaining for three years in occupied Kiev, the professor must have been disloyal and a collaborator.

Nekrasov's hero is beset by a number of emotional and practical problems: a triangle, clearly an accident of war, involving himself, his wife, and the wounded soldier with whom she lived while her husband was at the front; finding the right line of work (should he try for further education or take the easy way by becoming a taxi driver or physical training instructor?); how to deal with iniquity and corrupting influences within his local Party organization (the novel ends on a note of unresolved suspense – will the hero be excluded from the Party or merely reprimanded in some degree?). His more general and fundamental problem, however, is the psychological and moral one of learning how to live as a civilian, of overcoming the tremendous hold that front-line values and associations have over him, and of enduring his disillusionment in a postwar world that still contains much evil.

For all its civic import (there are, among other things, a fine satirical treatment of a Party careerist in action and a portrait of a nasty female petty bureaucrat), Nekrasov's novel is about private lives. He is a warm, loving writer who sees much good in people and is sympathetic toward honest human failings. Moreover, the novel displays a neat and tight narrative structure, an impressive command of sensory and psychological detail, and the ability to evoke a social atmosphere fully.

Yet a third novel on the theme of the returned soldier is Vladimir Tendryakov's *A Rendezvous with Nefertiti* (*Svidanie s Nefertiti*, 1965), whose hero's war experience was in one of Stalin's punitive detachments – to which he, as most others, had been unjustly sentenced. More specifically, overtly, and insistently anti-Stalinist than the works discussed above, the novel is loaded with ironic references to Stalin and the ubiquitous glorification of him, and with scenes and characters illustrating the pernicious workings of Stalinism – such as the midnight arrest of a collector of Western art. As a novel, *A Rendezvous with Nefertiti* has serious flaws. It is awkward, repetitious, sentimental, and wordily didactic in places. Still, it has color and the power of authoritative social criticism fostered by the campaign against the "cult of personality."

The hero has become an art student, and there is a discussion among four war veterans, all of them art students, who have just participated in a demonstration on Red Square over which Stalin, like a deity, has presided. One of the young men argues that Stalinism is a religion, necessary for the preservation of a sense of national purpose and order. Another, who believes completely in Stalin and everything he stands for, nevertheless maintains that Stalinism cannot be a religion because Stalin himself is mortal. As it develops, however, the whole dispute turns on the question of sacrifice in the name of future generations and one's willingness to suspend moral judgments for the sake of attaining communist goals:

> [You say] forget yourself completely, live for your great grandson. Can a man really live only on mirages of the future? There is an oppressive injustice in this – you are fertilizer! The heralds of a marvelous future – what right do they have to treat one with such scornful arrogance? . . .
>
> In order to have blind faith, I must have confirmation. The idea must manifest itself every day before I'll begin to be convinced that blood is flowing less and less, – and it must manifest itself now, and not after my death. Why must I believe blindly?

It is significant that the discussion quoted takes place among art students, for a vast quantity of the literature of recent years is devoted to problems of creativity, artists, and the arts. Conscious of having passed through a long period of creative drought, writers combed over this aspect of the past with almost masochistic thoroughness. In novel after novel, a painter, poet, or inventor – almost invariably a veteran who has proved his manhood and patriotic devotion at the front – struggles to find self-expression in the stifling, frustrating atmosphere of Stalin's Russia, which is dominated by an establishment of officially approved hacks who have prostituted their talents. Such novels usually have happy endings: Stalin passes from the scene, and after years of heartbreaking discouragement the hero gets his opportunity to contribute his gifts to society. However, this socialist-realist ingredient – the happy ending – does not in itself vitiate the substance of such works, and is not always present. What is important in these novels is their meticulous exposure of the falsity, shallow pretentiousness, and time-serving quality of the officially inspired art and literature that formerly prevailed and that still, though threatened, appear to have a long lease on life. Novels devoted to such themes abound not only in earnest dialogues about the nature and purpose of art but also in parodies of opportunistic writing and ironic descriptions of socialist-realist art. In *A Rendezvous with Nefertiti* the hero, who has just graduated from an art institute and is hungry for work, is offered a commission to do a painting to decorate a wall in a new Moscow hotel. To give the young artist an idea of what he wants, the hotel director shows him a photograph of a typical socialist-realist painting:

> under the open sky long tables, heaped with food, roast goose, hillocks of apples, around the tables the beards of venerable old men, the neckties of young ones, embroidered Russian blouses, girls' dresses in the city style. A reproduction of the familiar . . . "Collective Farm Wedding."
>
> "Create for us something like this picture. With all the, so to say, optimism and life-affirming quality of this work . . . a gala holiday in our Soviet countryside, sunny, joyful. In a word, in the spirit of this same work, but in your own style, so that it will be an independent work . . . One meter eighty centimeters by two meters twenty-five centimeters."

Although he is virtually starving, the hero flatly refuses this fat commission.

Two of the authors mentioned in this chapter are members of national minorities who do at least some of their writing in their native tongues. One is Bykov, whose novels are translated from the Byelorussian, and the other is Chingiz Aitmatov, a Kirghiz who writes both in his native language and in Russian. Nearly all of Aitmatov's work is ethnically oriented and displays a great love for his people, their habitat and their customs. At the same time, he is heavily concerned with problems of morality that far transcend Kirghiz culture – the cruelty and injustice that corrupt government and Party officials, as well as other evil individuals, can inflict on honest and innocent, simple people.

His novel *Farewell, Gul'sary* (*Proshchai, Gul'sary*, 1966), which won a

Lenin Prize in 1968, has for its protagonists Tanabai – an honest and direct but stubborn and impulsive peasant, a good Communist who had helped "dekulakize" his own brother in the 1930s and had been several times wounded during his army service in World War II – and his horse Gul'sary, formerly Tanabai's own but now the property of the local kolkhoz. The careers of man and horse (a superior but much-abused animal whose life is affectionately chronicled from birth to death) run parallel, in their ups and downs, in many respects. Framed by a recurring scene in which the two are walking together along a dusty road as the worn-out horse approaches death, the novel is based on a series of flashbacks that permit a flexible alternation of temporal planes and contrasting episodes. A prominent element is the setting – the beautiful but harsh steppe and hills – together with violent weather that produces many catastrophes.

The central plot of the novel tells the story of Tanabai's victimization by arbitrary and self-serving Party officials. Although he has no experience he is ordered to become a shepherd and, as a Communist, is pledged to raise a ridiculously and impossibly large number of lambs. When lambing season comes, it turns out that the authorities have provided no shelter for the newborn. In the ensuing, powerfully dramatized catastrophe, Tanabai and his family fight valiantly but hopelessly to save them, but hundreds die. The regional prosecutor – an utter Stalinist cynic – comes to investigate the catastrophe: "What do you think you're doing, comrade" – he nodded in the direction where Tanabai had carried away the dead suckling lamb – "a shepherd-communist, and the lambs die?" To which the hero replies: "Apparently they don't know I'm a communist." To cover up their own mistakes, the local authorities stage a show trial, as a result of which the hero is expelled from the Party.

Through local intrigue between secretly rival Party officials, and through his own undiplomatic behavior and refusal to defend himself, Tanabai is declared an enemy of the people. The only ray of light has been a young Komsomol official's unsuccessful attempt to defend Tanabai in the name of proper Party justice. Several years later, this same young man, who by now has become the regional Party Secretary, invites Tanabai back into the Party. From political and ideological standpoints, this is the silver lining, the socialist-realist happy ending. But it seems obviously tacked on.

Farewell, Gul'sary, then, is a work of ingenious socialist realism, which provides a rich and fascinating account of Kirghiz folkways, severely criticizes the kolkhoz system, comes down hard on abuses in the Party's dictatorial and unjust conduct of public affairs in Stalin's time, but manages to suggest that the Party and the system it represents will eventually purify themselves.

In the present context it has been impossible to consider all of the interesting and important literature that reexamines the past. Notable omissions are the valuable and moving memoirs of Evgenia Ginzburg, *Krutoi marshrut* (translated as *Journey into the Whirlwind*, 1967), and the works of Sinyavsky, Solzhenitsyn, and certain poets and prose writers dealt with elsewhere in the present volume. Other writers whose works *in part* concern the past fall more properly in different sections of the present book.

Most of the literature mentioned in this chapter has in common an awareness that during the first thirty-five years after the Revolution a massive falsification of the record took place – that historical events, social, economic and political conditions and developments, cultural institutions, popular beliefs and attitudes and, in fact, the very nature of human beings were fundamentally distorted in Soviet writing. The distortion continues to this day, but large numbers of writers have striven to correct the record and to reinterpret the experience that their fellow countrymen underwent during that period. Their progress was fitful and halting; the information they had to work with was often poor and, at best, incomplete; and those writing with an eye to censorship often had to be satisfied with hints and indirection. Nevertheless, the opportunity to display a renewed moral awareness and heightened appreciation of human values enabled them to examine many phenomena in an altered, more truthful light.

10

Literature copes with the present

A vast amount of the fiction published following the death of Stalin was devoted to the contemporary scene, as previous chapters have indicated. Writing became increasingly involved with the actual problems of Soviet society and, at its boldest and frankest, with criticism of an ossified establishment that maintained itself through corruption, intrigue, lies, and naked force. Public hypocrisy, ritualistic glossing over of the truth, and the use of obfuscating ideological formulas were attacked sometimes directly, more often indirectly, through the portrayal of characters with troubled consciences or, conversely, highly developed powers of moral and ethical self-justification. Implicit in most of this writing was a plea that institutionalized myths be undermined by the truth. Literature was coming closer to life as it is actually lived under Soviet conditions and evaluating it more honestly. This development led many critics to complain that writers had now adopted a "one-sided approach to life phenomena," so that "gloomy and musty" episodes recurred in story after story. What really bothered these critics was the fact that, in opening and exploring previously forbidden areas, a new literature of critical realism was making serious inroads in canonical socialist realism.

The concept of socialist realism requires that the interests of the individual be closely identified, either explicitly or implicitly, with the interests of the state. As literature became more concerned with private lives, however, this identification became looser and more remote, and often disappeared altogether. Among the best writers, for example, the Communist Party virtually vanished from fiction. Until the middle fifties, party cadres had been omnipresent in works with a contemporary setting – solving problems, giving sage advice, inspiring by example, and often performing the role of a kind of collective *deus ex machina*. In the interests of "realism," of course, it had been necessary to attempt to characterize Party members as human beings, warts and all. But because they had a special moral function in the narrative, the temptation to sentimentalize them, or to make them unnaturally gallant, had usually been far too powerful to overcome. In actuality, the Party still dominates public life, and the proportion of characters in recent literature who happen to be Communists may well be nearly as large as it ever was. The difference is that they are not named as such. There are probably two reasons for this phenomenon. First, the liberalization of literary controls has made it easier for writers to portray examples of unpunished evil behavior on the part of characters in positions of responsibility, but to identify them specifically as Party members, which they undoubtedly are, would be to exceed the permissible limits of candor. Second, and more important, the new comparative freedom to treat humans as humans and not as social symbols, and the removal of the pressure on literature to trumpet the glory of the Communist Party, combined to permit the lifting of the Party label from fictional characters.

The quality of Soviet intellectual and cultural life came to be examined more closely. Such authors as Ehrenburg, Tendryakov, and Kazakov produced novels and stories about the creative problems, morals, and ethics of artists and writers – frustrated by ideological controls, the cultural isolation and backwardness of the country, and the vested interests of officially accepted schools and individual artists. Vladimir Soloukhin's novel *Mat'-Machekha* (*Coltsfoot*, 1964), whose hero is a nature poet, traces in detail the psychology of creativity and examines the position of the poet in society – his mission as a purveyor of culture and the limitations of his obligation to write for the masses. Although Soloukhin, in characteristic fashion, insists on the poet's obligation to cultivate his national cultural traditions and to preserve his uniquely Russian heritage, his novel is also a plea for the autonomy of art and the artist.

The first harbinger of these new trends was Ehrenburg's *Ottepel'*, which appeared in two sections, translated as *The Thaw* (1954) and *The Spring* (1956). Undistinguished as a work of literature, and relatively timid in the light of the social protest of later years, the novel nevertheless managed to touch upon most of the themes that were to become the burden of the new critical realism. Its main topic was the destructive influence of Stalin's regime on the arts. Two major characters are Volodya Pukhov, a hack painter who has made a good living and a local reputation in his small provincial city by turning out works of socialist realism, and his friend Saburov, a genuine artist who lives in obscure poverty because of his refusal to bend to the prevailing winds. Pukhov, who has good taste and much innate talent, is bitterly aware of his own sellout, and he envies the honest Saburov, who in turn pities him. As the novel develops, the change of climate after Stalin's death enables Saburov to emerge from obscurity and to become appreciated, and Pukhov himself begins to shed his commercialistic, opportunistic cynicism.

The theme of the need for creative freedom in the arts stands by itself, but it is complemented by the story of a brutal bureaucrat, the corrupt factory manager Zhuravlev. An intriguer who maintains his power by backbiting, falsifying production records, and stifling opinions opposed to his own, Zhuravlev gets a come-uppance of sorts when the central authorities discover that he has been cheating his workers by keeping them in woefully substandard housing. A variety of additional topics that were to become of major interest in the next few years are broached in Ehrenburg's novel. In the character of Dr. Vera Sherer he presents a victim, fortunately a survivor, of Stalin's anti-Semitism. The terror of the 1930s is mentioned; the existence of concentration camps is disclosed indirectly through mention of the release of prisoners. There is satire on official art criticism and the ideological clichés of Soviet journalism. And the generation gap, soon to become an important topic of literature, is represented by Pukhov's father, an Old Bolshevik regarded by his children as a romantic idealist.

For a Soviet novel, *Ottepel'* pays what would previously have been considered an inordinate amount of attention to love affairs (there are four of them) and the problems of marriage. This concern over emotional matters is characteristic of Ehrenburg's novel in general – its assertion of the literary importance of private lives and private feelings – and is reflected in its narrative method, which focuses on the psychology of individuals, chiefly through extensive use of interior monologue and shifting points of view. To a considerable extent, then, the novel is an implied polemic against the traditional interests and conventions of socialist realism. In another respect, however, it observes those conventions, for its general trend is optimistic: the negative phenomena of Soviet life that are depicted in *The Thaw* begin to be corrected in *The Spring* and, correspondingly, human relationships become warmer and more harmonious.

Another early indication of the literary "thaw" was Vera Panova's *Span of the Year (Vremena goda)*, published in 1953. Other writings of Panova have already been discussed, and here a few remarks about her career in general are appropriate. Panova was one of the most popular and widely published writers of the forties, fifties, and sixties. Several of her stories and novels were filmed, she was a prolific and successful playwright as well, and she received numerous state prizes for her works. In addition to her novels *The Train* (cf. p. 270) and *Sentimental Novel* (cf. p. 264), she wrote *Kruzhilikha* (1947) – a novel centering on the problems of a factory manager in the immediate postwar period – *Bright Shore* (*Yasnyi bereg*, 1949) – a novel set on a state farm – and the charming *Seryozha* (1955) – a novella portraying a small boy as he makes discoveries about himself, the people surrounding him, and the world about him.

Generally speaking, Panova is more concerned with people than with issues. Her focus is on intimate, individualized portrayals of the private lives and personal problems and feelings of ordinary individuals. She writes of the relations between parents and children, husbands and wives, and of young people in love and the throes of courtship. A particular forte of Panova is her ability to portray children and adolescents. The intimate style and warm tone of her writing are quite unique – friendly, sympathetic and, above all, feminine, in a motherly, sometimes grandmotherly, and often genially gossipy manner. Panova always pays due attention to the social milieu in which individual destinies are worked out and, in so doing, comments quietly on important contemporary social problems. Although mildly liberal and often subject to sharp attacks from critics on the right, Panova was politically a dutiful Soviet writer.

Span of the Year is Panova's best novel and, though less didactic, in many respects goes deeper into Soviet life than *The Thaw*. Its initial impact on Soviet readers and critics was not as sensational as that of Ehrenburg's novel, although many critics attacked it for excessive attention to the seamy sides of Soviet society (especially the criminal underworld) and for being too tolerant of families that permit lawbreakers to arise in their midst. For her objective, understanding treatment of such matters, Panova was accused of "neutralism" and "naturalism." But the novel became extremely popular with the public and was appreciated as an honest and authentic portrayal of Soviet existence.

Featuring a great variety of characters and points of view, with a suspenseful and intricate plot that depends heavily on such devices as flashbacks and diaries, *Span of the Year* is constructed as a kind of microcosm of Soviet upper middle-class life in the early 1950s. The novel begins on New Year's Eve and ends exactly one year later. In the course of the seasons that pass within this frame, contrasting pairs of characters (husbands and wives, brothers and sisters, friends), as well as contrasting families, are presented as they confront one another and otherwise interact. Frequently the omniscient narrator shares for a time the perspective of an individual character, providing an added sense of intimacy.

Loaded with fascinating and closely perceived details of daily life, the novel also provided what was, for its time, a surprisingly open depiction of corruption and embezzlement in high places. One of the major characters is Bortashevich, an important official who falls into crime because, as the author carefully points out, his natural moral vulnerability has been exacerbated not only by the need for money to satisfy his wife's expensive tastes but also by the *environment* of irresponsible power. There are numerous glimpses of life among the bureaucrats, a class unto themselves with well-cultivated bourgeois values and habits. But as an antidote to Bortashevich and his henchmen there is the honest and dedicated Dorofea, a former peasant who becomes a prominent Party official.

What is most interesting, however, about Bortashevich on the one hand and Dorofea on the other, is their relationships with their families. The teenage children of Bortashevich are pure and idealistic, in glaring contrast to their corrupt, materialistic parents. Particularly noteworthy is the young Seryozha Bortashevich, whose diary, generously quoted, provides a fascinating view of the psyche of a touchingly admirable Soviet youth. (Seryozha is the first, apparently, in a large crop of questioning adolescents who appear in the literature of the late fifties and sixties.) Dorofea's devoted husband is a simple, contented man who has not even aspired to match his wife's attainments. The history of this Soviet marriage, fundamentally a happy one, would delight any feminist. On the other hand, Dorofea has a son whom she has pampered and spoiled so badly that he becomes the pawn of a criminal gang. In portraying the Bortashevich family, in which socially undesirable parents produce good children, and Dorofea's family, in which socially exemplary parents produce a criminal son, Panova implicitly seems to question the conventional Soviet assumptions about the role of environment and training in shaping the characters of the young. Correspondingly, her entire, many-faceted novel suggests that truth is more unstable and elusive than the literature of the Stalin period admitted it to be.

Viktor Nekrasov's novel *Kira Georgievna* (1961) centers on a woman of forty-one who has flitted along the surface of life, seizing upon immediate experience and immediate satisfaction, avoiding personal responsibility, and refusing to recognize the unpleasant. She has merely played with life, pretended to live. Nekrasov portrays Kira compassionately and does not indict her for her superficial approach to existence. To a great extent, he suggests, she is a product of her environment, which has encouraged people to avoid facing facts. For Kira, who is among other things a sculptress, lives in a kind of socialist-realist dream world, forever youthful and "forward-looking," artificially optimistic.

The novel concentrates on Kira's relationship with three men: her husband Obolensky, an art professor twenty years her senior; her young lover Yurochka, nearly twenty years her junior; and her former husband Vadim, a poet and film writer recently returned from two decades of imprisonment and exile. All three men are superior to Kira in that they have stronger wills, deeper moral understanding, more sincere sympathies and antipathies, and do not deceive themselves. Obolensky, old and ill but still benign in his attitude to Kira, has become resigned to life's frustrations. Yurochka's conscience, reinforced by a gradual disillusionment with Kira, forces him to walk out of her life. Vadim, who has matured profoundly through hard and unjust experience, perceives that Kira has evaded the moral issues of the times, and that she is spiritually wanting. This realization makes him abandon his attempt to resume life with Kira. As the novel ends, Kira bleakly and guiltily begins to understand that her existence has been irresponsible and therefore empty. She has accomplished nothing worthwhile in her "optimistic" art, she is childless, and she has been unable to establish a deep and permanent emotional relationship with any of the men in her life.

Kira Georgievna was attacked by Party critics on a number of grounds. Some found it narrowly intimate in thematics, trivial in its portrait of a frivolous woman. Others protested that Kira was not typical of Soviet reality. Still others accused Nekrasov of failing to attack truly "contemporary" problems, argued that the novel lacked social resonance, and found the author guilty of emotional "vegetarianism" in constructing his novel without sharp dramatic conflicts.[1] These criticisms can be answered. The conflicts in the novel, although not dramatic on the surface, are fundamental, because they concern the need for social awareness and personal responsibility. (One of Vadim's reasons for turning away from Kira is her lack of interest in hearing the details of his life in the concentration camp.) *Kira Georgievna*, although not a didactic novel, is a subtly moral one. It is a closely realistic examination of the shortcomings of an individual. It explains without condemning, and ties these shortcomings to the malaise beneath the surface of social life.

By the middle sixties the search for veracity in fiction by amassing directly observed detail had produced an increasingly inclusive and multifaceted examination of the social environment. An example of the new objectivity was Vitali Syomin's novel *Seven in One House* (*Semero v odnom dome*, 1965). The novel is set in a neglected suburb of a large Soviet city (presumably Syomin's native Rostov-on-Don), where, because of the chronic housing shortage, families are jammed together in close quarters. The essence of the novel, however, is not its depiction of crowded housing (this is already a convention in Soviet literature), but its dispassionate portrayal of ordinary working-class Soviet citizens engaged in the business of daily living. A good proportion of them are shown to be as petty, selfish, unambitious, and indolent as the usual run of humans everywhere. Concerned with their own mundane affairs, they seem totally uninterested in ideology and devoid of the sense of lofty purpose and direction that Soviet citizens are traditionally supposed to feel. They work as much as they have to, they produce children, they gossip, they drink and occasionally brawl (an accidental murder takes place in the course of a senseless fight between street gangs). They are closely tied to, and bound by, a drab environment.

The central figure in the novel is Mulya Konyukhova, a middle-aged war widow who has managed to shelter simultaneously in her small, dilapidated house four generations of her family, including her stupid, eccentric mother and her dull, lazy, and generally worthless son. Although Mulya's life has been one of heroic sacrifice (during the war and for several years after, she had only one dress and nearly starved to feed her family), the author has been careful not to give her a saintly coloration. She is garrulous and earthy, despises her mother, and has coddled and spoiled her son. But her chief qualities are an ingrained sense of responsibility and a spunky independence. Here is part of her account of her job in a leather-goods factory:

> We took on socialist obligations – we were competing with a leather-goods factory in another district. Well, and how did they take on these socialist obligations? They set the production figures somewhere in the director's office or Party factory committee, and brought them to us in the shop to vote on. "Who's 'for'? Who's 'against'? Nobody?" I say, "I'm against." They didn't even believe me, they thought they must have heard me wrong: "Is there anyone against?" I say, "I'm against. You've got it written there that you're going to lower the cost-price and increase labor

productivity by twenty-five percent . . . But how to increase it? We don't have machines. We have manual labor. You write: increase productivity? By speeding up manual labor? You write: 'Insure by mechanization a hundred-percent increase in labor productivity – and I'm to agree a hundred percent." They yell at me: "You're not on our side!" "It's you," I say, "who are not on our side." Next day they call me up before the factory committee: "You said that the communists in the factory are not on our side?" – "And are you communists?" I ask. "Watch your words, Konyukhova! You're lucky it's not the old days. We'll take educational measures with you."

And what kind of educational measures do they take with me? They move me over from a high piece-work rate to a low one. They're turning everybody against me. But you see, I'm so fast. I work very fast. My organism is like that. I work as much as two young people. How can there be equality in manual labor? You are healthy, you are quick – for you one norm, for a weak person another. They put me to riveting straps – and in one shift I make as big a heap of them as two other people . . . The women get peeved at me, but I tell them: "Why did you vote for that agreement? I voted against it! And you're mad because the quotas are killing you."

The bosses don't like me. They don't like me, but they can't do anything about it – they can't give me a worse job because there isn't any, and I always overfulfill the plan.

Mulya's monologue continues with a complaint about the factory director, who is harsh and rude to the workers, who cares only about increasing production, and who refuses to replace broken windows that cause nasty draughts in the shop. What is significant about this passage, however, is not its criticism of factory mismanagement and working conditions (this has always been permissible, to a degree, in Soviet literature), but the fact that the *working* career of Mulya plays such a small, incidental role in the total narrative. Mulya is, after all, a very good factory worker, yet the author's treatment of this aspect of her life is confined to the brief passage just cited.

Mulya works because she has to earn a living. She works well because she is naturally quick and energetic, and not because of an awareness that the purpose of her labor is to build communism. Work is just one of the things that everybody does, and there is no particular reason to get excited about it. Syomin's failure to endow his heroine with an exalted feeling toward labor brought censure from orthodox critics, who also accused him of failing to show heroism among ordinary Soviet people. He was further criticized for "one-sidedness and narrowness" in his depiction of Soviet life and, because of his objective tone, of indifference to its negative aspects.[2]

Such criticisms are wide of the mark and ridiculous. Syomin's is a close and by no means unsympathetic study of a particular environment and the people in it. For his first-person narrator he chose a relatively detached observer – a journalist who happens to be married to Mulya's daughter. The narrator, who is an intellectual, does not, for the most part, share the culture and values of the people he is telling about. Nevertheless, he records their way of life with respect and fidelity, allowing them to speak for themselves in their own colloquial, substandard, but colorful idiom.

The most attractive feature of *Seven in One House* is its wealth of cultural detail. The novel is framed, for example, by a scene in which a group of neighbors, assembled to help renovate Mulya's house, are resting and drinking after their day of traditional communal effort. These suburban dwellers, although representatives of the contemporary blue-collar working class, still refer to themselves as *muzhiki* and *baby* – the peasant terms for men and women – a habit that emphasizes their lingering ties to the soil and folk customs. And Mulya's mother has disguised her Bible by encasing it in the binding of a biography of Stalin. Syomin's greath strength is in his ability to write about ordinary Russians without idealization or sentimentality.

Vasily Shukshin (1929–74) wrote with a flair for anecdote, a keen sense of what was timely, and a great diversity of interests. Born in a village in Altai territory, he left Siberia in 1954 to attend the Gorky Cinema Institute in Moscow. He became very prominent in films, directing his own scenarios and sometimes playing the leading parts as well. His first short story came out in 1961, and numerous collections have been published.

The stories are fast moving, with dynamic plots and, not infrequently, surprise endings. The narration is taut and racy, so economical that it often seems impressionistic, even glibly cinematic, but at its best it achieves a Chekhovian delicacy. The dialogue is extensive and often carries the main burden of narration. At times, the conflicts seem contrived and exaggerated, lacking in intrinsic weight that would justify Shukshin's versatile efforts to dramatize them. At others, Shukshin uses swift, precise

strokes to endow his conflicts with considerable social and spiritual profundity.

The main function of Shukshin's stories is to display characters in large
numbers, constituting, it would seem, a gallery of types and curiosities all
of whom are about equally worthy of the author's attention. Some of the
best are merely episodic, such as the typically bitchy, snappish salesgirl
with whom the well-meaning hero of "Boots" is forced into a spiteful
minor altercation. This character is himself typical of Shukshin – an ordinary kolkhoznik who, in a gesture of love, buys his wife a pair of boots
that turn out to be too small because of her extraordinarily large calves.

Shukshin's technique of developing a story counter to the reader's expectations is displayed in "Petya," a sketch of two unattractive ex-villagers
recently moved to town. Petya is uncultured and drunken, a self-satisfied,
fat rooster of a man. His posing, raucous scarecrow of a wife is equally
repulsive. It turns out, however, that what seems like spurious, affected
devotion on the part of Petya's wife is really love – pitiful, ugly, but genuine love. Also typical of Shukshin is his choice of two newly arrived im-
migrants from the countryside, for his favorite topic is the transition from
rural to urban life and the resulting shock and sense of alienation it produces. His attitude is not one of protest, but merely one of interest. But in
his depiction of the ungainliness, unease, and disorientation of the ex-
peasant there is implicit a wistful respect for the simple, healthy, and self-
justifying way of life he has left. In later stories Shukshin introduced characters who are more openly and consciously troubled over the quality,
meaning, and content of their existence. The hero of "In Profile and Full
Face," a young chauffeur of village origin, discloses this feeling as he converses over a bottle with an old peasant. He cannot accept the somnolent
rural life, he wants more "scope," and still he does not know why he is
doing what he is: "Indeed, I don't know why I live." The dilemma is not
new in literature, but for Shukshin it is directly related to the disappearance of a rural order of things.

Shukshin, however, is far more than a chronicler of the awkward and
painful transition from rural to urban values, for he often features the
harsh truth about human suffering in general. His characters represent a
broad spectrum of ordinary Soviet people – not only peasants but workers
and city dwellers as well. A large number of them have been given a raw
deal, are unsuccessful or trapped in unjust circumstances that make them
feel dislocated, and some have become criminals. Many are the prisoners
of their frustrated dreams, too weak or too unlucky to realize them. Others, including narrators who speak for the author himself, are burdened
by thoughts about the inevitability of death. Occasionally, human suffer-

ing erupts into violence, as in the story "Two-Fingers," in which a newly married man discovers his wife making love with his cousin. In a rage, he tries to kill her with an axe: she escapes, but in the process he cuts off two of his own fingers. Although Shukshin's emotional vignettes are presented without obvious commentary, his situations of suffering are usually a device for highlighting serious moral and social problems.

Shukshin's most celebrated work is the film *The Red Guelder Rose* (*Kalina krasnaya*), which he originally published as a story written for cinema. The story itself was little noticed but, as a film directed by the author – who also played the leading role – it attracted wide and controversial attention. The hero is a former criminal released from prison, a strong but tormented personality who makes an effort to repudiate his past and his former criminal associates, and dies in the attempt. His striving to find a place in the ordinary world, to communicate with normal people, and to assert that which is decent in him, is thwarted by his inability to understand a nonpredatory existence – an inability caused largely by a childhood of deprivation and early exposure to the underworld. Despite the tender help of a good woman and ample opportunities to make a positive adjustment to society – an adjustment he profoundly desires – he is defeated by self-destructive impulses.

Near the end of his life, Shukshin began writing allegorical fantasies with a strong satirical bent. In the story "Point of View" he uses some of the magical apparatus of the folk tale to satirize the conventions of Soviet writing. A Russian ritual matchmaking, involving a meeting between the families of the bride and groom, is first described as if written by a pessimist, then as if by an optimist. In both cases the truth is distorted to conform to preconceived notions, including those of official literary doctrine. Finally, parts of the confrontation are depicted from a "mixed" and then from a "neutral" point of view. The function of the story, however, is not to find a "correct" view, but rather to expose the unreliable eye of the indoctrinated and biased beholder. The long story "Until the Third Cockcrow," in similarly satirical vein, parodies the Russian fairy tale in sending the traditional character Ivan The Fool in search not of wisdom but of a *certificate* of wisdom. Various figures from Russian literature (Poor Liza, Oblomov) and folklore (Baba Yaga) enliven the allegory, which extensively lampoons Soviet literature, ideology, and mores.[3]

Since the inception of the Russian novel of production and construction in the 1920s, work and technological processes have always been a major, and often an obligatory, theme of Soviet writers. Traditionally the Soviet production novel has been loaded with detailed descriptions of industrial processes and working techniques – the operation of railroads, blast furnaces, rolling mills, and electrical circuits. Narrative interest was intended to be derived, in large part, from the intrinsic fascination of the machinery itself, its deployment and maintenance, and from the means of organizing the labor force to meet production quotas. In theory, the production novel was supposed to concentrate on the human element, on the developing psychology and social attitudes of the individual worker, but in practice such novels often degenerated into popular sociotechnological textbooks. Because ideological prescriptions and restrictions made the human element extremely difficult to handle with any degree of persuasiveness, writers tended to avoid human problems by padding their works with industrial detail. Over the years production proved to be a limited source of aesthetic interest, boring to both writers and readers.

The theme of work and production remains important in Soviet literature. In some recent fiction, however, there have been changes in emphasis and focus. Work is still generally recognized as having a special importance in human life, but it is sometimes viewed differently and in a more balanced fashion than before. Like Syomin's Mulya, increasing numbers of major characters in Soviet fiction who take pride in their occupational skills nevertheless do not endow their competence with ideological significance. At times the central figure is a misfit, an outsider who will not accept the rules of the enterprise or do things in the prescribed, orthodox way. At other times the figure is not a production leader but, rather, a morally sensitive individual who has reservations about the purpose, quality, and social priority – the human implications – of a given enterprise. Perhaps the most interesting development related to the theme of work, however, is a new concern with the problem of individual creativity. This concern centers most frequently on the issue of innovation, in which the hero struggles to invent some badly needed technological device or process, against the opposition of entrenched interests. The innovator in such situations is akin to an artist striving, in the face of powerful obstacles, to make the benefits of his talent and originality available to mankind.

This concern was stated early in the post-Stalin period by Daniil Granin in his novel *Iskateli* (1954), translated as *Those Who Seek*. Granin was born in 1918, is a decorated war veteran, and an engineer by training. His first story was published in 1949, and he became a full-time writer with the publication of *Those Who Seek*. Since then he has also been a prominent official in the Writers' Union, whose Leningrad section he headed for a number of years. He has journeyed abroad a great deal and has published numerous essays on his travels. Among other concerns, as he indicated in an article in 1967, he shares the fears of Western scientists that the human race may heedlessly exhaust the resources of the planet. Granin's novels and stories, always timely and usually controversial (see his story "One's Own Opinion," discussed on pp. 176–7), focus primarily on science and technology as they bear on the vital problems of the day. His chief interest is in the inquisitive, creative mind and personality and the way they fare in the contemporary world.

The hero of *Those Who Seek* is Andrei Lobanov, a young inventor whose main problem is how to adjust to the realities of Soviet life while maintaining his integrity, ideals, and creative drive. By nature he is a pure scientist, but he conceives of a project (the invention of a device for locating breaks in power lines) that requires him to leave his university to become an administrator in an institute for applied research. To win the respect and cooperation of his colleagues, he must develop leadership qualities and curb his tendency to "go it alone." In the end his enthusiasm proves infectious and his impulsiveness is compensated for by his scientific honesty, courage, unwillingness to compromise his principles, and devotion to his work. At the same time he becomes less a machine, more humane. And though he ceases to be an individualist, he retains his individuality.

Lobanov's invention becomes a symbol of the search for truth and the advancement of civilization, and the novel's main conflict is between the forces that encourage scientific and technological progress and those that retard it. (In opposition to Lobanov are individuals representing the undesirable features of the scientific establishment: Potapenko, a smooth bureaucrat with a taste for luxurious living, a talent for intrigue, and ambition to become a minister; and Professor Tonkov, who defends his vested interest by using his empire of disciples to machinate against potential rivals. Both Potapenko and Tonkov are expert in-fighters, specialists at slander and ideological name calling.) Related, but subordinate problems in the novel are those of reconciling experimental with applied science and research with production, as well as the problem of promoting teamwork between universities and industry.

Those Who Seek provides many insights into Soviet ways of doing things – for example, back scratching, influence and exchange of favors in industrial management; the workings and defects of the system of "socialist emulation;" and the machinery of the Plan, with its power both to foster and to impede creative research. There are interesting portraits of Soviet women: a typical working housewife with her onerous cares and duties, and an upper-class wife who rebels against her soft life. For its time, the novel was innovative in its criticism of living conditions, its treatment of questions of sexual morality, marriage, and the family, its expression of doubt as to the desirability of automatic reliance on collective wisdom, and its airing of moral and ideological issues that were to be developed more thoroughly a few years later. To a great extent, however, *Those Who Seek* is also a conventional Soviet novel.

Its criticism of Soviet life is, for all its candor, moderate and low key. It does not question established social goals or the methods of achieving them; rather, it points out certain imperfections in the machinery. The novel dramatizes, in traditional fashion, the trial-and-error process of training in leadership. Lobanov, initially a loner, eventually becomes an exemplary and inspiring worker in the collective, a positive hero. He is aided, moreover, by a sympathetic Party official, who undertakes to pave the way for him but disciplines and instructs him at the same time. It is largely through this official's efforts that the novel has a happy ending.

In 1958 Granin published the novel *After the Wedding* (*Posle svad'by*), which deals with the problems of a pair of newlyweds and, on the social level, with various industrial and agricultural issues. He returned to the theme of creativity in science with the novel *I Enter the Storm* (*Idu na grozu*, 1962). This novel is about researchers who fly into the centers of storm clouds, studying them with the aim of controlling thunderstorms to help aviation. Once again there is much concern with conflicting views on the nature of scientific research and the best approaches to it, with the career rivalries of various scientists, and with the ethical principles involved in scientific activity.

Like *Those Who Seek*, this novel features a stubborn maverick hero, a diamond in the rough whose firm and honest adherence to principle involves him in trouble with bureaucratic authorities and turns public opinion against him, but who eventually triumphs by virtue of perseverance and enterprise. His strength is in his *individualistic* refusal to follow the easy, accepted, respectable path, his striving to preserve his ideals, and his devotion to his work. The novel has a distinctly liberal slant. For one thing, the Party is completely absent: the hero and his scientific colleagues rely solely on themselves for inspiration and guidance. Among these young scientists, moreover, there are attractively presented intellectual iconoclasts who display a new irreverence toward the state and its apparatus and a frank admiration for Western culture. Careerism and charlatanism in Soviet science – attributed to the lingering effects of Stalinism – are portrayed with powerful irony. But *I Enter the Storm* is deficient in plot interest and character development, and it is excessively laden with scientific detail. In this latter respect, Granin was unable to avoid the pitfall of the traditional production novel.

The most controversial novel of this type, by far, was Vladimir Dudintsev's *Not by Bread Alone (Ne khlebom edinym)*. Published in the fall of 1956, it immediately caused a sensation. The public, and especially the student generation, read it avidly, while Party officials attacked it as a distortion of Soviet reality, convened meetings to denounce the author, and attempted in various other ways to discredit him. Khrushchev called the author a "calumniator" who took a "malicious joy in describing the negative sides of Soviet life." Dudintsev was also duly accused of "individualism" and failure to understand the positive value of the collective.

The plot centers around the efforts of the young inventor Lopatkin to develop a new kind of pipe-casting machine. Drozdov, the head of an industrial combine, has promised to help Lopatkin. When Drozdov discovers that Professor Avdiev, the influential chief of a scientific group, has the support of a ministry for developing an inferior machine of his own design, he withdraws his aid from Lopatkin. Helped only by a handful of obscure and powerless allies – including Drozdov's estranged wife, who has fallen in love with him – Lopatkin continues working on his invention, enduring extreme poverty as well as bullying and trickery from the Establishment. In time a large amount of state money is squandered on Avdiev's machine, but Lopatkin's is proved superior. To cover up, the authorities responsible frame Lopatkin and railroad him to a concentration camp. After years of abuse and discouragement, Lopatkin is released from camp through the intervention of the military, who become interested in his invention, and his machine is successfully produced. But the ending is not the conventional happy one: the real villains, especially Drozdov, are not punished and presumably will continue to thrive.

Lopatkin is an idealist who goes it alone for the benefit of mankind and who desires only "to give without being interfered with." For him material well-being means nothing, and he takes a kind of spiritual satisfaction in self-abnegation and disdain for creature comforts. Drozdov, on the other hand, is an avowed materialist, proud of the high standard of living he enjoys as a reward for helping to create society's material "basis." The opposition between these two characters is both ideological and moral: Drozdov believes that "matter comes first," calls himself one of the "building ants," and justifies his opportunism and ruthlessness in the name of the goal of communism; Lopatkin believes that man does not live by bread alone, calls the Drozdovs "monopolists" for whom communism means merely filling one's belly, and abhors their brutality, scheming, and dishonesty.

Dudintsev's novel was sensational in its time because it was frankly a work not of socialist realism but of critical realism. It portrays a rigid Soviet social structure, dominated by a privileged class of "bosses" isolated from the people who maintain their power through corruption. Moreover, the novel undermines many of the assumptions and much of the terminology that have been used to justify this order of things. Lopatkin's enemies, for example, call him an "individualist" and therefore an enemy of the people and of communism. They take pride in their ostensible allegiance to the collective through whose united, selfless efforts communism is presumably being built. But it is these "collectivists" who are most concerned with their own personal careers and welfare and who stifle creativity by their persecution of nonconformists like Lopatkin. And it is the individualist Lopatkin who obviously has the loftier ideals and is more closely in touch with the common people.

Dudintsev's novel is conventional in that it deals with several themes similar to those of Ehrenburg, Panova, and Granin, but it is more outspoken and militant than theirs. Although it is too polemically and mechanically devoted to its thesis to be a formidable work of art, it is important in the history of post-Stalinist literature because it offers no assurance that the Soviet system is capable of overcoming the evils that the novel depicts.

Traditionally the central situation of a production novel is a job of work: the building of a large industrial enterprise or a section of it, the development and perfecting of some separate process, or a drive to increase production. Characters are measured in terms of their attitudes toward the job, and enthusiasm for the job springs from infection with the collective spirit. An essential ingredient of such a novel is the presence of one or more "positive heroes," leaders whose example of zeal and initiative inspires other workers to greater accomplishments. The major intrigue of the novel revolves either around the formation of such a hero through the awakening of his consciousness of social purpose or the successful efforts of such a hero, already formed, to inspire his fellow workers with mounting enthusiasm for the job.

A traditional function of the production novel has been to demonstrate the therapeutic or educational value of work in forming the personality and social outlook of the individual. This didactic element has been particularly prominent in literature about young people. The typical situation has been one in which a youth who has done poorly in school, or who has rebelled against his parents, turns up at some construction site, usually in a remote region. When he first begins work, he is uncooperative, lazy, arrogant, and generally obstreperous. (Sometimes he is merely uncertain of his goals and inexperienced.) Sooner or later there ensues a crisis, usually involving some construction mishap or particularly challenging production problem, in which, almost against his will, the young hero performs a feat of courage or quick thinking that discloses his better self. It is revealed that the spirit of the collective has been subtly infecting his rebellious soul. The school of hard knocks, as well as his fellow workers' example of socialist behavior, has made a man of him, and he is now prepared to reenter society with a mature and positive outlook on life.

As we have seen, however, many stories and novels of the post-Stalin period have dispensed with such traditional plot formulas and characters. Syomin's Mulya and the truck drivers of Nagibin and Tendryakov, for example, are not "enthusiasts" about their work, nor are they consciously concerned with the building of communism. Moreover, in the course of the narrative they do not develop more positive sentiments about the collective and its goals. Their pride in their competence is a purely personal matter. In some recent stories and novels the hero is a misfit, an outsider who does not accept the rules, who works well but in an unorthodox manner because he is incapable of adapting himself to the rhythm of the collective. In traditional production novels, such characters either develop proper social attitudes or emerge as clearly marked villains. Nowadays, however, there is less moral correlation between satisfactory workmanship and other socially desirable qualities.

Some writers have recently seemed to favor small, limited, less collective types of work to write about. Others have purposely ignored the details of work. Aksenov's story "Oranges from Morocco," for example, creates an impromptu worker's holiday in which the characters are shown at a moment when they are being *distracted* from their labors. They are all good workers, and yet one of them, who works on an oil prospecting rig, wants most of all to leave "this stupendous, enchanting, stinking valley." But even where work continues to be described, the emphasis is on the related human drama, the clash of personalities and attitudes, and not on the work itself. Finally, some writers have developed variations on the formula of the production story to raise entirely new questions. They utilize traditional and conventional, officially sanctioned forms, but re-shape them to emphasize moral and ideological issues that have previously been suppressed, underplayed or neglected.

At the time of his defection to the West in 1969, Anatoli Kuznetsov (born 1929) was one of the most widely read authors in the Soviet Union. His stories and novels were especially popular among young readers, and young people were usually the subjects of his writings. The work that es-tablished his fame in the USSR was the short novel *Sequel to a Legend* (*Prodolzhenie legendy*) published in 1957. Written in a brisk diary form, with deft character sketches, sensitive descriptions of places (notably the city of Irkutsk), and vivid accounts of work processes from a participant's point of view, it is in many respects a standard Soviet story of a young man "finding himself" with the aid of a sympathetic collective.

Tolya, who has just graduated from secondary school without distinc-tion, refuses to follow the normal work channels open to him in Russia and chooses to try his fortune in Siberia. (He is concerned about the inad-equacy of his schooling – and especially the study of literature – as prepa-ration for life.) He goes to Irkutsk and becomes a concrete worker in the construction of a power station on the Angara River. On the work site he faces not only the practical problems of learning an arduous semiskilled trade but also disillusionment as he views petty corruption and lack of en-thusiasm on the part of some of his fellow workers. Also, he receives oc-casional letters from his school friend Victor, who has entered an institute for training store managers and boasts of his cushy life in the big city and his own cosy, white-collared future. Ultimately, encouraged by the solici-tude of his colleagues and inspired by the example of a senior worker, Tolya overcomes his misgivings and elects to remain in Siberia. He has found his vocation and will make his contribution to society as a solid citi-zen.

In *Sequel to a Legend* the contrasts between the right and wrong direc-tions for young Soviet men to take are presented rather mechanically, and the amount of socialist moral uplift in the novel is standard. Still, the novel is relatively free of the starry-eyed glorification of work that is the hallmark of the construction novel, and it debunks, to some extent, the platitudes of that genre. For example, the Kosomol is not portrayed as the eager, efficient, and alert organization that readers of orthodox novels have come to expect. But the clichés of the traditional construction novel are present in sufficient abundance to mark it as a work of socialist realism, albeit with an up-to-date liberal slant.

A much more unorthodox novel, of much greater literary distinction, is *The Ore (Bol'shaya ruda*, 1961), by Georgi Vladimov (born 1931). The setting is an iron mine, the hero a truck driver hauling ore. Pronyakin is a loner with a powerful urge to excel. He is so determined to make an outstanding individual record that he decides against working cooperatively with the other drivers to improve methods and thus alienates them. Although he has already impressed everyone on the site with his skill and energy, he attempts to make a big splash, get even with his enemies, and prove his superiority by hauling a prohibitively heavy load up a steep road of wet clay. In doing so he purposely tempts fate, overturns his truck, and is fatally injured. In the hospital, just before his death, there is a brief reconciliation with his fellow drivers, but no real resolution of Pronyakin's inner conflicts.

Pronyakin is not merely an individualistic show-off but a complex character. A former drifter and boozer, he has acquired a wife, with whom he wants to settle down in a normal, stable existence – the privacy of a house, perhaps a refrigerator and television. To find a "place" in life, he needs to make money, and the mercenary desire for personal gain accounts to some extent for his feverish zeal as a driver. But Pronyakin is also motivated by a selfless love of work and a genuine desire to make a social contribution. Moreover, his very aggressiveness has given rise to self-doubts, and he is puzzled by his inability to fit into the collective and adapt himself to its rhythms. He dies a tormented, paradoxical young man, a misfit who could have been a leader. That is all: Vladimov makes no attempt to draw a moral.

The Ore is written in an energetic style that is also psychologically subtle and suggestive. Vladimov endows the operation of the excavation itself with an epic grandeur without, however, overburdening his descriptions with excessive or redundant detail. Like Nagibin, he is adept at conveying the special affection of the truck driver for his machine and the sensation of managing it under hazardous conditions. Vladimov tells colorfully and precisely of the difficult techniques of driving up and down the slippery clay slopes of the mine, and the accident itself is described vividly from the point of view of the victim, in terms of his immediate physical sensations.

The novel is not entirely free of elements of the standard construction story, for example in its emphasis on the pioneering spirit behind the huge mining project and the last-minute reconciliation of the individual hero with the collective. But essentially *The Ore* is a construction novel that uses the standard formulas, as it were, in reverse. For one thing, its treatment of working conditions is starkly realistic, without the customary relieving emphasis on the promise of a better future. For another, it is free of didacticism: the Party plays no role, and there is no instruction in the problems and techniques of on-the-job leadership. Most important, the conflict between the individual and the collective is not presented in moral terms. Pronyakin is not an undisciplined egotist who needs to be shown the way; his problems are not amenable to the quick therapy of an ideologically correct and solicitous collective.

In 1969 Vladimov published a seafaring novel, *Three Minutes of Silence* (*Tri minuty molchaniya*). The settings are a small fishing trawler in the North Atlantic, the mother ship that supplies it and to which it delivers its catch, and the Russian port that is the trawler's home base. The characters are veteran seamen and a motley group of casual young sailors – essentially unskilled proletarians who are rootless and without stable goals. Senya, the hero, is a troubled young individual with good instincts and the courage to follow them, but without a sense of direction or meaning in his life. It is typical of his way of life that he signs on as a crewman on the trawler only because he has been "rolled" while drunk in port and is dead broke.

The novel climaxes during a mid-winter storm with the rescue, by the Soviet trawler, of the crew of a sinking Scottish fishing boat. Before this moment, Senya has saved the Soviet boat itself, risking criminal prosecution by cutting loose the submerged nets in defiance of the captain, who was too timid to do so. Violent action, however, is not the novel's main feature. Much of it is concerned with Senya's mixed emotions about the young women in his life and with his musings (the novel is told in first person) over what to do with his life. Portraits of individual crew members are prominent, notably a veteran ship's engineer – the voice of experience, wisdom, and integrity – who tries to persuade Senya to learn his trade. Changes in the crew's morale in the face of adversity are carefully traced. Probably the novel's greatest strength is in its local color. Through detailed description, abundant dialogue, and the hero's own monologues, all told in slangy, nautical vernacular and with considerable rough humor, the novel conveys a tangible sense of existence in the Soviet fishing fleet. Like Vladimov's previous novel of labor, *Three Minutes of Silence* is original precisely because it avoids the ideological clichés and stereotypes of the standard production novel. In the end Senya has gained experience but, without directly specifying it, Vladimov indicates that Senya still has little of the requisite, orthodox confidence in communal purposefulness. (Vladimov's novel *Faithful Ruslan* is discussed in Chapter 13.)

As we have seen in the works of Bitov, Aksenov, Voinovich, and others, a major concern of writers, developed during the middle 1950s, was puzzled, searching, restless youth. The adolescent heroes and heroines of such writers as Lyubov Kabo, Grigori Medinsky, Inna Goff, Anatoli Pristavkin, and Nina Ivanter all have rejected in varying degree the values, beliefs, and prejudices of their parents' generation and are trying to find for themselves a stable and reliable body of truth. In their search they feel compelled to rely only on their own instincts, because the authority figures around them – parents, teachers, and other elders – have largely been compromised by their record of submission to Stalinism.

Literature about young people, however, was not restricted to adolescents troubled by their historical circumstances. Many prominent contemporary authors, such as Nagibin (see pp. 154–7) and Panova (see pp. 177–8, 264, 287–9), wrote not about adolescents but children. One of the best strains in the literature of the 1960s was writing that dealt sympathetically with children as they faced injustice, disappointment, and troubles of a moral nature. The strongest writers in this vein were Nikolai Dubov and Chingiz Aitmatov.

Dubov (born 1910), who has also been a journalist and playwright, lives in the Ukraine, and most of his works are set in the south. He came to prominence in the early 1950s as a writer of novels for and about children: *At the Edge of the Earth* (*Na krayu zemli*, 1951), *Lights on the River* (*Ogni na reke*, 1952), and *The Orphan* (*Sirota*, 1955). His more recent works are clearly intended for more adult readers. "The Difficult Test" ("Zhestkaya proba," 1960) is a story about a young orphan, raised in a children's home, who becomes a factory worker, witnesses widespread corruption on the job, and is forced to develop his own honest code of ethics independently. The story belongs in the above-mentioned category of works about troubled adolescents.

A more profound and delicately tuned work, both tough-minded and touching in its exploration of youthful sensitivities, is Dubov's short novel *A Boy by the Sea* (*Mal'chik u morya*), published in 1963. Sashuk is a bright, curious boy who suffers increasing miseries through a combination of fate and the callousness of adults. He is constantly being insulted, ignored, shamed, and embarrassed by grown-ups who do not notice his feelings or even realize that a person his age has feelings that should be respected. The fact that Sashuk is a real charmer makes his situation all the more poignant. The world about him, however, is merely insensitive, not malevolent. And a few people are kind and attentive to him, notably an ex-convict (who had done five years for striking his boss) and a vacationing astrophysicist (the setting is the Crimean shore of the Black Sea) who tells Sashuk that he must "find his own star."

Much of the novel's attractiveness comes from its seaside setting and Sashuk's discoveries as he wanders alertly along the shore. The movement of the novel, however, is such that things grow worse and worse for the little hero, until he is nearly devastated. He has been repeatedly insulted and has suffered numerous disappointments, his mother is gravely ill in the hospital, his puppy has been senselessly killed, and he is alone in a world that is manifestly unjust. One feels, however, that although some of his goodness, sweetness, and idealism may be destroyed in the process, Sashuk will learn to cope with the adult world. He must find the star that the astrophysicist talked about: "Then surely he would know where the bad people are and where the good ones, whom to believe, whom not to, where the truth is and where the deception and what one must do."

The hero of Dubov's *The Runaway* (*Beglets*), published in 1966, is a boy somewhat older than Sashuk. Yurka, who also lives in the Crimea, has three younger brothers; a dim, drunken, quarrelsome father; a stupid, complaining mother; and a set of relatives of the same ilk. The only pleasantness in Yurka's life comes from the fascinating, remote seashore and his association with his little brothers. His first misfortune comes when his father, drunk, smashes the boy's bicycle beyond repair and injures Yurka in the process. When he arrives home, Yurka gets a beating from his mother. A ray of light appears with the arrival of a pair of campers – a man and woman from Moscow. They befriend the boys and, in particular, treat Yurka with a kindness and understanding to which he is unaccustomed. Soon the man, who is an architect, becomes a surrogate father for Yurka.

The turning point comes when the architect is accidentally drowned. It is then learned that his companion was not his wife but his illicit mistress, and that they were nonconformist runaways from respectable Moscow society. Yurka's family, who had fawned on the couple, now refuses to help the woman, and someone among them (probably Yurka's father) steals all of her money. Witnessing this two-faced viciousness, Yurka denounces his family, is severely beaten by both parents, and runs away. For two weeks he tries to fend for himself, but he soon discovers that the outside world, too, is coarse, cruel, and exploitative. Finally, hunger drives him homeward, although he has no intention of returning for good. He discovers, however, that his hated father has suddenly gone blind, and this knowledge, plus a glimpse of his brothers playing on the shore, triggers a decision to stay home and assume a new responsibility in the family.

The Runaway is technically inferior to *A Boy by the Sea* because the sections following Yurka's flight from home are too episodic and, in places, contrived. Also, the parallels and contrasts between Yurka and his architect friend – both runaways – are presented a bit too obviously. Nevertheless, the novel is just as powerful as its predecessor in its depiction of the suffering and trauma inflicted upon an innocent and uncomprehending boy by base and petty adults, and in its harshly realistic portrayal of the human race. Dubov has a clear-eyed comprehension of life, Chekhovian both in its sensitivity to detail and its lack of sentimentalism.

The stories of Chingiz Aitmatov about young people combine an interest in the universal problems of youth with a special concern for the author's native Kirghiz culture. Such is "The Camel's Eye" ("Verblyuzhy glaz," 1961), in which a boy whose history teacher has imbued him with a romantic fascination for the lore and traditions of his steppe ancestors, is confronted by his compatriots' complete indifference to their cultural heritage. A more complex and tragic work is the short novel *The White Ship* (*Bely parokhod*, 1970). The setting is endowed with a special importance – the lovely mountains and forests of Kirghizia with their fierce winds, and a large lake the white steamship plies. A major element in the story, inseparable from its plot, is the local folklore and its relevance for the community and its present way of life.

The central character is an exceedingly imaginative and sensitive little boy who lives in a tiny, remote community. Abandoned by both his mother and his father (a crewman on the steamship, which the boy occasionally sees in the distance), he has no other children to play with, and his closest associate is his gentle old grandfather. The boy lives a rich fantasy life (he imagines, for example, turning himself into a fish and swimming out to the ship to find his father), and is particularly impressed by the local legend of the Horned Mother Deer. In ancient times this doe saved the lives of the last two members of the Bugan clan, after all the others had been wiped out by rival clans. In return, their descendants protected deer, but later generations became forgetful and callous, slaughtering deer until they disappeared from the region altogether.

The immediate cause of the tragedy is the sudden return, after many years, of three deer. Enchanted, the boy instantly worships the animals, but soon his world is shattered when he discovers that his grandfather has been bullied into slaughtering one of them, a doe, for a feast. Heartbroken, crushed by this episode of human heartlessness, and bewildered by the gulf between his pure world of beautiful fantasy and cruel actuality, the boy drowns himself.

Steeped in Kirghiz mythology, drawing heavily on local traditions, customs, and natural surroundings for its atmosphere, *The White Ship* is a delicately integrated combination of elements: a study in the psychology of a child, a human tragedy, a poetic ethnographic portrait, a lament for a dying culture, and a multiple parable. It enters intimately into the private world of a boy by recounting his fantasies in interior monologue; the boy's innocent point of view is the story's moral index. The story has distinct political implications: its villain, the brutal forest warden who forces the killing of the doe, is a true Stalinist in temperament, morals, and attitude towards other human beings, and it is he and the power he wields that ultimately cause the boy's death. Also, this forest warden despises his Kirghiz national traditions and longs to live in a city. He exemplifies the corruption of modern man and the betrayal of a precious, threatened, national culture. Ultimately he represents a triumph of evil, backed by worldly power, over defenseless innocence.

The White Ship is an excellent work of literature, and it is not surprising that it disturbed official critics. The bone of contention was the triumph of evil over good, and the bleak implications of the boy's suicide. Aitmatov stoutly defended himself against his critics, affirming that truth in art is more important than happy endings, and arguing that in drowning himself the boy provided an inspiring example of uncompromising, unassailable integrity.

Most of the works discussed in the present chapter, and in previous chapters as well, illustrate how Soviet literature became more veracious after the death of Stalin. A concomitant of this trend was the erosion of socialist realism as a practical guiding principle for writers of talent. Aitmatov's *The White Ship*, for example, has absolutely nothing to do with socialist realism for a variety of reasons, the chief of which is that the novel is "gloomy" and "pessimistic." The same can be said, in greater or less degree, of the works of Panova, Nekrasov, Syomin, Dudintsev, Vladimov, and Dubov mentioned in this chapter.

During the fifteen years in which these works appeared, many Soviet critics were acutely worried over the immediate impression such works would leave with the reader: the mood they would create in him, the conclusions he might draw about Soviet society (and, by implication, its leadership), and about life in general. These critics feared that wide and deep explorations of the negative aspects of Soviet reality, and of the general human condition, would lead readers to attitudes of defeatism, indifference to official social standards, and lack of faith in the future. Although they conceded, ostensibly, the writer's right to investigate the seamy side of things, they insisted that ultimately he offer the reader a balance of confidence and hope.

In response to this urging, which had the weight of officialdom behind it, many Soviet writers provided their works with upbeat endings. Examples in the present chapter are Ehrenburg, Kuznetsov, and Granin. In fact, the only fundamental difference between Dudintsev's account of the vicissitudes of an inventor in Soviet society and Granin's treatment of the same theme is that the former fails to show an unalloyed triumph of good over evil while the latter takes pains to do this.

Another view, however, of the Soviet literature that concerned itself with the present and, by implication, with the future, might lead to the conclusion that the prescribed "happy ending" came, in the course of this fifteen-year period, to have little importance. The actual structure of works of fiction, the trend of its events pointing to a better, or worse, or ambiguous future may, in the view of both writers and readers, have lost much of its significance. One suspects that the major concern of writers dealing with the present was to describe it as accurately as possible. If, in order to publish a given work, it became necessary to provide it with a dutifully uplifting conclusion, this was a matter of secondary concern and relatively easy compromise. Thus, many works that conclude in an orthodox "healthy," "life-affirming" way implying that justice, reason, faith, and industry will conquer have included much material that negates such a message. Not only the statements of troubled, puzzled characters but also the *language* they use, and the cultural and social milieu they represent, contradict the sunny outcome with which the writer endows his story. All of this suggests that there may have developed an unspoken agreement between writers and readers – that both groups had become so inured to the conventions of socialist realism that they could be successfully observed and at the same time overlooked.

11

Aleksandr Solzhenitsyn

Aleksandr Solzhenitsyn is the most prominent literary heretic Russia has produced since Leo Tolstoy. Like Tolstoy, he is moved not only by a concern for spiritual values but also by a compelling corporeal interest in what is important for human fulfillment here on earth. He brings to Soviet literature a deep seriousness and reverence for humanity, a skeptical, exacting respect for the truth, and a passion for full disclosure. These qualities, enhanced by his enormous analytical powers and brilliant satirical talent, have made him intolerable to the Soviet establishment. But Solzhenitsyn is the kind of writer who would be dangerous to *any* establishment. He has a rare gift – a truly independent intelligence and a free, responsible spirit.

The basic psychological insecurity of a regime that cannot trust its most creative intellectuals has placed an interdiction on Solzhenitsyn during most of his public career. Only five of his works have been published in the Soviet Union. Of these the first four – the short novel *One Day in the Life of Ivan Denisovich* and the stories "Matryona's House," "An Incident at Krechetovka Station," and "For the Good of the Cause" – were published within a nine-month period in 1962 and 1963. The story "Zakhar-Kalita" – perhaps his weakest and least significant – was allowed publication in 1966. And that is all. His large novels, *Cancer Ward, The First Circle*, and *August 1914*, his *Sketches and Miniature Tales*, his plays, and a few additional fragments, have been published only in the West. Denied the freedom to communicate with his natural and intended audience – the Russian people – Solzhenitsyn has become known to merely a small fraction of them, through hand-to-hand circulation of his unpublished works in manuscript form. As a consequence of his exile, however, it is quite possible that Solzhenitsyn's voice is now heard more extensively in his native land than before his departure, through clandestine circulation of foreign editions of his works and through foreign radio broadcasts of his views.

Although the range of his topics and settings is ostensibly narrow, the sweep of his literary intelligence is enormous. His mastery of prose genres extends from delicate miniatures – the *Sketches and Miniature Tales* – to full-scale novels whose rhetorical majesty rivals that of the greatest Russian works of the nineteenth century. His most brilliant accomplishment in prose technique is the subtle and ingenious *One Day in the Life of Ivan Denisovich*. Every new work, however, seems to show additional stylistic dimensions. A measure of his versatility is that critics attempting to identify the Russian tradition from which his writing emanates have suggested such diverse models as Leskov, Remizov, Dostoevsky, Pilnyak, Klychkov, Bunin, Melnikov-Pechersky, Chekhov, Saltykov-Shchedrin, Turgenev, Babel, and Tolstoy. No one, however, has suggested that Solzhenitsyn is an imitator. The most "limiting" thing that could be said is that he is a synthesizer who partakes of many influences and adds much that is his own.

The predominant influence would seem to be that of Tolstoy, with whom Solzhenitsyn has many qualities in common: intense moral earnestness, a gift for precise psychological observation and analysis, a sense of environment, and a skeptical, ironical frame of mind. Like Tolstoy, he is sparing in his use of figurative language; he gives things their exact names and lets them stand for themselves. His occasional similes and metaphors are precise, clear, and disciplined, and only rarely is there a full-fledged symbol. Like Tolstoy, he is amazingly alert to the relevance of the objects that surround daily life. Things such as the interview table at Lefortovo prison or the worn stone stairs inside Lubyanka are examined carefully for the human significance that can be extracted from them. Tolstoyan stylistic devices abound: long, one-sentence paragraphs in *Cancer Ward*, with carefully balanced series of dependent clauses, word repetitions, and strings of parallel prepositional phrases and verb forms. Similarly, Solzhenitsyn does not shy away from involved syntax and parenthetical interpolations, particularly in passages of psychological analysis. His use of bodily movement to indicate mental attitudes and emotional responses, his employment of physical gesture as counterpoint in dialogue (as in the moving prison interview between Gleb Nerzhin and his wife), and his use of fixed attributes (Kostoglotov's scar, Shukhov's lisp, Rusanov's flashing glasses), all resemble Tolstoy's, as does his use of shifting point-of-view and interior monologue in characterization.

Of the numerous literary allusions in *Cancer Ward* and *The First Circle* by far the greatest number are to Tolstoy and his works. Clearly Solzhenitsyn reveres not only Tolstoy the craftsman but also Tolstoy the thinker. The reading of Tolstoy's moral tales transforms the outlook of the dying Efrem Podduev in *Cancer Ward* and leads directly to the novel's central ideological quarrel. There are several bitterly sarcastic references, in both novels, to the distortion, disparagement, and stifling of Tolstoy's ideas in official Soviet practice. (A secondary school teacher discourages her pupils from reading Tolstoy's novels because "they are very long and only obscure the clear critical articles about him.") At the same time, in his fiction Solzhenitsyn does not write as an advocate of a specific philosophy of life. He has Tolstoy's intense moral awareness without the latter's proclivity for theorizing and compulsion for intellectual formulations and prescriptions. Although Solzhenitsyn is usually closer to the civic, didactic Tolstoy of *Resurrection* than to the earlier Tolstoy of *War and Peace*, he lacks Tolstoy's scolding, evangelistic tone. Whereas the writing of the later Tolstoy was often self-lacerating, negative, and punitive, Solzhenitsyn's – if anything, even more thoroughly scathing in its social criticism – is tempered by robust mental health and freedom from neurosis, a sense of measure, and intellectual humility. (The same cannot be said, however, of his recent speeches and articles in the West, which, to many observers, seem didactic to the point of arrogance.)

A comparison of *Cancer Ward* with "The Death of Ivan Ilych" illustrates the differences. Both works are dominated by the same dread disease, both employ the ominousness of death as a device for moral exploration, and they have similar protagonists. (There are secondary resemblances as well: Rusanov's family is like that of Ivan Ilych, and the devices used in portraying the heroes' characters are similar – including dreams and their attendant symbolism.) But Tolstoy uses his medical situation to scare, to flagellate, and to preach; Solzhenitsyn uses his to observe and surely to criticize, but mainly to analyze in a less threatening, more compassionate manner. (I suspect, also, that Solzhenitsyn is a more *trustworthy* writer than Tolstoy. V. S. Pritchett has pointed out an implausibility in the portrayal of Stalin in *The First Circle* – the Leader thinks of Lady Anne in *Richard III* – but the portrait is probably less warped than, for example, Tolstoy's Napoleon.) Further comparison and contrast with Tolstoy will be found in the discussion of *August 1914*, later in this chapter.

On the basis of the thematic similarity between *One Day in the Life of Ivan Denisovich* and *Notes from the House of the Dead*, some critics have found affinities between Solzhenitsyn and Dostoevsky. His novels would seem to show, however, that although Solzhenitsyn has certain interests in common with Dostoevsky, the similarities are superficial. Although they share a mutual concern over the problem of evil, Solzhenitsyn lacks the metaphysical uncertainty of Dostoevsky and does not dwell on evil in such laborious profundity. Solzhenitsyn knows what is right and wrong: evil comes not from the Devil but from identifiable human weakness and the dislocation of the social order. His characters are more clearly defined, less extravagant in their thinking, and have fewer ideological and religious torments and options. There are no Karamazovs among them. Moreover, Solzhenitsyn does not indulge in dark hints, either as a novelist or an ideological strategy.

Solzhenitsyn does bring to the Soviet context, however, a concern that was prominent not only in Dostoevsky but also in many other nineteenth-century Russian writers, among them Goncharov, Turgenev, and Chekhov. Nearly every one of his novels and stories contains representatives of the dispirited Russian liberal intelligentsia – characters whose moral sensitivity, contemplative temperament, and preference for abstract thought over practical action makes them incapable of coping successfully with the harsh demands of reality. Such characters as Lieutenant Zotov in "The Incident at Krechetovka Station," the school principal Fyodor Mikheevich in "For the Good of the Cause," and the painter Kondrashev-Ivanov in *The First Circle* are the inheritors, in Soviet times, of a peculiar and persistent strain of ineffectuality among the intellectuals found in Russian literature. Admirable in their idealism and yearning for pure justice, they have traditionally been defeated by men of action and reduced to an underground existence of impotent frustration. In the works of Solzhenitsyn, their plight is complicated and aggravated by sinister contemporary social conditions: their isolation is largely involuntary. Nevertheless, they are direct descendants of the alienated heroes of the nineteenth century.

The moral problems Solzhenitsyn treats are nearly always socially oriented; he seems determined to make a full and detailed disclosure of the truth about Soviet life and to examine its moral essence. "Matryona's House" concerns official abuse of the peasantry and, incidentally, corruption in the Soviet educational system. *One Day* focuses on a concentration camp. *The First Circle* concerns other dramatic evils of the Stalin period: the secret police system of informers, false arrest, and arbitrary administrative justice; the harsh penal system; privilege, corruption, and luxurious living in the ruling class. *Cancer Ward* deals with the immediate aftermath of Stalin's rule. "For the Good of the Cause" is an exposure of careerism and bureaucratic disregard of popular aspirations and public welfare.

One of Solzhenitsyn's main concerns is the all-pervasive lie. In *The First Circle* the key to the character of Gleb Nerzhin (autobiographical in many respects) is that from his boyhood he has been aware of relentless, systematic official deception. Problems of conscience, and dialogues about its role, are prominent in the novels and stories. Lieutenant Zotov in "An Incident at Krechetovka Station" turns in to the authorities a man who *may* be a spy for the Germans. Whether the man is guilty or not, he is virtually certain to be disposed of as one. In performing a military duty, Zotov may have destroyed an innocent man; the thought will torment him for life. In *Cancer Ward* the Party bureaucrat Rusanov dismisses conscience by asserting that immoral acts are merely "bourgeois vestiges." Leninism has taken care of the problem of conscience "once and for all." Rusanov's opponent, Kostoglotov, insists that the human spirit demands an ideal of individual moral perfection and that the conscience is its touchstone.

A related theme is personal responsibility, to which Solzhenitsyn applies a variety of subtle shadings. In *The First Circle*, Volodin – a basically decent Soviet diplomat who has put his conscience to sleep by developing a half-baked "Epicurean" philosophy – activates his latent revulsion against the Stalinist terror by performing a humane deed that sends him to Lubyanka. Rubin, an imprisoned philologist, has persuaded himself in all good conscience that the higher aims of the state oblige him to help crush such men as Volodin. One of the most pathetic characters in *Cancer Ward* is Shulubin, bitter in the realization of his passive guilt of a lifetime in failing to challenge corruption and injustice. Solzhenitsyn is delicately venomous in his exposure of the vast Soviet vocabulary of obfuscation and cant – for example the much abused Russian word *oshibka* (mistake) as a moral dodge.

No clear political ideology has yet emerged from Solzhenitsyn. This is not to say that the works themselves are politically shallow. The author shrewdly undercuts, for example, all basically materialist political philosophy. Solzhenitsyn's own awareness of the organic dilemmas of communism – which places him in the tradition of skeptics from Dostoevsky to Zamyatin and Sinyavsky – is exemplified ironically in the "law of big numbers" of the careerist Lansky in *The First Circle*, who rationalizes Stalin's crimes in the name of progress ("As the traffic increases, so will the number of traffic victims") and, without irony, in the quarrel between Rubin, the convinced Leninist and the fiery skeptic Sologdin over the "morality of revolutionary means." And even Rubin senses that humans need the moral sustenance and discipline that comes from religious institutions and ritual. He conceives a "Project for Civic Temples," complete with a priesthood and liturgy, holiday ceremonies, and aesthetic appurtenances designed to formalize and solemnize the state religion.

Cancer Ward and *The First Circle* have an element of combative abusiveness that is largely absent from the other works of fiction. In these two novels Solzhenitsyn emerges as an angry, often bitter writer, merciless toward his enemies, openly despising the evil they represent. The novels abound in vignettes such as this one, about one of the *zeks* (Soviet slang for "prisoners") in *The First Circle:*

> Even his first sentence was gotten absurdly. At the beginning of the war they jailed him for "anti-Soviet agitation" – some neighbors who hankered after his apartment denounced him (and then got it). True, it turned out that he hadn't done any agitating, but he *could* have done it, because he listened to the German radio. True, he didn't listen to the German radio, but he *could* have listened, since he had a forbidden radio receiver at home. True, he didn't have such a receiver, but he *could* have had one, since he was a radio engineer by profession, and when he was denounced they did find two radio tubes in a box at his place.

Solzhenitsyn's most powerful weapon is irony – deft but seldom gentle. He performs intellectual judo on the official cliché, as in *Cancer Ward* when he explains the rise of a bureaucrat and his simultaneous estrangement from the population in terms of the "dialectical interconnections of all phenomena of reality." He makes sarcastic sport of habits of moral evasiveness, as when the prosecutor Makarygin in *The First Circle*, discomfited by his idealistic daughter's dinner-table accounts of social injustice, concludes that the stories are "untypical." The most consistently effective irony, in fact, is in Solzhenitsyn's ridicule of the cruel lunacy of Stalinism and his relentless exposure of the absurd rationalizations that justify injustice. Rusanov, for example, concludes that it is "inhumane" to "agitate" the lives of political exiles by returning them from the banishment to which they have become accustomed. His daughter finds something "ruthless" in the "painful, tormenting process" of political rehabilitation. Besides, one "cannot turn back the wheel of history." Solzhenitsyn's talent for pointing out the screaming nonsense and wild immorality of attitudes that people have come to consider unexceptionable makes him in this respect a worthy successor to Saltykov-Shchedrin. There is also a more extravagant kind of irony, as in the fully developed burlesque fantasies of *The First Circle:* the mock trial of Prince Igor for anti-Soviet activities and Eleanor Roosevelt's visit to Butyrskaya prison, which has been prettified, Potemkin-style, for the occasion. Sometimes sarcasm is combined with hyperbole, as in this parenthetical comment on prison regulations in *The First Circle:*

> No zek had the right to stay one second in his workroom without the supervision of a free employee, since vigilance prompted that the prisoner would surely use this unsupervised second to open the steel safe with the aid of a penciil, photograph its secret documents with the aid of a pants button, explode an atomic bomb and fly to the moon.

There are other ironic devices of a more purely comic nature – anecdotes, plays on words, and small portions of mild scatology. And irony at times dictates the very structure of the works. Just as in "Matryona's House," where the good that the heroine does brings about her destruction, so in *The First Circle* each character who makes an honest or humane moral choice is rewarded with a worsening of his situation. This is not, however, the "irony of fate." The source of the evil is clearly the Stalinist system, with its perverted view of human nature, its absurd deification of the lie, and its compulsion to waste and destroy human resources.

In the miniature "Lake Segden," Stalin is the subject of allegory as a cruel, squint-eyed king who has seized the motherland and terrorized its people. Stalin also permeates *The First Circle* and *Cancer Ward.* He is present both for thematic reasons and as a literary device. He dominates *The First Circle* as a living presence, through the direct effects of his policies and whims, through a constant ironic refrain of adulatory phrases ("Nearest and Dearest," "Father of Western and Eastern Peoples," etc.), and in an extensive direct portrait that shows him both in contact with his subordinates and alone with his thoughts. He emerges not as a demon but as a sick, fearful, psychologically identifiable individual with purely human dimensions – paranoiac, cruel, cunning, enormously vain, arrogant, self-deluded, and totally cynical. In *Cancer Ward,* set in 1955, the presence of Stalin is residual but powerful: many wounds are still fresh, many minds still stunned. Thematically in both novels the image of Stalin is a distillation of elements that are developed more fully in other parts of the narrative in scenes of frustration, cruelty, and suffering. His role in the narrative structure of *The First Circle* is, first, as a character and, second, as the evil genius whose caprice determines the fate of every other character in his Inferno and thus motivates the novel. In both *The First*

Circle and *Cancer Ward*, he serves as a device for characterization (attitudes toward Stalin vary), as an ironic narrative refrain, and as the sinister symbol of a way of life and system of belief. Stalinism provides much of the cement that holds these two novels together; reactions to Stalinism provide much of their tension.

Solzhenitsyn's first three novels are explorations of a system of insult in which good men are crushed, the human potential is thwarted, and the spirit is not permitted to flower. In *The First Circle* Gleb Nerzhin and his beloved Nadya agonize over whether to get a divorce, which will free her of the paralyzing stigma of being a political prisoner's wife. In the same novel the *zeks* solemnly debate over whether it is better to be imprisoned in youth or old age – since, they feel, every man must do ten years or more, which segment of a man's life is more expendable? Deprived of his birthright in a world of institutionalized bestiality where things are more important than people, man can only survive through moral toughness.

In all three of these novels there are fleeting images of exceptional human dignity in the midst of pain and horror, such as the anonymous, bald, and toothless old man in *One Day* – a perpetual prisoner – who always sits ramrod-straight in the mess hall and does not bend over his bowl like the others but brings his spoon up to his mouth. The hero of this novel, Ivan Denisovich Shukhov, preserves his dignity through resignation and calculated submission. Shukhov is a peasant, and his sentence is a long one, easily extendable. To maintain his mental composure he has cut his emotional ties with the outside world, and to endure physically he has developed a number of adroit means of living within the camp system. His ultimate self-preservation is in his ability to get along with his fellow *zeks*, his patience, and his love of physical work. In his peasant simplicity, resilience, and meek acceptance of his lot, Shukhov resembles Platon Karataev of *War and Peace*. Tolstoy's character, however, is a didactically conceived paragon of peasant virtues and a somewhat idealized abstraction. Shukhov, a more completely realized character, is a product not of his author's advocacy but of his observation. Like the heroine of "Matryona's House," who is also long-suffering and finds salvation in selfless labor, Shukhov is to a degree an idealized image of the Russian peasant, an inheritance from nineteenth-century tradition. But also like Matryona, Shukhov is richly individualized and is as memorable for his peculiarities as for his virtues.

Shukhov and Matryona endure oppression through a kind of primordial submissiveness. In other works, alternative responses are developed more fully. There are characters, such as Klara Makarygina in *The First Circle* and Yura Rusanov in *Cancer Ward*, who are just becoming aware that their world is out of joint and whose impending moral crises will surely alienate them from the existing order. The degree of their future spiritual isolation and the shape of their attitudes are unpredictable, but there are numerous patterns. The independent and defiant Bobynin in *The First Circle*, for example, survives morally through the courage of despair. Gleb Nerzhin, still hopeful, preserves his spiritual integrity by acting on principle, knowing it may destroy him. Rubin withstands his humiliation by clinging stubbornly to his faith in the dialectic. In any event, Klara and Yura will avoid the fate of the morally bankrupt Rusanov, Yura's father, who does not even admit that he has been living in a cesspool.

Solzhenitsyn's most fully developed hero, and his most thoroughly conceived embodiment of man's earthly plight, is Kostoglotov of *Cancer Ward*. He, too, is a casualty of Stalinism (first, long imprisonment and now perpetual exile) and, at age thirty-four, has been robbed of much of his life – an education, a profession, a wife and family, personal freedom. But in addition he has cancer, and the hormone therapy that is curing it will also emasculate him. Thus deprived, he must decide whether life is worth living. Kostoglotov is highly intelligent, an honest thinker with a fine sense of irony and justice, a courageous and uncompromising individualist, and a fighter. Hemmed in and battered, he nevertheless succeeds in preserving the modicum of volition that will give his life meaning. (He exerts this volition, sadly, in renouncing tenderly the two women who offer him love.) He is clearly Solzhenitsyn's finest tribute to the nobility and endurance of the human spirit.

Kostoglotov's opposite – and Solzhenitsyn's finest negative character – is Rusanov, a middle-echelon functionary who has denounced (secretly), bullied, and blackmailed his way (the author calls it "poetico-political work") to privileged affluence. A smug former proletarian who has lost his calluses, Rusanov has isolated himself and his family from the vulgar crowd, has shielded himself from reality in paper-shuffling and government statistics, and subsists on a steady diet of propaganda. He brings to the cancer ward limitless arrogance and unswerving orthodoxy. A prudish hypocrite with a strong proclivity for self-deception, he is a repository of wistful Stalinist prejudice. What makes him interesting is not so much the mental and moral wasteland he represents as the vigorous, strangely disarming spontaneity of his philistine reflexes: he always provides the cheap, the obtuse, the brutish response. Truly an original, Rusanov belongs in such diverse company as Porphyry Golovlyov and Chekhov's man-in-a-case.

Although Rusanov seems incapable of friendship, he is somewhat attracted to two other patients: Vadim, a dedicated young geologist and Chaly, a small-time speculator. With his cold honesty, Party idealism, single-minded ambition and devotion to the future, Vadim is the New Soviet Man whom the softer Rusanov mistakenly thinks himself to be. At the same time, Vadim, in his arrogance and spiritual blindness, is a subtle, terrifying parody of Rusanov. In Chaly, Rusanov senses a kindred spirit, a fellow crook; but Chaly is embarrassing because he is not a hypocrite like Rusanov. Vadim and Chaly are examples of Solzhenitsyn's brilliant use of foils: each character is a subtle commentary on all the others. A similar use of foils is in *One Day*, where two opposites – Buynovsky, the Party idealist and Alyosha, the devout Baptist – are presented through the neutral but skeptical eyes of Shukhov.

All of the first three novels are carefully designed and meticulously integrated portrait galleries. Each character is given a biography and limned in terms of his physical appearance, his behavior in the collective, and his relationship to other characters. Most are further individualized by intellectual, moral, ideological, or cultural idiosyncrasies, by a variety of quirks of personality, and by speech traits. In all three novels, however, characterization is governed mainly by setting: individuals respond variously to the challenge of a common milieu or circumstance – the disease of cancer and the ward environment; the concentration camp in *One Day*; and, in *The First Circle*, the *sharashka* (a research institute staffed by prisoners) and the Moscow upper-class world. This is all done systematically, but not mechanically. The art of Solzhenitsyn is one of subtle juxtaposition, shifting point of view, and change of pace. He seldom does the same thing twice in the same way.

Solzhenitsyn adds dimensions to his characters, for example, through ingenious methods of review. One chapter of *Cancer Ward* surveys the patients through the eyes of Vadim, whose particular kind of Soviet mentality filters out things about them that the reader has not previously perceived. In the process the character of Vadim is also reinforced and vivified. Somewhat similarly in *The First Circle*, Nerzhin on the day of his departure from the *sharashka* must decide who will get his precious volume of Esenin. In doing so he reviews the tastes of his comrades and provides an implicit evaluation of each of them. In *Cancer Ward* what keeps Rusanov from becoming merely a brilliant caricature is that we first experience the atmosphere of the ward through his own sensations on arriving there. This humanizes him, and only as we are gradually liberated from his point of view do we see that, in addition to the flesh and blood he shares with us all, he has a monstrous perspective on the world. Characterization in *One Day* is conditioned by a strategy in which narrative responsibility is divided between a third-person objective narrator and the hero Shukhov. The characters become known, as in other novels, by what they do and say, but because the only individualized point of view is that of Shukhov, there is a special "insider's" evaluation of each of them. The *zeks* are interpreted in terms of their positions in the camp's hierarchy of power and influence and, more importantly, their place as either workers or parasites in the camp organism.

The vividness of Solzhenitsyn's characters, and of his narration in general, comes from a rich but judicious selection and arrangement of detail and an extraordinary feel for the relationship between the part and the whole. One of the major strengths of *One Day* is its documentary precision and eye-witness fidelity in giving the particulars of concentration camp existence – presented in the *zeks'* own vocabulary. Detail does not, however, merely provide background or atmosphere: it becomes an integral part of the novel's psychological structure. The minute description of miserable camp food, for example, shows its elemental and yet complex spiritual importance in the prisoners' world. The little piece of metal Shukhov finds and hides because it "may come in handy" – an object he would have ignored in the outside world – epitomizes the value system of the camps. Solzhenitsyn's lean description of a work process – Shukhov's bricklaying – differs fundamentally from those in the standard Soviet "production novel," in which the accumulation of technical detail often becomes an end in itself. Here, the very rhythm of Shukhov's work has profound psychological and moral significance.

Rusanov's traffic in questionnaires and dossiers, in *Cancer Ward*, is not just his occupation; it stands, metonymically, for the man. Detail provides a sense of how Soviet institutions really work – the mechanics of an arrest, the transport of prisoners, the running of a hospital, the compulsive window dressing that dominates Soviet officialdom, as well as the small private acts of kindness and love that make life endurable. Reading *Pravda* with Rusanov, we have an insider's guide to the Soviet press. A post-office glue pot, hidden against pilferage, the merchandise in a crowded Tashkent department store, a letter from a forgotten Central Asian place of exile, the interior of Matryona's peasant dwelling, all become imagery that lends authenticity. Solzhenitsyn is alert to the look, feel, smell, and rhythm of life.

Care for detail is particularly striking in Solzhenitsyn's use of the Russian tongue. The language of *One Day* – lean and vivid – is a mélange of colloquial Russian, neologisms, Shukhov's peasant dialect, and concentration camp jargon. *The First Circle* and *Cancer Ward* are narrated in standard literary Russian, but they too use methods that are sometimes similar, although not identical, to those in *One Day*. The very phraseology used in reporting Rubin's thoughts about "the people," for example, exactly corresponds to Rubin's Marxist–Leninist orientation. And the life story of the peasant *zek*, Spiridon, unobtrusively lards passages of standard literary Russian with the language of Spiridon's own cultural background. Not only does Solzhenitsyn tailor the language of his characters to suit them as individuals; his own narrative and expository language is lively, personalized and full of vividly expressive coinages. Solzhenitsyn is a formidable linguist, and the quality of the language of any given passage often tells its own story.

The earthy prison language of *One Day* called forth some rebukes from prudish critics. Had *Cancer Ward* been published in the USSR, its quantities of unpleasant clinical detail would inevitably have invited the charge of "naturalism." However, the novel is neither morbid nor sensational. It is a sober, sympathetic, tasteful story of medicine, told by a grateful patient. Some elements do appear gratuitous: a plea for the family doctor and private practice, the drawing of an extraneous dichotomy between therapy and research, and the excessive irony of having a cancer specialist, the heroic Dr. Dontsova, infected with cancer. There is a strong suggestion, emanating largely from Kostoglotov, that correct spiritual attitudes and folk remedies are more effective against cancer than scientific treatment. Solzhenitsyn does not share this view, but the intelligent humility of his doctors provides a constant reminder of the limitations of scientific medicine.

In one of his miniatures, "But We Shall Not Die," Solzhenitsyn deplores the present-day attitude toward death, which he considers to be irreverent, evasive, artificial, and fearful. Death, he argues, must be contemplated without fear, and there must be no pretense of unconcern. The main unifying force in *Cancer Ward* is the shadow of death. Although the patients seldom discuss it openly, their very taciturnity, the progress of their diseases (some are cured) and their concern for each other emphasize its presence. Under its threat they examine their lives, values, and aspirations and show varying shades of apprehension and resignation. The narrative attitude is serene and compassionate; death is frightening and unjust, but it must be faced with dignity.

Solzhenitsyn is equally compassionate in his treatment of sex. A main theme of *The First Circle* is the brutality of the police state in separating devoted couples forever. In *Cancer Ward*, the erosion of Kostoglotov's sexual powers is made subtly analogous to his political persecution. Exiled, he sometimes thinks of himself as a stream that is destined to disappear in the sand.

Many of the objects and episodes in the *Sketches and Miniature Tales* take on distinctly metaphorical meanings. In "The Bonfire and the Ants," for example, there is allegorical significance in the compulsive return of ants to certain destruction in a burning log from which they have just fled. A metaphorical interpretation is also tempting for *One Day*, in which the concentration camp seems to stand for something larger – surely Stalinist Russia, possibly the twentieth-century world in general or, perhaps, the human situation in the abstract. (Those who see *Cancer Ward* as a political symbol are surely mistaken.) For the most part, however, the imagery of the novels is solid, concrete, and down-to-earth; the primary, direct meaning of a word is sufficient.

Although symbols are few, there is a great resonance of images in each novel. A monkey is blinded with tobacco in the Tashkent zoo; a harmless dog is senselessly slaughtered by the police in Ush-Terek; Kostoglotov is nearly run down by the automobile of the departing Rusanov. The episodes – all in *Cancer Ward* – are totally disconnected but mutually reinforcing. In *The First Circle* the prisoner Nerzhin is put into civilian clothes for his last pathetic interview with his wife; at the end of the novel he is driven away in a police van disguised by a sign that reads "MEAT" in four languages.

Solzhenitsyn achieves similar suggestiveness and depth by the manipulation of point of view.[1] In *One Day* the primary narrator is a kind of disembodied, omniscient presence, who speaks in third person (in prison language) as a surrogate for the author himself. This narration is frequently supplanted by that of the hero Shukhov, usually in the form of interior monologue conveyed through indirect speech. The combination of these two narrative voices (which are often subtly interchanged within single paragraphs, or even sentences) achieves the immediacy of a first-person *skaz* in the tradition of Leskov, Remizov, and Babel. The reader shares the point of view of Shukhov by "seeing" through his eyes, but he has the advantage of the augmented perspective and understanding that the primary narrator simultaneously provides. Shukhov knows everything about camp life with a large peasant wisdom, but he is also pathetically naive about its larger implications. As a result of this delicately manipulated double point of view, the novel conveys with the closest intimacy and sympathy the bias of its central character, and at the same time transcends the limitations of his cognition.

Despite Shukhov's long camp experience, there is much about the camp and its varied inhabitants that seems strange to him, that he does not fully comprehend – partly because of his peasant naiveté but mainly because the whole camp system runs contrary to nature. The strategy of showing the camp from Shukhov's "unsophisticated" point of view produces a fresh and unconsciously critical view of reality, and therefore an ironical one. The same thing is done in *Cancer Ward*, when the exile Kostoglotov, wandering about Tashkent on his single free day, discovers in a pathetic mixture of perplexity and disgust that life in the outside world has become so opulent that men are expected to know, and to care about, their own shirt sizes.

Solzhenitsyn's first three novels, like most of his stories, are rigorously restricted in time and space. Time is particularly important in *One Day*. Its limited time span, from reveille to lights out, enhances the structural unity, intensity, and compression of the novel. More important, this one day – a relatively *good* one for Shukhov among the 3,653 to which he has been sentenced – becomes the ironic quintessence of the stagnant, hopeless, and preposterous camp existence. The ultimate, purposeless idiocy of the camps is quietly emphasized in remarks about how time passes: "It was a funny thing how time flew when you were working! He was always struck by how fast the days went in camp – you didn't have time to turn around. But the end of your sentence never seemed to be any closer."[2] Time has become a traditional theme in Soviet literature, most notably in the industrial novel, which stressed rapid work tempos: time must not be wasted, time means progress. In *One Day*, time is an evil joke; the authorities have robbed men of it, simply to squander it in colossal quantities of meaningless activity.

All of the first three novels are compressed and crowded and, although there are vents to the outside world, to other times and places, they often teem almost to the point of surfeit. The artistic habit of working in close quarters may come from the author's own experience of apprehending the world in the confinement of prisons, camps, and hospital wards. But it is also a strategic choice; by isolating and encasing large numbers of characters together and subjecting them to a common experience he achieves both intensification and democratization. The camp in *One Day* is a world in itself – strange, isolated by its remoteness and by the wire, floodlights, and guns at its perimeter. At the same time, the camp is made to seem extraordinarily, timelessly real, much more so than the outside world where men are able to create barriers against actuality. Like the camp, the *sharashka* and the ward are also levelers and reshufflers. They break down the artificial hierarchies of the outside world and replace them with a more fundamental scale of values. The transformation brings fresh perspectives and ironic contrasts, and the close interaction of characters with very diverse social, occupational, political, cultural, and ethnic backgrounds produces the effect of a microcosm.

The First Circle, however, is not as successful as *One Day* and *Cancer Ward* in these respects. Although its characters are carefully differentiated, they sometimes seem to blend into an amorphous mass. For one thing, they are mostly persons with special mental talents, who tend to interact on a purely intellectual plane. The main difficulty, however, is structural. *The First Circle* is a kind of static *collage*, without a prominent plot or the kind of suspense that fixes characters in the reader's mind. Furthermore, its four-day time span limits the possibilities for character growth and development. Solzhenitsyn's purpose in alternating between the "free" sector of Soviet society (Moscow apartments and offices) and the "unfree" sector (the *sharashka* and other prisons) would seem to be to show not only that the captives are morally superior to their captors but that the difference between the two sectors is largely illusory: everyone is in essentially the same trap. In pursuing this theme, however, he fails to compensate for the lack of unity in his setting by other means, and as a consequence the characters become unnecessarily ephemeral.

Although the consistently downward trend in the fates of nearly all the major characters of *The First Circle* does provide a certain structural coherence, the other two novels are more unified. The intentional plotlessness of *One Day* is compensated for by its strict observance of time sequence, its unity of setting, and the unison of its narrative voices. *Cancer Ward* is held together also by its circumscribed setting but, in addition, by a more distinct plot based on the developing relationships among the characters, the progress of their diseases, and the evolution of their views on morality, life, and death. Both of these novels, moreover, benefit from a more adroitly rhythmic shifting of points of view, which creates the impression of movement and is at the same time less jarring and confusing than in *The First Circle*.

The First Circle and *Cancer Ward* are strong polemics against the official norms of Soviet literature, not only in their topics and narrative means but also in their fiery satire against socialist realism and the literary establishment. There are numerous indictments of the emptiness and corruption of what Volodin in *The First Circle* calls a "literature created not for readers but for writers." Solzhenitsyn attacks Stalinist literary whoredom; in both novels he ticks off, by name, numerous wealthy and officially honored hacks. (A special place among them is reserved for the late Aleksei Tolstoy: the murderously orthodox Rusanov simply *assumes* he is greater than Leo, and the sophisticated *zeks* in *The First Circle* call him Aleksei *non*-Tolstoy.) *The First Circle* contains the half-contemptuous, half-pitying portrait of the Stalin Prize novelist Galakhov, who lives in fear of the watchdog critics. Here are the thoughts of Galakhov and his colleagues, all "kept" writers:

> Of course, one was forbidden to write much of the truth. But they consoled themselves that some day circumstances would change, and then they would return once more to those events without fail, reillumine them truthfully, and would re-issue and correct their old books. But now they would write that quarter, eighth, sixteenth, that, well – to hell with it – thirty-second part of the truth that was possible. Because better a little bit than nothing at all.

And there is Rusanov's terrifying daughter Avieta, a second-generation philistine and incipient poet who has cased the literary world and has a surefire formula for making her way in it. Ultimately, however, the most acid indictment of socialist realism is Rusanov himself: he subsists on the myth of the positive hero.

In Solzhenitsyn's writings to date there is no explicitly stated theory of literature. From the arguments of some characters about art, the pattern of his literary allusions, and his own creative practice, however, one can tentatively call him an eclectic with conservative leanings whose main preoccupation is with truth and honesty in literature.

Similarly, no pronounced philosophy of history is discernible, although *August 1914* features a running polemic against Tolstoy's determinism in *War and Peace*. There is a depth of cultural reference and respect for Russian tradition in the novels and stories, however, that indicates a profound sense of historical continuity. He is clearly skeptical of euphoric notions about the cleansing quality of 1917 and its aftermath, and he argues implicitly against the uniqueness of the New Soviet Man. In such prominent characters as Shukhov, Matryona, the eccentric Zakhar in "Zakhar-Kalita" and many others, he emphasizes the lingering of age-old Russian behavior patterns and attitudes. At the same time, his view of the past is hardheaded and rational; he does not blindly love the traditional. His sense of the tragic quality of Russian history, and his feeling of personal identification with it, are expressed most strongly in the *Sketches and Miniature Tales*. In "City on the Neva," for example – a variation on Pushkin's theme of the Bronze Horseman – he contemplates the architectural grandeur of Leningrad, built by the Tsars with the bones of slaves, and wonders whether the pain and torment of the present will produce, in the long run, a similar beauty and magnificence.

Solzhenitsyn's reverence for the Russian cultural heritage is evident most of all in his concern for preserving the purity of the Russian language and his frequent complaint of neglect and desecration of Russian churches. (His concern for preserving Russian antiquities resembles that of Vladimir Soloukhin, but he differs from Soloukhin in his greater emphasis on the religious heritage.) There is religious awe in the miniature "The Duckling," which tenderly describes a newly hatched fledgling, then mentions man's exploits in space, and concludes: "But never! never, with all our atomic might, shall we be able to synthesize in our retorts, even if they give us ready-made wings and bones – never shall we be able to assemble a weightless, tiny, pitiful yellow duckling." In another miniature, "Starting the Day," he notes ironically that Russians nowadays pay daily tribute to the human body in group calisthenics but are repelled by similarly ritualistic attention to the soul. His sketch "The Easter Procession" indignantly describes a tiny band of worshippers, insulted and terrorized by an inane and sloppy crowd of young Soviet toughs. And "Matryona's House" features a heroine whose strength is in her primitive Christian devotion to serving others. Until recently, Solzhenitsyn's solicitude for churches and religion, and his sympathetic portrayal of humble faith, did not, however, warrant conclusions about the degree of his possible belief in Christianity. He admired the ethical values of Christianity and shared its spiritual concerns, but there was no discernible symbolism, no firm structure of Christian doctrine. Rather, his interest seemed to lie in the maintenance of decency and kindliness in life on earth and the preservation of human dignity through freedom to pursue truth. He has now made it clear, in public statements and in the novel *August 1914*, that he in fact is a Russian Othodox believer.

In the miniature "Breathing," he likens freedom to rain-washed spring air – "sweeter than any food, wine, even a woman's kiss." And in "Sharik" a little dog is unchained to romp in the snow; when warm, fragrant bones are brought to him, he merely sniffs at them and dashes off: "I don't need your bones – just give me freedom." For Solzhenitsyn, freedom is clearly a spiritual matter. One of the prisoners in *The First Circle* remarks, "When you've robbed a man of *everything* he's no longer in your power – he's free again." Although the novels are of course a protest against physical bondage, their essential drama is in the striving for liberty of the spirit.

Deprivation of physical freedom, paradoxically, has contributed greatly to his strength and wisdom as a writer. His knowledge of "the people" – the fruit of his years of imprisonment, exile, and hospitalization – enables him to write of them with a dispassionate authority unexcelled even by such a celebrated plebian as Gorky. And although he shares the traditional respect for the peculiar intensity of suffering and spiritual struggle of the Russian people, he eschews the sentimental and condescending idealization of the peasant folk that has often been its concomitant. His most prominent representatives of the "folk" – Shukhov, Matryona and the *zek* Spiridon of *The First Circle* – are by no means wholly exemplary. All three are primitive, instinctive thinkers, with many of the brutish qualities of the herded animal. Calamity, love of labor, and closeness to the soil have strengthened them, but theirs is a passive strength that enables them to endure oppression, not to overthrow it. Solzhenitsyn's attitude toward the common peasant folk (industrial workers are notably absent in his works) is mixed.

In *The First Circle* he traces Nerzhin's pendular swing between contempt for and idolatry of "the people." Finally, Nerzhin's friendship with Spiridon (culminating in a scene strikingly similar to one in *Anna Karenina*) convinces him that generalized notions of "the people" are meaningless. In his treatment of another view of "the people" – the spurious and obscene official Soviet *narodnost'* – Solzhenitsyn is particularly devastating. He reports that the Rusanovs "loved the *narod* [the people] . . . but as the years went by they more and more could not bear the *naselenie* [the population]." Solzhenitsyn's survey of the Soviet population from top to bottom has brought him to a simple conclusion that is nevertheless heretical in its time and place: human beings must be judged as individuals.

The novel *August 1914* is a distinct departure from Solzhenitsyn's previously published writings – the first volume of a huge projected work of historical fiction that will investigate the sources of Russia's present circumstances. Devoted primarily to the Battle of Tannenberg in World War I, in which the Russian armies, advancing into East Prussia, suffered a crippling defeat that was ultimately to prove fatal, it is essentially a military novel. It may fascinate those with a taste for strategy and tactics and leave others quite indifferent. It is evident that the author is laying groundwork by introducing, but not developing, a large number and variety of characters, including whole families, who are destined for prominent roles in later novels. With a few exceptions, the characters at this stage, although potentially interesting, seem fragmentary and two-dimensional. Their appearances are too infrequent, often separated by hundreds of pages of narration and exposition of military events.

August 1914 centers on a national military catastrophe and explores its causes. Behind the inefficiency and ineffectuality of the armed forces lies a corrupt and ossified Tsarist regime. The heroism of the ordinary soldier is betrayed by a high command that is self-serving, sloppy, antiquated, and out of touch with military reality. Emblematic of this situation is the figure of General Samsonov, commander of the Second Army, a well-meaning but futile officer who is responsible for the disaster and commits suicide at its climax, but who is also shown to be a victim of circumstances he could not possibly have controlled. Solzhenitsyn's protagonist is Colonel Vorotyntsev, an intelligent and enterprising young officer who observes, from various battlefield positions, the effects of top-level blunders and does what little he can to counteract them. In the novel's culminating scene Vorotyntsev confronts an assemblage of generals, presided over by Grand Duke Nikolai Nikolaevich, denounces the entire conduct of the war thus far, and is angrily dismissed from the meeting.

Although the novel's concentration on the military prevents it from giving a full social panorama of the times, Solzhenitsyn makes some effort to trace contemporary political and intellectual currents. His characters seem to represent nearly the entire political spectrum. It is difficult to discern a specific bias as yet, but there is an evident sympathy for characters of a liberal persuasion. A number of supplementary formal devices, new for Solzhenitsyn, serve to reinforce his themes. The most effective of these – a mélange of newspaper clippings similar to the "newsreels" in John Dos Passos' *U.S.A.* – has the dual function of suggesting the general atmosphere of the times and, more pointedly, of demonstrating how the media lulled the public by misrepresenting the course of the war. There are also periodic summaries of the "general situation" — interpretive essays on military developments resembling those in Tolstoy's *War and Peace*. Through the reproduction of some of the actual communiqués used by army leaders in the attempt to cover up their blunders and losses, Solzhenitsyn provides a kind of ironic documentation. He also appends aphorisms and folk proverbs to the ends of many chapters. His least successful device is the "screen" sequence, written like a scenario, which he uses to portray episodes of an intensely dramatic nature.

On the whole, *August 1914* is a disappointment. The above-mentioned combination of devices often seems aesthetically redundant and even clumsy. Solzhenitsyn is not nearly as adept as Tolstoy at writing historical novels. This is primarily because he does not have Tolstoy's sure and subtle sense of character, or his ability to weave together history and fiction, story and argument. In view of Solzhenitsyn's strong affinity for

Tolstoy, it is interesting that in this particular novel he explicitly takes issue with the view of men and history expounded in *War and Peace* – the "Kutuzovism" that minimizes the role of the individual will in shaping the course of events.

August 1914 is an intensely patriotic book which, paradoxically, is capable of irritating and even angering Russian nationalists. Colonel Vorotyntsev, who is the author's mouthpiece on such matters, passionately loves his country, and another prominent character – the peasant soldier Blagodarev – is a tribute to the special qualities of the Russian folk, akin in spirit to such figures as Matryona and Ivan Denisovich. On the other hand, the book expresses deep admiration for the cleanliness, orderliness, vigor, enterprise, and efficiency of the enemy. The Germans have a superb military organization; the Russians seem scarcely able to plan.

One must tentatively conclude that Solzhenitsyn is better at using material that is close to his own experience, or that arouses his moral and ideological passions, than he is at epic historical representation. It is altogether possible, however, that the sequels to *August 1914* will show him to be a better master of epic materials than he now appears to be. We shall have to wait and see.

Since his arrest by the KGB and exile in February 1974, Solzhenitsyn has become a world figure of enormous moral and political importance. His huge, three-volume *Gulag Archipelago*, the product of prodigious historical research, provides massive documentation of the development and operation of the Soviet system of police terror and imprisonment. Despite its staggering array of facts and figures, *Gulag Archipelago* is anything but a dry work of historical description and analysis. It is a passionate, immensely moving work, employing the full array of Solzhenitsyn's talents as a publicist and conveying, often with great irony and dramatic intensity, the author's boundless indignation at the colossal inhumanity of the Gulag system, his compassion for its victims, and his sense of the profound, pervasive social corruption that the system entails.

As a public figure and prolific writer in exile (his account of his tribulations as a writer within the Soviet Union, *The Calf Butted Against the Oak*, was published in February 1975), Solzhenitsyn has worked energetically to influence world opinion about the USSR, as a means of compensating for the loss of influence within his country that was an inevitable consequence of his expulsion. He has surprised many of his admirers in the West by his political conservatism, his disdain for Western urban democratic industrialized society, his mystical, nationalistic faith in the superiority of the Russian people and their folk traditions, and his advocacy not of immediate democracy for Russia but rather, initially, of a benevolent authoritarianism. He is, moreover, as controversial among émigré dissidents as he was at home. Nevertheless, Solzhenitsyn remains a most eloquent advocate of truth, cultural and intellectual freedom, and a reign of justice and law for the Russian people.

12

The art of Andrei Sinyavsky

The imprisonment of Andrei Sinyavsky in 1965 stilled, in mid-career, the most original and enigmatic voice in contemporary Soviet literature. At the time of his arrest he was known in the USSR solely as a gifted, liberal, literary critic and scholar. Abroad he was known as Abram Tertz, a mysterious Russian author – possibly not even a resident of the Soviet Union – who had written a brilliant, devastating critique of socialist realism, two short novels (*The Trial Begins* and *Lyubimov*), six short stories, and a small collection of aphorisms (*Unguarded Thoughts*).

As Sinyavsky he had written (sometimes collaborating with A. Menshutin) reviews and essays on contemporary Soviet poetry, several articles in literary histories and encyclopedias, and a superb introduction to a collection of Pasternak's poetry. He had coauthored, with I. Golomshtok, a book on Picasso. Nearly all of these writings were remarkable for their intellectual discipline, liveliness, erudition, and aesthetic sensitivity. At the same time these writings, though often controversial in their liberal bias, were well within the prevailing ideological limits.

As Tertz, on the other hand, he was both the advocate and the practitioner of what he called, in his essay *On Socialist Realism*, a "phantasmagoric art," a literature of the grotesque, which strove to be "truthful with the aid of absurd fantasy." Such an art was not without precedent in Russian literature. The strain of the grotesque and fantastic, stemming primarily from Gogol, was prominent in the nineteenth century. It had been even more pronounced in the first two decades of the twentieth century, in such writers as Sologub, Bely, and Remizov, and it was prominent during the early years of the Soviet period in the prose fiction of Zamyatin, Olesha, and others. With the imposition of socialist realism as official doctrine in the early 1930s the use of the grotesque and the fantastic as artistic devices was suppressed. (One genre – science fiction – was somewhat exempt.) Only in the late fifties, in such a work as Dudintsev's *A New Year's Tale*, did they begin timidly to reappear. Tertz's advocacy of such means, if not altogether heretical, was well in advance of the times. It was understandable that one who held such views might, if he were a Soviet citizen, wish to mask them under a pseudonym.

Until Sinyavsky was unmasked by purely extraliterary means no one suspected on the basis of the texts alone that he was Tertz. The fine literary intelligence and sophistication of Sinyavsky are paralleled by the creative inventiveness of Tertz, but there the similarity between the two ends. Sinyavsky had mastered two quite distinct voices and had managed to keep them separate. This chapter will be concerned almost exclusively with the Sinyavsky who wrote as Tertz. But it should be kept in mind that a writer who is adroit enough to sustain two independent literary personalities may also be capable of launching and maintaining still others. Sinyavsky-Tertz is an exceedingly complex thinker and artist.

Sinyavsky's direct pronouncements on the fantastic in literature are few. His article on science fiction, published in a Soviet journal in 1960, urges Russian writers of this genre to be less "practical" and "earthly" and to give more rein to their imaginations. In the context of the times the article is at most mildly unorthodox, and it develops no real theory of the fantastic. *On Socialist Realism*, his genuinely bold and daring theoretical essay published abroad under the pseudonym Tertz, is almost totally devoted to demonstrating the bankruptcy of the official literary ideology of the past quarter-century. Only at the very end of this essay, as if in an ironic afterthought, does he explicitly advocate a "phantasmagoric art," and he does not elaborate on its principles. For his view of the fantastic, then, one must see what is implicit in his fiction and in his critique of socialist realism.

On Socialist Realism is a carefully reasoned indictment of the theory and practice of Soviet literature. Sinyavsky's polemic strategy is to describe and seemingly accept the ideological premises on which this state-controlled literature is based, while he simultaneously – through example, paradox, and arguments based on the history of Russian literature – undermines the whole concept of socialist realism by reducing it to absurdity. This basic strategy, however, is augmented by such a profoundly ironical treatment of the ideological premises underlying socialist realism that considerable doubt arises as to whether the author accepts even these premises. For the sake of argument Sinyavsky accepts the teleological notion that history has a direction, goal, and Purpose, and that it is a function of literature to serve this Purpose – the attainment of communism. He then proceeds to show that the literary models that have been arbitrarily selected as methodological guides for this purposeful literature – the nineteenth-century Russian realists – are ill suited to this function. The method of "realism," he argues, is inapplicable to the kind of heroic mythmaking that the building of communism requires. A more suitable model, he suggests, would be eighteenth-century Russian neo-classicism, which was rigid and stable, affirmative, expansive, and devoid of the poisonous subtlety of doubt and irony that are inherent in nineteenth-century realism. In Sinyavsky's opinion Mayakovsky was the only Soviet artist who had understood that literature that truly serves the Purpose must not aspire to be realistic: Mayakovsky relied on hyperbole.

Sinyavsky's essay is more than just a literary argument. It is a savage attack on Stalinism, among other things, and an examination, with copious illustrations from Soviet cultural history, of the problem of ends and means. The essay is so loaded with sarcasm, moreover, that it is often impossible to determine whether an assertion is serious or tongue-in-cheek. At times, he seems to burlesque his own ideas. The ostensible purpose of the essay is to find a viable communist literary *aesthetic*, but Sinyavsky comes very close to saying that this is *ethically* impossible. One could interpret his last-minute advocacy of a "phantasmagoric art," for example, as a statement of desperation: since it is impossible to write "realistically" in Soviet society (i.e., to tell the truth), let us stop fooling ourselves and frankly resort to fantasy. If this interpretation is correct, *On Socialist Realism* would best be considered a kind of Swiftian modest proposal. And perhaps that is what it is.

On the other hand, there was no evidence in Sinyavsky's writings to indicate that he was a conscious disbeliever in communism (which would in fact make a "communist art" inimical in his view) or that he thought that all avenues to the truth in Soviet literature are closed. What seems to disturb him is that socialist realism demands in the writer a pose of certainty, a dogmatic self-assurance that a truly intelligent and sensitive writer must find impossible to maintain. It is this feeling, I believe, that leads Sinyavsky to espouse, at the close of his essay, a "phantasmagoric art with hypotheses instead of a Purpose and the grotesque instead of a depiction of ordinary life." Truth in art, he seems to imply, can only be reached, if at all, through guesses, indirection, tentative exaggeration and distortion, and through the language of metaphor.

Sinyavsky's art, then, is based on an ironic understanding of his own uncertainty and confusion, a lack of teleological confidence in orderly and purposeful processes, and a fascination with the bizarre and the irrational. By dealing in opposites and incongruities and by creating ironic analogies, he seems bent on conjuring up actuality rather than describing it. Although there are patterns in his writings taken as a whole, his work at first produces an effect of extreme fragmentation, of polyphony without harmony. His apparently undisciplined and illogical swarms of impressions suggest an artistic personality that is intricate without being integrated. And it is true that some of his works – one thinks of the stores "You and I" and "Tenants" and of several passages in *Unguarded Thoughts* – seem hopelessly chaotic and abstruse. As a rule, however, his writings are not as disjointed and obscure as they at first appear to be. One suspects that his excesses come from the fact that he is an enemy of artificial coherence, of intellectual and artistic systems that sweep contradictions under a rug.

All of Sinyavsky's fiction has contemporary Russian settings. Soviet mores and linguistic peculiarities, Soviet institutions, mental habits, and attitudes are essential to its fabric. The problems and conflicts he depicts are recognizably those of contemporary Soviet civilization. *The Trial Begins*, for example, is set in Moscow at the time of Stalin's death and tells of specific events and places with considerable – if impressionistic – accuracy. There are allusions in several of the stories to actual public events and personages, and many of the details of Soviet life are set down with fidelity. Sinyavsky is therefore a "realist" in the sense that his works tangibly reflect the Soviet environment. At the same time, however, "plausible" characters, objects, and occurrences frequently blend into "implausible" ones, in violation of the laws of nature or commonly accepted principles of cognition. His method of shifting back and forth between the real and the grotesque or fantastic can perhaps best be called surrealism.

The most prominent surrealistic element in Sinyavsky's fiction is the supernatural. In "The Icicle," for example, the hero – an ordinary Muscovite – suddenly becomes clairvoyant. He is cursed with the ability to see both backward and forward in time so that he "lies adrift in the waves of time and space." He can read minds, foresees the circumstances of his own death and, because souls are transmigratory, he lives simultaneously with his and others' past and future incarnations. In *Lyubimov* the hero is magically endowed with the power of mass hypnosis, which enables him to delude the populace of a provincial town into believing, for instance, that he has turned mineral water into spirits, a tube of toothpaste into a fish, a river into champagne. With these powers he becomes the local dictator for a time, and improvises an illusory utopian state. The novel abounds in supernatural tricks and creatures, ghosts, spells, and folk magic, so that, in distinction to "The Icicle," it has many of the qualities of a fairy story or folk tale, and even seems in part to be a conscious exploitation and parody of that genre. A third and still different use of the supernatural is found in "Pkhentz," whose hero is a creature from outer space, a cactuslike vegetable who manages to exist on earth by disguising himself as a man.

Sinyavsky's friend Alfreda Aucouturier has testified to his fondness for "authentic accounts of witchcraft and magic" and has stated that "he believes in the power of fantasy to attempt by a trick to offer an explanation of reality, while simultaneously recording a mystery."[1] At the same time, she does not state flatly that he believes in the supernatural, and there is on record no statement from Sinyavsky himself to this effect. The question is moot, but whether or not Sinyavsky himself does "believe in ghosts," it is certain that the use of the supernatural in his fiction is rational, calculated, and sophisticated. Its employment is largely a matter of artistic strategy, in the tradition of Bely and Sologub. And like these two writers he sometimes makes it difficult to distinguish between patently supernatural phenomena and purely psychological ones, between demonic happenings on the one hand and dreams, delusions, and hallucinations on the other. The story "Tenants," for example, is entirely a monologue, apparently the ravings of a dipsomaniac writer who thinks he sees a woman turned into a rat, who fancies he can transform himself into a glass, and whose world is populated by sprites and spirits. He argues that industrialization has so polluted streams, rivers, and lakes that water nymphs have fled to the cities:

> What a lot of them perished! Countless numbers. Not entirely of course – after all, they are immortal beings. Nothing to be done about that. But the brawnier specimens got stuck in the water mains. You've probably heard it yourself. You turn on the kitchen tap, and out of it come sobs, various splashings, and curses. Have you thought whose antics these are? The voices are those of water numphs. They get stuck in a washbasin and it's murder the way they sneeze![2]

This story, then, may be the psychological portrait of a fevered imagination. But there is also much evidence to support the notion that the narrator is actually a goblin who has possessed the drunken writer, and that the story is this devil's monologue, in which case the tale would be basically supernatural.

Whatever the orientation of this particularly puzzling story, there are others, devoid of the supernatural, in which the fantastic element comes purely from the psychological derangement of the individual characters. Such is the case in "You and I," a story of divided personality, and in "Graphomaniacs," whose dominant note is paranoia. In still other works a fantastic effect is created through the detailing of normal workings of the imagination and the unconscious – dreams and reveries that have no particular pathological significance. Thus in *The Trial Begins* the prosecutor Globov and his idealistic schoolboy son Seryozha attend a symphonic concert. The music stimulates contrasting private fantasies in them. For Seryozha:

> The music was like his private image of the revolution. The flood drowned the bourgeoisie in a most convincing way.
>
> A general's wife in evening dress floundered, tried to scramble up a pillar and was washed away. The old general swam with a vigorous breast-stroke, but soon sank. Even the musicians were, by now, up to their necks in water. Eyes bulging, lips spitting foam, they fiddled frenziedly, randomly, below the surface of the waves.
>
> One more onslaught. A lone usher, riding on a chair, swept past. The waves beat against the walls and lapped the portraits of the great composers. Ladies' handbags and torn tickets floated among the jetsam. Now and then, a bald head, white like an unripe watermelon, slowly floated up out of the sonorous green depth and bobbed back out of sight.

Globov, on the other hand, thinks in images of authoritarian power:

> He, too, was fascinated by the flood, but he understood it better than Seryozha. What struck him was that his surge of music wasn't left to its own devices; it was controlled by the conductor.
>
> The conductor built dams, ditches, aqueducts, canalizing the flood; at the sweep of his arm one stream froze, another flowed forward in its bed and turned a turbine.
>
> Globov slipped into a seat in the front row. Never had he sat so close, never had he realized how hard was the conductor's work. No wonder! Think of having to keep an eye on all of them, from flute to drum, and force them all to play the same tune.

The reveries of both Seryozha and Globov are presented in grotesque patterns of imagery. In neither of them, however, is there an indication of mental illness. Rather, their thoughts are metaphorical expressions of their personalities.

Whether dealing with the supernatural, with hallucination and delusion, or with the normal subconscious, Sinyavsky makes extensive use of subjective, introspective modes of narration. His first-person narrators are usually engaged in confessing or complaining to an unspecified audience that seems either unsympathetic or uncomprehending. Sometimes his narrators appear to be mumbling to themselves. Moreover, these subjective voices often switch barely perceptibly, and sometimes imperceptibly, so that the reader cannot always be certain of the narrator's identity. This combination of subjective narration and ambiguity concerning the narrator emphasizes the aura of the fantastic.

Much of what *seems* fantastic in Sinyavsky is in fact simply grotesque. He distorts his material in order to find new angles, fresh emphases, unusual perspectives. The "unreality" of much of *The Trial Begins*, for example, comes from its technique of montage, its kaleidoscopic juxtaposition of scenes and characters to reflect the atmosphere of confusion that surrounded the demise of Stalin. A similar distortion for the purpose of intensifying thematic concepts and epitomizing feverish psychological states is found in the story "At the Circus." Like his predecessors in the writing of ornate prose – such as Bely, Remizov, Zamyatin, and Pilnyak – Sinyavsky makes special use of shapes, shadows, and reflections. In *The Trial Begins*, the beautiful, self-centered, and depraved Marina gazes at her reflection in the display window of a beauty shop:

> There she saw herself as in a distorting mirror. People walked across her, trolley-buses drove past, and flasks of scent and pyramids of colored soap drove through them.
>
> "All these beauty preparations only spoil your skin," she thought as she looked sulkily at her image. But her face, smudged with shame and temper, trodden by the shadows of the passersby, remained beautiful enough.

In this scene the world is not unreal or fantastic, but merely "strange." Much in the manner of Yuri Olesha (who, however, scrupulously avoided the supernatural), Sinyavsky portrays a "different" order of reality and suggests that things are not what they seem. He does this also by means of caricature, hyperbole, and downward comparisons, and by deliberately depriving phenomena – such as sex – of their conventional romantic overtones.

Despite his formal similarities to the Russian Symbolists, he is much less interested than they were in using art as an approach to metaphysics. For one thing, he seems too earthy and ironic by nature to commit his art to such solemn purposes. The absurd for him tends to be a source of satire, not of metaphysical speculation. At the same time, he is obviously in earnest when he uses the bizarre and the illogical as a device for exploring the world of common experience. He employs the unreal and the unusual to speak vividly and arrestingly about the real and the usual – to examine actual psychological states, spiritual and moral problems, historical and cultural essences. But his art is one of impressions and fragments rather than consistently unified generalizations, and this, I believe, is why he writes in *On Socialist Realism* of the importance of "hypotheses." In his view, art can only pursue the truth indirectly; the image is a kind of tentative proposition.

Sinyavsky is a self-consciously *literary* writer. His works are peppered with allusions, both overt and covert, to a wide variety of literary schools and figures, chiefly Russian and West European of the nineteenth and twentieth centuries. The temptress Marina in *The Trial Begins* is said, at thirty, to be of a "Balzacian age."[3] Lyonya Tikhomirov, the mesmerizing young dictator in *Lyubimov*, liberates the prisoners in the local jail and exhorts them to remember: "The word 'man' has a proud ring!" – Sinyavsky's sarcastic reference to Gorky's much abused line from *The Lower Depths*. There are zany misquotations and puns, such as one in which the title of Gogol's *Dead Souls* emerges as "The Dead Smother." Sinyavsky's most brilliant literary allusions, however, are in his parodies. A long apostrophe to Soviet railroads in "The Icicle," for example, is an exact parody of Gogol's famous apostrophe to the Russian troika. *Lyubimov* is largely patterned on Saltykov-Shchedrin's *History of One Town*, and this novel also has long passages of calculated, purple Gogolian rhetoric. In *The Trial Begins* there are numerous parodies of the jargon used in Stalinist literary criticism.

To a certain extent Sinyavsky's abundant literary references and parodies are simply a clever writer's game, a form of exuberant play. As a rule, however, these exercises also have a satiric purpose and constitute serious literary commentary, for the subject of much of Sinyavsky's fiction is literature itself. *The Trial Begins* is, among other things, a story about socialist realism: in its prologue the narrator is given an assignment to depict a group of characters and events in the prescribed official manner; the body of the story is his defiantly unorthodox response to the assignment; the epilogue describes his punishment. The novel as a whole is an implicit demonstration of the absurdity of socialist realism; the very nature of the characters and events with which the narrator is dealing – contemporary Soviet citizens in contemporary circumstances – is such that the formula does not work. Although *Lyubimov* is not as neatly programmatic as *The*

Trial Begins, it too is extensively concerned with literary problems as such. It is, in part, a novel about novel-writing, a novel that talks to itself. Within its loose and elaborate structure there are two primary narrators, whose styles clash, who interrupt one another and quarrel over strategy, fumble, and sometimes cancel each other out. His main narrator, a good-natured, pedantic philistine with literary pretensions, is given to confusion, false starts, and Sterne-like confessions to the reader (he dislikes the fantastic!) through which the author himself engages in wry and sophisticated spoofing of novelistic techniques and devices.

In other works Sinyavsky is more specifically concerned with the conditions under which literature exists in the Soviet Union. "Tenants" features a devastated, drunken writer – by no means a uniquely Soviet phenomenon, but under conditions that suggest that this peculiar society has caused his downfall. "Graphomaniacs" is, indirectly, about censorship. Its hero is a writer who has not published, surrounded by writers who are also unpublished:

> But do you know what we owe it to? To censorship. Yes, censorship is the dear old mother who's cherished us all. Abroad, things are simpler and harsher. Some lord brings out a wretched book of *vers libre,* and immediately it's spotted as crap. No one reads it and no one buys it, so the lord takes up useful work like energetics or stomatology. . . . But we live our whole lives in pleasant ignorance, flattering ourselves with hopes. . . . And this is marvelous! Why, damn it, the state itself gives you the right – the invaluable right – to regard yourself as an unacknowledged genius. And all your life, all your life you can –

In this situation of frustrated creativity, where everyone is possibly a stifled genius, the hero develops the paranoiac conviction that successful, *published* writers have plagiarized his works.

Literature traditionally examines itself, and fiction that is concerned with literary problems and conditions *per se* is not, of course, unusual. There is special significance, however, in Sinyavsky's overt preoccupation with problems of writing, with the psychology of art and the principles of creativity. His concern epitomizes the situation of a post-Stalinist literature that is trying to reassert and, to a great extent, remake itself, that is rediscovering techniques and approaches to artistic expression from which it has been cut off for more than three decades. More than any other contemporary Soviet writer, Sinyavsky represents a return to the devices and interests of the 1910s and 1920s.

In the structure of his works and in his stylistic devices Sinyavsky most strikingly resembles such early twentieth-century writers as Bely, Remizov, Pilnyak, and Zamyatin. His chief structural characteristic is a fondness for abrupt transitions and the scrambling of chronology, settings, and characters. Scenes and dialogues shift rapidly and sometimes barely perceptibly, without apparent bridging or connection. At times this gives his narratives a jerky, staccato quality. In most cases, however, passages that seem merely to be randomly juxtaposed turn out, on closer inspection, to be related thematically. *The Trial Begins,* for example, is a carefully constructed progression of scenes connected to each other not so much through their characters and the development of plot as through recurrent imagery and the ironic association of ideas. But even in this novel – Sinyavsky's most tightly knit and symmetrical work – there are authorial digressions, direct apostrophes to the reader, and flights of rhetoric that are strongly reminiscent of the loose and discursive structures of Bely and Pilnyak. In other works the narrators seem to be purposely unidentified or, at best, calculatedly unreliable or poorly individualized. The narrator of "At the Circus," for example, is omniscient, but sometimes gives the illusion of being confused and uncertain of his facts. The narration in "You and I" is shared by two halves of the same personality: they address each other, the point of view shifts constantly between them, but at times they are indistinguishable. In "Tenants," written in the form of a conversation in which only one side is recorded, the narrator lacks a consistent identity. It should be emphasized that these are not innovations in Russian literature: Gogol and Dostoevsky used similar techniques, and they became the stock-in-trade of writers in the first decades of the twentieth century. But they have been almost totally absent from Soviet literature for the past forty years.

Sinyavsky's most ambitious and, on the whole, most successful experimentation with narrative structure is in the novel *Lyubimov.* Its basic form is that of a historical chronicle, recorded by an eyewitness scribe. This scribe, Savely Proferantsov, is subjectively involved as a participant in the events he records and is, moreover, a blumbling, self-conscious stylist. He is particularly fond of and confused by the writing of footnotes. It is through the medium of these footnotes that a second narrator appears – the ghost of Samson Proferantsov, an eccentric nineteenth-century liberal intellectual. Samson's voice is first heard as the usurper of Savely's footnotes: he takes them over to criticize the way in which Savely is writing his chronicle, and a quarrel ensues between the notes (Samson) and the text (Savely). A few pages later Samson again intrudes into the notes, then leaps into the text to propose that he and Savely finish the story together by writing it "in layers." From here on, despite Savely's violent objections, his spectral collaborator periodically takes over the narration at will. In contrast to Savely's halting, clumsy, and bemused prose, Samson's is elegant in the finest nineteenth-century tradition. But there is yet a third voice, for occasionally the author becomes his own narrator, in passages of sharp and witty commentary. The existence of these three voices, which clash and yet amalgamate, is fundamental to both the themes and the structure of the novel. They offer a variety of perspectives on the fantastic events that take place and enhance the novel's narrative interest by providing a change of pace.

Lyubimov is also Sinyavsky's most versatile display of narrative devices and tricks, most of them, it would seem, tongue-in-cheek. Here again the footnotes play a prominent part. In describing the Soviet government's ineffectual attempt to bomb the revolutionary town of Lyubimov, for example, Savely portrays the approaching airplanes in the text itself and the town in the footnotes, alternating rapidly between the two in an awkward attempt to create a cinematic effect through the typography of the printed page. And when he is stumped over the problem of narrating two simultaneous events, Savely again trots out his footnotes to handle one of them. There are also numerous digressions in which Savely discusses his notions of literature and takes the reader into his confidence to talk over his methods of writing and his compositional difficulties. This mixture of candor and ineptness produces a good-natured spoof of bad writing.

In his approach to characterization also, Sinyavsky is reminiscent of Bely and Zamyatin. His characters are intentionally flat and two-dimensional. There is very little concrete description of them, a minimum of biographical detail, and little, if any, growth and development. Their distinguishing marks, as a rule, are a few carefully highlighted, often grotesque physical, mental, or verbal traits that serve as leitmotivs. Despite their lack of "roundedness," they are made vivid and striking by caricaturelike details of appearance, gesture, speech, and behavior. They are important not as individuals but as types, as personifications of elements, forces, and problems – they all "stand for something." In *Lyubimov* each of them represents – although not in rigidly allegorical fashion – aspects of the Russian national character, or particular traits of Russian political, cultural, or social behavior. *The Trial Begins* is a kind of symbolic organism, each of whose interlocking or carefully juxtaposed characters stands for a cardinal phenomenon in the Moscow society of 1953.

Sinyavsky makes extensive use of heavily laden images and symbols. At a soccer game in *The Trial Begins* a particularly aggressive attempt to score a goal becomes a metaphorical commentary on the novel's theme of sexual frustration and that of ends and means. When the goal is scored and then disallowed, additional symbolic meanings accrue that are related to the novel's themes of creativity, sterility, and abortion. In both *The Trial Begins* and *Lyubimov*, the KGB agents Vitya and Tolya dream of creating a "psychoscope" – a remotely operated mind-reading machine that resembles, in its general conception, fantastic instruments of thought control that serve as symbols in works of Zamyatin, Leonov, and Olesha. In the story "The Icicle" an icicle hanging menacingly above a Moscow sidewalk becomes the symbol of inescapable fate whose power transcends even that of the hero's clairvoyance and, as an ironic reminder of the ultimate freezing of the planet, of the absurdity of the "march of history." Like those of Zamyatin and Pilnyak, Sinyavsky's symbols tend to be either exceedingly primordial or supermodern, and his imagery ominous and violent. (Marina's announcement to Globov that she has had an abortion produces in her husband the effect of an atomic bomb exploding.) In common with the prose fiction of the Russian Symbolists, however, Sinyavsky's writing contains many prominent images whose associations are neither limited nor absolutely clear. In "At the Circus," for example, the circus symbol and the character named Manipulator suggest a multiplicity of meanings, some of them contradictory. Likewise, the pathetic, alienated, nonhuman hero of "Pkhentz" invites a wide variety of interpretations.

Ultimately it is Sinyavsky's prose style that brings him closest to the "ornamental school." Whole passages resemble, in their texture and devices, the prose of Bely, Remizov, and Pilnyak, and hark back to the stylistic father of them all – Gogol. The ingredients are various. Sinyavsky has, first of all, an extremely sensitive ear for contemporary Soviet speech and can both reproduce and parody it with great fidelity. The characters in *Lyubimov*, especially the hero Lyonya Tikhomirov, speak in clichés and use heavily the political and ideological jargon of Soviet newspapers. The language of "Pkhentz" is current pseudo-intellectual urban slang, larded with bureaucratese and, like that of the narrator Savely in *Lyubimov*, with archaic, high-flown, bookish expressions. Hackneyed slogans in *The Trial Begins* and *Lyubimov* are burlesqued and ironically distorted to add symbolic overtones and satiric nuances. In *The Trial Begins* Stalin speaks like Jehovah and his presence is always described in Biblical language. Many of the works, most notably *Lyubimov*, contain passages of brilliantly idiosyncratic, Gogolian *skaz*.

Another characteristic that attaches Sinyavsky to the ornamental tradition is his proclivity for mixing first-, second-, and third-person narration. In "Tenants" and "You and I" the narration alternates between first and second person, and "You and I" culminates in a bewildering mixture of the two. "At the Circus" combines all three persons. Moreover, Sinyavsky is capable of achieving great variety and complexity within the confines of a single mode. "Pkhentz," written in first person, combines reported dialogue, narrative monologue, and interior monologue. In the two novels Sinyavsky's interior monologue closely resembles that of Bely and Pilnyak, especially when it conveys fragmented, semicoherent thought and impressionistic representations of speech.

A hallmark of ornamentalism is exuberant verbal experimentation. Sinyavsky indulges in this with gusto, sometimes to create ironic effects, but often seemingly for the sheer fun of it. In the novels there are rhetorical passages whose syntax is so carefully balanced that the author seems to be proclaiming facetiously, "Here, readers, is prose rhythm." English, French, and German words are frequently inserted, producing a comic incongruity. There are numerous ridiculous and grotesque puns – to show stream-of-consciousness associations in the private fantasies of characters, to convey satiric authorial double meanings, and sometimes, apparently, just for the hell of it. There is much alliteration, sound repetition, and word repetition, at times for rhetorical effect and at others purely for decoration. Like Bely, Remizov, Zamyatin, and Pilnyak – and Gogol before them – Sinyavsky plays games with the letters of the Cyrillic and Roman alphabets, fascinated by their shapes and associations. The voluptuous Marina in *The Trial Begins* notices that the profile of her torso resembles the letter S. In the same novel a letter tries to squirm away from a secret police search:

> [The detective] ran his hand over the first page and, presumably by way of censorship, scooped up all the characters and punctuation marks. One flick of the hand and there on the blank paper was a writhing heap of purple marks. The young man put them in his pocket.
>
> One letter – I think it was a "z" – flicked its tail and tried to wiggle out, but he deftly caught it, tore off its legs, and squashed it with his fingernail.

In the person of Savely, the naive narrator of *Lyubimov*, Sinyavsky makes sport of his own creative processes:

> You write and don't understand what's happening to you, and where all these words come from, which you have never heard

> and haven't thought of writing, but have suddenly emerged from
> the pen and swum, swum over the paper like some kind of ducks,
> some kind of geese, some kind of black-winged Australian swans.
> . . .
>
> At times you write in such a way that terror seizes you and the
> fountain pen falls out of your hands. I didn't write this! Honest,
> it wasn't I! But you read it over, and you see that it's all correct,
> that this is the way it was. . . . Lord!

But for the erudite Sinyavsky, inspiration is obviously only partly a fortuitous matter. His vocabulary – at all levels – would seem to be enormous. He has an impressive command of colloquial, vulgar (including
scatological) language, he exploits fully and ironically the stale words of
official propaganda and ritual, and he is a master of archaisms and ecclesi-
astical lexicon.

His language, moreover, is exceedingly figurative, with bizarre tropes
that frequently develop, as do those of Mayakovsky, into elaborately extended metaphors. Whole stories, such as "At the Circus," are based on a
central metaphor (a restaurant, sexual activity in a bathhouse, religion, society, and life itself are portrayed as a circus). In contrast to Solzhenitsyn,
for whom the image is a direct quintessence, an epigram, Sinyavsky assiduously exploits his images for their secondary and tertiary meanings.
There is a multiplicity of meanings, for example, in the fact that the hero
of "Pkhentz" is not an earthling but a cactuslike vegetable who subsists on
water. Not only is he an alien, he is also cleaner and, in his physical and
mental purity, intrinsically superior to the filthy human race. His
estrangement is something like that of the artist Sinyavsky, whose lack of
dogmatic self-assurance compels him to communicate by means of ironic
indirection:

> How could they understand me, when I myself am quite unable
> to express my inhuman nature in their language. I go round and
> round it, and try to get by with metaphors, but when it comes to
> the main point – I find nothing to say.

In his oblique manner Sinyavsky does, of course, have "something to
say." In sum, he is saying, like Dostoevsky, that the world is more complex and mysterious, good and evil less tangible, human nature more intricate, human behavior less rational, than we generally suppose them to
be. And he is likewise saying that the human situation is more pathetic
and absurd than the official Soviet literature of mandatory affirmation can

show it to be. One of his major themes is alienation, the estrangement of the individual not only from society at large but also, at times, from his immediate neighbors, his family and sexual partners, and even from himself. The collective is hostile and confusing, one's intimate associates (especially those of the opposite sex) disgusting and irritating. Life itself is a desperate and lonely muddle, governed by weird and incomprehensible, mischievous, and malevolent forces. This theme is not totally consistent throughout all of Sinyavsky's fiction, of course, and the emphasis on its various aspects fluctuates from story to story. In *Lyubimov*, for example, it is lightened by a vein of rollicking satire, and in such works as *The Trial Begins* and "Graphomaniacs" it is narrowed and localized by the element of civic protest. Nevertheless, the portrait of the individual as a victim, isolated from his fellow men by suspicion, incomprehension, and fear, and powerless to shape his destiny, is a consistent one. Sinyavsky seems particularly fascinated by Jewish characters and the phenomenon of anti-Semitism; his choice of a Jewish pseudonym – Abram Tertz – is in keeping with his preoccupation with those whom the world crazily singles out for abuse.

The atmosphere of alienation is emphasized by Sinyavsky's use of the grotesque. To his bewildered and suffering characters, the ordinary world seems strangely predatory, ugly, and distorted. The divided, paranoiac hero of "You and I" feels that his fellow guests at a dinner party are transvestites, clicking their knives and forks and thereby communicating with each other in a secret code. The lonely hero of "Pkhentz," who has a number of plantlike arms, which he conceals by strapping them tightly to his body, is, in human terms, deformed; in his eyes, however, the human female figure is repulsive and terrifying. In *The Trial Begins*, the mutual isolation of nearly all the characters is underlined by a myriad of grotesqueries. A banquet of secret police starts with animated conversation; as the drinking increases the participants all fall discreetly silent.

It is tempting to interpret Sinyavsky's theme of alienation, in its various forms, in terms of the opposition between the individual and the centralized, omnipotent state. Surely, much of the psychic disaffection in *The Trial Begins* is shown to be attributable to the personality of Stalin and to the ponderous, corrupt, inhumane machine he created. The maladjustment of the hero in "Graphomaniacs" is triggered by the ubiquitous state censorship of literature. One could conclude that the hero of "At the Circus" turns criminal in protest against the deadening routine of a rigidly controlled social system. The nervous, suspicious, conspiratorial atmosphere of the police state permeates the fantasy of "The Icicle" and "You and I." And the hero of "Pkhentz" is a creature who has fallen into a conformist society where individualism is suspect, and who must therefore conceal his identity: he is, metaphorically, an "internal émigré." But despite this sampling of evidence from the stories, it would be erroneous to conclude that Sinyavsky is attempting to demonstrate that alienation is exclusively, or even primarily, the product of the Soviet political and social system. More likely, the Soviet scene simply provides material-at-hand, to be used in conjuring up a more generalized vision of the contemporary human situation.

At the center of Sinyavsky's art, one suspects, there is a fierce ethical consciousness, a thirst for moral certainty, and a deeply frustrated idealism and sense of what is rational and just in human affairs. He exaggerates, and arranges observed and imagined data into ugly and ridiculous patterns, to express his dismay and ironic wonderment at the gulf between human pretensions and human actuality. As an artist he is motivated by the associative powers of metaphor and hyperbole, but as a moralist and satirist he uses them to startle and shock. To a certain extent Sinyavsky's world of fantasy is private and closed, like the "third world" of Olesha and the darkly grotesque one of Sologub, but like theirs it also has an intrinsic moral relevance.

The Trial Begins is a systematic exploration of the problem of ends and means, with tightly interwoven references to ideology and religion, sex, politics, art, and history. As a kind of fictional counterpart of the essay *On Socialist Realism* it presents a society in which authoritarian means have so corrupted the pursuit of the Glorious Purpose that the Purpose itself has become perverted. Every character in the novel has either been infected with the falsity and brutality of this way of life or has been psychologically traumatized by it. Even the innocent and idealistic schoolboy, Seryozha Globov, who asks callow and honest – and therefore excruciatingly difficult – questions of his elders, and who is ultimately imprisoned for his naive rebellion, can only conceive of a revolutionary utopia in which "any man who hurts another man's feelings will be shot." *Lyubimov* is a similarly ironic treatment of misguided idealism, in which a village bicycle mechanic, suddenly given magic powers, sets up a benevolent dictatorship based on deception, which rots and crashes under its own weight.

Although Sinyavsky's writings are not explicitly anti-Marxist (they stress heavily, in fact, the element of determinism in history), they debunk the notion that the course of history is "scientifically" measurable and predictable. We have seen that in *The Trial Begins* and *On Socialist Real-*

ism he calls in question the smug assumption that everything can be justified in terms of the Purpose. He seems to be making further sport of the
activist Leninist notion of historically aware volition in "The Icicle,"
where the hero is given the occult ability to foresee the future but is unable
to do anything about it, despite the urgings of a colonel of the secret
police, who is anxious to speed up the inevitable victory of communism.
The hero says that the colonel "was evidently confusing me with God."

At the same time, Sinyavsky is acutely conscious of history. Although
Lyubimov is set in the Soviet period, the novel so resounds with references
to the Russian past and the Russian cultural tradition that it becomes a
kind of fantastic, impressionistic historical compendium. A word might
be said here about the frequent interpretations of this novel, in Western
reviews and commentaries, as a parabolic satire on the Revolution or an allegorical history of Russian communism. Such interpretations simply do
not withstand close scrutiny. It is true that the novel makes many specific
allusions to developments and figures in Soviet history – including
Lenin – and that it treats ironically many Soviet policies, slogans, institutions, prejudices, phobias, and patterns of behavior. There are likewise
Aesopian or metaphorical treatments of topics that relate to the Soviet experience. But neither the direct nor the figurative references are comprehensive or systematic. Attempts to read this novel as a kind of *Animal
Farm* are doomed to failure; the evidence is too random and fragmentary.
On the other hand, as an examination of the Russian national character
that *includes* the Soviet experience and draws heavily upon it, *Lyubimov*
does suggest some historical conclusions: the arrogant attempts of individuals to meddle with the natural, and unchartable, course of history culminate in disaster. And one of the reasons is that the human race – as illustrated in this instance by the Russians – is ultimately too intractable and
primordially perverse to tolerate such interference.

In *Lyubimov* and elsewhere, Sinyavsky's observations about the Russian
national character are so numerous, varied, and often contradictory that it
is impossible to make a consistent composite of them. If one were to ex-
tract from Lyubimov, for example, a catalogue of Russian qualities, the
most prominent of them would probably be backwardness, indolence, ir-
responsibility, drunkenness, superstitiousness, and deceptiveness. Such
an exercise would be pointless, however, for *Lyubimov* is obviously a work
of hyperbolic satire, in which one might well expect to find a low estimate
of human nature. But there is another source – *Unguarded Thoughts*, which
is not fiction – in which Sinyavsky makes similarly uncomplimentary remarks about his countrymen. Under duress at his trial, Sinyavsky seemed

partially to disavow the views expressed in *Unguarded Thoughts* when he testified that this was "not entirely" the author speaking. Nevertheless, these views must be considered as representing the general cast of his thought. Here is one of his observations:

> Drunkenness is our most basic national vice, and more than that our *idée fixe*. The Russian people drink not from need and not from grief, but from an age-old requirement for the miraculous and the extraordinary – drink, if you will, mystically, striving to transport the soul beyond earth's gravity and return it to its sacred noncorporeal state. Vodka is the Russian muzhik's White Magic; he decidedly prefers it to Black Magic – the female. The skirt-chaser, the lover take on features of the foreigner, the German (Gogol's devil), the Frenchman, the Jew. But we Russians will surrender any beauty (consider the example of Sten'ka Razin) for a bottle of pure spirits.
>
> Together with our propensity for theft (the absence of firm faith in actual, concrete ties), drunkenness gives us a certain wanderer's familiarity and places the *lumpen* in a suspicious position in the eyes of other nations. As soon as the "centuries-old principles" and the class hierarchy crumbled and were replaced by amorphous equality, this devious nature of the Russians pushed up to the surface. Now we are all devious (who among us does not feel something knavish in his soul and fate?). This gives us unquestionable advantages in comparison with the West, and at the same time it gives the life and strivings of our nation the stamp of inconstancy, frivolous irresponsibility. We are capable of putting Europe in our pocket or of loosing an interesting heresy there, but we simply are incapable of creating a culture. As with a thief or a drunkard, one must be prepared for anything from us. It's easy to knock about, to direct us by administrative measures (a drunkard is inert, incapable of self-direction, he drags along in the direction they pull him). And one should also keep in mind how difficult it is to rule this wavering people, how oppressive this direction is for our administrators!

In other passages of *Unguarded Thoughts* there are mitigating statements of admiration and praise, but most of Sinyavsky's profound brooding over the Russian national character has a similarly somber hue. What is important, however, is not the degree of praise or censure but the quality of the meditation that underlies it. Sinyavsky's thought has a Dostoevskian intricacy and spiritual charity; his deep concern over Russia's failings is the concomitant of an equally deep love of Russia. In an age in which the official image of the New Soviet Man is tinged also with prominent vestiges of Russian chauvinism, Sinyavsky's painful efforts to understand his countrymen in their true complexity are remarkable for their tonic, demythologizing flavor.

Because of its aphoristic nature, *Unguarded Thoughts* presents few fully developed ideas, and many of the entries are exceedingly cryptic. They do serve, however, to mark out areas of Sinyavsky's concern that are also treated in his fiction. One of these is sex, which he treats with a candor never found in works published in the Soviet Union. Sinyavsky is not an erotic writer. Sterility and impotence, and the ugly, perverse, and spiritually destructive features of sex are so heavily emphasized that sex as an aspect of love is almost totally excluded. In the novels and stories Sinyavsky employs sex not for its own intrinsic interest but as a device for characterization and thematic emphasis. In *The Trial Begins*, as we have seen, sexual imagery is brought to bear on the question of ends and means. The theme of abortion (including a grotesque fantasy involving the transformation of human fetuses into fish to increase the food supply) complements the novel's image of the state as a deadening institution that inhibits creativity. Similarly, Vitya and Tolya, a pair of secret police who crop up periodically in the novel, are presented as a homosexual couple. The emasculating effects of state servitude are suggested in the character of Karlinsky, a "liberal" but corrupt lawyer who, at the culmination of an elaborate campaign to seduce the beautiful and narcissistic Marina, proves impotent. And the presumptuous futility of Lyonya, the young dictator in *Lyubimov*, is underlined when he turns out to be an impotent husband, masochistically tormenting himself as his wife Serafima regales him with the details of her past affairs.

In other works – notably "At the Circus" – Sinyavsky portrays sexual activity as a nasty romp, inane and repulsive. To a certain extent he seems to do this to stress a general atmosphere of alienation. But in *Unguarded Thoughts* he expresses such a frank and explicit loathing of sex (although also, characteristically, a sinful appreciation of its charms) that his use of it in fiction seems not merely an aesthetic matter but one of conviction. In one passage he argues that the basic attraction of sex is its quality of shameful defilement, its reenactment of the Fall. Women are not only enigmatic (in sexual activity woman "becomes a priestess, guided by dark forces"), they are physically disgusting (there is even something repulsively libidinous in the way they eat sweets). Sex is a joyless burden: "If

only one could become a eunuch, how much one could accomplish!"
These and many other observations in *Unguarded Thoughts* do not necessarily indicate a striking abnormality in Sinyavsky. But they do show a
highly developed sense of the dichotomy between the flesh and the spirit.

In *Unguarded Thoughts* it is evident that Sinyavsky is a profoundly religious thinker who believes in God with a visceral faith that seems to be
based largely on wonder at the beauty of nature and the mystery of creation. He is distressed over modern man's lack of intellectual humility
and, like Dostoevsky, he mistrusts refined, abstract philosophizing. At the
same time, he maintains a small, Dostoevskian reservoir of intellectual
doubt. He asks, mischievously:

> Lord, let me know something of You. Affirm that You hear
> me. I don't ask a miracle, just some kind of barely perceptible sig-
> nal. Let, say, a bug fly out of that bush. Let it fly out right now.
> A bug is a most natural thing. No one will suspect. And it will be
> enough for me to be able to guess that You hear me and are letting
> me know it. Just say it: yes or no? Am I right or not? And if I am
> right, then let a train whistle four times from beyond the forest.
> There's nothing difficult in that – to whistle four times. And then
> I shall know.

Despite his intellectual's love of paradox (God is "unknowable and recognized everywhere, inaccessible and nearer than close, cruel and kind, absurd, irrational and utterly logical"), he values the simple and intuitive
faith that he attributes to the ordinary Russian. At the same time, his faith
is not so solemn as to prevent ironic or blasphemous treatment of religion.
(*Lyubimov*, for example, is full of comic references to the very same folk
belief that he extols in *Unguarded Thoughts*.) He is preoccupied with death,
but not morbidly so: his numerous remarks about death emphasize its
finality and stress the importance of a life of dignity on earth.

In his criticisms of the quality of contemporary life – its excessive materialism, frantic complexity, blind reliance on scientific progress, hostility
to quiet contemplation, and inhibition of sincere communication between
individuals – there is an implicit longing for some other, spiritually purer
culture. Only the dim outlines of this hypothetical superior culture can be
deduced: his only utopia, *Lyubimov*, is a negative one. Surely it would not
be modeled along Western lines: Sinyavsky is unmistakably opposed to
capitalist ethics, and he suggests that the liberal concept of "freedom of
choice" is an illusory one. If he believes in the goal of communism, his acceptance of it is undoubtedly qualified by strong ethical reservations. He

seems to believe that man's nature is so sinful that it is not amenable to institutional measures. His ideal culture, then, would be governed by a charitable acceptance of human imperfectibility. It would also embody large elements of the Russian cultural tradition for, despite his satiric treatment of Russians, he obviously views his cultural heritage with nostalgia and feels that Russians as a nation have a uniquely profound – if tragic – understanding of life. All of this would suggest that Sinyavsky is ultimately a conservative with strong neo-Slavophile tendencies.

Any summary of Sinyavsky's personal philosophy based on his fiction, his literary criticism, and his motley collection of aphorisms is bound to do him an injustice. One can speak with some assurance about his art, but not about his beliefs. As a true ironist, he is so inconsistent and self-contradictory that his convictions are bound to elude a firm definition.

Sinyavsky was released from prison in 1971 and lived quietly in Moscow until 1973, when he was allowed to leave for Paris. He is now (1976) teaching at the Sorbonne. Although he is reported to have continued writing fiction, his major publications since leaving the Soviet Union are a large critical work on Gogol (*In the Shadow of Gogol*), a similarly important study of Pushkin (*Walks with Pushkin*), and a *Voice from the Chorus* (1973), based on his long semimonthly letters to his wife from the camps in which he was incarcerated. *A Voice from the Chorus* is a complex work written in a loosely diaristic form, combining impressions of camp existence with speculations on life and death, literature, philosophy, history, and the Soviet people as exemplified by his fellow prisoners as individuals and in the mass. The "Voice" of the title represents the consciousness and point of view of Sinyavsky himself as he observes, reacts, meditates, or narrates, whereas the "Chorus" serves as a contrapuntal, generalized emanation from the camp population, consisting of stories, anecdotes, sayings, and quotations from prison slang and songs. The work amply demonstrates that his camp experience did not diminish Sinyavsky's originality and that in the course of it his talent further matured.[4]

13

Underground literature

Underground literature is writing that cannot legally be published in the USSR. It circulates through the medium of *samizdat* – handwritten or typewritten (and carbon copied) manuscripts, distributed on something like a chain-letter principle. The borderline between underground and "above-ground" literature is not always distinct. It sometimes happens that, because of a sudden switch in official policy or merely an arbitrary bureaucratic decision, a writer whose works are usually acceptable for publication will run into censorship difficulty with a given work and be forced to resort to underground channels. Also, some writings that the censors would probably find innocuous nevertheless circulate through *samizdat* simply because their authors choose not to submit them for publication. Some of the works of authors no longer living, such as Mandelstam and Pasternak, are still prohibited by censorship and thus have become underground literature. And many works no doubt circulate underground for the reason that editors have rejected them for lack of literary merit. The most significant underground literature, however, is that which has been found unacceptable for political and ideological reasons.

Despite occasional compromises and relaxations of controls, the Soviet regime has always been at odds with liberal writers, and the regime became increasingly hostile toward them during the last decade of the period with which the present study is concerned. At times, works of direct and open social protest or satire had found their way into print, such as Evtushenko's "Baby Yar" and Tvardovsky's *Tyorkin in the Netherworld*. These were allowed to appear, however, only because their sentiments happened to coincide with, or at least not seriously conflict with, those of responsible officials at the given moment. Their publication represented merely a kind of officially harnessed protest – merely a licensed dissent.

Moreover, writers' purely aesthetic explorations, their attempts to break away from prescribed patterns, had been constantly hampered. Although they were granted somewhat greater freedom of stylistic experimentation, the cramping limitations on aesthetic innovation remained severe.

The growing freedom of thought in the latter half of the 1950s and the first half of the 1960s reinforced the desire to tell the truth openly in accordance with one's personal understanding of it. As a result of the Twentieth Congress of the Communist Party, with its partial revelation of the deceit, brutality, and criminality of the Stalin regime, Soviet literature was officially encouraged to discuss the evils of the past. But there were strings attached to the new permissiveness: large areas of the past were still not open to examination and, as always, discussion of present evils was strictly limited. For many writers, the atmosphere was as frustrating as it was encouraging. When it became evident that the liberal expectations aroused by the Congress had been too high, the discouragement and rage among Soviet intellectuals found an outlet in literature of a kind that could not be published and thus went underground. Underground literature was the result of rising, and then frustrated, expectations.

The system of official censorship was the chief reason for the existence of underground literature. Another reason was that the authorities themselves did not respect the law and were simply arbitrary in their control over the printed word. As the regime resorted increasingly to severe repressive measures against dissidents – expulsion from the Writers' Union, blacklisting, various forms of harassment by the KGB, sedition trials, punishment in prison camps and mental hospitals, and exile – a great amount of literary activity was forced underground.

The underground literary movement was not an organized or coordinated one. With the exception of a few ephemeral small magazines of tiny circulation and the *Chronicle of Current Events* (which was not literary in nature, although it had the support of some writers), it was essentially a loose and random phenomenon. For those who participated in the movement, however, life was arduous and nerve racking, just as it was for their friends from other dissident sections of the population. Although *samizdat* in itself does not violate any statutes and is thus not illegal, the authorities exerted great pressure in the effort to suppress it – attempting to link it to foreign intelligence services or anti-Soviet political organizations among Russian émigrés, infiltrating it with KGB agents as a means of terrorizing, and arresting and imprisoning its participants on a variety of pretexts.

Although there had been previous isolated examples of underground literature, the movement became distinctly noticeable toward the end of

1956. In the next few years it grew rapidly, stimulated by such events as the suppression of *Doctor Zhivago* and the persecution of its author. By 1964, *samizdat* had received a further stimulus when it became impossible to publish sharply anti-Stalinist works. The decision of Khrushchev's successors to reverse the trend of liberalization provided even greater incentive for underground literature. The trial of Andrei Sinyavsky and Yuli Daniel in 1966, for example, sharply increased the number of literary dissidents, as did the trial of Yuri Galanskov, Aleksandr Ginzburg, and others in 1968.

Very little of the underground writing during these years was intentionally subversive. By 1970, however, the emphasis of *samizdat* had changed from literature to articles and documents of a primarily political cast. Nevertheless, the memory of the period of liberalization of literature and its accompanying hopes remained strong. Between 1970 and 1975, despite the heightened police activities that marked the continuing reversal of de-Stalinization, and the forced emigration of many leading underground writers, *samizdat* continued to reveal remarkably interesting works of literature.

Although most underground literature was not explicitly anti-Soviet and was not directed against the regime as such, it frequently protested against the authorities' violations of both the letter and the spirit of Soviet law. On an ideological level it often took up the question of ends and means, militated against the hallowed Marxist–Leninist concept of class morality and ethics, and argued the necessity for moral principles common to every man. Satire, especially, dwelt on the discrepancy between official pretense and practice and on the excessive moral flexibility of persons in positions of power. The purely literary quality of underground writing was on roughly the same level as that of officially published works. In the early years of the movement its style was largely conventional, in the spirit of Russian literature of the first two decades of this century, with the exception of some experimentation, especially by the poets. Later, as more prominent and talented writers such as Solzhenitsyn, Sinyavsky, and Voinovich, together with other stylistic experimenters, joined the movement, the quality rose markedly.

Many of the works discussed in previous chapters are, of course, underground literature. These include, among others, Pasternak's *Doctor Zhivago*, the fiction of Sinyavsky and Chukovskaya, Grossman's *Forever Flowing*, Brodsky's poetry, and the memoirs of Nadezhda Mandelstam. Solzhenitsyn's early works, which once were published in the Soviet Union, have now *become* underground literature, together with everything else he has written. Additional underground writings of great merit will be discussed subsequently. First, however, a word about one of the earliest and, in its way, most heroic manifestations of *samizdat:* the underground magazines.

These periodicals appeared sporadically, usually in only one or two issues of, at most, two or three hundred copies. Usually their content was unsensational, and they were seldom intensely political, although their ideological complexions varied. Nearly all of them published at least some *belles-lettres,* much of it material that could easily have passed the censors. (To some extent, it would seem, the publication of these journals was purely a gesture of defiance against the censorship.) Their editors were, as a rule, loosely knit groups of young people – some of them still teenagers – in Moscow and Leningrad. Their literary contents were chiefly poetry, fiction, essays, and criticism emanating from their own amateur circles, but quite often they included works by well-known writers that apparently could not be published in legally established journals. The aesthetic standards of these underground magazines – with some exceptions – were quite high, but the editorial process itself was evidently, and probably of necessity, haphazard.

The existence of many of these magazines – with exotic names such as *Boomerang* and *Cocktail* – was known outside the Soviet Union only by word of mouth. The first substantial journal, whose contents are a matter of record, was *Syntaxis* (1959), edited by Aleksandr Ginzburg. Essentially nonpolitical, the magazine nevertheless expressed discontent with the quality of contemporary life, skepticism about institutionalized values and, often, feelings of melancholy not in keeping with the forward-looking spirit urged by literary officialdom. Aesthetically eclectic and self-consciously individualistic, the contributors to *Syntaxis* often displayed an inclination to emulate the poetry of the Silver Age (Khlebnikov, Bely) or semirehabilitated but still suspect poets such as Tsvetaeva and Zabolotsky. As editor, Ginzburg was arrested and sentenced to two years' imprisonment in September 1960.

Syntaxis was succeeded in 1961 by *Phoenix.* Similarly eclectic and formally experimental, *Phoenix* was more explicitly political and at the same time expressed a greater variety of attitudes and moods, ranging from despairing gloom to passionate summons to revolution. The most notable single work published in *Phoenix* was the poem "A Human Manifesto," in which the magazine's editor, Yuri Galanskov, expressed not only his personal frustration and disorientation in the contemporary world but also his generation's anxiety about the future. *Phoenix* also contained bitter criticism of contemporary Russian culture and laments over the state of the arts in the Soviet Union. Its most gifted contributor was the young poet Natalya Gorbanevskaya. For editing *Phoenix*, Galanskov was expelled from Moscow University and sent to a mental institution.

In 1965 the journal *Sphinxes* appeared, edited by an older writer, Valery Tarsis. Nominally the organ of a group of youthful dissidents, it also included contributions from senior underground writers. In 1966 Galanskov resumed his editorial activities with *Phoenix-66*. (He was arrested in January 1967, tried a year later with Ginzburg and others, and sentenced to seven years in concentration camps. He died in camp in 1972 at the age of 33, the victim of physical deprivation and intentionally inadequate medical treatment.) Another underground journal that appeared in 1966 was *The Russian Word*, founded by a group that called itself the Ryleev Club in honor of a poet who took part in the Decembrist uprising of 1825. This was the last of the significant underground *literary* journals. Its most famous successor was the *Chronicle of Current Events*, established in 1968 for the purpose of registering and protesting against the state's illegal suppression of dissidents, national minorities, and religious groups. Under extreme pressure from the KGB the *Chronicle* ceased publication at the end of 1972, but it resumed its clandestine circulation in the spring of 1974.

Numerous writers who have been discussed in previous chapters are known, in large measure, because of manuscripts that have made their way to the West and been published there both in translation and in the original Russian. Western publication of Russian-language books of Soviet origin has in fact become an important supplement to *samizdat*. (It has even been argued, only partly in jest, that *samizdat* has been *crippled* by Western publishers, because Soviet authors now wait for their works to return from the West in hard covers before circulating them.) Some authors, such as Pasternak with *Doctor Zhivago* and Sinyavsky and Yuli Daniel, who published under pseudonyms, deliberately made their works available for publication abroad. The works of others, however, were taken abroad without the consent or knowledge of the authors: this was inevitable, because once a work begins circulating in *samizdat* the author loses control over it.

A special stimulus to foreign publication of underground works has been the "third emigration" of Soviet nationals. (The first emigration was that which followed the Revolution; the second took place during and immediately after World War II.) This group began leaving the Soviet

Union in the late 1960s and their numbers increased markedly in the early 1970s, because the authorities had either expelled them or permitted them to emigrate. Its numbers represented much of the finest Soviet literary talent and included such figures as Solzhenitsyn, Nekrasov, Brodsky, Maksimov, Korzhavin, Sinyavsky, Aleksandr Galich, and Gorbanevskaya. This growing exile community maintained a degree of contact with dissidents who remained behind. Through Russian-language publishing houses and periodicals, chiefly in West Germany, France, and the United States, the exiles printed not only works of their own that they had been unable to publish in the USSR but also manuscripts that kept arriving from the motherland. Although there was no Soviet law prohibiting the sending of manuscripts abroad for publication, the authorities fought the practice through a number of sanctions and pressures against authors, including criminal prosecution for "anti-Soviet agitation and propaganda." Also in the 1970s the Soviet accession to the Universal Copyright Convention and some accompanying internal legislation seemed designed, among other things, to hamper the publication of unauthorized Soviet works abroad. But the flow of underground literature to the West (and, to a lesser degree, back again to the Soviet Union) continued.

For centuries Russian poets have been writing between the lines, conveying dissident messages through recondite hints and allusions. As this practice requires not only a skillfully subtle writer but also an especially informed and well-trained circle of readers, the number of those who fully understand its subversive shadings is relatively small. Evidently, from the point of view of the authorities, this kind of masked protest constitutes a kind of safety valve that enables a relatively harmless number of discontented intellectuals to voice certain complaints to an innocuously small group of initiated readers. It is tolerated because it is unlikely to produce widespread ferment. Thus, in the Soviet Union over the past two decades there has been an officially *published* poetry of a subversive nature – although never frankly and unambiguously so. On the other hand, this kind of poetry is not politically or ideologically insignificant: from time to time over the past twenty years the authorities have been moved to chastise, suppress, or even banish poets who threatened to increase the numbers of the discontented.

The subjects of *samizdat* poetry are both universal and local. Like many poets throughout the world, the Russians expressed anxiety over the loss of individual identity in the age of technology. Likewise, they wrote against militarism and war, and voiced terrible fears of a possible nuclear catastrophe. As for their own country, they protested against the absence of freedom of expression and freedom of information, and the ubiquity of official propaganda. One poem, by N. Nor, includes the following lines:

> We are not allowed to travel about Europe.
> We are not allowed to see the wide world.
> We get our knowledge from Utopias
> And build our world from gossip and newspapers.[1]

A favorite topic of satirical verse was the smug bureaucratic mentality that dominates much of contemporary Soviet life and marks a revolution gone stale. Another frequent topic is chronic Soviet anti-Semitism. The most prominent topic of underground poetry over the years, and one that lingered with great persistency, was the state security apparatus.

Long after the concentration camps ceased to be an integral *mass* feature of Soviet life, underground poetry on this theme continued to be popular. Much of it was in the form of songs or ballads composed by inmates of the camps. Taken as a whole, poems about the camps are a protracted cry of misery, compounded of the dull pain of prolonged suffering and of hatred and contempt for those who run the system. They are, at one and the same time, dirges for those who have been destroyed and proud testaments of men who are determined to survive. Poetry on this theme, however, is not limited to brooding over the vast national catastrophe of the past. Although in much smaller numbers, Soviet dissidents were still being sent to prisons, camps, and exile. In 1966, the twenty-year-old Vladimir Batshev, on his way to a five-year exile in Siberia, wrote these lines in Moscow's Lefortovo prison:

> Everything is strange, just seems to be . . .
> What is there for me to tell you?
> Here only the walls cough
> through the green throat of the cell.
> Now, insidious sleep comes,
> free, without bars . . .
> And, like the footsteps of the guards,
> water-drops tap in the gutter,
> and, like applause,
> the peephole clicks in the door,
> and there are moans in the damp walls . . .[2]

Imprisonment and exile, however, inspired not only laments and melancholy but also defiance, as in these lines by Nor:

If suddenly you come for me,
To throw me in an iron cage,
I shall leave the world with head unbowed,
And not regret what I have done.
I'll stride into the cold void
Without pleading for mercy, without complaints and tears,
And bear with me there the dream
That I have carried with me many years.
And far from friends, among thick walls
My dream and I await the day of freedom
Your long imprisonment does not terrify me,
Without killing my dream you can't kill me.[3]

Camp poems form a wide spectrum, ranging from resigned sadness to abusive, bitter attacks against the regime, laced with obscenity and the language of the criminal underworld. The sophisticated sarcasm of an intellectual is evident in the following excerpt from the cycle of poems entitled "And At That Time," which Yuli Daniel wrote during his imprisonment. Exploiting the Soviet practice of contracting long phrases, usually of a bureaucratic nature, into single words, Daniel examines the term "concentration camp" (*kontsentratsionnyi lager*) and its contraction "kontslager." (To comprehend the full implications of these lines, one should understand that the word *lager* by itself means "camp," not necessarily with a prison connotation, that the root prefix *kants* refers to "chancery" and the whole range of bureaucratic activity, and that the word *konets* means "the end"):

What is a "kontslager"? This strange hybrid of words
burns like a slap on the century's visage.
"Lager" – we know that: ". . . we set up camp near
                              Yassa,
the cock crowed from morning, and we chopped branches
                              for firewood. . . .
"Lager" – that's familiar: "we made our camp in the
                              forest,
dried out the dew, boiled brook water in the pot. . . .
What then does the prefix mean, this unnatural
                              addition – "konts,"
which makes the word crash down the slope in a final
                              hiccup of death,

and then, turning, rattling its greedy guts,
it rises, like a vampire, a werewolf, a bloodsucker?
Maybe the girl who typed the Secret Decree, –
mistook "a" for "o" and one should read it "kants"?
The longed-for sum-total of centuries of bureaucratic
                                                    ways.
A veritable heaven, a paradise, where the paragraph
                            is omnipotent, like God.
Where the "out-basket" is smaller than the "in-basket,"
Where, when a directive goes round – don't move,
                            don't stand, don't sit.
Perhaps some young typesetter, not too bright, spoiled
                            it in a hurry,
let it slip? And one should read it – "konets"?
To creation – "konets." To satisfaction – "konets."
                            And to everything
that disturbed the darkness, that beckoned to the soul
                            and to the mind.
To man – "konets." To humanity – also "curtains."
A bowl of thin soup you'll get. Nothing more.
True or not, I don't know. But this mongrel syllable
lives in every house, it has made itself common.
Well, what about it, philologist? Come on, answer,
                            speak up,
with whom did you beget this word, how did you help it
                            crawl into the dictionary?
And when, at last, will you attack this stagnation,
                            turned norm,
and kill this syllable, marking it red?[4]

The poetry of the camps may well have been the purest and most authentic literary expression of Stalin's times, because the rest of Soviet literature had abetted the evils of Stalinism by maintaining a prudent silence. The flood of anti-Stalinist poetry that appeared in 1956 and immediately thereafter was, as a consequence, heavily guilt ridden. In their attempts to express their shock and horror at the realization of how the nation had become perverted, the poets excoriated themselves as sellouts, or dupes at best.

Anti-Stalinist poetry was not, however, merely self-castigating and retrospective. The theme of a need for moral renewal, intellectual and spiritual awakening, and a fundamental shakeup of values was prominent. The poet Shug argued the need for greater emotional integrity and daring:

> Give me
>   a lively
>   robust life
> without clever
>   Party wailing,
> Without objective lies.
> You will tell me
>   in pious tones,
> What is right,
> What is not,
> But I shout:
> Long live extremes,
> The planned
> And smooth
> Is not for me.
> For you feelings
> Are nonsense.
> For me a means
> Of throwing the heart
> Into the furnace of time.
> I hate
>   your sensibleness
> Which knows no doubts.[5]

Vladimir Batshev proclaimed that poets were fed up with writing to formula and pleaded for a clean slate: "We must start again from the beginning." Underground poetry, in fact, may have been without precedent in the self-conscious intensity of its search for purification. It aspired, among other things, to a new semantic integrity and freedom from the obligation to lie, as expressed in this poem by M. Mertsalov:

> Words, words, an undistinguished quantity
> Of lofty words of civic fervor;
> I have ceased fearing these words,
> For them I have paid dearly.
>
> Words, words – where is the measure of these words?
> What right have I to poems and the truth?
> For them men have been tortured with lies and poison.

For them,
For a handful of ringing words,
For someone's reflection, some sort of shading,
Lives have been shattered,
Hearts have wasted away in cells and torture chambers.

Words, words – menacing and evil
Are the gaping cellars of Lubyanka.
I have ceased fearing these words,
For them I have paid dearly.[6]

This preoccupation with "words" (there were many other poems, published as well as underground, on the same theme) indicated an urgent desire not only for a moral but also a cultural renewal. Underground poetry contributed to that renewal in the sense that it expanded the topical range of Russian verse and the variety of its viewpoints. As has been mentioned in connection with *samizdat* magazines, many of the underground poets also aspired to stylistic innovations and even greater aesthetic individuality, as a protest against the norms of socialist realism. A great deal of this experimentation seemed merely naive and inept. With a few exceptions, none of the underground poets displayed as much originality or technical competence as the best published poets, such as Martynov and Voznesensky. Nevertheless, these attempts at innovation (and renovation) indicated that the restlessness that gave impetus to underground poetry was not only social and political but also cultural.

Numerous underground poems expressed alienation, anxiety, frustration, and despair. In a poem written in 1966, Natalya Gorbanevskaya compared Russia to an insane asylum:

In the madhouse
wring your hands,
your white brow against the wall
like a face against a snowdrift.[7]

Probably the most talented of the underground poets, Gorbanevskaya always integrated her political themes into a more generalized view of life. Her images are often violent, involving pain and separation from others, including loved ones, and extreme fluctuations between anguish, depression, and joy. Terse and technically versatile, she is a poet of mood rather than philosophy, but she displays a deeply engaged concern over the future of Russian culture and the fate of mankind in the atomic age. (In 1968 Gorbanevskaya participated in a small demonstration against the Soviet invasion of Czechoslovakia. Arrested and released, she compiled a book about the demonstration and the trials of her fellow participants. For this she was arrested in 1969, found "mentally disturbed" and confined to an asylum. Released in 1972, she was allowed to emigrate in 1975.)

Disillusionment and unbelief, pessimism extending to cynicism, and images of gloom and morbidity are prominent in *samizdat* poetry. Occasionally there have been suicidal notes, as in these lines by S. Krasovitsky:

> But I hear the sound of iron –
> A pistol's black flower has arisen,
> And when my time comes,
> Like not just any lover with his beloved,
> I shall transfix my temple
> With a remarkable wild red rose.[8]

There are also expressions of a more generalized pessimism, a kind of cosmic malaise, as in Yu. Stefanov's "Song About A Spider," which concludes:

> God trembles,
> The leader leads,
> Wanderers seek bread,
> Time flows aimlessly,
> Like a stream of sand.
> And lips are bitten
> And fingers clenched,
> And in the glance the same
> Mute anguish.[9]

The incidence of purely political themes in underground poetry is fairly low. Very little of it seems to be directed against the Soviet regime as such, and even less of it constitutes an appeal for immediate and specific political activity. Even the poems that evidently spring from profound political discontent lack the immediately hortatory quality of a sharp call to action. In a poem of A. Vladimirov there are ominous, if vague, predictions of violent change to come:

> A murmur is approaching,
> There's trouble ahead,
> A rumble is crawling
> Over land and water.[10]

There are defiant, although unspecific, notes of revolt from Nor, who proclaims:

So there are few of us!
　　　　　We're waiting! We believe!
So we may die!
　　　　　Our time will come![11]

The most sweepingly revolutionary of the underground poets was Galanskov, who was clearly in revolt not only against Soviet conditions but
also against conditions throughout the world – against the age in which he
lived. His "Workers of the World, Unite," for example, is not only a plea
against war and oppression but also a summons to universal insurrection:

But I affirm that somewhere there lurks
A huge
Worldwide
Rebellion.[12]

For the most part, however, the poets expressed merely a longing, a
wistful hope that Russians have not lost the aspiration to overthrow oppression. Some of them, nationally conscious with strong Slavophile inclinations, devoted verses to "Holy Russia." The verses of others urged a
religious revival. The image of the Decembrists is extremely prominent in
underground poetry, notably that of Batshev and Evgeny Kushev. Some
youthful verses by A. Mikhailov, although unpolished and technically
crude, summarize in concrete and vigorous images many of the concerns
of underground poetry:

If you have never been in a concentration camp,
If you have never been tortured,
If your best friend has never written an anonymous
　　　　　　　　denunciation against you,
And if you have never crawled out from under a heap
　　　　　　　　　　　of corpses,
Surviving the firing squad by a miracle,
If you do not know the theory of relativity
And tensor calculus,
If you cannot ride a motorcycle at 200 kilometers
　　　　　　　　an hour,
If you have not murdered your beloved, obeying someone
　　　　　　　　　　else's orders,
If you do not know how to assemble transistor radios,
If you have not belonged to any sort of Mafia

And don't know how to forget yourself and shout
                    "hurrah" along with everybody,
If you can't hide from an atomic explosion in two
                                        seconds,
If you don't know how to dress at the expense of eating,
If you can't live together with four other people in
                            five square meters
And don't even play basketball,
Then you are not a man of the twentieth century![13]

Another source of relief from the artificial sentiments of official art were the songs of contemporary balladeers. These songs, circulating chiefly by means of tape recorders, supplanted the large public poetry readings that flourished in the early sixties and then ceased under official pressure. The phenomenon was not a musical one in a strictly conventional sense: the tunes, sung to guitar accompaniment, were simple and unpretentious, and the music was intentionally subordinate to the words. Expressing popular emotions, outlooks and hopes, the balladeers were an outgrowth of underground poetry. Their enormously enthusiastic reception in the sixties and seventies would indicate, in fact, that their "songs" had become culturally a more important form of underground art than poetry itself.

The first important bard of this nature, and the earliest to be widely tape-recorded, was Bulat Okudzhava. (For a discussion of his poetry, see pp. 98–104.) His songs were lyrical and romantic in cast, intimate in intonation, conveying moods of nostalgia, love, and quiet sadness. Their manner was simple, sincere, and conversational, full of humane concern and tenderness for trusting little people with their hopes and aspirations, their individual happiness and sorrows. At the same time, Okudzhava was a sly and subtle satirist, and a major source of his popularity was the contemporary relevance of his allegorical statements.

A bolder, much more caustic and vicious satirist was Aleksander Galich. His songs lacked Okudzhava's romanticism, were more dramatic, and packed with bitterly clever, socially conscious black humor. Like Okudzhava he often wrote about the "little man," the underdog, but he stressed the strange and often shocking misfortunes which the Soviet system brings to such a person. The world of his songs is one of anti-Semites, neo-Stalinists, secret police, and informers, and the language is often correspondingly crude or obscene. Uncompromising in his social criticism, pessimistic in his portrayal of the low state of popular morale, Galich, who is a playwright and scenario writer by profession, was expelled from the Writers' Union in 1971, then from the Union of Cinematographers and the Literary Fund. Thoroughly blacklisted, he was finally allowed to emigrate in 1974 and now lives in Munich.

On anti-Semitism Galich ironically remarks:

> If you'll be a useful Jew,
> They'll let you call yourself a Russian . . .[14]

One ballad takes the form of a monologue by a man who has been released after a twenty-year stretch in concentration camps:

> And I sit in this beer-hall like a lord,
> And I even have my teeth left.[15]

In another ballad, Galich thinks about the multitude of his friends who have disappeared into the camps:

> But nevertheless, I don't weep for the dead,
> I don't even know who's dead or alive.[16]

He writes sarcastically of those who long for a return of Stalinism, and of opportunists who play it cosy:

> Let others cry out from despair,
> From insult, from sorrow, from cold!
> In silence we know there's more profit,
> And the reason is – silence is gold.
>
> That's how you get to be wealthy,
> That's how you get to be first,
> That's how you get to be hangmen!
> Just keep mum, keep mum, keep mum.[17]

Other popular balladeers were Novella Matveeva (see pp. 127–30), and the satirists Yuli Kim, Mikhail Nozhkin, and Vladimir Vysotsky. A well-known stage and screen actor, Vysotsky was thematically versatile and wrote about numerous aspects of life. His focus, however, was essentially the same as that of Galich. One song, for example, tells of the unsuccessful attempt of two prisoners to escape from their concentration-camp hell, and another describes the horrible lives of dissenters who have been punished by incarceration in a madhouse. Although Vysotsky's tone is not as consistently bitter as that of Galich, his protest can at times be just as powerful. One song tells of how a hoodlum finds respectability by becoming an active anti-Semite:

> I'm ready for everything:
> Robbery and violence,
> And I'm saving Russia
> By beating up Yids.[18]

As in *samizdat* poetry, a favorite topic of underground prose writers has been the Soviet internal security system. The most famous works on this topic are those of Solzhenitsyn, but there are also moving and valuable autobiographical accounts of arrest, grim concentration camp life, and almost unimaginable survival in Evgenia Ginzburg's *Journey into the Whirlwind* (*Krutoi marshrut*, 1967) and Anatoly Marchenko's *My Testimony* (*Moi pokazaniya*, 1969). *Ward No. 7*, Valery Tarsis' autobiographical novel about the use of a mental institution to torment political offenders, and the short stories of Varlam Shalamov, all of them set in concentration camps, further illuminate the cruel, corrupt and absurd institutions with which the Soviet regime disciplines the population and attempts to exterminate opposition.

After Solzhenitsyn's *One Day in the Life of Ivan Densiovich*, the finest work of fiction about the camps is Georgi Vladimov's novel *Faithful Ruslan* (*Vernyi Ruslan*), which made its way to the West in 1964, but was first published in 1975. Its hero, Ruslan, is a dog trained to guard prisoners. When his camp is evacuated, Ruslan and the other dogs are simply turned loose. When his master – a guard – also departs, Ruslan takes up with a freed prisoner who has not left the area and "guards" him – the only thing he knows how to do. He also learns to forage in the forest for his own food and becomes a freer, healthier, and nobler animal. However, a contingent of free construction workers arrives at the camp site, and Ruslan and the other dogs can only assume that these too are prisoners. Using the tactics in which they have been trained, the dogs try to keep the workers in line. A bloody battle between people and dogs ensues, in the course of which Ruslan is killed. He dies valiantly, thinking he has resumed his duty.

Ruslan has been trained to do only one thing, and this he has done faithfully to the end. He knows only the master–dog and dog–prisoner relationships. In contrast to some of the other dogs and the guard who was his master, he is not bloodthirsty but, as in the struggle that precedes his death, he is a fierce fighter. His tragedy is that, with his strongly ingrained sense of "service," and with his native bravery, vigor, and intelligence, he has not been trained for anything constructive. Moreover, nobody has bothered to retrain him for the new circumstances. He is a dutiful individual whose best traits have led to his victimization.

The novel has wide figurative and symbolic meanings, and great social resonance. The waste of Ruslan by the camp system parallels the waste of good, faithful humans by the same means. There are numerous comparisons between two-legged and four-legged creatures, always in favor of the latter. In this sense the story is akin to Tolstoy's story "Yardstick" and Chekhov's "Kashtanka," but it is superior to both of them in many respects – most notably its moral connotations and its aesthetic use of an animal's-eye view of the world. As an allegory the novel uses the camp world and its human and animal population as a kind of microcosm of Stalinist Russia. Each of the dogs suggests individual aspects of the Soviet personality, attitudes toward life, patterns of behavior, and the social hierarchy. The allegory, however, is not mechanical or strained, for the novel is of remarkably high literary quality. Its use of flashbacks to episodes of camp life, for example, provides sensitive and profound portrayals of that existence. The writing throughout is remarkably imaginative and compassionate. Vladimov's "underground" novel is clearly his best.

Numerous other works of moral and social exploration have emerged from underground. One is Vladimir Maksimov's *Quarantine* (*Karantin*), which was published in the West in 1973. The novel's structure is somewhat similar to that of Maksimov's *The Seven Days of Creation* in that it is composed of a number of short stories related by a central situation. A train that has left Odessa is stopped and quarantined because of an epidemic of cholera that has broken out in the city. For six days the passengers, representing various social groups, tell their individual stories, which usually bespeak aimlessness, moral trauma, and disillusionment resulting from degrading experiences. Alcohol and sexual activity seem to have been the only solace in their empty lives, devoid of freedom or spiritual foundations. The two central characters are a young officer and his mistress, whose relationship passes from a stage of purely physical love, through one of indifference, to one of spiritual love, and who thereby experience moral salvation. Cumulatively, the stories of the other characters portray an embittered existence of frustration and suffering, for which the only relief, the author indicates, is Christian selflessness and mercy. An extra dimension is provided to the novel by numerous excursions into Russian history, designed to portray the evolution of a society through moral crises.

"My Apologia," a presumably autobiographical story by a person who wrote under the pseudonym Victor Velsky (and is reported to have died in 1964), is the account of a sensitive, lonely, alienated young intellectual who, under pressure, betrays some of his fellow university students to the KGB, which in turn tries to recruit him as a steady informer. After great moral torment, he decides to escape to the West and makes his way into West Berlin but, after wandering about the city for a few hours, he loses his nerve and returns. He concludes that he is "a Russian in my thirsting after the ideal! A miserable, eternal Russian nomad!" The only thing left is suicide, but he lacks the necessary courage. With Dostoevskian undertones the story gives interesting commentary on both the dismal moral climate of Stalin's times and the atmosphere of spiritual void under Khrushchev, with the latter's dominant emphasis on material values.

In the early 1970s the brothers Arkadi and Boris Strugatsky, the Soviet Union's most popular writers of science fiction, began finding difficulty in publishing their stories, which had recently taken on strong allegorical and satirical qualities, with obvious political references to the present. Their novel *The Nasty Swans* (*Gadkie lebedi*) went into *samizdat* and was published abroad in 1972. A satirical, sometimes surrealistic, anti-utopian fantasy that cuts in many directions, it tells of a group of independent-thinking outcasts confined to a special compound because they carry a peculiar genetic disease. Joined by a number of restless children who are dissatisfied with the state and with their parents' attempts to indoctrinate them in false values, they rebel against the immoral, corrupt existing order and drive it out. The story ridicules, among other things, literary prostitution, sloganeering, machinelike glorification of political leaders, military aggrandizement, and governments that lie to the people.

Among the earliest works of *samizdat* to be sent abroad were the stories of Yuli Daniel. His "Atonement" is the story of the ostracism of a man wrongly accused of having "informed" on a friend. The friend spent many years in concentration camps after having been convicted of spreading "malicious anti-Soviet propaganda." Gradually boycotted by everyone he knows, including his mistress, the central character finally suffers an emotional collapse and winds up in a mental hospital. The story is a study in the atmosphere of suspiciousness that grips the citizens of a police state (these are all members of the "liberal intelligentsia") and of the sense of guilt that builds up in even the most well-meaning individuals. Another treatment of the moral consequences of terrorist policies is Daniel's story "Hands." Told retrospectively in first person, its main action takes place shortly after the Revolution. A young man, drafted by the Cheka to execute "counterrevolutionaries," is assigned to shoot a priest. As a grim joke, his comrades have loaded his rifle with blanks, so that although he shoots many times, the priest does not fall. As a result the hero has a nervous breakdown and for the rest of his life suffers a tremor in his hands so severe that he can only do limited work.

Daniel's talent for satire is displayed in "This is Moscow Speaking," a story based on a grotesque situation: the Soviet government's proclamation of a Public Murder Day. On this day anyone over the age of sixteen may kill, unpunished, anyone else, with the exception of members of the military and certain classes of officials. Most of the story is concerned with the reactions of persons from the Moscow literary and artistic world to the announcement, which first comes over the radio and is followed by a supporting barrage of propaganda from the media. The literati make various attempts to guess the reason for the coming event, to joke about it, to rationalize it ideologically and justify it morally. Most striking is the passive way in which these intellectuals, and the Soviet populace as a whole, accept the decree. The story is not only a sardonic satire on Soviet captive intellectuals but also a lampoon of many features of the Soviet system: the press, the sheeplike gullibility of the populace, and widespread hypocrisy.

The finest satire among works unpublished in the Soviet Union is that of Vladimir Voinovich. The hero of his story "By Mutual Correspondence" is a soldier, essentially an obtuse lout, who amuses himself by writing love letters to women he does not know – a practice that eventually traps him into marrying a woman twelve years his senior and settling down to a miserable civilian life in a backward village with his growing brood. His naiveté and weakness for vodka have made him an easy mark for a scheming woman aided by her bullying brother. Both the language and the characters in the story are crude and earthy, and very funny. The satire, which often has the flavor of Zoshchenko, is directed at conventional Russian targets such as drunkenness and petty greed, but it also touches on Soviet institutions, notably the internal passport system.

Voinovich's masterpiece thus far is the novel *The Life and Extraordinary Adventures of Private Ivan Chonkin* (*Zhizn' i neobychainye priklyucheniya soldata Ivana Chonkina*, 1975), of which only the first two sections had appeared as of 1976. A satirical mixture of the realistic, the fantastic, and the absurd, it is a study of delusion on a mass scale. Its plot is basically simple: a small Soviet military airplane makes a forced landing near a village deep in the heart of Russia. The soldier Chonkin is sent to guard the plane until it can be repaired and restored to duty. Apparently forgotten by the army, Chonkin, who is himself a peasant boy, settles down to life in the village, takes up with Nyura, the local postmistress, and moves in with her. While

Chonkin is waiting to be noticed by the army, Hitler's forces invade the Soviet Union.

In time, the NKVD receives a tipoff that an unknown soldier is living in this remote village, and an eight-man detachment is sent out to bring him in. Chonkin does his duty by defending his plane against these attackers. With Nyura's help he captures the entire detachment, together with the local NKVD captain, who has gone out to find out what has happened to his men. Using his captives as forced labor, Chonkin establishes a Stakhanovite record for harvesting potatoes. Disturbed by wild rumors of a "Chonkin band" that is reportedly terrorizing the countryside, the army sends out a regiment to destroy them. The NKVD captain escapes, mistakes the approaching regiment for Germans, and tries to ingratiate himself by passing as a Gestapo officer. (His interrogation by the equally confused Soviet army officers is a high point in the novel.) Ultimately Chonkin is captured. At first he is decorated for bravery in guarding his plane against what is thought to have been German paratroopers and then, when the facts become a bit clearer, is arrested as a deserter.

Chonkin is ostensibly a poor soldier – clumsy, physically unprepossessing, not very energetic and supposedly not very bright. His apparent ineptitude, however, comes not from a lack of intelligence but from a native inability to understand or accept the absurd conditions and institutions which the army and society consider normal. He is a child of nature, whose spiritual health and common sense in a world that is ridiculously warped make him seem a fool. As the story accumulates a number of grotesque characters and hilarious episodes, Chonkin's surroundings seem increasingly bizarre and Chonkin himself increasingly normal.

In this novel Voinovich's style and arsenal of narrative devices place him in the tradition of Gogol, Zoshchenko and Ilf and Petrov. The dialogue is sharp, earthy, and wildly funny; the narrator himself is at times vulgar and naive, at others a sly and witty caricaturist and parodist of ideological clichés and political jargon. Occasionally the narrator becomes discursive and engages in intimate conversations with the reader. Odd characters abound – drinking, expounding, quarreling, jostling, or viewing one another with amazement. Surrealistic dreams and fantasies enhance the novel's atmosphere of strangeness, illogicality, and comic distortion. All of these devices have the function of satirizing totalitarian culture, provincial ignorance, backwardness and suspiciousness, and specific institutions such as the collective farm, the secret police, and the Party.

Although there are satirical features in every line of the novel, its satire tends to cluster in individual characters. There is, for example, the harried, dipsomaniac collective-farm president Golubev who, when Chonkin arrives on the scene, can only assume that he has been denounced and that this soldier has been sent to report on him. An account of life in a concentration camp does not distress Golubev: perhaps the living there is better than on his own collective farm! He welcomes the war; life at the front is bound to be better than at home. There is also Gladyshev, the flower of the local intelligentsia, who, as a self-taught geneticist along the lines of Lysenko, aspires to cross the tomato with the potato, and who has filled his and his family's living quarters with various kinds of dung for experiments with fertilizers. And there is the man whom the local authorities, on orders to liquidate spies and saboteurs, have arrested as a scapegoat. They are amazed at his insolent defiance until they discover that his name, which police everywhere have been begging him to change, is Moses Solomonovich Stalin. The prisoner is immediately released.

The influence of such officially forbidden or frowned-upon writers as Proust, Joyce, and Kafka, and of "modernist" tendencies in general, is evident in some recent *samizdat* prose. There has also been an influence from Daniil Kharms, a Russian absurdist writer and verbal experimenter of the 1920s. The spirit of Kharms is evident in a number of satirical plays written in the 1960s by Andrei Amalrik, who also acknowledged the influence of Beckett and Ionesco. In Amalrik's plays irrationality and paradox predominate, as symptomatic of the deformity and moral debasement of contemporary life.

A somewhat similar attitude of disillusionment is found in the stories of Vladimir Maramzin, whose stylistic experimentation, however, is in the tradition of Zoshchenko and Andrei Platonov. Like those writers, Maramzin specializes in combining linguistic levels – elevated language with vulgar speech – and featuring the ordinary Soviet man as his narrator and central character. Ironical often to the point of cynicism, Maramzin turns Soviet slogans and propaganda against themselves and uses the incorrect, rough, and clumsy language of the man in the street as a commentary on the alienation and moral obtuseness which, Maramzin feels, Soviet life has induced in him. An interesting and original stylist, fond of puns and colorful, pungent, off-beat expressions, Maramzin, who emigrated to France in 1975, was one of the most promising products of the underground.

14

Conclusion

When the idea of writing this book was conceived in the mid-1960s, Soviet literature appeared to be on the upswing. A new, bold generation of poets and prose writers, reinforced by an older generation recently released from decades of frustration, was in the process of introducing a variety of fresh topics, ideas, and styles into a literature that had been virtually moribund. The present book, then, was planned as the chronicle and analysis of a literary renaissance. The events and developments of the ensuing decade, however, have been so disappointing that the process can now be best described as a renaissance in reverse. What began as a great burst of liberated creative energy subsided into something fragmented, depressed, and lifeless.

There is reason to hope that the setback is only temporary. For one thing, a great amount of literary talent remains in the Soviet Union – most of it now silent, timid, or underground, but nevertheless alive. For another, the recent emigration of many of Russia's most powerful and accomplished writers has at least preserved their lives, their opportunities to publish and, in a limited way, to continue communicating with the countrymen they left behind. In addition, although the literary horizon has darkened profoundly, the conditions under which the Soviet literary world must live are still far better than they were under Stalin. Finally, the solid accomplishments of many Soviet writers in the past twenty years, and the general learning process that these accomplishments involved, cannot be easily erased.

It must be remembered that in the early 1950s Soviet literature was constricted by an extremely narrow conception of human nature, human affairs, and historical processes, and was governed ultimately by the whim of the world's most powerful dictator. For the most part, writers, in order to be published at all, had been forced to become dishonest, or superficial, or both. Political expediency and the mandate of official optimism forbade the mention of large areas of social evil; others were glossed over as incidental terrain, crossed in the inevitable march of progress. The result was a mass literature of social and emotional make-believe under the guise of socialist realism. As reading matter it was dull, unimaginative, and predictable. Moreover, the writing community had developed a huge sense of collective guilt for having participated, for more than a quarter-century, in the systematic suppression and distortion of the facts of Soviet life and for having rationalized the injustice, inhumanity, and betrayal of ideals that were characteristic of Stalin's times.

A major feature of the writing of the post-Stalin period was its effort to settle accounts with the past, to correct the record and to atone, as far as possible, for the failure of literature to act as the conscience of the nation during its years of most extreme corruption and suffering. The process involved both a renewed sense of civic duty and a recognition of the need for cultural – and specifically aesthetic – rehabilitation. Writers understood that unless the literary community cultivated the habit of honesty and developed the freedom to pursue its goals with integrity it could not achieve aesthetic fulfillment. In resuming its candid exploration of human affairs, Soviet literature began to restate propositions that are taken for granted in the literature of the West: the uniqueness of the individual personality; the right of the conscience to question institutionalized morals and ethics; the dignity of introspection, of private thoughts and tastes; the recognition of a common humanity in art, independent of political and social systems.

The rules continued to be set and administered, however, by political authorities; the censorship remained in force. Directors of publishing houses and editors of magazines were still subject to centralized Party discipline. Controls over the translation and importation of literature from abroad continued to restrict opportunities for contact with foreign literatures. The freedom of writers to question, to shake up preconceptions, to startle, disturb, and mystify, remained limited. A prudish antiseptic attitude prevented the full exploration of dark sides of human nature; social alienation could be described sympathetically only at great peril.

Writers in the fifties, sixties, and seventies clearly aspired to much greater freedom to examine questions of existence, personality, and ideology than they did in fact achieve. They could not be as satirical, or downright subversive, as they wanted to be. Much Soviet writing suffered not only from the officially imposed constraints of the given moment but also from the debilitating cultural *habit* of observing constraints. Also, the authorities invariably followed a loosening of constraints with a retightening. It is heartening that under such circumstances writers, at least for a time, managed to fight their way, against massive, glacial resistance, to some degree of autonomy. They achieved this by stubbornly pushing against the controls, expanding into every unguarded vacuum, and exploiting to the utmost every opportunity to develop greater literary latitude and depth.

As a result of these efforts, Soviet literature in these two decades won a number of important new positions from which it cannot easily be dislodged. The ironical manner of writing, reminiscent of Russian literature of the twenties and similar to that of the contemporary West, has become established, although several of its best practitioners have recently been forced underground or into exile. Lyricism and attention to the writer's "inner world," formerly disparaged and officially discouraged, is now quite acceptable. In dealing with private lives, writers can now penetrate into causes, motives, and implications more freely than before. Moreover, it is widely, although by no means universally, recognized that the Revolution and the political system that followed it have not succeeded in creating a unique, Soviet human nature. The "positive hero" (the kind of emblematic figure whom Viktor Nekrasov wryly suggests in his Kira Georgievna's sculpture of a young man with "a firm glance that knows no doubt, directed into an unknown future") remains a standard fixture in the writing of orthodox hacks, but in the works of most talented writers he has changed almost beyond recognition or disappeared altogether.

Many writers, reacting against the banality of the literature of the Stalin period, engaged in a search for originality of style. They sought chiefly in the realm of language, attempting to make it more colorful, concrete, and veracious. Especially among younger writers there was an evident contempt for the "Party language" of Lenin and Stalin and for official and bureaucratic jargon – all of which became the subject of parody – and a fascination with the richness of slang and contemporary colloquial patterns of speech. At the same time, most writers adhered to the stylistic traditions of nineteenth-century Russian realism with its emphasis on rational, logical methods of narration and its avoidance of mystification. Moreover, the socialist-realist convention of clarity and simplicity continued to influence writing styles, so that literature tended to be lacking in richness of verbal texture, density, and evocativeness. As a rule, even the best writing lacked the power to startle and disturb the imagination. It was almost never stylistically "difficult." In this respect it is noteworthy that the fantastic, the grotesque, and the surrealistic were rare and almost exclusively the province of underground literature.

The main reason for the lack of allusiveness, density of imagery, and richness of metaphor, was the lingering isolationism of Soviet literature. Too rarely did it reflect in depth either the Russian cultural past or the existence of a modern international literature. To some extent the writers' inclination to confine their attention to their own environment, their own time and place, and to avoid the references and cultural echoings that characterize contemporary Western literature, came from their lack of education and erudition. The Soviet system simply did not permit them to be as knowledgeable as they might otherwise have been. However, even those who had managed to educate themselves were discouraged, by political inhibitions and the fear of committing ideological error, from displaying the depth of their culture. As previous chapters have indicated, the influence of the first three decades of twentieth-century Russian literature, and of modern Western literature, did increase in the post-Stalin period. But the increase would undoubtedly have been much greater had there been no official controls.

An important feature of this period, and one that could quite possibly play a decisive role in the development of Soviet culture in years to come, was writers' revived interest in the Russian national tradition and the Russian national character. This trend was best exemplified in the village writers, with their respect for folkways, antiquity, and even religion. The poets, too, displayed a concern for the destiny of *Russia as a nation*, in distinction to the Soviet Union as a whole and, in their allegorical use of historical events and settings, seemed to be seeking spiritual succor in a consciousness of Russia's past.

During these two decades the range and variety of literary topics increased markedly. The most important of these for the moral welfare of the nation were the prison camps – the essence and end-product of the police state and the most prominent single symbol of Stalinism. In published literature, unfortunately, the topic had an extremely short life but, as we have seen, the camps became the outstanding theme in underground literature. There were, however, many other reminders – notably but not exclusively in village literature – of the injustice with which the Soviet state had treated its citizens and violated their human dignity. Inherent in most references to injustice, and sometimes discussed with considerable explicitness, was the question of ends and means – the ancient ethical concern whose revival was essential for the rehabilitation of Soviet literature.

Works of fiction about construction and technology often raised related questions: what are we building for? Why, and at what cost? In Stalinist literature such questions were seldom asked, because the answers were axiomatic.

These two decades also produced a deeper and more honest examination of social and moral problems. Values such as personal honesty and responsibility, loyalty to friends, attention to one's conscience, concern for those less fortunate than oneself, and kindness and liberality in dealing with people and in forming one's opinion of them were all given fresh emphasis. Concerns of this nature were particularly prominent in the abundant literature directed to the problems of children, adolescents, and young adults, and in the problem of the "generations" – the relations of the young to their compromised and betrayed parents of the Stalin generation. Writers also dealt with individual behavior without concern for its moral implications, engaging in psychological portraiture for its own intrinsic interest. Intimate feelings of love or isolation, for example, were now described with complete freedom from didacticism. At the same time, many writers clearly displayed a strengthened devotion to spiritual values and a disdain for the previously standardized and orthodox measures of personal achievement.

As of the year 1976 it was evident that Soviet Russian literature had *not* been killed by Stalinism. Although it was in deep trouble, it was better off in many ways than it had been in 1953. Lyric poetry had been revived. Experimentation both in poetry and in the short story, resembling that which had taken place in the 1920s, had resumed. Socialist realism, with its prescriptions and programmatic distortion of the truth, had been largely supplanted by critical realism, with its propensity for posing questions and describing the world authentically.

The novel in the Soviet Union was still lifeless; its only talented practitioners had been forced abroad or underground. Large, systematic, critical examinations of experience were still intolerable to those who controlled Soviet publishing. The crippled condition of the novel was, in fact, symptomatic of the critical situation of literature in general. The exciting days of iconoclastic, protesting poetry had passed. After years of apparent indecision, marked by alternating harassment and cajoling, terror and restraint, pampering writers on the one hand and imprisoning and exiling them on the other, the Soviet rulers seemed to have stabilized the situation by steering literature into a semidoldrum. Writing that was critical in tone was limited to traditionally "safe" areas, avoiding serious ideological confrontations. The Soviet authorities had come to realize that, in their own interests, a genuinely liberal policy toward literature was an impossibility, and that any permissiveness must be highly selective.

By 1976, then, literature in the Soviet Union was more profound than it had been two decades before, but its investigations were oriented to questions of behavior and not to questions of ideological belief. Good and evil were measured pragmatically, in terms of their effects on the individual or society, and not in relation to the intangible, the elusive, the abstract forces that have always tormented the world's most creative literary minds.

NOTES

Chapter 1. The literary situation

1 Ol'ga Berggol'ts, "Razgovor o lirike," *Literaturnaya gazeta*, April 16, 1953.
2 Il'ya Erenburg, "O rabote pisatelya," *Znamya*, No. 10, 1953, pp. 160–83.
3 Vladimir Pomerantsev, "Ob iskrennosti v literature,"*Novyi mir*, No. 12, 1953, pp. 218–45.
4 "Gumanizm i sovremennaya literatura," *Voprosy literatury*, No. 11, 1962, p. 26.
5 M. Kuznetsov, "Sotsialistichesky realizm i modernizm,"*Novyi mir*, No. 8, 1963, p. 220.
6 "Zhizn' – istochnik tvorchestva!" *Voprosy literatury*, No. 8, 1963, p. 12.
7 V. Shcherbina, "Glavnoe napravlenie," *Voprosy literatury*, No. 2, 1963, p. 10.
8 I. Fradkin, "Replika T. Motylevoi," *Voprosy literatury*, No. 6, 1959, p. 59.
9 Kuznetsov, "Sotsialistichesky realizm," p. 220.
10 Shcherbina, "Glavnoe napravlenie," p. 10.
11 Yu. Borev, "Modernizm, chelovek, razum," *Voprosy literatury*, No. 3, 1963, p. 67.
12 *Ibid.*, p. 71.
13 Shcherbina, "Glavnoe napravlenie," p. 9.
14 *Ibid.*, p. 10.
15 I. Zventov, "Smekh – priznak sily (Zametki o satire),"*Voprosy literatury*, No. 7, 1962, p. 23.
16 "Na perednyi krai ideologicheskoi bor'by," *Voprosy literatury*, No. 4, 1963, p. 5.
17 Shcherbina, "Glavnoe napravlenie," p. 8.

Chapter 2. The oldest poets

1 Nikolai Aseev, "O strukturnoi pochve v poezii,"*Den' poezii*, Moscow, 1956, pp. 155–7.
2 Anna Akhmatova, *Sochineniya* (Tom vtoroi), Inter-Language Literary Associates, 1968, p. 107.
3 *Ibid.*, p. 121.
4 Anna Akhmatova, *Sochineniya* (Tom pervyi), Inter-Language Literary Associates, 1967, p. 328.
5 *Ibid.*, p. 327.
6 *Ibid.*, p. 346.

7 *Ibid.*, p. 329.

8 *Ibid.*

9 Vladimir Lugovskoi, *Seredina veka*, Moscow, 1958, pp. 238–9.

10 *Ibid.*, p. 244.

11 Nikolai Tikhonov, "Nash vek proidyot . . . ," *Znamya*, No. 11, 1969, p. 6.

12 Nikolai Aseev, *Lad*, Moscow, 1963, pp. 17–18.

13 *Ibid.*, p. 83.

14 Semyon Kirsanov, *Iskaniya*, Moscow, 1967, pp. 14–16.

15 *Ibid.*, pp. 72–3.

16 Semyon Kirsanov, "Sem' dnei nedeli," *Novyi mir*, No. 9, 1956, pp. 16–32.

17 Semyon Kirsanov, "Zerkala," *Znamya*, No. 3, 1967, pp. 78–9.

18 Semyon Kirsanov, "Kletka," *Znamya*, No. 1, 1969, p. 68.

19 S. Marshak, *Sobranie sochinenii* (Tom pyatyi), Moscow, 1970, p. 213.

20 *Ibid.*, p. 77.

21 Mikhail Svetlov, *Stikhotvoreniya*, Leningrad, 1968, p. 116.

22 Vladimir Ognev and Dorian Rottenberg (compilers), *Fifty Soviet Poets*, Moscow, 1969, p. 398.

23 *Ibid.*, p. 394.

24 *Ibid.*, p. 400.

25 Boris Pasternak, *Stikhi 1936–1959*, Ann Arbor, 1961, p. 67.

26 *Ibid.*, p. 76.

27 Boris Pasternak, *Poems*, translated from the Russian by Eugene M. Kayden, Ann Arbor, 1959, p. 177.

28 Boris Pasternak, *Fifty Poems*, translated with an introduction by Lydia Pasternak Slater, London and New York, 1963, p. 75.

29 *Ibid.*, p. 29.

30 Pasternak, *Poems*, p. 172.

31 Pasternak, *Stikhi 1936–1959*, p. 61.

32 *Ibid.*, p. 81.

33 P. Antokolskii, "My vse, laureaty premii . . . ," *Grani*, No. 56, 1964, p. 182.

34 P. Antokolskii, "Posle poemy," *Novyi mir*, No. 2, 1970, pp. 71–2.

35 P. Antokolskii, "Dva soneta (I)," *Novyi mir*, No. 8, 1969, p. 6.

36 Nikolai Zabolotskii, *Stikhotvoreniya*, Washington, D.C. and New York, 1965, p. 99.

37 *Ibid.*, p. 235.

38 N. A. Zabolotskii, *Stikhotvoreniya i poemy*, Moscow–Leningrad, 1965, p. 145.

39 Ognev and Rottenberg, *Fifty Soviet Poets*, p. 198.

40 Zabolotskii, *Stikhotvoreniya*, p. 174. It is interesting that the concluding line of this poem, originally published in *Novyi mir* in 1956, contains the phrase "resurrected earth" (*zemlya voskreshaya*), and that this phrase is changed, in the posthumous Soviet edition of Zabolotsky (1965) to "ill-fated earth" (*zemlya zlochastnaya*). Evidently both the religious and the political connotations of the former phrase, tolerable to the Soviet censorship in 1956, had become intolerable by 1965.

41 *Ibid.*, p. 189.

42 Leonid Martynov, *Pervorodstvo*, Moscow, 1965, p. 225.

43 Leonid Martynov, *Stikhotvoreniya i poemy* (Tom vtoroi), Moscow, 1965, p. 108.

44 Leonid Martynov, *Stikhotvoreniya i poemy* (Tom pervyi), Moscow, 1965, p. 253.

45 *Ibid.*, pp. 254–5.

46 Martynov, *Pervorodstvo*, p. 343.

47 George Reavey (ed.), *The New Russian Poets: 1953 to 1966*, New York, 1966, p. 20.

48 Martynov, *Stikhotvoreniya i poemy* (Tom pervyi), p. 195.

49 Martynov, *Pervorodstvo*, p. 30.

50 Martynov, *Stikhotvoreniya i poemy* (Tom pervyi), p. 364.
51 *Ibid.*, p. 365.

Chapter 3. The first Soviet generation of poets

1 Ol'ga Berggol'ts, *Vernost'*, Leningrad, 1970, p. 78.
2 Ol'ga Berggol'ts, *Uzel*, Moscow–Leningrad, 1965, pp. 127–8.
3 *Ibid.*, p. 130.
4 *Ibid.*, p. 46.
5 *Ibid.*, pp. 104–9.
6 Margarita Aliger, *Stikhotvoreniya i poemy v dvukh tomakh* (Tom vtoroi), Moscow, 1970, pp. 150–1.
7 *Ibid.*, p. 156.
8 *Ibid.*, p. 115.
9 Margarita Aliger, "Pravota," *Iz zapisnoi knizhki 1946–1956*, Moscow, 1957, p. 131.
10 Aliger, *Stikhotvoreniya i poemy* (Tom vtoroi), p. 167.
11 *Den' poezii*, Moscow, 1962, p. 52.
12 Vikto Bokov, *Izbrannoe*, Moscow, 1970, p. 229.
13 *Ibid.*, p. 173.
14 Aleksandr Yashin, *Izbrannye proizvedeniya* (Tom pervyi), Moscow, 1972, p. 314.
15 *Ibid.*, pp. 390–2.
16 *Ibid.*, p. 385.
17 *Ibid.*, p. 270.
18 *Ibid.*, p. 280.
19 *Ibid.*, p. 456.
20 *Ibid.*, p. 234.
21 *Ibid.*, p. 474.
22 Arsenii Tarkovskii, *Zemle-Zemnoe*, Moscow, 1966, p. 41.
23 *Ibid.*, p. 85.
24 *Ibid.*, p. 159.
25 *Ibid.*, p. 19.
26 *Ibid.*, p. 151.
27 A. Tvardovskii, *Za dal'yu dal'*, Moscow, 1961, p. 86.
28 *Ibid.*, p. 171.
29 A. Tvardovskii, "Tyorkin na tom svete," *Novyi mir*, No. 8, 1963, p. 21. Translated by Leo Gruliow in *Current Digest of the Soviet Press*, September 18, 1963, p. 25.
30 A. Tvardovskii, *Stikhotvoreniya, Poemy*, Moscow, 1971, p. 228.
31 A. Tvardovskii, "Po pravu pamyati," *Posev*, October 1969, p. 54.
32 *Ibid.*, p. 53.

Chapter 4. Poets formed during the war

1 Evgenii Vinokurov, *Lirika*, Moscow, 1962, pp. 12–13.
2 *Ibid.*, p. 214.
3 Evgenii Vinokurov, *Kharaktery*, Moscow, 1965, pp. 3–4.
4 Evgenii Vinokurov, "Chelovek mne etot nepriyaten . . . ," *Nash sovremennik*, No. 4, 1966, p. 2.
5 Evgenii Vinokurov, *Lirika*, p. 289.

6 Evgenii Vinokurov, "Chudaki," in V. Koblikov *et al.* (eds.), *Tarusskie stranitsy*, Kaluga, 1961, p. 130.

7 Vinokurov, *Lirika*, p. 213.

8 Evgenii Vinokurov, "Svet," *Stikhotvoreniya*, Moscow, 1964, p. 253.

9 Vinokurov, *Lirika*, p. 282.

10 *Ibid.*, p. 239.

11 Boris Slutskii, "Kak ubivali moyu babku?" *Rabota*, Moscow, 1964, pp. 93–4.

12 Boris Slutskii, "1945 god," *Segodnya i vchera*, Moscow, 1963, p. 162.

13 *Ibid.*, p. 161.

14 Boris Slutskii, "Tridtsatye gody," *Rabota*, pp. 108–9.

15 Yevgeny Yevtushenko, *A Precocious Autobiography*, New York, 1963, p. 78.

16 Boris Slutskii, "Bog," *Rabota*, p. 106.

17 *Ibid.*, pp. 53–4. Translated by Max Hayward in Patricia Blake and Max Hayward (eds.), *Half-way to the Moon*, London, 1964, p. 148.

18 Boris Slutskii, *Izbrannaya lirika*, Moscow, 1965, pp. 13–14.

19 Boris Slutskii, "Banya," *Segodnya i vchera*, Moscow, 1963, pp. 168–9.

20 *Ibid.*, p. 27.

21 Konstantin Vanshenkin, *Izbrannoe*, Moscow, 1963, p. 153.

22 *Ibid.*, pp. 138–9.

23 "Nasha anketa," *Voprosy literatury*, No. 5, 1965, p. 50.

24 *Ibid.*, p. 49.

25 D. Samoilov, *Vtoroi pereval*, Moscow, 1963, pp. 17–20.

26 *Ibid.*, p. 26.

27 D. Samoilov, "Smert' poeta," *Novyi mir*, No. 3, 1967, p. 131.

28 Quoted in B. Sarnov, *Rifmuetsya s pravdoi*, Moscow, 1967, p. 168.

29 D. Samoilov, "Aleksandr Blok v 1917-m," *Novyi mir*, No. 12, 1967, pp. 41–2.

30 Samoilov, *Vtoroi pereval*, p. 57.

31 N. Korzhavin, *Gody*, Moscow, 1963, p. 31.

32 *Ibid.*, p. 36.

33 *Ibid.*, p. 43.

34 *Ibid.*, p. 73.

35 *Ibid.*, pp. 68–70.

36 *Ibid.*, pp. 63–4.

37 *Ibid.*, pp. 20–1.

38 Yuliya Drunina, *Trevoga*, Moscow, 1963, p. 28.

39 *Ibid.*, p. 99.

40 *Ibid.*, p. 39.

41 *Ibid.*, p. 114.

42 Bulat Okudzhana, *Proza i poeziya*, Frankfurt/Main, 1968, p. 129.

43 *Ibid.*, p. 125.

44 *Ibid.*, p. 155.

45 *Ibid.*, p. 210.

46 *Ibid.*, p. 176.

47 *Ibid.*, p. 183.

48 *Ibid.*, pp. 233–4.

49 *Ibid.*, pp. 235–6.

Chapter 5. The younger generation of poets

1 A. Men'shutin, A. Sinyavskii, "Za poeticheskuyu aktivnost' (zametki o poezii molodykh)," *Novyi mir*, No. 1, 1961, p. 224.

2 Evgenii Evtushenko, *Idut belye snegi* . . . , Moscow, 1969, p. 61.
3 *Ibid.*, p. 62.
4 Quoted in Lev Ozerov, "Kratkii traktat o yabloke (Evgenii Evtushenko i drugie)," *Voprosy literatury*, No. 2, 1968, p. 101.
5 Evtushenko, *Idut belye snegi* . . . , pp. 61–2.
6 Evgenii Evtushenko, *Vzmakh ruki*, Moscow, 1962, p. 10.
7 *Ibid.*, pp. 19–20.
8 Evtushenko, *Idut belye snegi* . . . , p. 92.
9 *Ibid.*, p. 151.
10 Evtushenko, *Vzmakh ruki*, p. 170.
11 B. Sarnov, *Rifmuetsya s pravdoi*, Moscow, 1967, p. 314.
12 George Reavey (ed.), *The New Russian Poets 1953 to 1966*, New York, 1966, p. 110.
13 Ozerov, "Kratkii traktat," pp. 95–109.
14 Reavey, *The New Russian Poets*, p. 76.
15 Evgenii Evtushenko, "Khochu ya stat' nemnozhko staromodnym . . . ," *Novyi mir*, No. 7, 1964, p. 112.
16 Bella Akhmadulina, *Oznob*, Frankfurt/Main, 1968, p. 193.
17 *Ibid.*, p. 114.
18 *Ibid.*, p. 162.
19 *Ibid.*, p. 141.
20 *Ibid.*, p. 113.
21 *Ibid.*, p. 64.
22 *Ibid.*, p. 65.
23 *Ibid.*, p. 45.
24 *Ibid.*, pp. 136–7.
25 *Ibid.*, pp. 102–7.
26 *Ibid.*, p. 15.
27 *Ibid.*, pp. 9–10.
28 *Ibid.*, p. 18.
29 *Ibid.*, pp. 83–4.
30 *Ibid.*, pp. 142–54.
31 *Ibid.*, pp. 157–8.
32 *Ibid.*, p. 162.
33 Andrei Vosnesensky, *Antiworlds and "The Fifth Ace"* (Patricia Blake and Max Hayward, eds.), New York, 1967, p. 162.
34 *Ibid.*, p. 150.
35 *Ibid.*, p. 106.
36 *Ibid.*, pp. 199–245.
37 Quoted in N. A. Zakharova (ed.), *Voprosy sovietskoi literatury*, Leningrad, 1968, p. 28.
38 Vosnesensky, *Antiworlds and "The Fifth Ace,"* p. 239.
39 Viktor Sosnora, *Yanvarskii liven'*, Moscow–Leningrad, 1962, p. 16.
40 *Ibid.*, p. 59.
41 *Ibid.*, p. 35.
42 Viktor Sosnora, "Moi dom," *Oktyabr'*, No. 1, 1963, p. 86.
43 Novella Matveeva, *Dusha veshchei*, Moscow, 1966, p. 117.
44 Novella Matveeva, *Izbrannaya lirika*, Moscow, 1964, pp. 12–14.
45 Matveeva, *Dusha veshchei*, p. 15.
46 *Ibid.*, p. 103.
47 *Ibid.*, p. 114.
48 Aleksandr Kushner, *Nochnoi dozor*, Moscow–Leningrad, 1966, pp. 5–6.
49 *Ibid.*, pp. 22–3.

50 Vladimir Tsybin, *Au!*, Moscow, 1967, p. 21.

51 Vladimir Tsybin, "Vozrast," *Den' poezii*, Moscow, 1962, p. 111.

52 Vladimir Tsybin, *Glagol*, Moscow, 1970, pp. 17–18.

53 Iosif Brodskii, *Ostanovka v pustyne*, New York, 1970, p. 168. Translated by Jamie Fuller in *Russian Literature Triquarterly*, No. 1, Fall 1971, pp. 68–9.

54 Reavey, *The New Russian Poets*, p. 268. Translated by Mr. Reavey on p. 269.

55 *Ibid.*, p. 260. Translated by Mr. Reavey on p. 261.

56 Brodskii, *Ostanovka v pustyne*, p. 140.

57 *Ibid.*, pp. 21–6.

58 Reavey, *The New Russian Poets*, p. 264. Translated by Mr. Reavey on p. 265.

59 Brodskii, *Ostanovka v pustyne*, p. 111. Translated by George L. Kline in *Joseph Brodsky: Selected Poems*, Baltimore, 1974, p. 81.

60 *Ostanovka v pustyne*, p. 164. Translated by George L. Kline in *Joseph Brodsky: Selected Poems*, p. 124.

Chapter 6. The rise of short fiction

1 For a discussion of this and other stylistic phenomena, see Deming Brown, "Narrative Devices in the Contemporary Soviet Russian Short Story: Intimacy and Irony," *American Contributions to the Seventh International Congress of Slavists*, Vol. 2, *Literature and Folklore*, The Hague and Paris, 1973, pp. 53–74.

2 "Molodye – o sebe," *Voprosy literatury*, No. 9, 1962, pp. 117–58.

3 Yurii Trifonov, "Predvaritel'nye itogi," *Novyi mir*, No. 12, 1970, p. 110.

Chapter 8. The village writers

1 Fyodor Abramov, "Luidi kolkhoznoi derevni v poslevoennoi proze," *Novyi mir*, No. 4, 1954, pp. 210–31.

2 G. Lomidze, "Sila realizma (Zametki o sovremennoi proze)," *Voprosy literatury*, No. 5, 1963, p. 66.

3 V. Chalmaev, "Neizbezhnost'," *Molodaya gvardiya*, No. 9, 1968, p. 287.

4 Efim Dorosh, "Ivan Akrikanovich," *Novyi mir*, No. 8, 1966, p. 260.

5 V. Chalmaev, quoted in I. Dedkov, "Stranitsy derevenskoi zhizni," *Novyi mir*, No. 3, 1969, p. 242.

6 *Ibid.*, p. 245.

Chapter 9. Literature reexamines the past

1 Translated from *Literaturnaya gazeta*, October 25, 1958, in *The Current Digest of the Soviet Press*, December 3, 1958, p. 6.

2 *Ibid.*, p. 11.

3 L. Lazarev, "Pamyat'," *Voprosy literatury*, No. 5, 1965, p. 62; A. Bochkarov, "Proverno voinoi," *Novyi mir*, No. 7, 1970, p. 232; L. Plotkin, *Literatura i voina*, Moscow–Leningrad, 1967, pp. 123–4.

Chapter 10. Literature copes with the present

1 D. Nikolaev, " 'Po kakoi pravde zhit'? . . ,' " *Voprosy literatury*, No. 10, 1961, pp. 88–98; V. Kamyanov, "Eticheskoe i esteticheskoe," *Voprosy literatury*, No. 8, 1962, pp. 16–17.
2 V. Oskotskii, "Chto mozhet chelovek," *Literaturnaya gazeta*, August 5, 1965; L. Novichenko, "Tvorcheskaya positsiya pisatelya i nekotorye cherty sovremennoi literatury," *Literatura i sovremennost'* (Sbornik sed'moi), Moscow, 1967, pp. 114–15; Z. Kedrina, "Kakaya ona, pravda obraza," *Voprosy literatury*, No. 2, 1966, pp. 6–7.
3 I wish to acknowledge my indebtedness to Geoffrey Hosking, who has kindly permitted me to read the manuscript of his very perceptive article on Shukshin. It is entitled "The Fiction of Vasily Shukshin" and is scheduled to be published in Vasily Shukshin, *Snowball Berry Red and Other Stories*, edited by Donald M. Fiene, Ardis Publishers, 1977.

Chapter 11. Aleksandr Solzhenitsyn

1 The author is indebted to the following two articles for valuable insights into the narrative structure of *One Day:* Vladimir J. Rus, *"One Day in the Life of Ivan Denisovich:* A Point of View Analysis," *Canadian Slavonic Papers (XIII)*, Nos. 2–3, 1971, pp. 165–78; Richard Luplow, "Narrative Style and Structure in *One Day in the Life of Ivan Denisovich,*" *Russian Literature Triquarterly*, No. 1, Fall 1971, pp. 339–412.
2 The quotation from *One Day in the Life of Ivan Denisovich* is taken from the translation of Ronald Hingley and Max Hayward, Frederick A. Praeger, Inc., New York, 1963. In translating from the *Sketches and Miniature Tales*, I found the rendition of Harry Willets extremely useful: Alexander Solzhenitsyn, "Breathing," *Encounter*, March 1965, pp. 3–9.

Chapter 12. The art of Andrei Sinyavsky

1 Alfreda Aucouturier, "Andrey Sinyavsky on the Eve of His Arrest," in Leopold Labedz and Max Hayward, eds., *On Trial: The Case of Sinyavsky (Tertz) and Daniel (Arzhak)*, London, 1967, p. 343.
2 Professor Assya Humesky has suggested to me that this passage may be a reference to a popular parody of the prologue to Pushkin's *Ruslan i Lyudmila* that circulated in the Soviet Union in the 1920s as an ironic protest against the new regime's attacks on romanticism.

In quoting from the works of Sinyavsky I have used the following translations, altering them occasionally on the basis of my own interpretation of the original Russian: Abram Tertz, *Fantastic Stories* ("You and I" and "The Icicle," translated by Max Hayward, "Graphomaniacs," "At the Circus," and "Tenants," translated by Ronald Hingley, New York 1963; "Pkhentz," trans. Jeremy Biddulph, in Peter Reddaway, ed., *Soviet Short Stories*, Vol. 2, Baltimore, 1968, pp. 214–63; Abram Tertz, *The Trial Begins*, translated by Max Hayward, New York, 1960; "Thought Unaware" [*Unguarded Thoughts*], translated by Andrew Field and Robert Szulkin, *The New Leader*, July 19, 1965, pp. 16–26.

3 This may also be a reference to Lermontov, who uses the same term in *A Hero of Our Times*.

4 The author wishes to express his indebtedness to three of his seminar students, whose interpretations are reflected in this chapter: Ray J. Parrott, Jr. ("Pkhentz"), Susan Wobst ("At the Circus"), and the late Guy W. Carter (*Lyubimov*).

Chapter 13. Underground literature

1 N. Nor, "Nam ne dano poezdit' po Evrope . . .," *Grani*, No. 52, 1962, p. 126.
2 Vladimir Batshev, "Teper' ya gosudarstvu nuzhen . . .," *Grani*, No. 61, 1966, p. 13.
3 N. Nor, "Esli vdrug za mnoyu yavites' vy . . .," *Grani*, No. 52 (1962), p. 125.
4 Yulii Daniel', *Stikhi iz nevoli*, Amsterdam, 1971, pp. 73–4. Trans. Vera S. Dunham and Deming Brown in *Encounter*, April 1972, p. 43.
5 A. Shug, "V otvet na eto . . .," *Grani*, No. 52, 1962, p. 136.
6 M. Mertsalov, "Slova, slova – bezlikoe chislo . . .," *Grani*, No. 52, 1962, p. 124.
7 Natal'ya Gorbanevskaya, "V sumashedshem dome . . .," *Stikhi*, Frankfurt/Main, 1969, p. 95.
8 S. Krasovitskii, "O, vesna! . . .," *Grani*, No. 52, 1962, p. 116.
9 Yu. Stefanov, "Pesnya o pauke," *Grani*, No. 52, 1962, p. 101.
10 An. Vladimirov, "O poslushai, poslushai! . . .," *Grani*, No. 52, 1962, p. 179.
11 N. Nor, "Nas ochen' malo . . .," *Grani*, No. 52, 1962, p. 126.
12 Yu. Galanskov, "Proletarii vsekh stran, soedinyaites!," *Grani*, No. 52, 1962, p. 156.
13 Artemii Mikhailov, "Esli ty ne byl v kontslagere . . .," *Grani*, No. 59, 1965, p. 47.
14 Aleksandr Galich, *Pesni*, Frankfurt/Main – Sossenheim, 1969, p. 28.
15 *Ibid.*, p. 34.
16 *Ibid.*, p. 94.
17 *Ibid.*, p. 10. Translated by Gene Sosin in Rudolf L. Tokes (ed.), *Dissent in the USSR: Politics, Ideology, and People*, Baltimore and London, 1976, p. 291.
18 Quoted in Russian by Alexander Malyshev in "Soviet Underground Literature: A Discussion," *Studies on the Soviet Union*, Vol. 8, No. 3, 1969, p. 75.

SELECT BIBLIOGRAPHY

Many hundreds of books, articles and reviews – each devoted primarily to an individual author – have been consulted in the preparation of this study. These works are too numerous to list in the present context. The following bibliography consists of larger and more comprehensive studies, which I have found useful in designing the scheme of this book.

Anninskii, L., "Zametki o molodoi poezii," *Znamya*, No. 9 (1961), pp. 197–212.

"Tak prosto, chto ne veritsya," *Voprosy literatury*, No. 10 (1965), pp. 30–45.

Banketov, A., "Lirika v epose," *Voprosy literatury*, No. 7 (1967), pp. 80–94.

Baranov, V., "Za zhanrovuyu opredelennost'," *Literatura i sovremennost'*, sbornik 6 (Moscow: Khudozhestvennaya Literatura, 1965), pp. 280–89.

Blake, Patricia, "Introduction," in Patricia Blake and Max Hayward (eds.), *Half-Way to the Moon* (London: Weidenfeld and Nicolson, 1964), pp. 7–39.

Bocharov, A., "Istoki pobedy," *Znamya*, No. 5 (1965), pp. 233–47.

"Iz chisla ukrashayushchikh mir," *Voprosy literatury*, No. 10 (1965), pp. 69–78.

"Provereno voinoi," *Novyi mir*, No. 7 (1970), pp. 232–52.

Borshchagovskii, Aleksandr, "Poiski molodoi prozy," *Moskva*, No. 12 (1962), pp. 193–211.

Brovman, G., "Nravstvennye kriterii i khudozhestvennaya kontseptsiya," *Literatura i sovremennost'*, sbornik 6 (Moscow: Khudozhestvennaya Literatura, 1965), pp. 316–27.

Brown, Edward J., *Russian Literature Since the Revolution* (London: Collier-Macmillan, 1969).

Buznik, V. V. and V. A. Kovalev (eds.), *Vremya, pafos, stil'* (Moscow-Leningrad: Nauka, 1965).

"Cherty literatury poslednikh let," *Voprosy literatury*, No. 7 (1964), pp. 3–48.

Chudakova, M. and A. Chudakov, "Iskusstvo tselogo," *Novyi mir*, No. 2 (1963), pp.239–54.

"Sovremennaya povest' i yumor," *Novyi mir*, No. 7 (1967), pp. 222–32.

Dedkov, I., "Stranitsy derevenskoi zhizni," *Novyi mir*, No. 3 (1969), pp. 231–46.

Dement'ev, Valerii, "Bessonitsa veka," *Nash sovremennik*, No. 8 (1965), pp. 108–15.

Dmitriev, S., "Debyuty goda (Zametki o molodoi proze i ee geroe)," *Literatura i sovremennost'*, sbornik 3 (Moscow: Khudozhestvennaya Literatura, 1962), pp. 262–90.

El'yashevich, Ark., "Nerushimoe edinstvo," *Zvezda*, No. 8 (1963), pp. 185–202.

Ershov, L., *Sovetskaya satiricheskaya proza* (Moscow–Leningrad: Khudozhestvennaya Literatura, 1966).

Gibian, George, *Interval of Freedom: Soviet Literature During the Thaw, 1954–1957* (Minneapolis: University of Minnesota Press, 1960).

"Soviet Writers of the 'Little World'," in George Thomas (ed.), *Cultural Scene in the Soviet Union and Eastern Europe* (Hamilton, Ontario: McMaster University, 1973), pp. 35–64.

Glinkin, P. and P. Sidorov (eds.), *Sovetskaya literatura nashikh dnei: stat'i* (Moscow–Leningrad: Khudozhestvennaya Literatura, 1961).

"Gumanizm i sovremennaya literatura," *Voprosy literatury*, No. 11 (1962), pp. 3–49.

Gusev, Vladimir, *V seredine veka* (Moscow: Sovetskii Pisatel', 1967).

Hayward, Max, "Themes and Variations in Soviet Literature," in Milorad M. Drachkovitch (ed.), *Fifty Years of Communism in Russia* (University Park and London: The Pennsylvania State University Press, 1968), pp. 262–83.

"The Decline of Socialist Realism," *Survey*, (Winter 1972), pp. 73–97.

Hayward, Max and Edward L. Crowley (eds.), *Soviet Literature in the Sixties* (New York: Praeger, 1964).

Hayward, Max and Leopold Labedz (eds.), *Literature and Revolution in Soviet Russia, 1917–1962* (London: Oxford University Press, 1963).

Holthusen, Johannes, *Russische Gegenwartsliteratur II, 1941–1967* (Bern: Francke Verlag, 1968). Translated as *Twentieth-Century Russian Literature: A Critical Study* (New York: Ungar, 1972).

Hosking, Geoffrey, "The Search for an Image of Man in Contemporary Soviet Fiction," *Forum for Modern Language Studies* (October 1975), pp. 349–65.

Isakovskii, M. "Dokole? (o stikhakh i talentakh)," *Voprosy literatury*, No. 7 (1968), pp. 67–82.

Johnson, Priscilla, *Khrushchev and the Arts: The Politics of Soviet Culture, 1962–1964* (Cambridge, Mass.: MIT Press, 1965).

Kardin, V., " 'Vechnye voprosy' – novye otvety," *Voprosy literatury*, No. 3 (1961), pp. 25–48.

Kogan, A., "Prodolzhaya razgovor," *Literatura i sovremennost'*, sbornik 6 (Moscow: Khudozhestvennaya Literatura, 1965), pp. 290–315.

Kovalev, V. A. (ed.), *Russkii sovetskii rasskaz: ocherki istorii zhanra* (Leningrad: Nauka, 1970).

Kozhinov, V., "Novoe poeticheskoe pokolenie," *Voprosy literatury*, No. 7 (1970), pp. 22–32.

Kuznetsov, F., "Nastuplenie novoi nravstvennosti," *Voprosy literatury*, No. 2 (1964), pp. 3–26.

Kuznetsov, M., "Sotsialisticheskii realizm i modernizm," *Novyi mir*, No. 8 (1963), pp. 220–45.

Lakshin, V., "Pisatel', chitatel', kritik," *Novyi mir*, No. 4 (1965), pp. 222–40; No. 8 (1966), pp. 216–56.

Lavlinskii, L., "Ritmy zhizneutverzhdeniya," *Znamya*, No. 6 (1966), pp. 205–15.

"V kom brodit gordyi dukh grazhdanstva," *Znamya*, No. 8 (1967), pp. 236–46.

Lazarev, L., "Eto stalo istoriei," *Novyi mir*, No. 6 (1967), pp. 235–50.

"K zvezdam (zametki o 'molodoi proze')," *Voprosy literatury*, No. 9 (1961), pp. 13–36.

"Pamyat'," *Voprosy literatury*, No. 5 (1965), pp. 58–78.

Levin, F., "Deistvitel'no – ne veritsya," *Voprosy literatury*, No. 10 (1965), pp. 45–51.

"Otkrytie," *Literatura i sovremennost'*, sbornik 6 (Moscow: Khudozhestvennaya Literatura, 1965), pp. 328–37.

Levin, V. D. (ed.), *Voprosy yazyka sovremennoi russkoi literatury* (Moscow: Nauka, 1971).

"Literatura i yazyk," *Voprosy literatury*, No. 6 (1967), pp. 88–156.

Lominadze, S., " 'Vechnyi dvigatel' ili 'vopros o zhizni'?," *Voprosy literatury*, No. 10 (1965), pp. 59–69.

Makarov, Ya., *Pokoleniya i sud'by* (Moscow: Sovetskii Pisatel', 1967).

Makedonov, A., "Pravda poezii," *Voprosy literatury*, No. 7 (1968), pp. 86–95.

Marchenko, A., " 'Chto' i 'kak' v poezii," *Voprosy literatury*, No. 12 (1962), pp. 36–45.

"Ispytanie rabotoi," *Literatura i sovremennost'*, sbornik 3 (Moscow: Khudozhestvennaya Literatura, 1962), pp. 239–61.

"Ne ob eksperimente . . .," *Voprosy literatury*, No. 5 (1962), pp. 42–53.

"Puteshestivya i vozvrashcheniya," *Voprosy literatury*, No. 5 (1964), pp. 18–38.

"Chto takoe ser'eznaya poeziya?," *Voprosy literatury*, No. 11 (1966), pp. 35–55.

Mathewson, Rufus W., Jr., *The Positive Hero in Russian Literature* (second edition), (Stanford, Calif.: Stanford University Press, 1975).

McLean, Hugh and Walter N. Vickery, "Introduction" in Hugh McLean and Walter N. Vickery (eds.), *The Year of Protest, 1956* (New York: Random House [Vintage Books], 1961).

Men'shutin, A. and A. Sinyavskii, "Davaite govorit' professional'no," *Novyi mir*, No. 8 (1961), pp. 248–52.

"Za poeticheskuyu aktivnost'," *Novyi mir*, No. 1 (1961), pp. 224–41.

Mikhailov, Al., "Vesti pritsel'nyi ogon'," *Voprosy literatury*, No. 9 (1963), pp. 23–39.

"Poezii – kachestvo!," *Znamya*, No. 10 (1964), pp. 229–40.

"Plenitel'naya vlast' traditsii," *Znamya*, No. 9 (1968), pp. 206–21.

Mikhailov, I., "Raznymi putyami," *Zvezda*, No. 2 (1965), pp. 194–201.

Mikhailov, O. and S. Chudakov, "Zametki o poezii 1959 goda," *Voprosy literatury*, No. 4 (1960), pp. 36–63.

"Mnogoznachnost' poeticheskogo slova," *Voprosy literatury*, No. 4 (1967), pp. 48–86.

Motyashov, Igor', "Logika bor'by," *Moskva*, No. 3 (1967), pp. 201–9.

"Otvetstvennost' khudozhnika," *Voprosy literatury*, No. 12 (1968), pp. 3–32.

Nikolaev, D., " 'Po kakoi pravde zhit'? . . .," *Voprosy literatury*, No. 10 (1961), pp. 78–106.

Ninov, A., *Sovremennyi rasskaz* (Leningrad: Khudozhestvennaya Literatura, 1969).

Novikov, V., "Novoe v sovetskoi poezii," *Znamya*, No. 9 (1964), pp. 229–48.

"Aktivnost' khudozhestvennogo tvorchestva," *Moskva*, No. 5 (1967), pp. 185–95.

"Obsuzhdaem problemy poezii," *Voprosy literatury*, No. 10 (1968), pp. 70–92.

Ognev, V., *U. karty poezii* (Moscow: Khudozhestvennaya Literatura, 1968).

Osetrov, Evgenii, "Poeziya vchera i segodnya," *Nash sovremennik*, No. 12 (1966), pp. 96–104.

Ozerov, Lev, "Kratkii traktat o yabloke (Evgenii Evtushenko i drugie)," *Voprosy literatury*, No. 2 (1968), pp. 95–109.

Ozerov, V., "Molodost' chuvstva, zrelost' mysli," *Voprosy literatury*, No. 9 (1962), pp. 3–24.

Pankov, V., "Poemy nashikh let," *Moskva*, No. 1 (1965), pp. 195–205.

"Vremya, dela, poeziya," *Literatura i sovremennost'* (Moscow: *Khudozhestvennaya Literatura*, 1960).

Pertsovskii, V., "Osmyslenie zhizni," *Voprosy literatury*, No. 2 (1964), pp. 27–44.

Plotkin, L., *Literatura i voina* (Moscow–Leningrad: Sovetskii Pisatel', 1967).

"Poeziya 1964 goda," *Voprosy literatury*, No. 2 (1965), pp. 19–77.

"Poeziya 1965 goda," *Voprosy literatury*, No. 3 (1966), pp. 16–91.

Polyak, L. M. and V. E. Kovskii (eds.), *Zhanrovo-stilevye iskaniya sovremennoi sovetskoi prozy* (Moscow: Nauka, 1971).

Protchenko, B. I., "Sovremennaya povest' o derevne," *Russkaya literatura*, No. 4 (1970), pp. 62–79.

"Proza 1964 goda," *Voprosy literatury*, No. 1 (1965), pp. 18–77.

Rassadin, St., *O stikhakh poslednykh let* (Moscow: Znanie, 1961).

"Chelovechnost' poezii," *Voprosy literatury*, No. 11 (1962), pp. 50–68.

"Zakony zhanra," *Voprosy literatury*, No. 10 (1967), pp. 66–80.

Sarnov, B., *Rifmuetsya s pravdoi* (Moscow: Sovetskii Pisatel', 1967).

Sememov, Vladimir, "Rodniki b'yut iz glubin," *Nash sovremennik*, No. 2 (1969), pp. 104–13.

Shubin, E., "Zhanr rasskaza v literaturnom protsesse," *Russkaya literatura*, No. 3 (1965), pp. 27–52.

"Printsipy raskrytiya kharaktera v sovremennom rasskaze," *Russkaya literatura*, No. 2 (1966), pp. 29–43.

Sinyavsky, Andrei, *For Freedom of Imagination*, translated and with an introduction by Laszlo Tikos and Murray Peppard (New York: Holt, Rinehart and Winston, 1971).

Skvortsov, L. I., "Ob otsenkakh yazyka molodezhi (zhargon i yazykovaya politika)," *Voprosy kul'tury rechi*, Vyp. 5 (1964), pp. 45–70.

Sokolov, Vadim, "Chudaki i planimetricheskaya yasnost'," *Voprosy literatury*, No. 10 (1965), pp. 52–9.

Solov'ev, Boris, *Poeziya i kritika* (Moscow: Sovetskaya Rossiya, 1966).

Solov'ev, Grigorii, "Chtoby shelest stranits, kak shelest znamen! . . .," *Nash sovremennik*, No. 11 (1968), pp. 104–10.

Soviet Literature: A Reappraisal (Studies on the Soviet Union, Vol. 8, No. 3, 1969).

Starikova, E., *Poeziya prozy* (Moscow: Sovetskii Pisatel', 1962).

Surganov, Vs. "Chelovek na zemle," *Literatura i sovremennost'*, sbornik 9 (Moscow: Khudozhestvennaya Literatura, 1969).

"Tugie uzly," *Znamya*, No. 2 (1971), pp. 214–37.

Svetov, F., "O molodom geroe," *Novyi mir*, No. 5 (1967), pp. 218–32.

Swayze, Harold, *Political Control of Literature in the USSR, 1946–1959* (Cambridge, Mass.: Harvard University Press, 1962).

Terts, Abram (A. Sinyavskii), "Literaturnyi protsess v Rossii," *Kontinent*, No. 1 (1974), pp. 143–90.

Toper, P., "Chelovek na voine," *Voprosy literatury*, No. 4 (1961), pp. 20–51.

Urban, A., "Geroi i stil'," *Znamya*, No. 3 (1962), pp. 196–211.

"Moda, shtamp i poet," *Voprosy literatury*, No. 9 (1962), pp. 73–89.

"Pryamo v zhizn' . . . (Zametki o poezii)," *Voprosy literatury*, No. 1 (1964), pp. 28–50.

"Zametki o nezamechennom . . .," *Zvezda*, No. 5 (1964), pp. 195–203.

Vozvyshenie cheloveka (Leningrad: Khudozhestvennaya Literatura, 1968).

"Sud'ba voiny – sud'ba stikhov," *Zvezda*, No. 6 (1970), pp. 193–202.

Vickery, Walter N., *The Cult of Optimism: Political and Ideological Problems of Recent Soviet Literature* (Bloomington: Indiana University Press, 1963).

Vladimirov, S., *Stikh i obraz* (Leningrad: Sovetskii Pisatel', 1968).

Zaitsev, V. A., *Sovremennaya sovetskaya poeziya* (Moscow: Prosveshchenie, 1969).

Zamorii, T. P., *Sovremennyi russkii rasskaz* (Kiev: Naukova Dumka, 1968).

Zekulin, Gleb, "Aspects of Peasant Life as Portrayed in Comtemporary Soviet Literature," *Canadian Slavic Studies* (Winter 1967), pp. 552–65.

"The Contemporary Countryside in Soviet Literature: A Search for New Values," in James R. Millar (ed.), *The Soviet Rural Community: A Symposium* (Urbana: University of Illinois Press, 1971), pp. 376–404.

Zhovtis, A., "Granitsy svobodnogo stikha," *Voprosy literatury*, No. 5 (1966), pp. 105–23.

"V rassypannom stroyu (Grafika sovremennogo russkogo stikha)," *Russkaya literatura*, No. 1 (1968), pp. 123–34.

ACKNOWLEDGMENTS TO PUBLISHERS

Acknowledgment is made to publishers and holders of copyright for permission to quote from the following translations:

Boris Balter: From *Goodbye, Boys*, by Boris Balter, translated by Felicity Ashbee. English translation copyright © 1967 by E. P. Dutton & Co., Inc., and Harvill Press. Reprinted by permission of the publishers, E. P. Dutton & Co., Inc.

Joseph Brodsky: "In villages God does not live only" and "Two Hours in an Empty Tank" from Joseph Brodsky: *Selected Poems* trans. George L. Kline (1973) pp. 81, 124. Translation © George L. Kline, 1973. Reprinted by permission of Penguin Books Ltd. *Also:* From *Selected Poems* by Joseph Brodsky, trans. by George L. Kline. English translation and Introduction copyright © 1973 by George L. Kline. Reprinted by permission of Harper & Row, Publishers, Inc.

"The Wheelwright Died," "The Sky's Black Vault," "Thrushlike, the Gardener," trans. by George Reavey, October House. Reprinted by permission of Mrs. George Reavey.

"A Stop in the Wilderness," trans. by Jamie Fuller, *Russian Literature Triquarterly.*

Yuli Daniel: "And At That Time," translated by Vera S. Dunham and Deming Brown, *Encounter.*

Efim Dorosh: "Fifteen Years Later," *Radio Liberty Research.*

Aleksandr Galich: "The Prospectors' Little Waltz," translated by Gene Sosin, The Johns Hopkins University Press.

Vasili Grossman: *Forever Flowing*, trans. by Thomas P. Whitney, Harper & Row, Publishers, Inc.

Boris Pasternak: "When It Clears Up" and "After the Storm," from Boris Pasternak: *Fifty Poems* trans. by Lydia Pasternak Slater (1963) pp. 75, 85. Reprinted by permission of George Allen & Unwin Ltd and Barnes and Noble, Inc.

"Hayricks" and "Fame" translated by Eugene M. Kayden.

Boris Slutsky: From "A Footnote to the Debate about Andrei Rublyov" from *Half-Way to the Moon* edited by Patricia Blake and Max Hayward. Copyright © 1963 by Encounter Ltd. Reprinted by permission of Holt, Rinehart and Winston, Publishers.

Aleksandr Solzhenitsyn: From *One Day in the Life of Ivan Denisovich*, trans. by Max Hayward and Ronald Hingley (1963). Reprinted by permission of Praeger Publishers, Inc.

Abram Tertz (Andrei Sinyavsky): From "Thought Unaware," trans. by Andrew Field and Robert Szulkin, as published in The New Leader, July 19, 1965, pp. 16–26. Reprinted with permission of The New Leader. Copyright © The American Labor Conference on International Affairs, Inc.

From "Pkhentz," trans. by Jeremy Biddulph in *Soviet Short Stories*, edited by Peter Reddaway (1968) p. 68, © Penguin Books, 1968. Reprinted by permission of Penguin Books Ltd.

From *The Trial Begins* and *On Socialist Realism*, trans. by Max Hayward, pp. 24–25, 7–8, 120, and from "Graphomaniacs," in *Fantastic Stories*, trans. by Ronald Hingley, p. 176. Reprinted by permission of Pantheon Books, A Division of Random House, Inc.

Aleksandr Tvardovsky: From "Tyorkin in the Other World," trans. by Leo Gruliow, *Current Digest of the Soviet Press.*

Andrei Voznesensky: From "Oza," trans. by William Jay Smith and Max Hayward, Doubleday and Company.

With the exceptions noted here, all translations from the Russian are those of the author. The author's translations from poetry are literal, and do not attempt to convey the phonetic qualities, rhyme, or meter of the originals. The line and stanza structure, however, are preserved.

Large portions of the chapters on Aleksandr Solzhenitsyn and Andrei Sinyavsky were originally published in *Slavic Review.*

INDEX

The main discussions of individual authors and topics are indicated by page numbers in italics.

GALLAUDET UNIVERSITY
891.709B7s, 1978
Soviet Russia

gal,stx

3 2884 000 480 383

891.709 B7s 1978   180098

DEMCO